ADOLESCENT DEVELOPMENT AND SCHOOL ACHIEVEMENT IN URBAN COMMUNITIES

"A well-conceived, comprehensive resource . . . I like the emphasis on what is positive and effective for urban youths rather than on deficits and negative dysfunction."
Annette Hemmings, University of Cincinnati, USA

"This exciting volume contributes much to our understanding of adolescents who grow up in and develop in urban communities. It is unique in that it does not rely solely on traditional theories of development but actually addresses topics that reflect the everyday lived experiences of urban youth today."
Sandra Winn Tutwiler, Washburn University, USA

This timely volume explores essential themes, issues, and challenges related to adolescents' lives and learning in underserviced urban areas. Distinguished scholars provide theoretically grounded, multidisciplinary perspectives on contexts and forces that influence adolescent development and achievement. The emphasis is on what is positive and effective, what can make a real difference in the lives and life chances for urban youths, rather than deficits and negative dysfunction. Going beyond solely traditional psychological theories, a strong conceptual framework addressing four domains for understanding adolescent development undergirds the volume:

- Developmental continuities from childhood (such as competencies, internal working models of relationships and self in relationships, values and beliefs)
- Primary changes (biological, cognitive, social)
- Contexts of development (personal characteristics, interpersonal relationships, macrosystems)
- Adolescent outcomes (transformations in relationships, identity, emotional health and autonomy, competent conduct in school, work, and daily life)

A major federal government initiative is the development of programs to support underserviced urban areas. Directly relevant to this initiative, this volume contributes significantly to gaining a realistic understanding of the contexts and institutions within which urban youths live and learn.

Gary L. Creasey is Professor of Psychology, Illinois State University, USA.

Patricia A. Jarvis is Professor of Psychology, Illinois State University, USA.

ADOLESCENT DEVELOPMENT AND SCHOOL ACHIEVEMENT IN URBAN COMMUNITIES

Resilience in the Neighborhood

Edited by Gary L. Creasey
and
Patricia A. Jarvis

Routledge
Taylor & Francis Group

NEW YORK AND LONDON

First published 2013
by Routledge
711 Third Avenue, New York, NY 10017

Simultaneously published in the UK
by Routledge
2 Park Square, Milton Park, Abingdon, Oxon OX14 4RN

Routledge is an imprint of the Taylor & Francis Group, an informa business

Library of Congress Cataloging-in-Publication Data
Adolescent development and school achievement in urban communities : resilience in the neighborhood / edited by Gary L. Creasey and Patricia A. Jarvis.
      p. cm.
   Includes bibliographical references and index.
   1. Urban youth–Education–United States. 2. Youth with social disabilities–Education–United States. 3. Academic achievement–United States. 4. Youth development–United States. 5. Urban youth–United States–Social conditions. I. Creasey, Gary. II. Jarvis, Patricia A.
   LC5131.A35 2012
   370.9173'2–dc23   2012021549

ISBN: 978–0–415–89415–9 (hbk)
ISBN: 978–0–415–89416–6 (pbk)
ISBN: 978–0–203–81386–7 (ebk)

Typeset in Bembo by
Swales and Willis Ltd, Exeter, Devon

Printed and bound in the United States of America by Publishers Graphics, LLC on sustainably sourced paper.

We dedicate this book to our students who have welcomed our efforts to better prepare them to work with adolescents in urban underserviced areas. We hope this volume will be a useful tool in that regard. We also dedicate this book to our sons Zachary and Alexander Jarvis-Creasey and our beloved pug, Maggie, who enrich our lives in all ways and inspire us daily.

CONTENTS

PREFACE

The central theme of this volume concerns achievement in urban adolescents in underserviced areas. This addresses a critical topic that resonates at the community, state, and national levels. One of the major initiatives of the Obama administration is the development of a White House Office on Urban Policy that provides federal initiatives and support for health care, education, law enforcement, housing, and families living in underserviced, urban areas. The latter term is significant, because simply living in an urban area/cluster does not mean one lives in an underserviced neighborhood.

Rather, underserviced urban areas are generally high-density contexts that are often pressured by poor economic conditions, ethnic segregation, gentrification, high family mobility, sub-standard or difficult to access health care, and inadequate living conditions. Children and adolescents are often at added risk because living in an underserviced neighborhood generally means they are attending hard-to-staff schools. Such schools are marked by high percentages of students who are significantly below grade level and are taught by teachers who are difficult to retain and/or lack appropriate certification requirements. In certain underserviced cities, such as Chicago, Houston or Detroit, almost all of the public schools have significant percentages of children and adolescents who are not meeting state academic standards (in many cases, over 85% of the students are below standards).

A number of resources highlight the plight of adolescents who reside in underserviced urban communities and most professionals are aware that these youth live in impoverished, sometimes dangerous communities, attend substandard schools, routinely witness violent behavior (even in their own households) and are at risk for disordered eating, delinquency, school drop-out, gang activity, and significant developmental, physical, and emotional problems. The co-editors of the volume, on recent visits to several underserviced urban schools, wondered how any of the students could meet state academic standards, given that 99% of them lived in impoverished households, suffered from high rates of developmental and emotional disorders (e.g.,

PTSD), witnessed daily violence in the schools and visits from law enforcement officials, and were routinely exposed to curriculum that was three grades below their present grade-level. Such observations underscore why the Obama Presidential administration is focused on improving these conditions, and why most books and popular media portray such a pessimistic prognosis for youth residing in these schools and communities.

However, despite these concerns, there are sometimes wide pockets of resiliency in urban areas that contain under-serviced neighborhoods. When considering the term "resiliency," one can focus both on the adolescent and the range of supports in an urban neighborhood. In terms of the former, some adolescents are very robust individuals who find a way to cope with the daily challenges that face them in the community. Thus, although many youth who reside in these areas have academic, interpersonal and psychological problems, it is also true that some do not. Further, there is great diversity in the schools and neighborhoods in urban areas. Some schools are "failing," others are not, and sometimes these institutions are only blocks apart. Neighborhood "A," while technically "underserviced," may have an emerging economic base, strong community support and an expanding business corridor with locally owned businesses. Inexplicably, adjoining Neighborhood "B" may appear just the opposite, and have few economic opportunities, a dilapidated business corridor, crime, gang activity and virtually no community support. The former context reflects a resilient community, whereas the latter reflects a risky, disordered neighborhood. Because the lessons learned from successful schools and neighborhoods could be potentially applied to struggling communities, a central focus on successful applications (particularly those that are educational in nature) represents a theme of this book.

In this volume, the chief objective is to raise awareness of pressing issues that face adolescents in underserviced urban communities, focusing on the potential for healthy adolescent development and school achievement. We consider urban, as opposed to suburban or rural, communities as most adolescents in the United States reside in such communities and we do not want the focus too broad for this effort. A contemporary conceptual framework for understanding positive adolescent development crafted by Grotevant (1998) (see Chapter 2) will guide the central organization of the book. In particular, this framework stresses the importance of environmental context and how support from families, peer groups, teachers and community members can encourage positive youth development in adolescents who live in underserviced communities.

By embracing central elements of this framework for healthy adolescent outcomes, a logical organization for the book can be elucidated. Each chapter addresses various components of this framework, and includes contemporary theory, research, and application. We hope that this volume will set the tone for much-needed work in this area, and that professionals can move from a descriptive focus on underserviced communities to one of prescription. The latter seems to be brought in sharp focus by the authors, who stress the importance of strong partnerships between families, schools, and community organizations and the realization that adolescents themselves can function as critical change agents in their schools and communities.

Gary L. Creasey
Patricia A. Jarvis

ACKNOWLEDGMENTS

The editors gratefully acknowledge first and foremost Naomi Silverman at Routledge for seeing our vision as we see it, believing in it, and helping us every step of the way to make an idea into a reality. We are indebted to you for your expertise, professionalism, guidance, patience, support, and especially for obtaining thorough reviews of the prospectus for this work so that we could deliver on a volume that we are so proud of. We also acknowledge Routledge staff: Kevin Anderson, Julie Ganz and Madeleine Hamlin, as well as the production team at Swales & Willis for expert work in all areas. Finally, we thank the following individuals who helped us in innumerable ways with so many details along the way as we worked on this project: Suzanne Ferrara, Mackenzi Harmon, Martin Gallegos, Annie Leahy, Jessica Stahl, and Alexandra Fisher. Further, the editors were supported in part, via a grant from the United States Department of Education (Teaching Quality Enhancement Office of Innovation and Improvement). Our training in adolescent development under John Hill must also be acknowledged, as John's legacy lives on in this work in many ways.

1

URBAN AND UNDERSERVICED COMMUNITIES

Theoretical and Conceptual Considerations

Gary L. Creasey and Patricia A. Jarvis

Where do you live? As former residents of Virginia, one of the authors would argue he grew up in a "small town"; however, size is relative to some degree. Whereas his definition of "small town" was about 20,000 residents, we discovered when we moved to the Midwestern region of the United States that there are many "small towns" that possess fewer than 300 inhabitants. Further, we have also discovered that definitions such as "poor small town" or "urban areas" are also subject to personal opinions. One of our students indicated that he grew up in a "poor, underserviced city" in Illinois. During a recent visit, we discovered that many residents of this city make very good salaries, and the town itself has a low foreclosure rate, several thriving businesses and a regional medical center. Due to such strong differences of opinion, it is evident that we need better definitions concerning the neighborhoods we live in.

What is "Urban"?

What is meant by the term "Urban"? The United States Census Bureau (2010) provides useful definitions concerning the distinction between urban and rural areas of the country that are based on population and population density, or number of inhabitants per square mile. Urbanized areas are defined as densely populated regions marked by more than 50,000 inhabitants and are often part of relatively crowded, highly interconnected metropolitan regions that have strongly linked economic ties within the area. Large cities such as New York, Atlanta, Los Angeles, Chicago and Detroit are rather easy to locate; however, the metropolitan area extends past these cities. Within these regions, economies are somewhat tied by the residents, who may commute across the area to their jobs and spend money across the region. As an example, certain regions of the country—such as, New York, New Jersey, and sections of Pennsylvania and Connecticut—almost seem to share a common metropolitan area.

Whereas census and population data are useful in defining urban versus nonurban regions of the country, many adolescents who live in the "Washington DC Area" may not be markedly different from youth who live in smaller cities, such as Toledo, Ohio or Aiken, South Carolina. In contrast, although residents of Chicago, Joliet and Downers Grove, Illinois may all lay claim to living in the "Chicagoland" metropolitan area, they might not share much in common other than an affinity for the Chicago Cubs.

Even making vast comparisons between adolescents who live in heavily populated urban areas is difficult because the conditions within these areas can be dramatically different. Perhaps a better mechanism to ascertain the actual impact of living in different urban areas is to consider the broader demographics of the regions. For example, living in an underserviced urban area is dramatically different from growing up in affluent neighborhoods in urban communities. Indeed, population density, economic health, and access to good health care and schools are more likely to influence adolescent adjustment than just being from an urban, suburban or rural community, or growing up in the "North" versus the "South." Thus, whereas it is important to make distinctions between urban, suburban and rural areas, embedded within these regions are often distinct neighborhoods that can range from great affluence to extreme hardship and poverty.

What is an Underserviced Neighborhood?

Scholars have begun to identify variables that are characteristic of certain neighborhoods, or areas with distinct demographic (e.g., wealthy versus poor; Italian versus Polish), geographical (e.g., "Southside," "Garden District"), or politically defined (e.g., "Lower Ninth Ward") identifiers that could affect adolescent development. To more precisely define neighborhood boundaries, researchers may rely on local census data, administrative data sources (e.g., the way city leaders or law enforcement classifies boundaries), or some combination of the two (Leventhal & Brooks-Gunn, 2000). Local residents, who may indicate that there are distinct divisions within census- or administratively-defined neighborhoods, may augment these data and provide more useful refinements.

What markers of neighborhoods are frequently used to predict adolescent developmental adjustment? These variables can be classified using the following dimensions (Leventhal & Brooks-Gunn, 2000):

1. Income or social economic status (SES), ranging from affluent/high SES to poverty/low SES.
2. Racial/ethnic diversity, often assessed by concentrations of African American, Latino and foreign-born residents.
3. Residential stability, marked by either geographic mobility (people moving in and out of the neighborhood), or numbers of residents who have lived in their houses for more than 10 years and proportion of owner-occupied (versus rented) residents.

By combining these data with other indicators, one can begin to determine if a neighborhood is underserviced. It is sometimes difficult to "picture" what we mean

YBP Library Services

ADOLESCENT DEVELOPMENT AND SCHOOL ACHIEVEMENT IN
URBAN COMMUNITIES: RESILIENCE IN THE...; ED. BY
GARY L. CREASEY.   Paper   265 P.
NEW YORK: ROUTLEDGE, 2013

TITLE CONT: NEIGHBORHOOD. ED: ILLINOIS STATE
UNIVERSITY. COLLECTION OF NEW ESSAYS.
LCCN 2012-21549
  ISBN 0415894166   **Library PO#** /ID

	List	44.95 USD
8395 NATIONAL UNIVERSITY LIBRAR	**Disc**	5.0%
App. Date 8/27/14 SOE-K12 8214-08	**Net**	42.70 USD

SUBJ: 1. URBAN YOUTH--EDUC.--U.S. 2. ACADEMIC
ACHIEVEMENT--U.S.

CLASS LC5131   DEWEY# 370.91732   LEVEL ADV-AC

YBP Library Services

ADOLESCENT DEVELOPMENT AND SCHOOL ACHIEVEMENT IN
URBAN COMMUNITIES: RESILIENCE IN THE...; ED. BY
GARY L. CREASEY.   Paper   265 P.
NEW YORK: ROUTLEDGE, 2013

TITLE CONT: NEIGHBORHOOD. ED: ILLINOIS STATE
UNIVERSITY. COLLECTION OF NEW ESSAYS.
  LCCN 2012-21549
  ISBN 0415894166   **Library PO#** /ID

	List	44.95 USD
8395 NATIONAL UNIVERSITY LIBRAR	**Disc**	5.0%
App. Date 8/27/14 SOE-K12 8214-08	**Net**	42.70 USD

SUBJ: 1. URBAN YOUTH--EDUC.--U.S. 2. ACADEMIC
ACHIEVEMENT--U.S.

CLASS LC5131   DEWEY# 370.91732   LEVEL ADV-AC

by the term "underserviced." Consider media portrayals of urban neighborhoods that contain high-rise housing projects, litter strewn yards and packs of young men lurking on street corners. However, such images really do not inform us as to what is really going on in a community or neighborhood.

When we ask our college students to consider underserviced communities, the vast majority point to racial, ethnic and socioeconomic variables, such as family or community income levels. Indeed, race, ethnicity, English proficiency and socio-economic status are all variables that are used to identify at risk or marginalized groups of people (Peterman, 2008). However, it is important to marry these personal characteristics to other indicators of school and community functioning to arrive at the term "underserviced." That is, a defining feature of this term concerns barriers to health care, economic opportunity and educational choices. Thus, underserviced populations live in communities that have difficult access to good health care, jobs and schools. This could be due to population density, economic resources for the schools and community, and the time it takes to pursue health care options (Weitz, Freund, & Wright, 2001).

The educational barriers that face adolescents who live in underserviced communities can be realized by examining the obstacles that are encountered in the residing school systems. For example, an underserviced school is likely to contain large percentages of students on reduced or free lunches (a common demographic variable to assess family poverty) and significantly below grade level (Chou & Tozer, 2008). To illustrate, there are many schools in the City of Chicago in which 99% of the students receive free or reduced lunches and less than 10% are meeting or exceeding state academic standards (Illinois Interactive Report Card, 2012). Further, one major concern in this case is whether or not teachers, staff, and administrators are effectively trained to work with these students.

Indeed, these students are also robbed of effective instructors. For example, two more variables that mark underserviced schools are high teacher turnover and large percentages of teachers who are in emergency or temporary positions (Chou & Tozer, 2008). Thus, the students who are the most in need of high quality instruction often do not receive it.

So, personal characteristics such as race or ethnicity are only part of the picture when considering underserviced communities. The bigger picture concerns how these variables are interwoven with broader demographic and community variables— the reason that some picture underserviced populations as African American or Latino is because they are overrepresented in underserviced communities. However, poverty does not just affect adolescents of color. As an example, the Appalachian area, which marks vast regions of western Pennsylvania, Virginia, North Carolina and West Virginia, contains high rates of poverty, substandard health care, schools and housing—these regions are populated by high percentages of Caucasian residents.

As will be determined in this book, the interrelationships between these variables have been consistently linked to adolescent adjustment. Youth who live in relatively affluent neighborhoods marked by high resident stability display better psychosocial outcomes (e.g., achievement; positive mental health) than their counterparts who live in poverty-stricken neighborhoods marked by high resident instability and ethnic segregation (Leventhal, Dupéré, & Brooks-Gunn, 2009). Further, the adolescents who live in the more affluent neighborhoods engage in less risk-taking behavior (e.g., unprotected sexual activity) than youth who live in poorer neighborhoods, particularly when these latter residents are economically and racially/ethnically segregated (Baumer & South, 2001).

It is important to consider what we mean by the latter comment. Whereas most readers are familiar with neighborhoods and towns that contain a mix of residents from different demographic brackets, it appears that risk to adolescents increases when poverty is more concentrated and marked by racial/ethnic/social segregation. Based on such concerns, what social forces are at work to produce such economic disparities?

Underlying Mechanisms of Neighborhood Affluence

There are numerous reasons that there are high concentrations of poverty in the United States and worldwide. One risk factor concerns a sudden increase in a community population, often predicated by a promise of economic opportunity (e.g., low-cost housing) or jobs. Although such opportunities may bode well for a community for some time, difficulties arise if major employers go out of business or leave the community entirely (Wilson, 1987). Such deindustrialization then leaves a void in the community, as there may be sudden unemployment and a heavy concentration of low-paying jobs with few benefits. As an example, consider the plight of cities such as Detroit, Michigan—and what has transpired in and around this city—due to the collapse of the automobile industry.

Beyond sudden population increases and deindustrialization, another difficulty arises if more affluent, educated adults and families leave the community. This is often due to decreased occupational, economic and educational opportunities. This process then leaves behind a relatively poor, uneducated group of individuals that may find it difficult to find employment because they might not be qualified to assume good job opportunities, or, such jobs may have left the community entirely. This was a process that affected a number of major cities in the last century (Wilson, 1987).

As one example, as affluent, well-educated, urban dwelling African American families left the southern United States and settled in Midwestern urban areas, their White counterparts subsequently moved out of these same areas to settle into outer suburbs. Whereas these newly arrived African American families (and their adolescents) thrived, they too quickly left these urban areas as a new wave of poor, relatively uneducated African Americans from the rural south arrived during a second migration period. Although these new migrants were also African American, they were culturally very different from their predecessors (who were better educated and from southern United States cities) who quickly vacated when these new residents moved to the Midwestern urban areas. When these relatively affluent, educated African American families left, the jobs went with them (Black, 2003). This transition then left high concentrations of poor, uneducated African American families with few job or economic prospects.

Partly to combat this difficulty across the country, federal and local policies were instituted to protect these relatively isolated, poor, heavily segregated communities largely inhabited by African American (and later, Latino) families. One such example concerns the development of low-cost, public housing. Whereas this housing may have temporarily addressed some of the aforementioned problems, such housing was often isolated from more affluent urban neighborhoods and in many instances, created problems for residents due to poor architectural design. Consider high-rise buildings with non-working elevators (forcing residents to negotiate long walks up narrow, poorly supervised stairwells), or low-rise structures with isolated courtyards that invited drug dealing or gang activity.

What ramifications does such neighborhood poverty have on adolescents? As neighborhood poverty increases, so do resident perceptions of social isolation and local violence. The concentration of poverty—whether it is rural or urban—also creates a very low personal property tax base that creates problems for public schools that rely on such resources to properly function. Further, adolescents see little evidence for success, as there are few viable jobs, and limited positive role models in the neighborhood.

Despite these grim realities, it is also true that some communities adjacent to one another can be poor and demographically similar, yet, contain adolescents that are functioning at very different levels. This finding must mean that some neighborhoods have community assets and "protective factors" at work, whereas others lack these resources. What exactly are the characteristics of neighborhoods that we should assess that might positively or negatively influence adolescent development?

Assessing Neighborhood Characteristics

When defining neighborhood characteristics, as well as boundaries, one can rely on census information and educational or law enforcement districting data to provide a picture of neighborhood dimensions and density, as well as resident social class (marked by educational and occupational status), racial/ethnic diversity and residential stability. As indicated earlier, residential stability is akin to "turnover" and marks the tendency for people to stay or vacate the community. Such stability is greatly affected by economic conditions. For example, when there are dramatic increases in home foreclosures then it tends to drive out families with children and adolescents (who have lost their homes) and leaves younger (who rent or live with their aging parents) and older adults (who own their homes). Beyond disrupting the lives of the "displaced" adolescent—who must cope with the family move, new school, etc.—such movement also disrupts school organization and enrollment as there is less property tax collected and fewer neighborhood children attend the school. In any case, social class, racial/ethnic diversity and residential stability represent variables that researchers frequently assess to provide an initial landscape of how neighborhood characteristics influence adolescent development (Leventhal & Brooks-Gunn, 2000).

However, one difficulty with simply relying on demographic variables to define a community is that a neighborhood may have considerable diversity within its borders (Furstenberg, Cook, Eccles, & Sameroff, 1999). As an example, we work in a neighborhood largely inhabited by poor, Latino families. Whereas there seems to be little diversity in the community, it turns out that the neighborhood contains two rival gangs. Each gang stakes territory to the east or west of a central avenue and these territories completely shape the landscape of the neighborhood. Further, the west side of the neighborhood contains the only community park; adolescents who live on the east side often will not venture across the central street to go to the park or any of the events hosted by the west-side school.

How do we know this information? We use a process called community mapping and rely on the input of community organization leaders, as well as data collection involving children and parents within the community to better understand both neighborhood characteristics and conditions. The latter approach is important because it allows one to assess neighborhood disorder or the relative stability and safety of the community. It is now suspected that neighborhood order or disorder is more heavily predictive of adolescent adjustment than residential stability, income level or ethnic segregation (Roche & Leventhal, 2009). Thus, identifying variables that buffer adolescents from neighborhood disorder is a critical research question. In any case, now that important neighborhood characteristics have been identified, what impact do these variables actually have on youth development?

How Neighborhoods Influence Adolescents

The adolescent outcomes that are often commonly associated with neighborhood conditions are achievement, social/psychological functioning and sexual behavior (Leventhal et al., 2009). In evaluating all three outcomes, there are two findings that predominate. First, when considering various demographic variables, social class rather than racial/ethnic characteristics or residential stability have more profound influences on adolescent development (Duncan, Ziol-Guest, & Kalil, 2010). This makes sense, in that affluent neighborhoods generally contain well-educated adults with prestigious occupations and there may be an abundance of resources in the communities. Note too that the impact of social class is also the strongest when children and adolescents reside in affluent or poor communities for long periods of time. Thankfully, most youth who live in impoverished conditions normally do so temporarily; the negative influence of poverty is more likely to exert a toll on youth when it is long term and chronic in nature (McLoyd et al., 2009).

A second finding that predominates is that the relative order or safety of the community also is an important correlate of adolescent adjustment. This finding makes sense in that if it is "too dangerous to go outside" then personal safety and daily survival may trump the importance of school, physical fitness and other activities important to children and adolescents. Again, whereas neighborhood socioeconomic status is a correlate of neighborhood conditions and order, there are wide disparities in poor communities on this issue—poverty alone does not cause neighborhood disorder.

However, the two aforementioned findings beg the question of whether it is the conditions in the neighborhood (e.g., safety, cultural opportunities, abundant green space) that are affecting these youth, or if the influence is due to living in a high or low social class household. Indeed, it has been estimated that the relative impact of neighborhood characteristics is modest at best (Leventhal et al., 2009). That is, living in a poor or wealthy neighborhood does make a difference in an adolescent's life, but the relative impact of family functioning might have a more profound impact.

To sum, neighborhood characteristics, such as poverty and safety seem to be predominately associated with adolescent achievement, externalizing behavior problems, early sexual activity and female childbearing. These findings are not consistent for stages of adolescence, and are somewhat less pronounced in Latino youth. In addition, because not all "at risk" adolescents who reside in poor communities experience difficulties, there must be other variables that moderate or mediate the association between community characteristics and adolescent developmental outcomes. We turn to these potential variables in the next section.

Neighborhood Mechanisms

What accounts for the finding that neighborhood conditions, such as high rates of poverty and unemployment, are related to important adolescent development outcomes? There are two theoretical perspectives reviewed by Leventhal and colleagues (2009) that may explain such findings.

The first orientation, the sociological perspective, suggests that broad, demographic characteristics of the community, such as community affluence or safety, create a set of conditions that can facilitate or dampen adolescent adjustment and development. The second approach, which is more ecological in nature—and thus reflects the general orientation of the book—acknowledges the relative impact of community characteristics, but argues that other important contexts, such as family, peer, or school variables also can play a role in the process.

To start, sociological theories posit that adolescents living in high social class neighborhoods are more developmentally advantaged than their counterparts living in poorer communities, due to the culture or climate of the context. That is, in a more affluent, educated community, there is more community order and organization, greater institutional resources (e.g., high paying jobs, less burdened law enforcement) and a general, positive attitude amongst its residents (e.g., community pride; collective disapproval of gang activity and substance abuse) (Jencks & Meyer, 1990; Sampson & Groves, 1989). This in turn dictates the safety and "order" of the community; as indicated in previous sections, neighborhood order is closely tied to adolescent adjustment.

In terms of interventions, this approach would suggest that attempts to "build the community," through stronger community organization, increased law enforcement presence and neighborhood enhancement projects (e.g., creating more park areas, or "green space") led to more neighborhood organization and community pride that would translate to more positive adolescent development. Moving a neighborhood from disordered to "ordered" seems like a good idea when one considers the variables associated with neighborhood disorder.

Of course, the stance in this book is that the neighborhood is a major context for development, but there are other possible supports, such as the family and peer group that could possibly moderate the impact of community influences on adolescent development. This theory, which is more ecological in nature than sociological approaches, would suggest that positive parent behavior, or strong school systems could provide vital resources to offset the effects of neighborhood poverty or disorganization (Leventhal et al., 2009). While this theory recognizes the importance of neighborhood quality in the lives of adolescents, it also implies that conducting interventions in the family or school contexts may have as strong, or even stronger impacts on youth adjustment.

Both theories have received empirical support. For example, when considering sociological theories, neighborhood poverty is also associated with certain neighborhood conditions, such as gang and drug activity, community violence and physical markers of poverty, such as foreclosed homes and a general lack of green space. When community members perceive their neighborhood is dangerous and disordered, there is less collective efficacy, or less sense of "community pride" and cohesion (Sampson, Morenoff, & Earls, 1999).

Thus, it is not surprising that adolescents who live in impoverished, disordered communities are at a high risk for achievement problems, early sexual onset and sexual risk-taking behavior, and psychological difficulties (Natsuaki, Ge, Brody, & Simons, 2007; Roche & Leventhal, 2009). Further, living in disordered neighborhoods is also associated with poor dietary habits, less access to green space and highly sedentary behavior in adolescents—it is not surprising they are at risk for disordered eating and obesity problems (Burdette & Hill, 2008). These matters worsen in disordered communities where collective efficacy is low and adult stress is extremely high (Hill, Ross, & Angel, 2005; Natsuaki et al., 2007). When adults themselves do not "buy into" their community, such disengagement has extremely negative effects on adolescents who reside in the neighborhood (Mayberry, Espelage, & Koenig, 2009).

Finally—and particularly in impoverished communities that contain high rates of ethnic segregation and neighborhood disorder—there may be a collective distrust of various institutions (e.g., law enforcement) and populations (e.g., members of other ethnic groups) that are not viewed "as part" of the community (and may be viewed as partly to blame for the difficulties in the neighborhood) (Caughy, O'Campo, Nettles, & Lohrfink, 2006). If adolescents adopt such appraisals, it may be more difficult for members of different helping professions (e.g., teachers, social workers, psychologists) to offer assistance in such communities if they are collectively viewed as part of the problem rather than the solution.

While community conditions are closely tied to adolescent development, do these conditions outweigh the importance of more immediate variables in an adolescent's life, such as their family, friends, teachers and school conditions? If so, this conclusion would indicate we should work more on improving neighborhood conditions than studying and conducting interventions in these other contexts. Such a direction is not tenable. While community conditions do play a role in adolescent development, there is much research that supports a broader, ecological approach for understanding contextual support to such development (Leventhal et al., 2009). Indeed, there is much work to suggest that peer and family relationships, as well as school conditions have as much of a role, or even a greater role in shaping adolescent outcomes than the conditions of the community. For example, in one study, the prediction of adolescent substance abuse activity was best accomplished by collecting data on family and peer influences, as well as school and community data (Mayberry et al., 2009). These data suggest that when attempting to predict or forecast adolescent outcomes, it is best to use multiple sources of data from multiple contexts for development in doing so.

A final consideration—and one somewhat ignored via the theoretical approaches broached thus far—rests with the concept of resiliency, or the tendency to function positively in the face of adversity. There are certain families and adolescents who function very well despite very poor community conditions. Some of the characteristics that describe such families/adolescents will be discussed throughout this book as well as successful interventions and programs that have been implemented to improve adolescent, family, school and community conditions.

Conclusions

What are some conclusions that can be gleaned from this chapter? The first concerns how the communities we live in and their conditions probably have a greater impact on our development than whether or not we live in a certain region of the country (e.g., North vs. South) or in a city, suburb, or rural area. As an example, some neighborhoods in an urban area may be thriving and its residents have a strong community efficacy, and easy access to great schools, businesses and health care. In contrast, severe poverty, unsafe conditions and inadequate schools and employment opportunities may mark adjacent communities. Thus, the socioeconomic conditions and order/disorder of the community probably have a stronger, more sustainable impact on an adolescent's development than whether the community is urban, suburban or rural.

In this chapter, it was concluded that abundant community assets, economic growth and population stability often create a set of conditions that convince residents to stay in the neighborhood and develop a sense of collective efficacy or community pride. Further, such communities are often perceived as stable and safe by their residents; beyond offering an important source of support for youth they also allow "adolescents to be adolescents." In other words, adolescents have the time to concentrate on activities that are central to their development, such as exercise, community involvement, extracurricular activities and relationship building with family members and peers. Such involvement empowers adolescents to focus on positive development, as opposed to avoiding trouble and danger (Hirsch, Deutsch, & DuBois, 2011).

In contrast, communities that have few assets—often due to a chronic population exodus of affluent, educated citizens and few employment prospects for adults—place neighborhoods at risk for disorder and diminished community efficacy. Unfortunately, such conditions place adolescents at risk for achievement and social/psychological problems as well as sexual risk-taking behavior. Further, it was concluded that several variables often "work together" to place adolescents at a potential disadvantage.

For example, at the community level, poverty-stricken unsafe neighborhoods may possess few role models for success and limited possibilities for adult employment—consider how such conditions influence the adolescents' view of their future success in life. In addition, in such communities, adolescents have less time to "be adolescents" as safety and survival skills may take precedence over other contexts central to their development. Finally, such neighborhood conditions also seem to take a toll on one of the adolescent's primary supports as extreme poverty and unsafe conditions appear to affect adult/parental personal health, inter-parent relationship functioning and caregiver behavior (Leventhal et al., 2009).

It is suggested, too, that community organizations can take the lead—ranging from attracting more businesses, to foreclosure prevention programs, to green space creation—in making neighborhoods more attractive to live in. These organizations (as well as area schools) may also offer mentorship programs to adolescents; such programs, when using best practices, have been shown to have positive impacts on adolescent social and cognitive development.

In addition—and representing another theme of the book—there is great promise in school- and community-based programs that encourage adolescents themselves to become involved in, and advocates for, neighborhood improvement. It is theorized that such efforts may encourage positive youth development and promote the development of civic engagement. Indeed, working to improve community conditions could be a mechanism to improve the lives of all adolescents—whether in affluent or less affluent neighborhoods—as there may not be a lot of opportunities for youth in general to learn how to become a good citizen and a contributor to their society. While there is sometimes great motivation for youth in underserviced communities to leave the neighborhood, such community involvement may represent a compelling variable that motivates youth to remain in the neighborhood as positive change agents.

References

Baumer, E. P., & South, S. J. (2001). Community effects on youth sexual activity. *Journal of Marriage and Family, 63*, 540–554.

Black, T. (2003). *Bridges of memory: Chicago's first wave of black migration, an oral history.* Evanston, IL: Northwestern University Press.

Burdette, A. M., & Hill, T. D. (2008). An examination of processes linking perceived neighborhood disorder and obesity. *Social Science and Medicine, 67*, 38–46.

Caughy, M. O., O'Campo, P. J., Nettles, S. M., & Lohrfink, K. F. (2006). Neighborhood matters: Racial socialization of African American children. *Child Development, 77*, 1220–1236.

Chou, V., & Tozer, S. (2008). What's urban got to do with it?: The meanings of urban in urban teacher preparation and development. In F. P. Peterman (Ed.), *Partnering to prepare urban teachers* (pp. 1–20). New York: Peter Lang.

Duncan, G. J., Ziol-Guest, K. M., & Kalil, A. (2010). Early-childhood poverty and adult attainment, behavior, and health. *Child Development, 81*, 306–325.

Furstenberg, F. F., Cook, T. D., Eccles, J., Elder, G. H. Jr., & Sameroff, A. (1999). *Managing to make it: Urban families and adolescent success.* Chicago: University of Chicago Press.

Hill, T. D., Ross, C. E., & Angel, R. J. (2005). Neighborhood disorder, psychophysiological distress, and health. *Journal of Health and Social Behavior, 46*, 170–186.

Hirsch, B. J., Deutsch, N. L., & DuBois, D. L. (2011). *After-school centers and youth development: Case studies of success and failure.* New York: Cambridge University Press.

Illinois Interactive Report Card (Online). Available: http://iirc.niu.edu/ (May 14, 2012).

Jencks, C. S., & Meyer, S. E. (1990). The social consequences of growing up in a poor neighborhood. In L. Lynn, & M. McGeary (Eds.), *Inner-city poverty in the United States* (pp. 111–186). Washington, DC: National Academy Press.

Leventhal, T., & Brooks-Gunn, J. (2000). The neighborhoods they live in: The effects of neighborhood residence on child and adolescent outcomes. *Psychological Bulletin, 26,* 309–337.

Leventhal, T., Dupéré, V., & Brooks-Gunn, J. (2009). Neighborhood influences on adolescent development. In R. M. Lerner, & L. Steinberg (Eds.), *Handbook of adolescent psychology*, Vol. 2 (pp. 524–558). Hoboken, NJ: John Wiley & Sons.

Mayberry, M. L., Espelage, D. L., & Koenig, B. (2009). Multilevel modeling of direct effects and interactions of peers, parents, school, and community influences on adolescent substance use. *Journal of Youth and Adolescence,* 38, 1038–1049.

McLoyd, V. C., Kaplan, R., Purtell, K. M., Bagley, E., Hardaway, C. R., & Smalls, C. (2009). Poverty and socioeconomic disadvantage in adolescence. In R. M. Lerner, & L. Steinberg (Eds.), *Handbook of adolescent psychology*, Vol. 2 (pp. 444–491). Hoboken, NJ: John Wiley & Sons.

Natsuaki, M. N., Ge, X., Brody, G. H., Simons, R. L. (2007). African American children's depressive symptoms: The prospective effects of neighborhood disorder, stressful life events, and parenting. *American Journal of Community Psychology, 39,* 163–176.

Peterman, F. P. (2008). *Partnering to prepare urban teachers: A call to activism.* New York: Peter Lang Publishing.

Roche, K.M., & Leventhal, T. (2009). Beyond neighborhood poverty: Family management, neighborhood disorder, and adolescents' early sexual onset. *Journal of Family Psychology, 23,* 819–827.

Sampson, R. J., & Groves, W. B. (1989). Community structure and crime: Testing social-disorganization theory. *American Journal of Sociology, 94,* 774–780.

Sampson, R. J., Morenoff, J. D., & Earls, F. (1999). Beyond social capital: Spatial dynamics of collective efficacy for children. *American Sociological Review, 64,* 633–660.

U.S. Census Bureau. (2010). 2005–2009 American Community Survey 5-Year Estimates. Retrieved from http://factfinder.census.gov/servlet/GCTTable?_bm=y&-geo_id=&-ds_name=ACS_2009_5YR_G00_&-_lang=en&-mt_name=ACS_2009_5YR_G00_GCT1701_US37F&-format=US-37F&-CONTEXT=gct.

Weitz, T. A., Freund, K. M., &Wright, L.W. (2001). Identifying and caring for underserved populations: Experience of the National Center's of Excellence in Women's Health. *Journal of Women's Health and Gender-Based Medicine, 10,* 937–952.

Wilson, W. J. (1987). *The truly disadvantaged: The inner city, the underclass, and public policy.* Chicago: University of Chicago Press.

PART I

The Adolescent as an Individual: Theory and Contexts

2

ADOLESCENT DEVELOPMENT IN UNDERSERVICED COMMUNITIES

A Conceptual Framework

JulieAnn Stawicki and Barton J. Hirsch

The purpose of this volume is to examine resilient adolescent development, with a focus on programs and interventions that support academic success within the context of underserviced urban neighborhoods. The impact of the social, economic, and political neglect on youth who call these communities home is well documented (e.g. Leventhal & Brooks-Gunn, 2000; Leventhal, Dupéré, & Brooks-Gunn, 2009; Murry, Berkel, Gaylord-Harden, Copeland-Linder, & Nation, 2011). Large amounts of funding, programming, and research related to youth in urban areas are focused on the intervention or prevention of negative outcomes such as reducing drug use, teen parenting, etc. Numerous studies of risk and negative youth outcomes apply deficit-based assumptions about the youth and their communities. Yet deficit models alone fail to explain why many youth not only have an absence of problem behaviors but are successful despite the risk and limited opportunities they face. Framing the context of urban neighborhoods exclusively from a risk perspective limits the scope of productive action.

Underserviced neighborhoods are often defined by structural and sociodemographic characteristics, such as persistent/intergenerational poverty, geographic and social isolation from majority culture, under/unemployment, and ethnic/racial segregation (Brooks-Gunn, Duncan, Aber, 1997). In addition, institutional resources, such as the quantity and quality of schools, access to health care and recreational facilities, are often limited (Leventhal et al., 2009). Yet, structural and institutional resources are only one aspect of urban neighborhoods that impact youth and families. While many underserviced, urban communities are characterized by poverty and violence, they may also contain networks of neighbors looking out for one another, adults that serve as positive mentors and strong linkages to history and culture that are important predictors of the positive development of youth. Some communities have high rates of poverty, ethnic segregation and unemployment, and feature strong community efficacy, the social connections within neighborhoods and the capacity of residents to work together toward common goals. Other neighborhoods may be demographically similar, but marked by low social organization, poor community efficacy and high rates of criminal activity. The outcomes for adolescents are different in these demographically similar, but socially different communities (Leventhal et al., 2009). There is a need to acknowledge both the risk within the environment as well as the potential strengths and assets of the neighborhood and youth themselves. Context and social systems are crucial to understanding the complex environment of urban settings, where policy, economics, religion, and neighborhood affect youth, their development and opportunities for the future (see Brooks-Gunn et al., 1997; Leventhal & Brooks-Gunn, 2000).

There is an urgent need for a more comprehensive examination of youth living in underserviced, urban communities. Our challenge as researchers and practitioners is to better understand the contexts of youth in high-risk, urban neighborhoods and how these factors can be leveraged to influence change for the youth and families within these communities. This volume is unique in that it highlights the positive outcomes of youth in urban areas and examines the characteristics of those youth and the aspects of the schools and communities that support the positive development of all youth.

This chapter presents the organizing framework as described by Grotevant (1998), which provides a basis for the rest of the volume. His framework offers a systematic approach to understanding adolescent development that could be used to facilitate cross-discipline and research/practice communication. We will also draw on related adolescent development theory as well as highlighting research on the promotion of positive adolescent outcomes and interventions that support academic success in urban communities.

Importance of a Framework

There are several lenses through which different professions and fields of study examine the contexts and the outcomes of adolescent development. The study of adolescent development is made up of several disciplines, each interested in similar aspects of this period of life. For example, how youth become interested, prepared for, and integrated into the work force can be understood from many angles. Psychologists may concentrate on the individual's vocational identity. Sociologists may focus on the history of apprenticeship and roles for adolescents in the labor force. Educators and educational researchers may focus on vocational education and the skills needed to be hired for a job, and anthropologists could examine what is considered valued work in a given cultural context. Though each perspective has a distinct line of theory and research, they all have important information to contribute to the discussion of best practice and policy.

When each discipline has its own vocabulary and develops its own line of research, dueling concepts and terminology hinder communication and the ability to move the entire field forward. Translational research emphasizes a need for unified language between disciplines and levels of analysis. A common theoretical framework facilitates cross-discipline collaboration, provides a basis for merging research and practice, and creates a new language for all those interested in improving conditions for human development (Guerra, Graham, & Tolan, 2011).

A common framework can highlight the complex nature of human development and offers a way to organize and provide focus for further investigation and development of programs. Researchers often reduce complexities as a means to systematically investigate variables and hypotheses. However, this can result in losing the holistic approach to understanding the individual within multiple, interacting contexts. Theory grounds researchers and practitioners and keeps the focus on the complexities of environment.

Frameworks create meaning, organize existing knowledge, and help researchers/ practitioners find opportunities to intervene. In designing interventions, one needs to choose a level of intervention with a mind on the whole context. Successful programs support the whole person, and strengthen families, institutions and communities while at the same time they are able to report specific outcomes of intellectual and academic growth (Lerner & Castellino, 2002).

Grotevant's Framework of Adolescent Development

In the *Handbook of Adolescence*, Grotevant (1998) synthesized the history of major developmental theories and relevant research on adolescence, focusing on adolescence as a developmental period rather than a single context or outcome. He captures the dynamic processes that contribute to normal development and suggests a conceptual framework to structure cross-discipline communication and identify gaps in the research literature.

Grotevant's framework is the basis for the organization of this book and the remaining chapters of the book will illustrate how the concepts relate to academic success and urban context. We will first briefly present the concepts of Grotevant's framework which include: (1) Developmental continuities from childhood, (2) Primary changes, (3) Contexts of development and (4) Adolescent outcomes.

Developmental Continuities from Childhood

Youth do not arrive into adolescence as blank slates waiting to be transformed. They have accumulated a set of experiences, relationships, identities and skills that shape the opportunities and relationships in the next stage of adolescence. The changes in adolescence alter the development that has already taken place. Grotevant describes development as unfolding over time and earlier development sets the stage for subsequent changes. For example, by middle school, youth have had contact with school systems that have already passed judgment on their academic capabilities through grades, test scores and a history of behavior met with acceptance or disciplinary action. These experiences are carried with the young person into the next phase of development and shape their future possibilities.

Primary Changes

Adolescence is a cultural concept, yet the years around physical maturity are universally recognized as a distinct time period (Rogoff, 2003). Grotevant defines adolescence as characterized by three primary changes in the individual: the biological changes associated with puberty, the potential for cognitive change, and a redefinition of social roles. Although adolescence is based in biological changes, the accompanying changes and meaning are dependent on cultural community. For example, a 15-year-old is physically able to reproduce, but in mainstream American culture, teen-aged child bearing is not accepted as the norm.

Contexts of Development

Bronfenbrenner (1979) suggested that to better understand human development we have to go beyond direct observations of one person/one place to look to larger multi-person systems and interactions. Ecological theories describe development as unfolding within multiple contexts (biology, family, neighborhoods, time and culture). In his framework, Grotevant discusses three levels of contexts that influence adolescent development: the individual, interpersonal, and macrosystems.

Individual

The first level of ecological context begins with the personal characteristics of the adolescent. This includes factors such as the young person's gender, race, ethnicity, and sexual orientation. As with Bronfenbrenner's ecological model, individuals are in the center of their own development. Personal characteristics influence other contexts of development, such as family dynamics, friendships, and opportunities within society. Research literature suggests that individual characteristics (e.g. pubertal timing or personality traits) predict risk or resilience within the context of under-serviced neighborhoods (see Leventhal et al., 2009). For example, being an African American male may influence his decision or likelihood to speak up to give an answer aloud in a classroom environment. His individual confidence can contribute to his comfort in speaking up. His size, voice, and mannerisms may influence how others respond to him in return.

Interpersonal

The second level includes the interpersonal relationships and settings of which the individual adolescent is a part. This level includes both the direct relationships within the adolescent's life (*microsystems*), and the settings in which these other individuals do or do not interact with each other (*mesosystems*). An individual is part of a family or peer network; family and peers are part of greater interpersonal contexts such as schools, neighborhoods, and leisure activities—settings where family and peers, or teachers and parents interact with the young person and with each other.

Building on the prior example, the response that the African American student receives from his teacher will contribute to his school engagement. School engagement, along with other factors contributes to his academic performance: e.g., whether he has a parent actively involved in his school; whether he is involved in extra-curricular activities in the community; or the peer group to which he belongs. His answer to the question in the first example, along with his history of interactions with his teacher, impacts the teacher's assessment of his academic ability. The teacher's perception or interpretation of that student's skill is also influenced by the teacher's own background and experience of the capability of similar students.

Macrosystems

Lastly, Grotevant includes macrosystems as the third level of context of development. The macrosystems in his framework incorporate culture, societal norms, and the period of history in which the individuals and the systems are situated. The macrosystems and exchanges between them are contained within formal and informal structures, such as government, media, the economy, and political environment.

In the continuing example of the teen, his teacher, and his school performance, all exist within a particular community, political environment and period of history. Whether a parent is available to monitor homework would depend on whether someone is home during the after-school hours. Parent availability after school is, in turn, influenced by several factors, for example whether the family is headed by a single parent or the parents' work schedules. His participation in an after-school program depends on whether one is available at the school (which may depend on funding or political support for such programs in the area), whether he has trans-portation home, or the safety of his neighborhood. How his teacher praises or corrects students is dependent on his/her culture of origin, prior schooling, or the accepted professional norms, to name only a few factors.

As this example illustrates, the effect of ecological contexts on development is not unidirectional. Each of the contexts is shaped by and shapes the other contexts of development. Relatedly, more than one context contributes to development at the same time and unfolds over time. That is, the interaction of these contexts results in developmental outcomes and further transformed contexts, which, in turn, shapes future development.

Adolescent Outcomes

Along with the challenge of understanding the multiple, interacting contexts of development, defining adolescent outcomes is equally significant. Grotevant's framework provides a means of organizing the large body of literature that exists in this area. Each of these concepts will be discussed in depth in the following chapters of this book. For the purpose of introducing the concepts, we will briefly describe the outcomes defined by Grotevant, that include transformations in relationships; development of identity; emotional health; and competence.

Transformation in relationships. Adolescent relationships change in response to the growth and development of adolescents themselves and to the varying contexts of which they are a part. Important transformations are occurring in an adolescent's life, including emerging friendships, intimate relationships, and connections to the larger community. In turn, parents and children change their relationships in response to new romantic relationships, increased time spent with peers, school and work obligations, etc.

Development of identity. Identity is the subjective description of one's own personality as well as the social persona that defines self in relation to others. Identity development is a social process that emerges across ecological systems expressed differently across levels, and complicated by biology (e.g. timing of puberty), social (e.g. class and race), and historical meaning (e.g. immigration patterns). Adolescents face multiple choices of identity, such as what career to pursue, and the values or religious beliefs they hold. They also need to understand the worth of one's assigned identities such as gender, class, race, ethnicity, adoptive status, and sexual orientation. The successful development of identity, as defined by Grotevant, is the sense of continuity from one's identity in past and prospects for the future and reconciling identities of choice with assigned characteristics.

Emotional health. Described as a continuum, Grotevant defines emotional health outcome as a measure of "adjustment." On one end there is the development of self-esteem and self-worth; on the opposite end there is the development of internalizing disorders, such as depression and suicide ideation. Health is more than the absence of disorders, yet at the time of the publication of his framework in 1998, Grotevant pointed to a need for more research on the positive emotional development end of the spectrum.

Competence. Competence is the development of desired behavior, and the skills that can be used during the hours of school, work, or daily life. Grotevant includes a broad set of outcomes, such as culturally appropriate behavior and preparation to enter the world of work. As with emotional health, he conceptualizes competence on a continuum from prosocial behavior on one end to delinquent behavior or externalizing behavior on the other. There is a need for further differentiation of positive behavior as distinct from merely the absence of negative behaviors.

Grotevant's framework is compatible with a positive youth development approach. With a shared foundation in ecological theory, the positive youth development approach to human development defines development as a process of growth and increasing competence (Larson, 2000). The study of youth development focuses on the development and enhancement of social and personal assets to create pathways for youth to become motivated, directed, socially competent, compassionate, and "psychologically vigorous."

Grotevant's organization of adolescent outcomes aligns with outcomes defined from the study of community-based youth programs, social policy, and interventions that promote positive youth development. Lerner et al. (2005) organized adolescent outcomes into five areas of interest, known as the "Five C's": the development of *Connection*, favorable bonds with other people or institutions in which both parties contribute to the relationship; *Compassion*, the sense of empathy for others; *Character* is the description of the existence of favorable cultural values and a respect for social norms which is similar to the framing of Grotevant's development of identity; *Confidence* is a sense of positive self-worth, and is on the positive side of the spectrum of emotional health; finally, *Competence* defined as the perception of positive or skill action in specific areas (such as academic, social, vocational, etc.) is similar across conceptualizations. The presence of these factors over time will result in young people able to contribute to their family, community, and society at large (Lerner, Phelps, Forman, & Bowers, 2009).

Culture and Urban Neighborhoods

Blending anthropological work and ecological theories, Rogoff (2003) posits that human development can only be understood through analysis of the cultural practices and circumstances of their communities. Researchers, educators, and programmers need to be aware of the cultural lens through which adolescent outcomes are understood. This volume is dedicated to examining adolescent development in the context of underserviced urban communities; yet it is important to acknowledge that the majority of human development research is largely based in middle-class European American culture. We must go beyond traditional frameworks to incorporate an understanding of the unique cultural nature of development within low-income, ethnic minority communities.

In their ethnographic study of urban, African American neighborhoods, Burton, Allison, and Obeidallah (1995) identified the unique cultural construction of adolescence for youth living in these neighborhoods. The authors propose an alternative understanding of successful development. For instance, most adolescents experience role inconsistencies as they begin to take on adult responsibilities while they are still regarded as children in many settings. Yet, within low-income and/or single-parent families, a teenager likely has even greater adult responsibilities, such as working to provide income for the family, responsibility for the care of younger siblings, or the adolescent may already be a parent him- or herself. Additionally, patterns of teen childbirth lead to narrowed generational gaps within families, with an average of 14 years between generations in their study. Age-condensed families result in overlapping teen and adult worlds where they are competing for the same jobs, have similar aged romantic partners, or similar child care responsibilities. When the young person assumes these adult roles it can be difficult for the adolescent's parent to set limits or discipline their child. Lastly, the authors found that every family in the study had a young male family member who had died or was incarcerated. Most youth in their study stated that they did not expect to live past the age of 21. Teens perceived an accelerated life course as a result of entering the work force, early reproduction, and shortened life expectancy.

The ambiguity of adolescent development within the context of urban neighborhoods results in alternative definitions of successful outcomes by community members and by the adolescents themselves. According to ecological theories of development, adolescent outcomes are a product of overlapping contexts with congruent or possibly incongruent cultural meanings. The potential for conflicting cultural meanings of these roles is heightened for underserved, low-income and minority youth (Spencer, Swanson, & Cunningham, 1991). Burton et al. (1995) highlighted the alternative priorities for youth who are responsible for providing for immediate needs and who expect to die young. Young people focus on present well-being over long-term success, on being self-sufficient and on their ability to take on adult roles. Community members also emphasize additional outcomes of value such as religious participation, creative abilities, or connectedness to family. The meaning and prioritization of these outcomes, and their implications for the future can be in conflict with one another and with the majority culture.

Consider a youth from a low-income family who is working a regular job to contribute to the family income or is providing care for relatives, and, as a result, fails to attend school on a regular basis. Within the school context alone, researchers or educators may consider this student a casualty of the urban environment. However, within the context of the family, this same youth may have developed close, supportive relationships, and within the community this youth might be viewed as a success story. Yet, whatever cultural acceptance this adolescent has obtained, he or she still faces another cultural reality that will limit future options. Without a high school diploma, he/she faces a low-wage future. Success in one context does not necessarily translate into success in another; youth in urban areas must bridge multiple contexts and balance the cultural meanings of success.

Culture, Identity Development and Academic Success

Ethnicity and cultural identity have a significant impact on the experiences and development of minority youth (Spencer et al., 1991). The effects of structural inequality, racism, and poverty in the context of urban, underserviced communities are often ignored in developmental theories (Lerner et al., 2009). The Phenomenological Variant of Ecological Systems Theory (PVEST) accounts for unique experiences of injustice and inequity that contribute to urban African American identity development (Spencer, Dupree, & Hartmann, 1997). Individual encounters in diverse cultural contexts influence how adolescents perceive and experience the self and contribute to their ability to cope with high-risk contexts (such as dangerous neighborhoods) and with undervalued minority status in the larger culture. Identity and self-perception continue to shape the individual's competences and predict future outcomes. This framework has been used to expand and contextualize positive youth development outcomes of low-income, minority youth. This theory has been applied in research examining the link between ethnic identity, competence, and school outcomes in African American adolescents and suggests that the development of positive identity is a key to improving school adjustment for youth in urban educational settings (Lerner et al., 2009; Spencer, 1999).

Applying this broader ecological and cultural framework to school settings assists in understanding the complex interactions between levels of influence and provides opportunities for researchers and educators to design effective programs. Research suggests that youth who balance the demands and expectations of academic success (defined by the majority culture) while, at the same time, maintaining pride in their own ethnic, cultural, and social group demonstrate the greatest gains in academic, social, and emotional outcomes (Carter, 2006). Educators are challenged to analyze cultural practices (e.g. language, relationships and social support structures) in order to help youth bridge academic expectations within relevant contexts. Urban schools that take into account the cultural context of the learner and develop assets in support of positive development have been shown to increase the academic success of their students (Foster, Lewis, & Onafowora, 2003; Lewis et al., 2011).

Culture in the Classroom

Educators are teaching in increasingly diverse classrooms and the need for culturally competent instruction is a challenge faced by all urban school districts (Garcia, Arias, & Harris Murri, 2010). To meet this challenge, educational research has encouraged the investigation of how practices promoting achievement within urban, and racial and ethnic minority students are compatible or conflict with dominant educational practices. Culturally responsive education goes beyond training new instruction techniques; it requires multicultural preparation and professional development for teachers and school administrators (Villegas & Lucas, 2007; Weinstein, Tomlinson-Clarke, & Curran, 2004). Intervention strategies have been designed to coach teachers to recognize the cultural construction of knowledge and use this insight to improve classroom management and instruction. These comprehensive initiatives have resulted in increased teacher competence as well as improved student academic performance.

For example, a classroom intervention described by Wheeler (2008) encourages teachers to understand that students using the language of their culture are not making "errors" but are following the language pattern of their community. Teachers lead students through a critical thinking process to build on vernacular language use to increase understanding and knowledge of Standard English. Children are instructed to compare and contrast the grammar patterns of Vernacular African American English and Standard English, what rules are applied in speech and in writing and when they should be used. Teaching using so-called "linguistic code-switching" has resulted in enhanced cognitive development and improved test scores in students and an increased confidence in teachers (Wheeler, 2008).

Youth as Agents of Change

As highlighted by the transactional nature of Grotevant's framework, individuals are not simply created by culture or subject to its influences. Youth are at the center of their own development and help to shape the contexts and culture to which they belong. Programs promoting positive youth development engage youth in challenging, authentic activities to increase their skills and motivate them to take charge of their lives (Larson, 2000).

Specifically designed to promote positive development for youth in urban contexts, the social justice approach to youth development engages youth in reflection of complex social and ecological factors that comprise their own experience and asks them to participate in shaping their own environment (Ginwright & Cammarota, 2002; Ginwright & James, 2002). Importantly, it includes a focus on building awareness of how sociopolitical influences contribute to their own identity development.

It emphasizes analysis of power relationships, strategies to create social change, and collective action.

Participatory action research is one example of a program based in the social justice approach. Teachers are trained to help students identify concerns in their schools and communities. Partnering with adults, youth design and carry out research to better understand the nature of the problems and take action to improve the conditions in which they live. This approach has been applied in several urban schools (see Brown & Rodriguez, 2009).

For example, McIntyre (2000, 2003) engaged adolescents in urban areas to describe their perceptions of their neighborhoods, their understanding of violence and its impact on the school and community. As a result of their research, teachers and other adults in the community gained a better understanding of the complexities that shape the lives of inner-city youth. The youth themselves became engaged and motivated to build community capacity for change; and, in turn, adults were provided an opportunity see the positive assets in the youth themselves.

Youth social action has the potential to produce impacts at multiple contextual levels: individuals, communities and social conditions. For youth, community organizing promotes psychological empowerment and leadership development through engaging with peers around common issues (Christens & Dolan, 2011). Youth development interventions often incorporate expectations of contribution and social change as a mechanism to develop personal competence in youth. In these programs, positive outcomes are found not only for youth; schools, families, and community systems are also significantly impacted (Durlak et al., 2007). A social justice approach is unique within youth development programs, as it specifically addresses engaging low-income minority youth in political action by examining the institutional, historical, and systemic forces that limit or promote their future opportunities. This approach is theoretically posed to positively impact youth identity, problem solving, decision making, community well-being, and spiritual development in a culturally grounded way (Ginwright & James, 2002).

Conclusions

There is much research on the risks of growing up within underserviced urban communities. There is a need for synthesizing the existent research and determining the characteristics of youth, schools and communities that support the positive development of all youth. The strength of a common framework allows for a cross-disciplinary collaboration that can ground practice in sound theory and methodology.

Our chapter provides an overview of the Grotevant framework used as the organizing structure for the remaining chapters. Based in ecological theory, his framework provides a lens for researchers and practitioners to examine larger influences of social, political, and economic forces that influence human development. For those working in urban contexts there is a need to give more specific attention to the cultural basis of human development.

Although most adolescent development research and theory is based in middle-class, European American culture, there have been investigations of adolescent development within urban neighborhoods and alternative meanings of success. Positive school adjustment of minority youth is related to identity development and the perception of self in diverse cultural contexts. More research is needed to better understand how students broker multiple cultural contexts and how educators, school, and students can effectively incorporate and integrate culturally meaningful opportunities for success.

As schools systems look to facilitate positive development within high-risk, urban communities, attention must be paid to the implications of designing programs/interventions that target different ecological levels. There are cultural meanings applied to defining deficits and assets of development as well as designing individual or institutional interventions. We must consider factors beyond individual- and family-level influences, such as the larger social-level factors that impact behavior rather than point to problems of individual behavior or choice. The positive youth development approach emphasizes the strengths and potential of young people and identifies a role for young people to contribute to and change their environment. Our challenge as researchers, practitioners, educators, advocates, and citizens is to understand the full context of urban neighborhoods, the risks, assets, and resilience that exist within these communities and residents who call them home.

References

Bronfenbrenner, U. (1979). *The Ecology of Human Development*. Cambridge, MA: Harvard University Press.

Brooks-Gunn, J., Duncan, G. J., & Aber, J. L. (Eds.). (1997). *Neighborhood poverty*. New York: Russell Sage Foundation.

Brown, T. M., & Rodriguez, L. F. (Eds.). (2009). Youth in participatory action research. *New Directions for Youth Development, 123*, 19–34.

Burton, L., Allison, K., & Obeidallah, D. (1995). Social context and adolescents: Perspectives on development among inner-city African-American teens. In L. Crockett, & A. Crouter (Eds.), *Pathways through adolescence: Individual development in social contexts* (pp. 119–138). Mahwah, NJ: Lawrence Erlbaum.

Carter, P. L. (2006). Straddling boundaries: Identity, culture, and school. *Sociology of Education, 79*, 304–328.

Christens, B. D. & Dolan, T. (2011). Interweaving youth development, community development, and social change through youth organizing. *Youth & Society, 43*, 528–548.

Durlak, J. A., Taylor, R. D., Kawashima, K., Pachan, M. K., DuPre, E. P., Celio, C. I., . . . & Weissberg, R. P. (2007). Effects of positive youth development programs on school, family, and community systems. *American Journal of Community Psychology, 39*, 269–286.

Foster, M., Lewis, J. L., & Onafowora, L. (2003). Anthropology, culture, and research on teaching and learning: Applying what we have learned to improve practice. *Teachers College Record, 105*, 261–277.

Garcia, E., Arias, M. B., Harris Murri, N. J. (2010). Developing responsive teachers: A challenge for a demographic reality. *Journal of Teacher Education, 61*, 132–142.

Ginwright, S. & Cammarota, J. (2002). New terrain in youth development: The promise of a social justice approach. *Social Justice, 29*, 82–95.

Ginwright, S. & James, T. (2002). From assets to agents of change: Social justice, organizing, and youth development. *New Directions for Youth Development, 96*, 27–46.

Grotevant, H. D. (1998) Adolescent development in family contexts. In W. Damon, & N. Eisenberg (Eds.), *Handbook of child psychology (5th Ed.), Vol. 3. Social, emotional, and personality development* (pp. 1097–1149). Hoboken, NJ: John Wiley & Sons, Inc.

Guerra, N. G., Graham, S., & Tolan, P. H. (2011). Raising healthy children: Translating child development research into practice. *Child Development, 82*, 7–16.

Larson, R. W. (2000). Toward a psychology of positive youth development. *American Psychologist, 55*, 170–183.

Lerner, R. M., & Castellino, D. R. (2002). Contemporary developmental theory and adolescence: Developmental systems and applied developmental science. *Journal of Adolescent Health, 31*, 122–135.

Lerner, R. M., Lerner, J. V., Almerigi, J. B., Theokas, C., Phleps, E., Gestsdottir, S., . . . & von Eye, A. (2005). Positive youth development, participation in community youth development programs, and community contributions of fifth-grade adolescents. *The Journal of Early Adolescence, 25*, 17–71.

Lerner, J. V., Phelps, E., Forman, Y., & Bowers, E. P. (2009). Positive youth development. In R. M. Lerner, & L. Steinberg (Eds.), *Handbook of adolescent psychology (3rd ed.), Vol. 1 Individual bases of adolescent development* (pp. 524–558). Hoboken, NJ: John Wiley & Sons, Inc.

Leventhal, T. & Brooks-Gunn, J. (2000). The neighborhoods they live in: The effects of neighborhood residence on child and adolescent outcomes. *Psychological Bulletin, 126*, 309–337.

Leventhal, T., Dupéré, V., & Brooks-Gunn, J. (2009). Neighborhood influences on adolescent development. In R. M. Lerner, & L. Steinberg (Eds.), *Handbook of adolescent psychology (3rd ed.), Vol. 2. Contextual influences on adolescent development* (pp. 411–443). Hoboken, NJ: John Wiley & Sons, Inc.

Lewis, J., Duke, A., Hilgendorf, A., Brown, D., Jackson, J., & Agnew, R. (2011, August). *Supporting relationships for positive school change in urban schools.* 2010–2011 Final Report to the Wisconsin Department of Public Instruction.

McIntyre, A. (2000). Constructing meaning about violence, school, and community: Participatory action research with urban youth. *The Urban Review, 32*, 123–154.

McIntyre, A. (2003). Participatory action research and urban education: Reshaping the teacher preparation process. *Equity & Excellence in Education, 36*, 28–39.

Murry, V. M., Berkel, C., Gaylord-Harden, N. K., Copeland-Linder, N., & Nation, M. (2011). Neighborhood poverty and adolescent development. *Journal of Research on Adolescence, 21*, 114–128.

Rogoff, B. (2003). *The cultural nature of human development.* New York: Oxford University Press.

Spencer, M. B. (1999). Social and cultural influences on school adjustment: The application of an identity-focused cultural ecological perspective. *Educational Psychologist, 34*, 43–57.

Spencer, M. B., Dupree, D., & Hartmann, T. (1997). A phenomenological variant of ecological systems theory (PVEST): A self-organization perspective in context. *Development and Psychopathology*, 817–833.

Spencer, M. B., Swanson, D. P., & Cunningham, M. (1991). Ethnicity, ethnic identity, and competence formation: Adolescent transition and cultural transformation. *Journal of Negro Education*, 60, 366–387.

Villegas, A. M., & Lucas, T. (2007). The culturally responsive teacher. *Educational Leadership, 64*, 28–33.

Weinstein, C. S., Tomlinson-Clarke, S., & Curran, M. (2004). Toward a conception of culturally responsive classroom management. *Journal of Teacher Education, 55*, 25–38.

Wheeler, R. S. (2008). Becoming adept at code-switching. *Educational Leadership, 65*, 54–58.

3

THE IMPORTANCE OF HOUSING, NEIGHBORHOOD AND COMMUNITY CONTEXTS

Kevin W. Allison, Robert S. Broce and Alecia J. Houston

This chapter considers physical and structural characteristics of the housing within which youth and their families live, including considerations of housing quality, the stability of housing (e.g., homelessness and mobility), and residence in publically supported housing. Our second unit of focus, neighborhood, has been defined as geographically bounded groupings of households and institutions connected through structures and processes (Coulton, Korbin, & Su, 1999) or the smallest geographic areas with a name known to its residents and outsiders (Bursik & Grasmick, 1993). Our third context, "community," has been considered with respect to the psychological and social sense of belonging, emotional connection or membership with a group or place (e.g., McMillan & Chavis, 1986). In our examination of community, we focus on the more social and relational factors relevant to developmental context, leaving the physical aspects of context to our consideration of neighborhood.

Historically, we have had the benefit of the work of multiple scholars supporting a new appreciation and deeper understanding of the role of context (e.g., Crane, 1991; Leventhal & Brooks-Gunn, 2000; Mayer & Jencks, 1989; Sampson, Morenoff, & Gannon-Rowley, 2002; Wilson, 1987). Indeed, students residing in affluent neighborhoods demonstrate greater cognitive competencies and more positive academic outcomes than children who lived in non-affluent neighborhoods (Leventhal & Brooks-Gunn, 2001). There is also a link between neighborhood risk and developmental trajectories involving early parenting or violence, drug use and incarceration (e.g., Schonberg & Shaw, 2007; Caspi, Taylor, Moffitt, & Plomin, 2000; Vazsonyi, Cleveland, & Wiebe, 2006) which have been associated with lower educational performance. In the current chapter, we will not duplicate those reviews and conceptual integrations. This body of work has also built on a range of measurement strategies, including use of census and other administrative data, youth and parental assessments of perceptions of neighborhoods, mapping and windshield surveys. Again we will not duplicate those methodological reviews, but do note that the employment of more distal operationalizations of context (e.g., census- or zip-code-level data) and cross-sectional examinations of context may limit the understanding of critical proximal factors and processes (e.g., the effects of national policy interpretation and implementation at the local level). These processes may be especially important to strengthening our conceptual understanding of contextual influences and the processes that shape the environments in which adolescents grow and develop. In addition, understanding local "micro-environments" may be critical in shaping effective interventions. In the following sections we review relevant research on each level of context.

Housing and Housing Quality

Physical characteristics of housing, such as age of the structure, housing type (e.g., single-family and multi-family housing), and density play critical roles in youth development (Jacobs, Wilson, Dixon, Smith, & Evens, 2009). Older homes have a higher risk for elevated mold levels, poor ventilation, and high levels of dust mite and cockroach antigens that have adverse affects on physical and cognitive development. Youth residing in low-income urban communities are at disproportionate risk for asthma, due in part to their greater exposure and associated sensitization to irritants such as cockroach allergen (Basch, 2011). Related sleep disruptions and missed days of school associated with asthma among urban youth have been associated with poor academic achievement.

Lead exposure is another important environmental risk in urban environments. Data from the National Health and Nutrition Examination Survey (NHANES), indicated declines in blood lead levels for children younger than age 13 between 1976 and 2002, reflecting reductions in youth exposure to lead through lead paint (banned by the federal government for residential use in 1978), as well as lead gasoline (restricted from use in on-road vehicles by the 1996 Clean Air Act). Exposure may be greater in urban communities characterized by older housing stock and industrialization (Bailey, Sargent, Goodman, Freeman, & Brown, 1994). Ris, Dietrich, Succop, Berger, and Bornschein (2004) examined the longitudinal effects of childhood lead exposure in the Cincinnati Lead Study initiated in 1979, following an initial birth cohort of 300. The study found associations between blood lead levels at 78 months and neuropsychological assessments used to form learning/IQ and fine motor factors in the follow-up of 195 participants conducted when they were between 15 and 17 years of age. The effects of early environmental lead exposure persist into adolescence with these risks being greater for males.

Residence in Public Housing, Homelessness and Affordability

Empirical work has also examined the potential effects of residence in public housing on educational and other developmental outcomes. Schwartz, McCabe, Ellen, and Chellman (2010) examined school characteristics and performance of children living in New York City public housing. Children in public housing performed academically worse in math and reading than their peers not living in public housing, and attended schools where overall academic performance was lower. In work by Currie and Yelowitz (2000), children living in public housing developments, as compared to those living in other publically assisted living arrangements (e.g., housing voucher programs), were more likely to have changed schools, and Black children living in public housing complexes were less likely to experience school grade retention.

Discussions of housing and adolescent achievement have also considered issues of housing affordability and homelessness. Data from studies predating the *Stewart B. McKinney Homelessness Assistance Act of 1987*, and implementation of Education of Homeless Children and Youth (EHCY) programs, found more disruption and poorer school performance among homeless children and youth compared to poor youth in more stable housing. However, Buckner, Bassuk, and Weinreb (2001) indicate that although homeless children experience more residential moves than housed poor children, both groups had comparable rates of missed school days and similar levels of academic achievement. After controlling for child (age, gender and race/ethnicity) and parental factors (income, education and mental health), school mobility was a significant predictor of academic achievement. Rafferty, Shinn, and Weitzman (2004) compared adolescents who had experienced homelessness with a comparison group residing in public housing. Youth who had experienced homelessness had greater school mobility and grade retention. Although both groups had similar scores on cognitive ability assessments, youth who had experienced homelessness scored lower in both math and reading achievement.

Affordability and homeownership have become particularly salient in light of the economic crisis. The cost of housing can present significant financial challenges and limit a family's ability to meet the range of competing resource demands (Bratt, 2002). In addition, the inability to provide housing can also lead to other family disruptions (e.g., foster care placement; see: Harburger & White, 2004). Homeownership has been considered a reflection of residential stability, providing the opportunity for youth and their parents to develop stable networks and social connections and has been associated with higher rates of high school completion (Boyle, 2002; Galster, Quercia, Cortes, & Malega, 2003; Green & White, 1997).

Neighborhood Characteristics

Neighborhood characteristics can have various impacts on adolescent development. Lower-income neighborhoods have been characterized as more dangerous, have poorer public services, and contain more deteriorated physical infrastructure than that in middle- or high-income neighborhoods (Evans, 2004).

Economically disadvantaged school-aged children live in noisier environments than their middle-income counterparts (Haines, Stansfeld, Head, & Job, 2002). Children's reading abilities, cognitive development, physiological indicators, and motivational behaviors are affected by exposure to noise—most commonly transportation (e.g. cars, airplanes), music and crowds (Evans, 2006). Youth growing up in urban areas may face exposure to a range of other environmental risks. Pastor, Sadd, and Morello-Frosch (2002) examined the geographic patterns of toxic emissions which compromise air quality and potentially hazardous facilities in relation to school spatial distribution within Los Angeles. Latino children were more likely to comprise a larger proportion of students in schools located in closer proximity to toxic facilities and to attend schools in areas with higher levels of air-borne toxins. Asian and African American children and youth were at higher risk than European American youth to air toxins. In a geographic examination of air toxins in Michigan, air pollutants were at higher levels near schools with larger African American and Hispanic student populations (Mohai, Kweon, Lee, & Ard, 2011). Also, school attendance and student achievement in math and English were associated with air pollution concentrations, even after controlling for factors such as school expenditures and student demographics.

Other environmental stressors, such as exposure to violence, have also demonstrated detrimental effects on the academic achievement of urban adolescents. In a prospective study of urban, middle school students, Henrich, Schwab-Stone, Fanti, Jones, and Ruchkin (2004) found that witnessing violence was predictive of lower academic achievement. Milam, Furr-Holden, and Leaf (2010) similarly found neighborhood violence to be associated with lower reading and math achievement in urban students.

Neighborhood factors appear not only to affect current performance but also youths' perceptions of the future. Stewart, Stewart, and Simmons (2007) indicate that neighborhood disadvantage was negatively associated with aspirations for attending college, accounting for approximately 10% of the variance in the college aspirations in a sample of urban African American adolescents.

Neighborhood Infrastructure

The availability of learning opportunities in the community such as libraries, family resource centers, literacy programs and museums help stimulate children's learning and may promote school readiness and achievement outcomes (Leventhal & Brooks-Gunn, 2001). Further, community-based developmental programs can support positive school attitudes, cognitive skills, and academic achievement (Catalano, Berglund, Ryan, Lonczak, & Hawkins 2004; Durlak & Weissberg, 2007; Rhodes, Grossman, & Resch, 2000). These findings suggest that youth development opportunities can be an important resource to promote positive outcomes, but program quality is critical in supporting outcomes (Yohalem, Granger, & Pittman, 2009).

Youth and family are not passive recipients of contextual influences—residents actively shape the community setting. For example, Benson, Scales, Hamilton, and Semsa (2006) hypothesized that youth participation in service targeting their communities works not only to change the contexts in which these youth grow up, but also has a positive effect on the youth's behavior. The importance of the contextual resources relevant to positive youth development has been noted within the Search Institute's discussion of external developmental assets (e.g., support, empowerment, constructive use of time), the National Research Council's consideration of the features of positive developmental settings, the Alliance for Youth's reference to caring adults, opportunities to serve, and safe places, and The Forum for Youth Investment's emphasis on developmentally important connections (see Scales and Leffert, 2004).

An emerging body of work is considering neighborhood structural factors that are shaped by local administrative jurisdictions. Van Zandt and Wunneburger (2011) found moderate levels of economic segregation in urban areas and that housing characteristics (e.g., home ownership, median housing value) were associated with achievement for students overall, but not for economically disadvantaged students. Szapocznik et al. (2006), in an examination of public-school students living in East Little Havana Miami, found that youth living in mixed-use blocks were at lower risk of having low conduct-related grades compared to youth living in a residential block. These results are congruent with the tenets of New Urbanism, which recommends land use and community design principles that encourage limited car use and walking to support social interaction. These examinations underline the need to reexamine traditional considerations and operationalizations of residential "density" as related to developmental outcomes. Although higher residential density has been implicated as a human stressor, Churchman (1999) has suggested that there are both positive and negative aspects of density. For example, zoning and land use that reduces sprawl may also promote walking and reduce car use, resulting in lower levels of air pollution.

Community

Beyond the neighborhoods and the specific structures in which youth and their families live, context provides a set of social connections that are also important to development. One conceptual strategy for examining social connections of community involves considerations of community social capital. Woolley et al. (2008) found neighborhood-level "bonding" social capital (i.e., the social interactions internal to the youth's neighborhood with adults and other youth) to be positively associated with both math and reading achievement. Similarly, Plybon, Edwards, Butler, Belgrave, and Allison (2003) found neighborhood social cohesion to be associated with school self-efficacy among African American adolescent females. Alternative operationalizations of community social capital, such as indices of attending neighborhood schools and more densely connected parental networks, also appear to support adolescent academic achievement (Israel, Beaulieu, & Hartless, 2001). Beyond social capital, education interventions that emphasize one's cultural sense of connectedness, focusing on "emancipatory education," have demonstrated positive effects on achievement motivation and school connectedness among inner-city African American 8th-grade youth (Lewis, Sullivan, & Bybee, 2006).

Another way in which community has been considered is to examine the disruptions that occur with residential mobility (South & Haynie, 2004). Hofferth, Boisjoly, and Duncan (1998) used data from the Panel Study of Income Dynamics (PSID) to explore the impact of several variables related to parent factors, including residential mobility, on educational achievement. High-income children who only moved once during their adolescent years were more likely to attend college than those who had not moved, but they were less likely to graduate high school or attend college if they moved twice or more. Children from low-income families experienced negative effects with only one move, cutting the probability of college attendance in half and reducing schooling completed by 0.72 years.

In examining mobility, it is especially important to consider parental factors including the active or passive "selection" into neighborhood contexts within which an individual's family will live. An important tension exists in this discussion relative to the hypothesized benefit of access to increased resources and lower risk, as opposed to the disruptive and stressful aspects of moving. Part of the work and subsequent intervention studies on the potential benefit or risk of moving is traced to the promising results of the Chicago Gattreaux program which suggested that families who moved from areas of high poverty to areas with lower poverty had improved outcomes in terms of educational persistence and attainment, and employment (Rosenbaum, 1993). These findings were questioned, however, because data were not collected with a prospective experimental design (Clampet-Lundquist, Edin, Cling, & Duncan, 2006).

The Gattreaux program served as the critical precursor to the Moving to Opportunity Study (MTO) that was designed to examine the potential benefit of a policy intervention that supported family transitions to lower-poverty neighborhoods. The MTO study used an experimental design to test the effectiveness of an intervention that offered housing rental vouchers to families to move from high-poverty areas (over 40%) to neighborhoods with low concentrations of poverty (less than 10%). Approximately 5,300 families volunteered from within five public housing authorities (Baltimore, Boston, Chicago, Los Angeles, and New York City) and were randomly assigned to one of three groups (Goering, Feins, & Richardson, 2002). The *experimental group* received housing counseling and Section 8 housing vouchers to be used in areas with less than 10% poverty. The *comparison group* received Section 8 housing vouchers under the regular, geographically unrestricted program; and the *control group* did not receive vouchers but continued to receive project-based assistance.

Across cities, only 34 to 58% of families in the experimental group actually used vouchers to move to low-poverty neighborhoods. One to three years after entering the MTO program, only 34.5% of families in the experimental group still lived in low-poverty neighborhoods and outcomes have varied depending upon whether families actually used their voucher to move to a low-poverty area, the amount of time since the move, and the outcome variables studied (Goering et al., 2002).

Short-term results (e.g., those from 2–3 years follow-up) were generally positive for children's behavioral outcomes. Girls across sites had better mental health and education outcomes, and engaged in fewer risk behaviors than their female control peers (Kling, Liebman, & Katz, 2007). These girls also had more friends who did school activities. In Baltimore and Chicago, experimental girls were less likely to be pregnant or have children (Clampet-Lundquist et al., 2006). In an intermediate study of all of the sites (5–6 years) experimental boys showed more behavioral problems than the control boys. Experimental boys were more likely to be arrested for property crimes and have more school absences. They also engaged in more risky behavior (Kling, Ludwug, & Katz, 2005; Kling et al., 2007).

Educational outcomes have been somewhat disappointing. Experimental children from all sites did not demonstrate any better reading or math scores, behavior, or school engagement than their control peers (Clampet-Lundquist et al., 2006; Fortson

& Sanbonmatsu, 2010). In the NY site, experimental children spent less time on homework and reported lower grades and school engagement than the control children (Leventhal & Brooks-Gunn, 2005), and children in Baltimore and Chicago that received a voucher were more likely to drop out (Clampet-Lundquist et al., 2006). In light of these findings it is important to consider why, despite apparent positive behavioral effects for parents and girls, there have been less than optimal academic outcomes. Was the "dosage" or exposure to higher-quality neighborhoods too little or too late? Have moves resulted in substantial changes in context or to the contextual factors such as high-quality schools? Do disruptions in social connections, greater salience and potential targeting, or greater opportunity and reinforcement for deviance outweigh potential benefits?

Lessons from Community Interventions

Of recent initiatives working to build neighborhood infrastructure and capacity, one model receiving considerable national attention is the Harlem Children's Zone (HCZ) (see Tough, 2008). The HCZ, created under the leadership of Geoffrey Canada in 1997, is a comprehensive set of programs operating in a designated area of Central Harlem. Two charter schools within the HCZ make up the core of the school investment and include increased educational time (extended school days, year-round schools, Saturday school for remedial work), as well as high expectations for teachers.

Dobbie and Fryer (2009) examined data from the HCZ and demographic and outcome data from the New York City Department of Education to estimate outcomes for the HCZ programs. Taking advantage of the lottery system used by the HCZ charter middle school, a treatment group of lottery winners was compared to a control group of lottery losers. Results of the study showed that students who entered the HCZ charter middle school in 6th grade improved 0.8 of a standard deviation in math, representing a closure of the Black–White achievement gap, and an improvement of 0.25 to 0.33 of a standard deviation in English language arts by 8th grade, closing about half of the achievement gap. Students who entered a charter school at the beginning of elementary school showed that the achievement gap was completely closed in English language arts and math (gains of 0.8 and 1.5 standard deviations, respectively). HCZ charter students were also less likely to be absent, despite the increased instruction time. These results were consistent across ability levels. These academic benefits appear linked to the charter school experience as siblings who had access to other HCZ community programs, but who did not have access to these educational settings, experienced no gains in academic scores or attendance.

Conclusions

Underserviced urban environments expose the youth to a wider range of toxins and stressors that can compromise physical health and cognitive development. The disruption of social networks and discontinuities in school experiences are also associated with negative impacts on educational outcomes. Efforts to use neighborhood mobility as a portal to greater opportunity may have underestimated the importance of social relationships, the assets of support, or the possibility of marginalization and the potential negative effects of greater salience that may also be important. In addition, the relocation studies raise the critical question as to whether moving to lower-poverty neighborhoods substantially provides true access to improved opportunity. At base, the work reviewed suggests that positive educational outcomes appear to be explicitly linked to the building blocks of opportunity *within urban communities*, such as good schools and strong community efficacy.

If our goal is to support productive developmental outcomes for adolescents involving physical health, economic opportunity, civic engagement, and healthy relationships, we cannot continue to ground our work in a fragmented view of youth, their developmental contexts, social policy and the resulting community systems and infrastructure. This fragmentation may also extend to our conceptual models for examining neighborhood. Neighborhoods and communities are intentional human creations. These settings may be shaped by local, state and federal policy, community history, and are subject to the decisions of elected officials, urban planners, local school boards and administrators, public safety leadership and federal judges.

From an ecological perspective, processes such as ethnic succession support us in considering the ways that historical changes in our ecological contexts may influence development. For example, changes in neighborhood contexts grounded in school desegregation have been implicated in the residential mobility of European Americans, especially in the South. Conceptualizations of tipping point models, the role of in-group residential preferences for African Americans and European Americans, as well as the troubled history of redlining, mortgage discrimination and policy efforts such as the 1968 Fair Housing Act are important considerations in understanding the changing contexts that are relevant to the neighborhoods in which urban youth live and are educated (Boustan, 2011). These factors, supported by policy that reinforces jurisdictional boundaries, and transportation policies that result in community isolation, have resulted in the de facto dismantling of Brown (Clotfelter, 2004; Orfield & Eaton, 1996) and are grounded in our country's troubled racial history and present. In order to implement change in creating developmental contexts that support adaptive developmental outcomes, it will be necessary to engage with the complex sets of local, state and federal policies, as well as the relevant histories that undergird the measures of housing, community and neighborhood relevant to our work in urban developmental contexts.

The ways in which our society shapes the physical spaces, as well as the social and developmental resources and opportunities to which children and youth have access, may reflect the extent to which the individuals at each stage in life are seen as valued, included, prioritized or marginalized. If we desire youth growing up in urban settings to achieve and become contributing members of our communities, we must provide them access to healthy and adequately resourced developmental environments that support these outcomes.

References

Bailey, A. J., Sargent, J. D., Goodman, D. C., Freeman, J., & Brown, M. J. (1994). Poisoned landscapes: The epidemiology of environmental lead exposure in Massachusetts's children 1990–1991. *Social Science and Medicine, 39*(6), 757–766.

Basch, C. E. (2011). Asthma and the achievement gap among urban minority youth, *Journal of School Health, 81*(10), 606–613.

Benson, P. L., Scales, P. C., Hamilton, S. F., & Semsa, A., Jr. (2006). Positive youth development: Theory, research, and applications. In R. M. Lerner (Ed.), *Theoretical models of human development. Volume 1 of Handbook of child psychology* (6th ed.) (pp. 894–941). Editors-in-chief: W. Damon & R. M. Lerner. Hoboken, NJ: Wiley.

Boustan, L. P. (2011). Racial residential segregation in American cities. In N. Brooks, K. Donaghy, & G. Knapp (Eds.), *The Oxford handbook of urban economics and planning* (pp. 318–339). New York: Oxford University Press.

Boyle, M. H. (2002). Home ownership and the emotional and behavioral problems of children and youth. *Child Development, 73*(3), 883–893.

Bratt, R. G. (2002). Housing and family well-being. *Housing Studies, 17*(1), 13–26.

Buckner, J. C., Bassuk, E. L., & Weinreb, L. F. (2001). Predictors of academic achievement among homeless and low-income housed children, *Journal of School Psychology, 39*(1), 45–69.

Bursik, R. J., & Grasmick, H. G. (1993). *Neighborhoods and crime*. New York: Lexington.

Caspi, A., Taylor, A., Moffitt, T. E., & Plomin, R. (2000). Neighborhood deprivation affects children's mental health: Environmental risks identified in a genetic design. *Psychological Science, 11*, 338–342.

Catalano, R. F., Berglund, M. L., Ryan, J. A. M., Lonczak, H. S., & Hawkins, J. D. (2004). Positive youth development in the United States: Research findings on evaluations of positive youth development programs. *Annals of the American Academy of Political and Social Science, 591*, 98–124.

Churchman, A. (1999). Disentangling the concept of density. *Journal of Planning Literature, 13*(4), 389–411.

Clampet-Lundquist, S., Edin, K., Kling, J. R., & Duncan, G. J. (2006). Moving at-risk teenagers out of high-risk neighborhoods: Why girls fare better than boys. Working paper, Federal Reserve Bank of Cleveland. Retrieved from: http://www.clevelandfed.org/research/workpaper/2011/wp1101.pdf.

Clotfelter, C. T. (2004). *After Brown: The rise and retreat of school desegregation*. Princeton, NJ: Princeton University Press.

Coulton, C. J., Korbin, J. E., & Su, M. (1999). Neighborhoods and child maltreatment: A multilevel study. *Child Abuse & Neglect, 23*, 1019–1040.

Crane, J. (1991). The epidemic theory of ghettos and neighborhood effects on dropping out and teenage childbearing. *American Journal of Sociology, 96*(5), 1226–1259.

Currie, J., & Yelowitz, A. (2000). Are public housing projects good for kids? *Journal of Public Economics, 75*(1), 99–124.

Dobbie, W., & Fryer, R. G. (2009). Are high quality schools enough to close the achievement gap? Evidence from a social experiment in Harlem. Working Paper 15473, National Bureau of Economic Research. Retrieved from: http://www.nber.org/papers/w15473.

Durlak, J. A., & Weissberg, R. P. (2007). The impact of after-school programs that promote personal and social skills. Retrieved October 9, 2007, from Collaborative for Academic, Social, and Emotional Learning web site: http://www.casel.org/downloads/ASP-Full.pdf.

Evans, G. (2004). The environment of child poverty. *American Psychologist, 52*(9), 77–92.

Evans, G. (2006). Child development and the physical environment. *Annual Review of Psychology, 57*, 423–451.

Fortson, J. G., & Sanbonmatsu, L. (2010). Child health and neighborhood conditions results from a randomized housing voucher experiment. *The Journal of Human Resources, 45*(4), 840–864.

Galster, G. C., Quercia, R. G., Cortes, A., & Malega, R. (2003). The fortunes of poor neighborhoods. *Urban Affairs Review 39*, 205–227.

Goering, J., Feins, J., & Richardson, T. (2002). A cross-site analysis of initial Moving to Opportunity Demonstration results. *Journal of Housing Research, 13*(1), 1–30.

Green, R., & White, M. (1997). Measuring the benefits of home owning: Effects on children. *Journal of Urban Economics 41*, 441–461.

Haines, M. M., Stansfeld, S. A., Head, J., & Job, R. F. S. (2002). Multilevel modeling of aircraft noise on performance tests in schools around Heathrow Airport London. *International Journal of Epidemiology, 56*(2), 139–144.

Harburger, D.S., & White, R.A. (2004). Reunifying families, cutting costs; Housing-child welfare partnerships for permanent supportive housing. *Child Welfare League of America, 83*(5), 493–528.

Henrich, C. C., Schwab-Stone, M., Fanti, K., Jones, S. M., & Ruchkin, V. (2004). The association of community violence exposure with middle-school achievement: A prospective study. *Applied Developmental Psychology, 25*, 327–348.

Hofferth, S. L., Boisjoly, J., & Duncan, G. J. (1998). Parents' extrafamilial resources and children's school attainment. *Sociology of Education, 71*, 246–268.

Israel, G. D., Beaulieu, L. J., & Hartless, G. (2001). The influence of family and community social capital on educational achievement. *Rural Sociology, 66*(1): 43–68.

Jacobs, D. E., Wilson, J., Dixon, S. L., Smith, J., & Evens, A. (2009). The relationship of housing and population health: A 30-year retrospective analysis. *Environmental Health Perspectives, 117*(4), 597–604.

Kling, J. R., Liebman, J. B., & Katz, L. F. (2007). Experimental analysis of neighborhood effects. *Econometrica, 75*(1), 83–119.

Kling, J. R., Ludwig, J., & Katz, L. F. (2005). Neighborhood effects on crime for female and male youth: Evidence from a randomized housing voucher experiment. *Quarterly Journal of Economics, 120*, 87–130.

Leventhal, T., & Brooks-Gunn, J. (2000). The neighborhoods they live in: Effects of neighborhood residence upon child and adolescent outcomes. *Psychological Bulletin, 126*, 309–337.

Leventhal, T., & Brooks-Gunn, J. (2001). Changing neighborhoods and child wellbeing: Understanding how children may be affected in the coming century. In S. L. Hofferth, & T. J. Owens (Eds.), *Children at the millennium: Where have we come from, where are we going?* (pp. 263–301). Kidlington, Oxford: Elsevier.

Leventhal T., & Brooks-Gunn, J. (2005). Neighborhood and gender effects on family processes: Results from the moving to opportunity program. *Family Relations, 54*, 633–643.

Lewis, K. M., Sullivan, C. M., & Bybee, D. (2006). An experimental evaluation of a school-based emancipator intervention to promote African American well-being and youth leadership. *Journal of Black Psychology, 32*, 3–28.

Mayer, S., & Jencks, C. (1989). Growing up in poor neighborhoods: How much does it matter? *Science, 243*, 1441–1445.

McMillan, D. W., & Chavis, D. M. (1986). Sense of community: A definition and theory. *Journal of Community Psychology, 14*, 6–23.

Milam, A.J., Furr-Holden, C. D. M., & Leaf, P. J. (2010). Perceived school and neighborhood safety, neighborhood violence and academic achievement in urban school children. *Urban Review, 42*(5), 458–467.

Mohai, P., Kweon, B., Lee, S., & Ard, K. (2011). Air pollution is linked to poorer student health and academic performance. *Health Affairs, 30*(5), 852–862.

Orfield, G., & Eaton, S. E. (1996). *Dismantling desegregation: The quiet reversal of Brown v. Board of Education.* New York: The New Press.

Pastor, M., Sadd, J. L., & Morello-Frosch, R. (2002). Who's minding the kids? Pollution, public schools, and environmental justice in Los Angeles. *Social Science Quarterly, 83*(1), 263–280.

Plybon, L. E., Edwards, L., Butler, D., Belgrave, F. Z., & Allison, K. W. (2003). Examining the link between neighborhood cohesion and school outcomes: The role of support coping among African American adolescent girls. *Journal of Black Psychology, 29*, 393–407.

Rafferty, Y., Shinn, M., and Weitzman, B. C. (2004). Academic achievement among formerly homeless adolescents and their continuously housed peers. *Journal of School Psychology, 42*, 179–199.

Rhodes, J. E., Grossman, J. B., & Resch, N. L. (2000). Agents of change: Pathways through which mentoring relationships influence adolescents' academic adjustment. *Child Development, 71*, 1662–1671.

Ris, M. D., Dietrich, K. N., Succop, P. A., Berger, O. G., & Bornschein, R. L. (2004). Early exposure to lead and neuropsychological outcome in adolescence. *Journal of the International Neuropsychological Society, 10*, 261–270.

Rosenbaum, J. E. (1993). Closing the gap. Does residential integration improve the employment and education of low-income Blacks? In L. B. Joseph (Ed.), *Affordable housing and public policy: Strategies for metropolitan Chicago* (pp. 223–257). Chicago: Center for Urban Research and Policy Studies, the University of Chicago.

Sampson, R. J., Morenoff, J. D., & Gannon-Rowley, T. (2002). Assessing neighborhood effects: Social processes and new directions in research. *Annual Review of Sociology, 28*, 443–478.

Scales, P. C., & Leffert, N. (2004). *Developmental assets: A synthesis of the scientific research on adolescent development* (2nd ed.). Minneapolis: Search Institute.

Schonberg, M. A., & Shaw, D. S. (2007). Risk factors for boy's conduct problems in poor and lower-middle-class neighborhoods. *Journal of Abnormal Child Psychology, 35*(5), 759–772.

Schwartz, A., McCabe, B. J., Ellen, I. E., & Chellman, C. C. (2010). Public schools, public housing: The education of children living in public housing. *Urban Affairs Review, 46*(1) 68–89.

South, S. J., & Haynie, D. L. (2004). Friendship networks of mobile adolescents. *Social Forces, 83*(1), 315–350.

Stewart, E. B., Stewart, E. A., & Simmons, R. L. (2007). The effect of neighborhood context on the college aspirations of African American adolescents. *American Educational Research Journal, 44*(4), 896–919.

Szapocznik, J., Lombard, J., Martinez, F., Mason, C. A., Gorman-Smith, D., Plater-Zyberk, E., Brown, S. C., & Spokane, A. (2006). The impact of the built environment on children's school conduct grades: The role of diversity of use in a Hispanic neighborhood. *American Journal of Community Psychology, 38*, 299–310.

Tough, P. (2008). *Whatever it takes: Geoffrey Canada's quest to change Harlem and America.* Boston: Houghton Mifflin Company.

Van Zandt, S., & Wunneburger, D. F. (2011). The relationship between residential land use patterns and the educational outcomes of economically disadvantaged students in Texas. *Urban Education, 46*(3), 292–321.

Vazsonyi, A. T., Cleveland, H. H., & Wiebe, R. P. (2006). Does the effect of impulsivity on delinquency vary by neighborhood disadvantage? *Criminal Justice and Behavior, 33*(4), 511–541.

Wilson, W. J. (1987). *The truly disadvantaged.* Chicago: University of Chicago Press.

Woolley, M. E., Grogan-Kaylor, A., Gilster, M. E., Karb, R. A., Gant, L. M., Reischl, T. M., & Alaimo, K. (2008). Neighborhood social capital, poor physical conditions and school achievement. *Children and Schools, 30*(3), 133–145.

Yohalem, N., Granger, R. C., & Pittman, K. J. (2009). The quest for quality: Recent developments and future directions for the out-of-school-time field. *New Directions for Youth Development, 121*, 129–140.

4

PERSONAL CHARACTERISTICS ASSOCIATED WITH RESILIENCE AND VULNERABILITY IN URBAN ADOLESCENTS

Michael Cunningham, Natalie Papale, and Andrew Kim

The purpose of this chapter is to examine how personal characteristics are associated with resilience and vulnerability for African American adolescents. Resilience is defined as, "a dynamic process encompassing positive adaptation within the context of significant adversity" (Luthar, Cicchetti, & Becker, 2000, p. 543). Vulnerability is defined as, "when mental health or behaviors are weakened under challenging situations" (Luthar et al., 2000 pp. 547–548). Associated with both constructs is exposure to adversity. Stressful life events are used to examine adversity in the current study. Typically, stressful life events are associated with maladaptive behaviors and, in turn, produce maladaptive outcomes. However, not everyone exposed to stressful events experiences a negative outcome. The extant literature posits that self-esteem and/or social support can buffer the negative consequences of chronic stress exposure (Luthar, 2006; Spencer, 2006).

In the current chapter, the personal characteristics examined are: age, gender, family structure, and socioeconomic status (SES). These characteristics become more salient with age because of the development of formal operational thought (Keating, 1990) as well as increased social mobility (Spencer, 2006). Gender-specific trajectories are also associated with this developmental period; key differences between males and females are associated with resiliency, vulnerability, self-esteem, and perceptions of social support (Spencer, 2006; Trask-Tate, Cunningham, & Lang-DeGrange, 2010). During adolescence, males and females experiment with adult roles and identity. Notions of identity traditionally tend to be male focused, concerning independence and autonomy (Trask-Tate et al., 2010). Females cope more with relationships as interdependence becomes more important at this time. The gender-specific patterns are affiliated with one's family structure too. Family structure also predicts how adolescents perceive social support and interact within their respective families (McLoyd, 2011). For example, parental monitoring has a greater impact on the future expectations of males than females (Cunningham, Mars, & Burns, in press).

SES is another important personal characteristic because low SES is associated with chronic poverty and community disadvantage. Those with low SES can be exposed to frequent violence and deaths, taking a toll on adolescents (McLoyd, 2011; Trask-Tate & Cunningham, 2010). Therefore, SES is examined in this study because of the frequency of exposure to challenges.

Each personal characteristic is important on its own. However, literature often directly links these personal characteristics to outcomes. Consideration of the mechanisms associated with personal characteristics that lead to vulnerable and resilient outcomes is less noted (Spencer, 2006). This point is especially salient when examining research on racial/ethnic minority urban adolescents. The last decade has seen an increase in conceptual models that specifically address urban and racial/ethnic minority adolescents (see Garcia Coll et al., 1996; Spencer, 1995, 2006). The section below examines these models and associates them with relevant personal characteristics.

Theoretical Frameworks

The Ecological Systems Model (Bronfenbrenner, 1977; Bronfenbrenner & Morris, 2006) was one of the first theoretical models to provide a widely used conceptual framework to understand urban adolescents. Through interactions between the growing individual and the context (e.g., family, peers, community), one can examine how direct and indirect ecological systems are associated with developmental outcomes. However, not explicit in Bronfenbrenner's model is a consideration of how individuals make meaning of their experiences through a personal lens associated with the individual's racial, ethnic, and cultural backgrounds.

To address this issue, Garcia Coll and colleagues (1996) posit an Integrative Model of Development for the study of minority populations' competencies that considers personal characteristics such as social class, racial and ethnic background and historical considerations associated with skin tone and racial/ethnic heritage. Garcia Coll and colleagues refer to personal characteristics as *social position variables* (e.g., social class, ethnicity, and gender). These variables must be understood in relation to social constructs such as racism and discrimination, which influence contextual experiences such as segregation. These variables, in turn, are associated with facilitative or inhibiting environments.

Spencer's Phenomenological Variant of the Ecological Systems Theory (PVEST) (Spencer, 1995, 2006) adds phenomenology to the ecological theoretical perspective. Perception of the self and others is an essential aspect of development that is not fully addressed by Bronfenbrenner's theoretical perspective. Spencer, Dupree and Hartmann (1997) address this weakness by focusing on typical developmental processes simultaneously with how individuals "make meaning" of their experiences. A PVEST perspective posits that phenomena and experiences not only influence how much one feels valued or valuable (e.g., self-esteem), but these experiences also influence how one gives meaning and significance to different aspects of oneself (Spencer, 2006). More specifically, a PVEST perspective emphasizes that experiences and one's perception of experiences in diverse cultures and contexts influence how one perceives oneself and others. Urban adolescents must perceive themselves in many contexts, which require specific coping processes. For example, W. E. B. Dubois noted that Black Americans experience a "double consciousness" by living as a Black person and an American person (Spencer et al., 1997).

Personal characteristics fit into what Spencer defines as one's *"net vulnerability"* or characteristics a person cannot change. This is the first component of Spencer's PVEST. Spencer and colleagues (1997) note that "self-organization is determined not only by context, but by phenomenological experience of race, gender, physical status, and many other potential factors" (p. 820). Therefore, personal characteristics must be examined as the balance between risk and protective factors. For the Garcia Coll Integrative Model, personal characteristics are described as social position variables (e.g., skin color, racial features, hair texture) that are particularly salient to populations of color. For example, being an African American male is often considered a risk factor (Corprew & Cunningham, 2012; Cunningham, 1999; Swanson, Cunningham, & Spencer, 2003; Spencer, 2006); yet, male privilege may advantage males over females in terms of how they interact within social settings. Physical maturation may also be a risk or a protective factor. Early maturing African American males have more challenges because they are viewed as dangerous adult men (Cunningham & Meunier, 2004; Cunningham, Swanson, Spencer, & Dupree, 2003; Stevenson, 1997; Stevenson, Herrero-Taylor, Cameron, & Davis, 2002). However, African American females get better grades and are more successful in academics than African American males. Both PVEST and the Integrative Model posit that these variables are aspects that the individual cannot change, but must be considered, as they are associated with daily interactions.

Both models emphasize the importance of these personal characteristics, as they are associated with social challenges. Spencer's explains that the net vulnerability plays a major role in how individuals react to stressful events. Garcia Coll et al. (1996) emphasize the point that the personal characteristics are not additive but interact and/ or mediate relations to other structural processes associated with racism, discrimination, and oppression. For example, in PVEST, *net stress engagement* is the second component. Net stress engagement comprises of the challenges and/or supports present when an adolescent encounters a risk. Indeed, parents can socialize their children to adaptively cope with a stressful event. For example, African American males may have very different interactions with law enforcement than their White counterparts (Cunningham, 1999; Spencer et al., 1997). Knowing this, African American parents can share with their sons how to respond properly to police, thus making a negative event with police less likely (Cunningham et al., 2003; Spencer et al., 1997). On the other hand, if a parent does not socialize youth to deal with these types of experiences, this may contribute to a negative racial identity.

Teachers and peers also play a role in such ethnic socialization (Cunningham & Swanson, 2010; Hurd, Zimmerman, & Reischl, 2011). For example, urban, African American adolescents are inclined to look up to adults who they respect and frequently encounter in their everyday lives (Hurd, Zimmerman, & Xue, 2009). Similarly, Garcia Coll et al.'s (1996) Integrative Model links personal characteristics to residential settings, which are directly associated with environments that promote or inhibit exposure to structural opportunities (e.g., schools and neighborhoods). A major difference in the two models is that PVEST focuses on individuals within the social context and the Integrative Model focuses more on learning the environment in which individuals reside.

A balance of challenges and support from family, teachers, and peers is important and influences the *reactive coping strategies* of the adolescent, which is the third aspect of Spencer's PVEST model. If an adolescent has more challenges than supports, he or she might begin to adopt maladaptive coping strategies. This could occur if the adolescent does not have a positive racial identity and experiences conflict in school because of it. A maladaptive coping strategy in this case would be for the adolescent to stop going to school or doing schoolwork, for example. Yet, if an adolescent's supports are greater than his or her challenges, an adaptive coping mechanism may be developed. For example, a positive racial identity in African American adolescents has been associated with high self-esteem and academic achievement (Spencer, Noll, Stoltzfus, & Harpalani, 2001). In turn, students demonstrate high self-esteem and achievement goals in conjunction with high Afrocentricity. One reason an adolescent may have high Afrocentricity would be if parents, teachers, and/or peers instill this notion in the adolescent (Cunningham & Swanson, 2010; Trask-Tate & Cunningham, 2010).

The Integrative Model's discussion of adaptive culture is also important to consider here. Garcia Coll and colleagues (1996) also point out the fact that culture is lived through traditions, histories, migration patterns, acculturation and the current demands of one's context. PVEST focuses on how cumulative reactive coping responses become stable coping responses or "*an emergent identity,*" which is the fourth component of PVEST. Spencer (2006) identifies that an adolescent can form either a productive or adverse stable coping response, which is associated with an emergent identity. The identity is dependent on the feedback given to the adolescent from reactive coping strategies. If an individual receives positive feedback for a maladaptive reactive coping strategy, that individual may form an adverse stable coping response. For example, an adolescent who does not attend school may receive positive feedback from peers, thus continuing this reaction. On the other hand, receiving positive feedback from an adaptive reactive coping strategy may form a productive coping response. The formation of either an adverse or a productive coping response will contribute to the formation of an emergent identity. This stability in the individual is recognized, when situation response patterns become a stable identity (Spencer, 2006). The Integrative Model also transitions from more macro constructs such as culture and history to more micro constructs such as the child's characteristics and family structure and roles. Thus, the Integrative Model pushes researchers to consider interactive effects associated with developmental competencies of cognition, social, emotional, and linguistic competencies as well as how individuals incorporate their family culture to understanding life in the United States.

In examining outcomes, PVEST pushes researchers to understand how stable coping response and emergent identity are formed to impact *life stage outcomes* (PVEST's fifth component). The coping response or identity may be either adverse or productive, once again depending on the adolescent's reaction in the prior stages (Spencer, 2006). Several researchers acknowledge identity formation as a primary psychosocial goal of adolescence (Erikson, 1968; Sellers, Smith, Shelton, Rowley, & Chavous, 1998; Spencer et al., 1997). These life stage outcomes can be productive or unproductive. For example, if an adolescent has many challenges, maladaptive coping strategies, and the formation of negative coping responses, that individual may develop an unproductive life stage outcome. Unproductive life stage outcomes include mental illness or lack of intimacy (Spencer, 2006; Spencer et al., 1997). Yet, if an adolescent has many supports, adaptive coping strategies, and the formation of positive coping responses, that individual may possess high future expectations, good health, and effective parenting (Cunningham & Swanson, 2010; Spencer, 2006; Spencer et al., 1997).

Spencer's (2006) PVEST model does not end at the fifth category of life stage outcomes. This model is cyclical, so the life stage outcomes have an effect on the first category discussed, *net vulnerability*. If adolescents develop adverse life stage outcomes, such as school disengagement, they are perceived as the "disengaged student," which impacts their net stressors, reactive coping methods, emergent identity, and life outcomes. Conversely, positive life outcomes such as resilience and school engagement impact net vulnerability too. For example, resilient students are perceived as able to "beat the odds," which in turn impacts their net stressors, reactive coping, emergent identities, and life outcomes.

Empirical Example

We use PVEST in this present study to demonstrate the processes of resilience or vulnerability. If someone exhibits high future expectations, that individual will be identified as resilient. High self-esteem and/or strong social support can bolster strength and resilience in adolescents (Trask-Tate et al., 2010). In turn, resilience can help to buffer the relationship between a stressful life event and a positive outcome. On the other hand, if someone exhibits depressive symptoms, that individual will be identified as vulnerable. Low self-esteem and/or low social support can cause one to be more vulnerable (Luthar et al., 2000). This vulnerability can facilitate depressive symptoms after a stressful life event presents itself.

Self-esteem and social support from both the mother and the father are examined. Not all adolescents live with both parents, but support from both parents is still taken into account and is important (Garcia Coll et al., 1996). For example, non-custodial fathers as well as other significant adult men (e.g., uncles) may play important roles in the lives of children and adolescents (Hurd et al., 2011; Trask-Tate & Cunningham, 2010). As indicated in Figure 4.1, the study examines personal characteristics as they are associated with salient research associated with African American adolescents such as stressful life events, self-esteem, social support, future expectations, and depressive symptoms.

Our main hypothesis is that high self-esteem and social support buffer the negative effects of stressful life events has to high future expectations, whereas low self-esteem and lack of social support inhibit positive adaptation to stressful life events and result in depressive symptoms. Additionally, gender differences are expected. Females will report higher amounts of depressive symptoms and future expectations.

This study's participants consisted of 206 urban African American high school students (135 females, 71 males) ranging in age from 13 to 18 ($M = 15.77$, $SD = 1.17$).

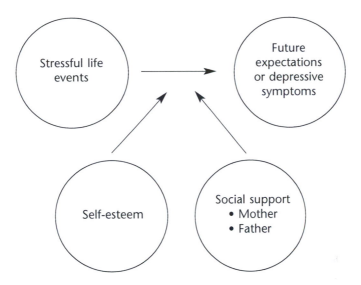

FIGURE 4.1   Conceptual model used in the study

The students lived in households where at least one family member was employed and the income of the household was either at or below poverty level. Also, 46% lived in single-parent households.

Personal Characteristics

To report *Single-Parent Household Status*, students answered the question, "Do you live all or most of the time in a single-parent family." Yes is coded as "1" and no is coded as "2." Students self-reported their parents' education. There was one question asking the students how often the mother worked while the student was growing up. *Gender* was self-reported. *Socioeconomic Status (SES)* was examined by combining single-parent household, mother's education, and mother's work history. Mother's education, father's education and single-parent household were summed and then averaged.

Stressful Events

The original *Life Events Questionnaire* was adapted by Spencer (1989) to accommodate inner-city adolescents in the southeastern United States. Spencer's version, called *Stressful Events*, included questions addressing events characteristic of high–risk communities, categorizing events as circumscribed events, life transitions, behavioral problems, positive events, and community violence. For this particular study, positive events were excluded and the survey given to these participants comprised of 46 items for circumscribed events, life transitions, behavioral problems, community violence, daily hassles, and other miscellaneous items (e.g., "dropped from a sports team").

Self-esteem

This study used the *Hare self-esteem scale* (Hare, 1996). The scale consists of a 4-point Likert scale with responses from 1 (strongly disagree) to 4 (strongly agree).

Social support

The *Social Support Scale* (Munsch & Blyth, 1993), measures how youth perceive support from individuals, such as their mother and father, teachers and school administrators. For the purpose of this particular study, the focus was perception of the importance of support from the mother and father. The students rated the importance on a scale consisting of 0 (none), 1 (somewhat), 2 (moderate), and 3 (a great deal). Each pair of items was summed and higher numbers indicated higher perceptions of support.

Future expectations

The *Future Expectations Scale* (Spencer, 1989), evaluated adolescent future expectations. All 15 items refer to expectations and goals within the next 10 years, such as whether or not they will "have a good job, a college degree, be a role model to youth," etc. Responses were recorded with a 4-point Likert scale ranging from 0 (unlikely) to 3 (very likely).

Depressive symptoms

The measurement of depressive symptoms was recorded with nine items of symptoms of psychological distress such as anhedonia, feelings of hopelessness, and frequency of worry. Included in the sample items were, "My family life is happy" and "At times, I think I am no good at all." Each item was rated on a scale from 1 to 5, including 1 (strongly agree), 2 (agree), 3 (not sure), 4 (disagree), and 5 (strongly disagree).

Results

Due to space limitations, we only report the results of the primary study hypothesis, that is, that self-esteem and social support would buffer the impact that the stressful events construct has to future expectations and depressive symptoms. Additionally, we examined if the personal characteristic variables impacted the relationships. All the variables were standardized and stepwise regression was used to examine the results. Stressful life events were only associated with psychological distress ($\beta = .15$, $p < .01$) as a main effect. The construct did not have a statistically significant association with future expectations nor did the construct have statistically significant interactions with the other variables.

The six sets of analyses examined psychological distress and future expectations as the outcome variables, respectively. Psychological distress as the dependent variable is shown in Table 4.1. The personal characteristics (PC) of SES, gender, and age were

TABLE 4.1 Regression models with personal characteristics, and psychological distress as the dependent variable

	Personal Characteristic (PC = Age)		Personal Characteristic (PC = gender)		Personal Characteristic (PC = SES)	
	SE	β	SE	β	SE	β
Step 1 – $F_{(202, 3)} = .18$, $R2 = -.01$			$F_{(202, 3)} = .18$, $R2 = -.01$		$F_{(202, 3)} = .18$, $R2 = -.01$	
Age	.07	-.01	.07	-.01	.07	-.01
Gender	.15	.01	.15	.01	.15	.01
SES	.07	-.05	.07	-.05	.07	-.05
Step 2 – $\Delta F_{(199, 6)} = 45.33$, *** $\Delta R2 = .41$			$\Delta F_{(199, 6)} = 45.33$, *** $\Delta R2 = .41$		$\Delta F_{(199, 6)} = 45.33$, ** $\Delta R2 = .41$	
Home self-esteem (HSE)	.06	-.61***	.06	-.61***	.06	-.61***
Mother support (Mom)	.06	-.01	.06	-.01	.06	-.01
Father support (Dad)	.06	-.08	.06	-.08	.06	-.08
Step3 – $\Delta F_{(195, 10)} = 1.71$, $\Delta R2 = .02$			$\Delta F_{(195, 10)} = 3.27$, $\Delta R2 = .02$		$\Delta F_{(195, 10)} = 1.13$, $\Delta R2 = .01$	
PC × Mom	.05	.30	.14	.11	.06	.05
PC × Dad	.05.	1.17	.13	-.10	.07	-.03
PC × HSE	.05	.27	.13	-.26**	.07	-.01
Mom × Dad	.06	-.11*	.06	-.11*	.06	-.10
Step 4 – $\Delta F_{(193, 12)} = .20$, $\Delta R2 = .00$			$\Delta F_{(193, 12)} = 1.77$, $\Delta R2 = .01$		$\Delta F_{(193,12)} = .06$, $\Delta R2 = .00$	
PC × HSE × Mom	.01	-.04	.09	.11	.06	.02
PC × HSE × Dad	.01	-.01	.07	.05	.06	-.01

* $p < .05$
** $p < .01$
*** $p < .001$

entered into Step 1. Support from mother and father as well as home self-esteem were entered in Step 2. Home self-esteem was used instead of self-esteem dimensions because more variance was accounted for in the relationships between home self-esteem and the support measures. The two- and three-way interactions were entered in Step 3 and Step 4, respectively. Out of the three models, the one with the personal characteristic of gender was the only set of the analyses that had a statistically significant relationship. Specifically, the two-way interaction of gender and home self-esteem suggests that boys were more vulnerable to psychological distress when their home self-esteem was low. Additionally, all of the models suggest that support from parents interact with one another. As support from the father increases, support from the mother decreases, or one could argue that support from the mother increases as support from the father decreases.

Table 4.2 displays the regression models with future expectations as the dependent variable. The analyses were the same as previously described. The results were similar for gender. Unlike the previous models, the interaction of age and support from the father was associated with future expectations, which suggests that older students who receive more support from their fathers have higher future expectations than younger students. Similar results are noted for students in higher SES families. Students from high SES families and who report high support from fathers have high future expectations. However, there is a statistically significant and negative interaction between support from mother and SES, which suggests that support from mothers is crucially important when SES is low.

Conclusions

Guided by Spencer's PVEST Model, the purpose of this chapter was to examine the association between resilience and vulnerability for African American adolescents. Spencer's model discusses normative development, but adds a phenomenological variant of perception to the theory. Adding meaning to life events is essential for understanding the occurrence of vulnerable and resilient outcomes. Stressful life events were used to examine adversity, noting that stressful life events are associated with maladaptive behaviors and outcomes as well as adaptive behaviors and outcomes. Both vulnerability and resilience can manifest themselves after a stressful life event occurs. Personal characteristics play a major role in the expression of either vulnerable or resilient outcomes.

The personal characteristics examined in this study were: age, gender, and SES. The variables observed were: stressful life events, self-esteem, social support, future expectations, and psychological distress. The results supported other research that has shown that an increased number of stressful life events are associated with increased psychological distress in adolescence (Ge, Lorenz, Conger, Elder, & Simons, 1994; Larson & Ham, 1993). Stressful life events have been shown to desensitize individuals to future stressful events, explained by the stress-sensitization model (Hammen, Henry, & Daley, 2000). Yet, it is possible that exposure to one stressful event can increase the probability of resilience, whereas more than one stressful event can be hindering.

TABLE 4.2 Regression Models with Personal Characteristics and Future Expectations as the dependent variable

	Personal Characteristic (PC = Age)		Personal Characteristic (PC = gender)		Personal Characteristic (PC = SES)	
	SE	β	SE	β	SE	β
Step 1 – $F_{(202, 3)}$ = .65, $R2$ = .01	$F_{(202, 3)}$ = .65, $R2$ = .01		$F_{(202, 3)}$ = .65, $R2$ = .01		$F_{(202, 3)}$ = .65, $R2$ = .01	
Age	.07	−.02	.07	−.02	.07	−.02
Gender	.15	.10	.15	.10	.15	.10
SES	.07	.02	.07	.02	.07	.02
Step 2 – $\Delta F_{(199, 6)}$ = 2.82,★ $\Delta R2$ = .04	$\Delta F_{(199, 6)}$ = 2.82,★ $\Delta R2$ = .04		$\Delta F_{(199, 6)}$ = 2.82,★ $\Delta R2$ = .04		$\Delta F_{(199, 6)}$ = 2.82,★ $\Delta R2$ = .04	
Home self-esteem (HSE)	.08	.01	.08	.01	.08	.01
Mother support (Mom)	.08	.16	.08	.16	.08	.16
Father support (Dad)	.07	.09	.07	.09	.07	.09
Step3 – $\Delta F_{(195, 10)}$ = 2.47,★ $\Delta R2$ = .05	$\Delta F_{(195, 10)}$ = 2.47,★ $\Delta R2$ = .05		$\Delta F_{(195, 10)}$ = 2.47,★ $\Delta R2$ = .05		$\Delta F_{(195, 10)}$ = 2.47,★ $\Delta R2$ = .05	
PC × Mom	.06	.65	.18	−.02	.07	−.14★
PC × Dad	.05	2.18★	.17	−.22	.08	.16★
PC × HSE	.05	−1.06	.16	.43★★★	.08	.10
Mom × Dad	.07	.15★	.07	.14★	.08	.10
Step 4 – $\Delta F_{(193, 12)}$ = .27, $\Delta R2$ = .00	$\Delta F_{(193, 12)}$ = .27, $\Delta R2$ = .00		$\Delta F_{(193, 12)}$ = .27, $\Delta R2$ = .01		$\Delta F_{(193, 12)}$ = .27, $\Delta R2$ = .05	
PC × HSE × Mom	.01	.034	.11	.04	.07	.04
PC × HSE × Dad	.01	−.05	.09	−.02	.08	−.01

★   p < .05
★★   p < .01
★★★ p < .001

This study's results are consistent with this research in that a statistically significant relationship was found between stressful life events and psychological distress. The adolescents in this study were exposed to a high number of stressful life events, possibly making them vulnerable to challenging outcomes. Research for self-esteem has shown that high global self-esteem may occur when a child grows up in an environment with adequate support systems. African American females have been shown to have lower self-esteem than males. Mediating effects examined in a study by Gaylord-Harden, Rugsdale, Mandara, Richards, & Petersen (2007) showed that perceived parental support for African American adolescents was a predictor of high self-esteem. High self-esteem was also shown to help lower internalizing difficulties, such as depression. Continuing with the consistency of previous research, this study showed an inverse relationship between self-esteem and stressful life events.

The regression analyses highlight the point that boys and girls have different experiences. Most interesting was the fact that home self-esteem had a larger impact on whether boys are vulnerable to psychological distress. Similar patterns were noted when examining future expectations. However, age and SES were also associated with future expectations. The results bring up additional questions that need to be addressed when examining resilience and vulnerability in urban adolescents. What is the motivation for when and how parents give support to their children? As discussed by Trask-Tate et al. (2010), support from mothers may be taken for granted, thus its impact is not as evident in the analyses.

This study does have its limitations. The findings were correlational and the measures were all self-reports. However, using Spencer's PVEST model requires perception to be taken into account and self-report is the only way to judge someone's perception. The students in this study were limited in geographic region, and thus the results may not generalize to lower-achieving populations and other regions. Past research and the current study show that resilience and vulnerability play a role in the life stage outcomes of stressful life events. Perceptions of different life contexts and experiences during adolescence are important in the development of resilience or vulnerability. More research must be done in order to fully examine the manifestation of why certain people are resilient and others are vulnerable.

The use of PVEST (Spencer, 1995, 2006) or the Integrative Model (Garcia Coll et al., 1996) is important too. Both models focus on individuals and their ecological context. PVEST encourages researchers to understand phenomena from the individual's perspective (i.e., phenomenology); whereas the Integrative Model encourages researchers to understand the structural conditions in which personal characteristics are associated with developmental competencies. Both models are important, but have implications for study designs. Single-informant studies can use PVEST to understand phenomena from the individual's perspective. Multiple-informant studies can use the Integrative Model to examine structural conditions as well as developmental competencies. Researchers who use mixed-method designs can benefit from both theoretical perspectives. Qualitative studies must consider how personal characteristics are associated with life outcomes. Likewise, quantitative studies must consider additional constructs that must be measured before making definitive statements about life outcomes. Ideally, both the methodologies and theoretical perspectives should be used because growing up in an urban context is complex and capturing the meaning of the individual and the ecological context is equally important.

References

Bronfenbrenner, U. (1977). Toward an experimental ecology of human development. *American Psychologist, 32,* 513–531.

Bronfenbrenner, U., & Morris, P. A. (2006). The bioecological model of human development. In W. Daman, & R. Lerner (Eds.), *Handbook of child psychology, Vol. 1: Theoretical models of human development* (6th ed., pp. 793–828). New York: Wiley.

Corprew, C. S., & Cunningham, M. (2012). Educating tomorrow's men: Associations between negative youth experiences, peer support, and academic achievement in high achieving adolescent African Americans. *Education and Urban Society.* doi: 10.1177/0013124511406534.

Cunningham, M. (1999). African American adolescent males' perceptions of their community resources and constraints: A longitudinal analysis. *Journal of Community Psychology, 27,* 569–588.

Cunningham, M., & Meunier, L. (2004). The influence of peer experiences on bravado attitudes among African American males. *Adolescent boys: Exploring diverse cultures of boyhood* (pp. 219–232). New York: New York University Press.

Cunningham, M., & Swanson, D. P. (2010). Educational resilience in African American adolescents. *Journal of Negro Education, 79,* 473–487.

Cunningham, M., Mars, D. E., & Burns, L. (in press). Gender differences in parental monitoring: Relations of stressful events and future expectations in African Americans. *Journal of Negro Education.*

Cunningham, M., Swanson, D., Spencer, M., & Dupree, D. (2003). The association of physical maturation with family hassles among African American adolescent males. *Cultural Diversity and Ethnic Minority Psychology, 9,* 276–288.

Erikson, E. (1968). *Identity: Youth and crisis.* Oxford: Norton & Co.

Garcia Coll, C., Lamberty, G., Jenkins, R., McAdoo, H. P., Crnic, K., Wasik, B. H., & Garcia, H. V. (1996). An integrative model for the study of developmental competencies in minority children. *Child Development, 67,* 1891–1914.

Gaylord-Harden, N., Ragsdale, B., Mandara, J., Richards, M., & Petersen, A. (2007). Perceived support and internalizing symptoms in African American adolescents: Self-esteem and ethnic identity as mediators. *Journal of Youth and Adolescence, 36,* 77–88.

Ge, X., Lorenz, F., Conger, R., Elder, G., & Simons, R. (1994). Trajectories of stressful life events and depressive symptoms during adolescence. *Developmental Psychology, 30,* 467–483.

Hammen, C., Henry, R., & Daley, S. (2000). Depression and sensitization to stressors among young women as a function of childhood adversity. *Journal of Consulting and Clinical Psychology, 68,* 782–787.

Hare, B. R. (1996). The HARE general and area specific (school, peer, and home) self-esteem scale. In R. Jones (Ed.), *Handbook of tests and measurements for black populations* (pp. 199–206). Hampton, VA: Cobb & Henry.

Hurd, N. M., Zimmerman, M. A., & Xue, Y. (2009). Negative adult influences and the protective effects of role models: A study with urban adolescents. *Journal of Youth and Adolescence, 38,* 777–789.

Hurd, N. M., Zimmerman, M. A., & Reischl, T. M. (2011). Role model behavior and youth violence: A study of positive and negative effects. *The Journal of Early Adolescence, 31,* 323–354.

Keating, D. P. (1990). Adolescent thinking. In S. S. Feldman, & G. R. Elliott (Eds.), *At the threshold: The developing adolescent* (pp. 54–89). Cambridge, MA: Harvard University Press.

Larson, R., & Ham, M. (1993). Stress and "storm and stress" in early adolescence: The relationship of negative events with dysphonic affect. *Developmental Psychology, 29,* 130–140.

Luthar, S. S. (2006). Resilience in development: A synthesis of research across five decades. In D. Cicchetti, & D. Cohen (Eds.), *Developmental psychopathology, Vol. 3: Risk, disorder, and adaptation* (2nd ed., pp. 739–795). Hoboken, NJ: Wiley.

Luthar, S. S., Cicchetti, D., & Becker, B. (2000). The construct of resilience: A critical evaluation and guidelines for future work. *Child Development, 71,* 543–562.

McLoyd, V. C. (2011). How money matters for children's socioemotional adjustment: Family processes and parental investment. In G. Carlo, L. J. Crockett, & M. A. Carranza (Eds.), *Health disparities in youth and families: Research and applications* (pp. 33–72). New York: Springer Science + Business Media.

Munsch, J., & Blyth, D. A. (1993). An analysis of the functional nature of adolescents' supportive relationships. *Journal of Early Adolescence, 13,* 132–153.

Sellers, R., Smith, M., Shelton, J., Rowley, S., & Chavous, T. (1998). Multidimensional model of racial identity: A reconceptualization of African American racial identity. *Personality and Social Psychology Review, 2,* 18–39.

Spencer, M. B. (1989). *Patterns of developmental transitions for economically disadvantaged Black male adolescents.* Proposal submitted to and funded by the Spencer Foundation, Chicago, IL.

Spencer, M. B. (1995). Old issues and new theorizing about African American youth: A phenomenological variant of ecological systems theory. In R. L. Taylor (Ed.), *African American youth: Their social and economic status in the United States* (pp. 37–70). Westport, CT: Praeger.

Spencer, M. B. (2006). Phenomenology and ecological systems theory: Development of diverse groups. In W. Daman, & R. Lerner (Eds.), *Handbook of child psychology, Vol. 1: Theoretical models of human development* (6th ed., pp. 829–893). New York: Wiley.

Spencer, M., Dupree, D., & Hartmann, T. (1997). A phenomenological variant of ecological systems theory (PVEST): A self-organization perspective in context. *Development and Psychopathology, 9,* 817–833.

Spencer, M., Noll, E., Stoltzfus, J., & Harpalani, V. (2001). Identity and school adjustment: Revisiting the "acting White" assumption. *Educational Psychologist, 36,* 21–30.

Stevenson, H. C. Jr. (1997). "Missed, dissed, and pissed": Making meaning of neighborhood risk, fear and anger management in urban Black youth. *Cultural Diversity and Mental Health, 3,* 37–52.

Stevenson, H., Herrero-Taylor, T., Cameron, R., & Davis, G. (2002). "Mitigating instigation": Cultural phenomenological influences of anger and fighting among "big-boned" and "baby-faced" African American youth. *Journal of Youth and Adolescence, 31,* 473–485.

Swanson, D., Cunningham, M., & Spencer, M. (2003). Black males' structural conditions, achievement patterns, normative needs and "opportunities." *Urban Education, 38,* 608–633.

Trask-Tate, A., & Cunningham, M. (2010). Planning ahead: Examining the relation between school support and parental involvement in the development of future academic expectations in resilient African American adolescents. *Journal of Negro Education, 79,* 137–150.

Trask-Tate, A., Cunningham, M., & Lang-DeGrange, L. (2010). The importance of family: The impact of social support on symptoms of psychological distress in African American girls, *Research in Human Development, 7,* 164–182.

PART II
The Fundamental Changes of Adolescence

5

ADOLESCENT PHYSICAL DEVELOPMENT AND HEALTH

Amanda S. Birnbaum and Miriam R. Linver

Adolescence is typically characterized by good physical health; consequently much of the focus in adolescent health is on health-related behaviors rather than health problems (e.g., Ozer & Irwin, 2009). Adolescents' eating, physical activity and sedentary behaviors have become central as the nation struggles with health consequences of poor diet, insufficient activity, and obesity (e.g., Ogden et al., 2006). These behaviors show marked changes in adolescence as autonomy increases and pubertal transformations occur (Jasik & Lustig, 2008; Patton & Viner, 2007). At the same time, there is evidence that lifetime physical activity and dietary habits are formed during this life stage, making it a critical window for lifelong health promotion (te Velde, Twisk, & Brug, 2007; Telama et al., 2005).

Urban communities vary in the resources, exposures, and norms they bring to bear on adolescents' eating and physical activity behaviors. Although underserviced urban environments may limit access to affordable and appealing fresh foods, there are farm-to-table and gardening programs in many urban communities (e.g., Ozer, 2007), along with efforts to improve food and beverage offerings in corner stores and bodegas (e.g., Song et al., 2009). The relationships between urban environments and adolescent physical activity are complex and only beginning to be elucidated by research (Spruijt-Metz, 2011). Some attributes of urban design are positively associated with adolescent physical activity—e.g., access to parks (Babey, Hastert, Yu, & Brown, 2008), and residential density (which increases the number of walkable destinations) (Kligerman, Sallis, Ryan, Frank, & Nader, 2007). Yet when parks and streets become settings for gang, drug, and other serious criminal activities, there is evidence of lower adolescent physical activity (e.g., Molnar, Gortmaker, Bull, & Buka, 2004). Socioeconomic and racial disparities in access to recreation facilities also contribute to lower physical activity levels in urban adolescents (Gordon-Larsen, Nelson, Page, & Popkin, 2006). This chapter synthesizes emerging evidence on urban environments and adolescents' diet and physical activity behaviors, emphasizing promising intervention strategies.

Interventions to promote health may be particularly salient during adolescence. Compared to children, adolescents are more capable decision makers about the desirability of health-promoting behaviors and more capable of acting on these decisions. Successful interventions may have long-lasting benefits as habits developed during adolescence may set patterns for future behaviors (Ozer & Irwin, 2009). Recently, adolescent interventions have focused on person–context interactions, recognizing adolescents as a resource to be nurtured, rather than a problem to be solved (Balsano, Theokas, & Bobek, 2009). Interventions that target positive youth development focus on adolescents' strengths, with the goal of contributing to the healthy development of young people and (as adolescents move into adulthood) at every level of society (Lerner, 2004). Below, we review major health issues of adolescence and, from a positive youth development perspective, describe promising interventions, concluding with implications and future directions.

Domains of Adolescent Health

Adolescent Health and Urban Environments

Although adolescence is one of the healthiest periods in the lifespan as measured by concrete outcomes, some domains of unhealthy behavior are of particular concern for adolescents in underserved urban environments, and may be responsive to intervention. These include (but are not limited to) nutrition, physical activity, and obesity.

Nutrition

Adolescents' food choices are influenced by peers, families, and demographic characteristics such as race and income (Story, Neumark-Sztainer, & French, 2002). Higher SES is associated with adolescents eating more fruits and vegetables and fewer snack foods (Cutler, Flood, Hannan, & Neumark-Sztainer, 2011). Wang and colleagues (2010) found low SES African American adolescents consumed more sugar-sweetened beverages, fried foods, and calorie-rich, low-nutrient snacks and fewer dairy products compared to a European American national sample. Adolescents in low SES neighborhoods are more likely than other adolescents to live in close proximity to convenience stores (Neckerman et al., 2010), which is associated with higher intake of unhealthy snacks and beverages, whereas proximity to farmers' markets is associated with healthier diets among adolescents (Leung et al., 2011).

Physical Activity

Overall, adolescents become less physically active with age, and females are less active than males. For example, 48% of 9th-grade boys and 30% of 9th-grade girls report being physically active for 60 minutes at least five days per week; by 12th grade, 40% of boys and 22% of girls report the same (Centers for Disease Control and Prevention, 2010). Living in an urban environment can impact physical activity both positively and negatively. Urban environments provide access to parks and connected street networks allow walking or biking to daily destinations, but high crime can prevent adolescents from using these facilities for physical activity (Davison & Lawson, 2006; Molnar et al., 2004). Adolescents in low SES neighborhoods have lower physical activity levels than those in higher SES neighborhoods, which Gordon-Larsen and colleagues (2006) linked empirically to reduced access to key physical activity facilities such as schools, public spaces (e.g., pool or recreation center), youth organizations, and activity programs (e.g., dance or martial arts studio, sport or recreational camps).

Obesity

Poor nutrition and inadequate physical activity are predictors of obesity; in turn, obesity is related to numerous health problems in adolescence and adulthood. Obesity-related health inequalities are such that obesity rates are higher among persons of low SES, African American background, and Hispanic ethnicities (Ogden et al., 2006). Neighborhood poverty plays a role by limiting economic opportunity, restricting access to healthy foods, and promoting obesity in already disadvantaged populations (Lovasi, Hutson, Guerra, & Neckerman, 2009). Adolescents are more vulnerable to these risks than adults, as they are developmentally more susceptible to environmental influences, e.g., television commercials glorifying unhealthy habits such as eating fast food. They also have limited disposable income and are likely to spend money on food that is inexpensive and easily available, such as candy and soda (Morland, Wing, & Diez Roux, 2002).

Yet adolescents in dense urban areas can also be resilient, e.g., creating neighborhood-based social activities that are inherently active, such as pick-up basketball or "tag"-like games, or using public transportation and walking to/from transit stops to a greater extent than adolescents who rely on cars. Although for urban adolescents, low SES is generally associated with poor diet and insufficient physical activity, the situation seems ripe for intervention, for example by matching adolescents with already existing or easily created physical activity programs in their immediate environments, or increasing access to farmers' markets and healthy foods.

Summary

Adolescents generally consume diets that do not align with nutritional guidelines, and exhibit declines in physical activity, making adolescence an essential time for intervention. The unique circumstances of urban adolescents offer a distinctive opportunity for interventions that specifically target obstacles and advantages inherent to underserved urban environments.

Interventions

We next discuss promising intervention strategies for promoting healthy eating and physical activity behaviors among adolescents in underserviced urban areas. As described below, traditional health education and persuasion approaches have had limited success in affecting these behaviors. Newer approaches have emphasized reciprocal determinism, the concept that individuals are both influenced by and exert their own influence upon their environments (Bandura, 1986). Such approaches, consistent with a positive youth development orientation (Lerner, 2004), create roles for adolescent participants that are more active and transactional, rather than casting adolescents simply as the audience.

Below, we describe such interventions as falling into three general categories: "traditional with a twist"—interventions that solely target adolescents themselves, but do so from a transactional perspective, and "environment plus education"—interventions that attempt to change adolescents' usual environments (e.g., schools, after-school programs) while also engaging adolescents directly with activities or lessons. Finally, another wave of interventions has been emerging, with the focus on policy or environmental changes without direct involvement of the adolescent. We refer to this type of intervention as "structural environment;" it takes into account that some structural factors can influence health behaviors directly, "without being mediated by a change in individual beliefs, skills, attitudes, or knowledge" (Cohen, Scribner, & Farley, 2000, p. 146). The discussion below is not a comprehensive review of the literature on interventions. Instead, we highlight strategies that are consistent with Grotevant and Cooper's (1998) developmental framework (see more in Chapter 2), and offer promise for promoting healthy contexts and behaviors for adolescents in underserved urban communities.

It is perhaps not surprising that interventions focused on modifying individual-level characteristics have had limited success (Cohen et al., 2000). Without addressing the social and environmental contexts within which the behaviors are enacted, such interventions are at best benign and weakly effective; at worst, by advocating behaviors that are unrealistic or impossible for the setting or context, they may convey a disconnect between the interventionists and the audience that undermines the very aims of the intervention. These concerns are especially salient when the audience is adolescents in underserviced urban communities, where healthier foods and beverages as well as resources and opportunities for safe physical activity may be less available and more expensive than in other communities (Gordon-Larsen et al., 2006; Lovasi et al., 2009). Interventions that exhort adolescents to change their behavior but fail to acknowledge environmental constraints have little promise of producing behavior change, and could foster alienation or exclusion.

Promising Interventions: Traditional with a Twist

Several recent interventions developed specifically for urban adolescents have woven an explicit focus on environmental and social contexts into more traditional, individual-focused education and persuasion techniques, and have produced positive evidence. These interventions address adolescents directly and include traditional elements such as curricula, hands-on activities, skill-building, and promotion of healthy choices. What is different is that the interventions also include capacity-building to help adolescents bring their own voices to bear, and imbue the interventions with issues and challenges that are salient to their contexts. These interventions employ methods such as youth creative arts, advocacy training, or mentoring that have not been extensively evaluated within the realm of dietary and physical activity promotion, so many have been tested in small-scale feasibility studies, demonstration projects, or small quasi-experiments. Therefore, the empirical evidence base is nascent, though promising.

Some approaches have used a twist on traditional health promotion by helping adolescents create and disseminate their own versions of healthy eating and physical activity messages. One group used a theater-based approach in an after-school intervention for African American early adolescents in an urban center in Georgia (Jackson, Mullis, & Hughes, 2010). Participants learned about healthy eating and physical activity while also developing theater skills. As they progressed, participants were guided to apply their new knowledge and competencies to develop a script for a culminating performance conveying healthy eating and physical activity messages. Notably, the adolescents took this opportunity to infuse the script with issues that were closest to them:

> The participants wanted the characters in the play to be like them and the play setting to be in their neighborhood, not like what they saw on television. They wanted to be the stars. The characters, therefore . . . acted as the youth would in their own surroundings.
>
> *(Jackson et al., 2010, p. 94)*

Participants reported positive changes in knowledge and behaviors in pre-post surveys ($n = 15$). In a similar vein, Carter and colleagues (Carter et al., 2005) taught technical and creative skills for media messaging along with nutrition and physical activity lessons to multiethnic urban 9–12-year-olds in after-school programs in several cities. The programs provided skills and opportunities to become advocates for healthy eating and physical activity. Pre-post knowledge surveys ($n = 93$) suggested improvements post-intervention.

Lubans, Morgan, Aguiar, and Callister (2011) incorporated leadership development and a youth accreditation process as novel elements in an intervention with 9th-grade Australian boys in disadvantaged schools. Low-active boys were identified and trained as Physical Activity Leaders (PALs), with a focus on how to use resistance bands and instruct and lead classmates in their use. At a six-month follow-up, favorable results for adiposity (fatness) measures were observed. This intervention is especially intriguing as the youth leaders were students who traditionally would not be expected to shine in the physical activity arena; however, longer follow-up is needed to determine the durability of changes.

The Challenge! program (Black et al., 2010) tested a different type of twist. Challenge! was developed for African American adolescents in an urban neighborhood and includes traditional elements: leader's manual based on Social Cognitive Theory, healthy snack preparation, taste-testing, and physical activity experiences. The twist is that the program addresses the critique that traditional programs fail to consider home and community settings. Challenge! is delivered in participants' homes and communities by mentors who are African American college students trained in motivational interviewing, mentoring, and intervention content. At the conclusion of the Challenge! trial, participants reported favorable dietary changes and those who were heaviest at baseline also reported more favorable physical activity behaviors.

Promising Interventions: Environment Plus Education

Another approach to intervention combines adolescent-focused interventions with environmental changes supporting the promoted behaviors. The SNaX (Students for Nutrition and eXercise) project in Los Angeles grew from a community-based participatory research partnership between academic researchers and community stakeholders (Bogart et al., 2011). A middle school pilot project was developed to address barriers to healthy eating and physical activity. Two simple food environment changes were implemented: sliced (vs. whole) fruit was added to the menu, and cafeteria signage with promotional and educational content was added. A peer advocacy program was also initiated, with 7th-grade peer leaders conducting taste tests in the cafeteria and promoting healthy food and beverages and physical activity. At the end of the pilot study, cafeteria sales of fruits and healthy entrées increased significantly. SNaX investigators also reported decreased sugar-sweetened beverage consumption, and favorable changes in students' self-reported cafeteria attitudes. Notably, after the pilot was completed, the school district allocated funding to continue offering sliced fruit (Bogart et al., 2011).

Another California-based project, the California Endowment's Healthy Eating Active Communities (HEAC) initiative, took the approach of engaging adolescents as actors in their own contexts, helping them develop agency to act not only *within* their environments but also to act *on* their environments (Yoshida, Craypo, & Samuels, 2011). HEAC was a large-scale effort focused on creating and implementing policy changes to increase opportunities for healthy eating and physical activity in six low-income urban areas throughout the state (http://healthyeatingactive communities.org/). HEAC included a youth advocacy component in which high schoolers worked with adult mentors to develop leadership and advocacy skills. Collectively, HEAC adolescents conducted community and school events, community assessments, policy work, media work, and nutrition education. HEAC adolescents reported positive outcomes in terms of personal growth, civic engagement, and development of leadership and writing skills (Yoshida et al., 2011). Teaching urban adolescents effective advocacy and policy-change skills requires an extensive commitment of time and resources. As the HEAC experience suggests, the processes are feasible and yield favorable results.

In a similar vein, though on a much smaller scale, the Food Justice project is a group of adolescents working in their own New York City neighborhood to promote nutrition education and healthy behavior, while also making environmental changes, specifically to the local community garden (http://www.foodjusticeproject.org/). As with the HEAC adolescents, Food Justice participants also engage in community research, including family interviews, peer surveys, and creating maps of locally available healthy foods. These activities suggest that youth engagement in advocacy for healthy eating is feasible even on a small scale.

Urban community gardening programs are an increasingly popular type of "environment plus education" intervention approach. These programs vary widely: some employ curricula while others do not; some are based in schools and some in community settings; some are solely garden-based; and some include activities in additional venues such as classrooms, kitchens, or produce distribution sites. Program aims also vary, from educating youth about nutrition, science, agriculture, and environmental issues, to promoting social interactions and community engagement, to producing crops for participants' own consumption, sale, or donation. Despite their popularity and conceptual appeal, much remains to be learned about garden programs' effectiveness and best practices for achieving adolescent and community health goals (Ozer, 2007; Robinson-O'Brien, Story, & Heim, 2009). Of the few published evaluations of garden programs for promoting healthy eating, most focus on elementary-aged children (Robinson-O'Brien et al., 2009), but favorable results have been reported with adolescents (e.g., Lautenschlager & Smith, 2007), with one program reporting positive influence on both nutrition and physical activity (Hermann et al., 2006). With the intense focus on obesity prevention and promoting healthy eating and physical activity, garden-based programs may be especially timely and strategic, because they address these public health priorities while also providing opportunities for targeting other social, behavioral, and educational goals. Such programs and their need for practical volunteer participation and support may also represent an opportunity to engage families who experience language, cultural, or logistical barriers to involvement with more traditional school activities. Ozer (2007) presents a conceptual model that specifies possible proximal and distal effects of garden program components engaging students, schools, families, and communities; her review also highlights considerations for implementation and sustainability.

Promising Interventions: Structural Environment

Because schools represent a common setting in which adolescents spend considerable time and consume one or more meals, the school food environment has been a major intervention focus. Modifying food availability in schools is a straightforward yet often controversial approach, prompting arguments about autonomy, "food police," negative financial impacts, and the likelihood that adolescents would compensate outside school, but research overall supports feasibility and effectiveness. In one pilot study, researchers evaluated an intervention in which middle schools limited the available snack foods and beverages based on nutritional criteria (Schwartz, Novak, & Fiore, 2009). Pre-post student surveys found decreases in students' consumption of snacks and beverages that did not meet nutrition criteria. Students did not appear to compensate outside school, so the alterations in school affected their overall diets. One promising model for addressing the cost barrier is Connecticut's Healthy Food Certification Program, a state education department initiative providing monetary incentives for districts to extend state nutrition standards to foods and beverages sold outside reimbursable meals (i.e., competitive foods) with initial evidence of success in reducing unhealthy competitive foods in participating districts (Long, Henderson, & Schwartz, 2010).

Beyond the school environment, interventions have also begun to target neighborhood food and beverage availability. Initiatives to expand and promote healthy choices in corner stores highlight opportunities and challenges for future interventions. In Sacramento, California, Jetter and Cassady (2010) piloted adding fresh produce to a convenience store in a low-income urban neighborhood not served by supermarkets. Their case study provides an insightful analysis of the process and barriers. Customers purchased the newly added produce, suggesting latent demand. However, beyond the fixed costs of initially installing and stocking a fresh produce section, the owners found management costs associated with ongoing stocking and maintenance of the produce section to be barriers threatening overall viability and sustainability (Jetter & Cassady, 2010).

A Healthy Stores initiative in Baltimore, Maryland took a different approach, increasing the stocking and promotion of healthy foods in neighborhood corner stores ($n = 7$) and supermarkets ($n = 2$), rather than adding new products. Based on formative evaluation with community members, investigators selected ten healthy foods to target. Stocking of some of the ten food items did increase, with corresponding increases in sales of those items (Song et al., 2009). Pre-post interviews with community members ($n = 84$) revealed improvements in some psychosocial and behavioral variables (Gittelsohn et al., 2010). Resources and additional ideas for promoting healthy food availability in small local stores are available from the Healthy Corner Stores Network (http://healthycornerstores.org/). Interestingly, this network promoted a youth engagement and advocacy model, arguing that because youth represent important customers, involving them in the selection and marketing of new healthy items can be helpful for sales and sustainability (The Food Trust, 2011), suggesting that an "environment plus education" approach may be an effective way to implement this strategy in underserved urban communities.

For promoting physical activity, structural approaches involve creating new venues or opportunities. One promising approach for urban communities is opening school facilities to community members during non-school times (Evenson & McGinn, 2004). Concerns about liability and costs are commonly cited barriers to this practice, referred to as "joint use," but creative approaches have been explored and model joint use agreements are publicly available (http://www.phlpnet.org/childhood-obesity/products/nplan-joint-use-agreements).

One intervention in a low-income New Orleans neighborhood suggests a joint use approach is feasible for increasing adolescents' physical activity. Investigators (Farley et al., 2007) opened an elementary schoolyard that had previously been locked during non-school hours, providing sport and recreation equipment, amenities, and adult attendants to prevent vandalism and bullying (but not to organize or suggest activities). About 20% of those who used the yard were adolescents (kindergarteners through 8th graders were eligible), and two-thirds of all users were observed engaging in physical activity. The authors noted another, possibly far-reaching, benefit: more children in the intervention than control neighborhood spent time outdoors, suggesting that the schoolyard experiences may have increased the overall sense of outdoors as safe recreation space (Farley et al., 2007). Similar approaches for older adolescents may be effective, and could be combined with health education or promotion activities. Another approach has been adopted in Chicago, where the charitable arm of a professional sports team has received federal funds to partner with community organizations and build school-based fitness centers accessible to students and their families (http://www.nba.com/bulls/community/energizabulls_100303. html).

Conclusions

Physical activity and diet are critical health behaviors during adolescence and across the life span, and urban underserved environments present challenges and opportunities for promoting healthy behaviors. We identified three types of intervention approaches with promise for addressing the unique contexts and needs of urban adolescents in such environments, using a positive youth development approach that emphasizes adolescents' transactional relationships with their environments. The first type, "traditional with a twist," implements traditional health education and persuasion approaches in a manner that allows adolescent participants to shape core elements to reflect their own contexts and realities. The second intervention type, "environment plus education," combines adolescent activities with changes to the food or physical activity environments that support the promoted behavior changes. The third type, "structural environment," effects environmental changes that can lead to behavior changes without being mediated by individual-level factors.

Although the evidence base is still growing, the literature suggests some lessons and considerations for future interventions. For interventions that incorporate environmental change, building on and promoting existing environmental resources— such as schoolyards (Farley et al., 2007) or healthy snacks already being stocked in stores (Song et al., 2009)—is a successful strategy for achieving modest improvements in a short time frame. There is limited evidence supporting the structural environment only approach for promoting physical activity among urban adolescents. This may reflect challenges in funding and evaluating such interventions, or might suggest that environmental changes need to be combined with education or physical activity programming.

For interventions that involve adolescents directly, it is important to strike a balance between autonomy and guidance. When encouraging adolescents to develop health promotion messages, interventions must also include instructional components so the messages address important topics with accurate content. When encouraging adolescents to engage in leadership or advocacy, interventions must include sufficient training and support throughout the learning and implementation processes. Using a motivational interviewing approach (e.g., Black et al., 2010), that affirms participants' experiences and helps explore ambivalence, may be a particularly effective way to support adolescents to bring their own issues and voices to bear in health promotion interventions.

Our review suggests that the most promising intervention approaches reach across contexts and constituencies, e.g., adolescents themselves, families, schools, communities, and neighborhood built environments. Although no single intervention can effectively include all audiences and settings, those that explicitly acknowledge what Bronfenbrenner (1979) described as interconnectedness across nested levels of influence have the greatest potential to foster lasting change. At the time of this writing, a movement to reshape the national approach to diet and physical activity is being driven by First Lady Michelle Obama. Her Let's Move initiative expands beyond traditional audiences such as youth, parents, and health care providers, to also include schools, chefs, community leaders, and elected officials (http://www.lets move.gov/). Let's Move makes explicit links between individuals' nutrition and fitness status, and the larger ways of life in our cities, promoting attention to community gardens, food systems, healthy school lunches, walkable neighborhoods, and joint use arrangements. If Let's Move can successfully shift the sense of collective responsibility for health to the broader community, the intervention approaches described in this chapter may be positioned for even greater success.

References

Babey, S. H., Hastert, T. A., Yu, H., & Brown, R. E. (2008). Physical activity among adolescents: When do parks matter? *American Journal of Preventative Health, 34*(4), 345–348.

Balsano, A. B., Theokas, C., & Bobek, D. L. (2009). A shared commitment to youth: The integration of theory, research, practice, and policy. In R. Lerner, & L. Steinberg (Eds.), *Handbook of adolescent psychology* (3rd ed., Vol. 2, pp. 623–650). New York: Wiley.

Bandura, A. (1986). *Social foundations of thought and action: Social Cognitive Theory.* Englewood Cliffs, NJ: Prentice-Hall.

Black, M. M., Arteaga, S. S., Sanders, J., Hager, E. R., Anliker, J. A., Gittelsohn, J., & Wang, Y. (2010). College mentors: A view from the inside of an intervention to promote health behaviors and prevent obesity among low-income, urban, African American adolescents. *Health Promotion Practice,* published online 29 December 2010. doi: 10.1177/1524839910385899

Bogart, L. M., Elliott, M. N., Uyeda, K., Hawes-Dawson, J., Klein, D. J., & Schuster, M. A. (2011). Preliminary healthy eating outcomes of SNaX, a pilot community-based intervention for adolescents. *Journal of Adolescent Health, 48,* 196–202.

Bronfenbrenner, U. (1979). The ecology of human development: Experiments by nature and design. Cambridge, MA: Harvard University Press.

Carter, B. J., Birnbaum, A. S., Hark, L., Vickery, B., Potter, C., & Osborne, M. P. (2005). Using media messaging to promote healthful eating and physical activity among urban youth. *Journal of Nutrition Education and Behavior, 37,* 98–99.

Centers for Disease Control and Prevention (2010). Youth Risk Behavior Surveillance— United States, 2009. *Morbidity and Mortality Weekly Report, 59* (No. SS-5).

Cohen, D. A., Scribner, R. A., & Farley, T. A. (2000). A structural model of health behavior: A pragmatic approach to explain and influence health behaviors at the population level. *Preventive Medicine, 30,* 146–154.

Cutler, G. J., Flood, A., Hannan, P., & Neumark-Sztainer, D. (2011). Multiple sociodemographic and socioenvironmental characteristics are correlated with major patterns of dietary intake in adolescence. *Journal of the American Dietetic Association, 111,* 230–240.

Davison, K. K., & Lawson, C. T. (2006). Do attributes in the physical environment influence children's physical activity? A review of the literature. *The International Journal of Behavioral Nutrition and Physical Activity, 3,* 19.

Evenson, K. R. & McGinn, A. P. (2004). Availability of school physical activity facilities to the public in four U.S. communities. *American Journal of Health Promotion, 18*(3), 243–250.

Farley, T. A., Meriwether, R. A., Baker, E. T., Watkins, L. T., Johnson, C. C., & Webber, L. S. (2007). Safe play spaces to promote physical activity in inner-city children: Results from a pilot study of an environmental intervention. *American Journal of Public Health, 97*, 1625–1631.

Gittelsohn, J., Song, H. J., Suratkar, S., Kumar, M. B., Henry, E. G., Sharma, S., . . . & Anliker, J. A. (2010). An urban food store intervention positively affects food-related psychosocial variables and food behaviors. *Health Education and Behavior, 37*, 390–402.

Gordon-Larsen, P., Nelson, M. C., Page, P. & Popkin, B. M. (2006). Inequality in the built environment underlies key health disparities in physical activity and obesity. *Pediatrics, 117*(2), 417–424.

Grotevant, H. D., & Cooper, C. R. (1998). Individuality and connectedness in adolescent development: Review and prospects for research on identity, relationships, and context. In E. E. Aspass Skoe, & A. L. von der Lippe (Eds.), *Personality and development in adolescence: A cross national life span perspective* (pp. 3–37). London: Routledge.

Hermann, J. R., Parker, S. P., Brown, B. J., Siewe, Y. J., Denney, B. A., & Walker, S. J. (2006). After-school gardening improves children's reported vegetable intake and physical activity. *Journal of Nutrition Education and Behavior, 38*, 201–202.

Jackson, C. J., Mullis, R. M., & Hughes, M. (2010). Development of a theater-based nutrition and physical activity intervention for low-income, urban, African American adolescents. *Progress in Community Health Partnerships: Research, Education, and Action, 4*, 89–98.

Jasik, C. B., & Lustig, R. H. (2008). Adolescent obesity and puberty: The "perfect storm." *Annals of the New York Academy of Sciences, 1135*, 265–279.

Jetter, K. M., & Cassady, D. L. (2010). Increasing fresh fruit and vegetable availability in a low-income neighborhood convenience store: A pilot study. *Health Promotion Practice, 11*, 694–702.

Kligerman, M., Sallis, J. F., Ryan, S., Frank, L. D., & Nader, P. R. (2007). Association of neighborhood design and recreation environment variables with physical activity and body mass index in adolescents. *American Journal of Health Promotion, 21*(4), 274–277.

Lautenschlager, L., & Smith, C. (2007). Understanding gardening and dietary habits among youth garden program participants using the Theory of Planned Behavior. *Appetite, 49*, 122–130.

Lerner, R. M. (2004). *Liberty: Thriving and civic engagement among America's youth.* London: Sage Publications.

Leung, C. W., Laraia, B. A., Kelly, M., Nickleach, D., Adler, N. E., Kushi, L. H., & Yen, I. H. (2011). The influence of neighborhood food stores on change in young girls' body mass index. *American Journal of Preventive Medicine, 31*, 43–51.

Long, M. W., Henderson, K. E., & Schwartz, M. B. (2010). Evaluating the impact of a Connecticut program to reduce availability of unhealthy competitive food in schools. *Journal of School Health, 80*, 478–486.

Lovasi, G. S., Hutson, M. A., Guerra, M., & Neckerman, K. M. (2009). Built environments and obesity in disadvantaged populations. *Epidemiologic Reviews, 31*, 7–20.

Lubans, D. R., Morgan, P. J., Aguiar, E. J., & Callister, R. (2011). Randomized controlled trial of the Physical Activity Leaders (PALs) program for adolescent boys from disadvantaged secondary schools. *Preventive Medicine, 52*, 239–246.

Molnar, B. E., Gortmaker, S. L., Bull, F. C., & Buka, S. L. (2004). Unsafe to play? Neighborhood disorder and lack of safety predict reduced physical activity among urban children and adolescents. *American Journal of Health Promotion, 18*, 378–386.

Morland, K., Wing, S., & Diez Roux, A. (2002). The contextual effect of the local food environment on residents' diets: The Atherosclerosis Risk in Communities Study. *American Journal of Public Health, 92*, 1761–1767.

Neckerman, K. M., Bader, M. D. M., Richards, C. A., Purciel, M., Quinn, J. W., Thomas, J. S., . . . & Rundle, A. (2010). Disparities in the food environments of New York City public schools. *American Journal of Preventive Medicine, 39*, 195–202.

Ogden, C. L., Carroll, M. D., Curtin, L. R., Mcowell, M. A., Tabak, C. J., & Flegal, K. M. (2006). Prevalence of overweight and obesity in the United States, 1999–2004. *The Journal of the American Medical Association, 295,* 1549–1555.

Ozer, E. J. (2007). The effects of school gardens on students and schools: Conceptualization and considerations for maximizing healthy development. *Health Education and Behavior, 34,* 846–863.

Ozer, E. M., & Irwin, C. E. (2009). Adolescent and young adult health: From basic health status to clinical interventions. In R. Lerner, & L. Steinberg (Eds.), *Handbook of adolescent psychology* (3rd ed., Vol. 1, pp. 618–641). New York: Wiley.

Patton, G. C., & Viner, R. (2007). Pubertal transitions in health. *Lancet, 369,* 1130–1139.

Robinson-O'Brien, R., Story, M., & Heim, S. (2009). Impact of garden-based youth nutrition intervention programs: A review. *Journal of the American Dietetic Association, 109,* 273–280.

Schwartz, M. B., Novak, S. A., & Fiore, S. S. (2009). The impact of removing snacks of low nutritional value from middle schools. *Health Education and Behavior, 36,* 999–1011.

Song, H. J., Gittelsohn, J., Kim, M., Suratkar, S., Sharma, S., & Anliker, J. (2009). A corner store intervention in a low-income urban community is associated with increased availability and sales of some healthy foods. *Public Health and Nutrition, 12,* 2060–2067.

Spruijt-Metz, D. (2011). Etiology, treatment, and prevention of obesity in childhood and adolescence: A decade in review. *Journal of Research on Adolescence, 21,* 129–152.

Story, M., Neumark-Sztainer, D., & French, S. (2002). Individual and environmental influences on adolescent eating behaviors. *Journal of the American Dietetic Association, 102(Suppl. 1),* S40–S51.

te Velde, S. J., Twisk, J. W., & Brug, J. (2007). Tracking of fruit and vegetable consumption from adolescence into adulthood and its longitudinal association with overweight. *British Journal of Nutrition, 98,* 431–438.

Telama, R., Yang, X., Viikari, J., Valmaki, I., Wanne, O. & Raitakari, O. (2005). Physical activity from childhood to adulthood: A 21-year tracking study. *American Journal of Preventive Medicine, 28*(3), 267–273.

The Food Trust. (2011, July). *Youth as change agents: Youth-focused corner store projects.* Retrieved from http://www.thefoodtrust.org/php/programs/Summer2011issuebrief.pdf.

Wang, Y., Jahns, L., Tussing-Hymphreys, L., Rockett, H., Liang, H., & Johnson, L. (2010). Dietary intake patterns of low-income urban African-American adolescents. *Journal of the American Dietetic Association, 110,* 1340–1345.

Yoshida, S. C., Craypo, L., & Samuels, S. E. (2011). Engaging youth in improving their food and physical activity environments. *Journal of Adolescent Health, 48,* 641–643.

6

COGNITIVE DEVELOPMENT

Improving Reasoning and Decision-Making Skills among Urban Youth

Bonnie L. Halpern-Felsher, Joann Lee, and Holly E. R. Morrell

Adolescence marks a time of rapid and extensive growth and development in cognitive, psychosocial, emotional and physical maturation. These changes have important implications for the development of reasoning skills and, ultimately, the ability to make competent decisions. Reasoning and decision-making occur within a complicated, interrelated context of mixed cultural messages, varying opportunities, differing levels of adult monitoring, peer pressures, and policy and legal restrictions. Compared to children, adolescents are provided with more opportunities to make decisions in a wide range of areas such as friendships, social activities, academics, extracurricular involvement, and consumer choices. Learning to make decisions, experience positive and negative consequences of those decisions, and derive insights from these outcomes are important, albeit challenging, developmental tasks for adolescents.

Adolescents living in underserved urban communities are faced with additional challenges that can affect their development, judgment, and decision-making. These challenges include poor economic conditions, gentrification, high family mobility, sub-standard or difficult-to-access healthcare, inadequate living conditions, greater exposure to physical and psychosocial stress, and inadequate adult supervision (Dearing, 2008). Unfortunately, studies on adolescent cognitive development, reasoning, judgment, and decision-making have rarely included samples of urban adolescents. When urban youth are included, the aims of the investigation are typically not focused on cognitive development or decision-making specifically among urban youth. The dearth of studies examining urban youth development represents a significant gap in our understanding of youth development and, in particular, our ability to generate findings that can inform strategies to improve urban adolescents' reasoning and decision-making skills and, ultimately, behavior.

In this chapter, we provide an overview of adolescent cognitive and psychosocial development, judgment, and decision-making. When possible, we highlight research concerning the challenges that adolescents face in underserved urban communities, including the lack of opportunities to stimulate intellectual growth, learning, and decision-making skills, as well as implications of adolescent decision-making that are relevant to health educators, healthcare providers, policy makers, and adolescent researchers concerned with developing novel efforts to reduce engagement in risky behavior among urban youth.

Adolescent Cognitive Development and Reasoning

Adolescents experience considerable cognitive change, in which thinking becomes more complex, more abstract, and less concrete. These cognitive changes allow adolescents to simultaneously consider multiple aspects of their actions and decisions, assess potential positive and negative consequences of a decision, and plan for the future. When coupled with psychosocial development (discussed next), these cognitive changes translate into adolescents' desire to participate in and eventually make their own decisions. In the next sections, the components of adolescent cognitive and psychosocial development that are most influential on decision-making are reviewed.

Psychosocial Maturity

Psychosocial markers of maturing include increased perspective taking, reduced susceptibility to peer pressure, reduced impulsivity, increased understanding of the future, sensation-seeking, and increased desire for autonomy. Although there are individual differences and within-age group variation in psychosocial factors, most adolescents reach a level of psychosocial maturity comparable to adults by age 16.

The ability to make one's own decisions is considered an essential component of decision-making competence. In order to make autonomous decisions, individuals must have the ability to resist undue pressure from others. Peer pressure can come in several forms. Most notable are overt forms of peer pressure, where adolescents actively encourage a peer to participate in a behavior or event. Peer pressure can also be subtle, such as when adolescents believe that all of their friends are engaging in a particular behavior, so they feel they should follow along.

While autonomy is certainly important, it does not negate the need to appreciate advice from others, and to be willing to seek advice. As such, adolescents must develop social perspective taking, or the ability to recognize how the thoughts and actions of one person can influence those of another, and to imagine how others might see oneself. Social perspective-taking also involves the ability to recognize that other people may have different points of view, knowledge, or intentions. The ability to acknowledge and utilize these different perspectives continues to develop in early adolescence, stabilizing and becoming similar to adults' abilities by age 16. It is plausible that perspective taking is dampened among urban youth who do not have positive role models to whom they can turn and rely on for advice. As such, urban youth tend to be more self-reliant, which is also an important aspect of decision-making. Adolescents, especially those from urban environments, must learn to not excessively rely on others, to have a sense of control over life, and to take the initiative. Not only does self-reliance provide an individual with the confidence to make decisions, it also allows one to move forward to actually make decisions, especially when obtaining advice from others is less possible.

Adolescents also need to take future possibilities into account in order to make competent decisions. Future perspective taking includes the ability to project into the future, to consider possible positive and negative outcomes associated with choices, and to plan for the future; these skills are generally acquired by age 16 (Steinberg, Cauffman, Woolard, Graham, & Banich, 2009). However, the ability to consider possible positive and negative outcomes develops much earlier, with adolescents able to recognize behavior-related risk, such as positive and negative outcomes associated with sexual behavior, by age 10–12 (Halpern-Felsher & Cauffman, 2001).

Making informed decisions also requires the ability to control desires to act impulsively. Impulsivity refers to making decisions in a quick fashion, without much thought or information. Impulsivity steadily declines starting at approximately age 10 (Steinberg et al., 2008). Resisting impulsive actions is less likely to occur during situations involving peers or when the decision to be made is emotionally charged (e.g., deciding whether to have sex with your partner; Gutnik, Hakimzada, Yoskowitz, & Patel, 2006). While impulsivity decreases during adolescence, youth are more prone to sensation-seeking, or the desire to seek out novel and exciting experiences (Cauffman et al., 2010). Further, as Maslowky and colleagues showed (Maslowsky, Buvinger, Keating, Steinberg, & Cauffman, 2011), adolescents higher in sensation-seeking perceived greater benefits to risky behavior, and as a result were more likely to take risks (see also Steinberg et al., 2008). Despite the dearth of research on urban youth impulsivity and sensation-seeking, one can speculate that opportunities for more impulsive decisions are abundant given the high-paced, high-stress environments facing many urban youth, as well as the lack of positive role models.

Decision-Making

Adolescents' cognitive changes, coupled with psychosocial development including increased social and peer comparison, reduced impulsivity, greater peer affiliation, reduced susceptibility to peer pressure, improved ability to understand and plan for the future, and greater ability to consider and acknowledge other people's perspectives on the behavioral options, translate into adolescents' desire to eventually make or participate in decisions. Making competent decisions is an essential milestone in adolescence, with the decision-making process influencing everything from what clothes to wear, high school and college courses to take, college plans, career choices, and engagement in risky behavior. There are several theoretical models of decision-making that have displayed considerable utility in explaining how individuals, including adolescents, make such decisions.

Normative Models of Decision-Making

Normative models describe decision-making as a deliberate, analytic process. Intentions to engage in a behavior are considered to be the most proximal predictor of engagement or non-engagement in any given behavior, and are determined by several factors. These behavioral intentions are shaped by the following. First, an assessment is made concerning both the potential positive and negative consequences of a behavior or choice, such as getting an STD from having unprotected sex, feeling more relaxed after drinking alcohol, getting into trouble for smoking marijuana, or joining a gang. Second, perceptions of vulnerability to those consequences, such as the likelihood of getting into an accident after driving drunk or going to jail, help determine what decision is ultimately made. Third, the desire to engage in the behavior is considered, despite the potential consequences (e.g., "I know that I can get an STD from having unprotected sex, but it is more important for me to keep my partner happy"). And, finally, decision-making is determined in part by perceptions of the extent to which similar others are engaging in the behavior (e.g., "Most of my friends smoke pot, so why shouldn't I"? or "Many of my friends are joining that gang, so I'll join, too").

Many theories of health behavior have incorporated elements of these normative decision-making models, such as the Theory of Reasoned Action, Theory of Planned Behavior, and the Health Belief Model. In general, these theories postulate (and empirical evidence supports) the idea that decision-making is at least in part the result of a deliberative, rational, and analytical process, with the outcome of this process leading to increased or decreased likelihood of performing a specific behavior. Not only is the chosen behavior the one that will yield the greatest expected utility, but also the rational choice will be based on the components that are most valued by the individual.

It is important to note that in this normative, rational decision-making process, a competent decision-maker not only considers engaging in a particular action, but also considers the consequences associated with *not* choosing to engage in the behavior or make the decision. This is especially important for adolescents, for whom the choice is often between engaging or not engaging in a risky behavior, both of which have positive and negative outcomes, especially social outcomes. For example, a study of adolescent sexual decision-making showed that, in addition to reporting some positive outcomes, such as feeling responsible for gaining a good reputation, adolescents who decided not to have sex, or to postpone sex, reported experiencing some negative consequences related to that decision (e.g., having a partner become angry), compared with adolescents who chose to have sex, and these negative experiences increased with age if the adolescent remained abstinent (Brady & Halpern-Felsher, 2007).

Dual-Process Models of Decision-Making

The decision-making models discussed in the above section have been useful in predicting a number of behaviors, especially those involving decisions that are less emotionally charged. However, the application of these models is limited when used to explain behaviors involving more irrational, impulsive, socially undesirable, or emotionally charged behavior such as drug use, unsafe driving, or risky sex. Urban youth are also faced with additional decisions, such as whether to sell drugs or join a gang. These normative decision-making models are also less applicable to adolescents and some young adults for whom the ability to analytically process information is not yet fully formed. To address the less deliberate and more social, emotional, and reactive process often employed by adolescents, theory and research support the adoption of dual-process models that reflect multiple paths to decision-making.

Dual process models challenge the notion that decision-making competence only involves a deliberate, analytic process, or that decision-making involves a continuum from intuitive to analytic processing. Instead, these models argue that both intuitive and analytic processing work in tandem, along two parallel paths. One path reflects the more analytic, rational processing, as discussed above with respect to the rational decision-making models. In this path, decision-making includes cognitive skills such as consideration of outcomes, perceptions of behavioral-linked risks and benefits, attitudes and values related to the behaviors and related outcomes, and beliefs in what others expect them to do (i.e., *injunctive social norms*). These factors are expected to predict intentions to behave, with intentions being the most immediate predictor of actual behavior. The second path in the dual process models represents the non-cognitive but more psychosocially and emotionally charged components involved in decision-making. This is the less planned and more heuristic, reactive, and affective path, and is often employed by adolescents. According to the Prototype Willingness Model (Gerrard, Gibbons, Houlihan, Stock, & Pomery, 2008), this second path includes *descriptive social norms* such as personal perceptions and misperceptions about the extent to which peers and other important groups are engaging in a behavior. This heuristic path also includes images or perceptions regarding others who have engaged, or are engaging, in a behavior.

For example, urban adolescents are more likely to join a gang if they believe they will look "cool," be more accepted by their peers, and that they will not get caught. Social norms and images are then expected to predict willingness to consider a behavior. Willingness to engage is differentiated from the planful notion of intentions. While adolescents may not have an active plan in mind to sell drugs, smoke, have unprotected sex, or engage in delinquent behavior, they often find themselves in situations in which they would consider engaging in the behavior even though they were originally committed to avoiding it. For example, a non-smoking adolescent may be offered a cigarette at a party, leading to a spontaneous decision to try smoking, or an urban adolescent may suddenly be asked to sell drugs, resulting in the decision to join a gang. This deflected trajectory in original intentions is thought to result in part from adolescents' psychosocial immaturity, including being more impulsive and susceptible to peer pressure than adults.

Emerging from the dual process models and research on cognition, affect, and developmental processes involved in decision-making, Reyna and colleagues (Reyna & Farley, 2006) have proposed the Fuzzy Trace Theory in which they have operationalized two paths of reasoning. One form of reasoning is gist-based, or rooted in the general meaning that the event or decision evokes for a particular individual. Reyna argues that gist-based reasoning is derived from experience and knowledge accumulated over time. She argues that adults are able to reference information to new contexts in the form of these gists, and that they tend to use these heuristics or intuition-based reasoning more than they rely on specific details. In contrast, less experienced decision-makers rely more on verbatim reasoning, which are literal representations guiding decisions. These verbatim representations are more detailed, in which the decision-maker focuses more on facts, details, and weighing of trade-offs to guide their choices. As a result, adolescents are more likely to make decisions using verbatim processing, given their lack of experience compared to adults. However, adolescents will increase their use of gist-based reasoning with age and experience. Reyna does note that adolescents tend to evoke both forms of reasoning, thus providing additional support for the dual-process involved in adolescent decision-making.

Judgment and Reasoning

While the entire decision-making process is important for our understanding of adolescents' decisions, and has implications for how we educate youth, research and educational efforts often focus more specifically on judgments or reasoning, including both positive and negative consequences. These judgments, also known as perceptions or expectations, and how they relate to decision-making and behavioral outcomes will be discussed in the following sections.

Judgments of Risks

The relationship between risk judgments and risk behavior has been particularly applied to adolescents, as descriptions of adolescent risk-taking almost invariably make reference to adolescents' beliefs in their own invulnerability to harm. There have been numerous studies, methodologies and measurement tools assessing adolescent risk perceptions and the relationship between perceptions and behavior. Several investigators have compared individuals' perceived likelihood of harm against actual risk statistics. For example, studies have compared the perceived chance of getting lung cancer against the actual odds of lung cancer among smokers (Borland, 1997; Kristiansen, Harding, & Eiser, 1983; Viscusi, 1990, 1991, 1992; Viscusi et al., 2000). Others have examined adolescents' perceived chance of dying in the near future (Fischhoff, Bruine de Bruin, Parker, Millstein, & Halpern-Felsher, 2010). These studies generally indicate that adolescents and adults overestimate their risk of experiencing a negative outcome, compared to actual statistics. However, some studies have shown the reverse; for example, some smokers will underestimate their risk of experiencing negative consequences of their smoking behavior (Schoenbaum, 1997; Sutton, 1999). These mixed findings might be due to differences in outcome experiences. Adolescents who engage in a risk behavior without experiencing any negative consequences might believe those risks are less likely to occur. In contrast, experiencing risks might increase perceptions of risks occurring again. These findings are particularly relevant for urban adolescents, as they may be more exposed to opportunities to engage in risk behaviors (e.g., greater access to drugs, selling and buying drugs), without experiencing relevant negative outcomes (e.g., getting arrested), which may contribute to the increased likelihood of engaging in risky behaviors among urban youth, more so than non-urban adolescents. As Matsueda and colleagues argue (Matsueda, Kreager, & Huizinga, 2006), risk perceptions are shaped by past and current experiences with the behavior and outcome.

Risk perceptions have also commonly been measured using the concept of optimistic bias, or the extent to which one believes that one is at risk compared to others. Optimistic bias is an underestimation of the likelihood of personally experiencing negative events, or an overestimation of the likelihood of personally experiencing positive events. Optimistic bias is typically assessed by asking youth to compare their level of risk to others', either directly (e.g., "Compared to another person my same age and gender, my risk of dying in a car accident is . . .") or indirectly (e.g., by comparing risk estimates for self and estimates for another person). The outcome is considered to be an optimistic bias if it is positive in value (i.e., if the risk judgment for other is greater than for self). Optimistic bias measures are not directly comparable to risk judgments, in that a person can be optimistically biased at any level of risk judgment. For instance, an individual can be biased even if he or she estimates the risks for both self and another as very low, or judges the risk for self and another as very high.

While adolescents in general experience optimism, urban youth are more likely to have pessimistic views and perceptions as a result of their experiences and environmental circumstances. Studies have provided evidence that urban youth and youth who have perceived or real direct threats to their safety, such as living in an unsafe neighborhood, having been or fearing being the victim of a violent crime, or reporting gang activity in the neighborhood, have more pessimistic views and perceptions, and therefore perceive that they are more likely to die in the near future or experience harm. These views stem in part from the fact that urban youth often live in resource-poor communities or witness violence and other hardships around them (e.g., Cobbina, Miller, & Brunson, 2008; Fischhoff et al., 2010; Matsueda et al., 2006).

Benefit Perceptions

As indicated earlier, decision-making involves consideration of both the risks and the benefits of engaging and not engaging in a given behavior. Nevertheless, most studies have focused predominantly on perceptions of risk. More recently, the importance of considering positive outcomes or benefits in adolescent decision-making has resurfaced, thus yielding a surge of research on the role of benefit perceptions. Benefit perceptions are likely to yield important information regarding what motivates adolescents to engage in or refrain from behavior, especially when they are fully aware of the risks associated with a given behavior but still choose to engage (e.g., an adolescent may decide to join a gang to gain popularity, protection and a sense of family, despite knowing that it is possible to be killed or go to jail). Decisional balance, a construct of the Transtheoretical Model (Prochaska & Velicer, 1997a, 1997b), incorporates a weighing of both the benefits (pros) and risks (cons) in predicting behavior and behavior change. The model encompasses three factors: social pros (e.g., kids who drink alcohol have more friends), coping pros (e.g., smoking relieves tension), and cons (e.g., marijuana smells). This construct includes a number of social and short-term outcomes rather than solely relying on long-term health outcomes, which may be less salient to adolescents. Using this inventory, research by Prokhorov found that scores on the smoking pros scale increased and con scores decreased as adolescents' susceptibility to smoking increased. Focusing just on perceptions of benefits, it has been shown that adolescents with the highest perceptions of smoking-related benefits were more than three times more likely to smoke cigarettes (Song et al., 2009). Others have shown that adolescents value sexual benefits such as intimacy, sexual pleasure, and elevated social status, and adolescents expect that their sexual relationships will satisfy these goals.

It is important to note that research suggests that decision-making is domain-specific. That is, the ability to judge risks and benefits and make a decision in one domain does not necessarily reflect or mirror the decision-making or judgment that might occur within a different domain or regarding a different type of behavior (Albert & Steinberg, 2011; Halpern-Felsher & Cauffman, 2001). The notion of domain-specificity is especially important when trying to understand reasoning among urban youth, for whom the types of decisions to be made are not often the same as those faced by rural or suburban youth. Some decisions, such as deciding whether to engage in a risky behavior or enact a crime, are often made quickly, impulsively, and are influenced by opportunities to engage in a risk as well as by peers and others. Youth in urban settings often have more pressure and stress to engage in certain risky behaviors than do other youth. Further, while often reaching cognitive maturity, adolescents who commit crimes, especially those with mental disorders, are typically not psychosocially mature enough to understand the decision-making process, and often lack resources to assist in their decision-making.

Conclusions

Understanding adolescents' cognitive development and reasoning skills, and the implications of their development on reasoning, judgment, and decision-making among all youth, and in particular urban youth, is of great importance to researchers and practitioners in many fields such as the behavioral sciences, medicine, social work, law, and social policy. Interest in these topics derives largely from our desire to understand, predict, and ultimately mitigate negative consequences by preventing adolescents' engagement in risky and delinquent behavior. Understanding adolescents' competency to make decisions also has important implications for policies and laws concerning adolescents' ability to consent for research, consent for medical treatment, refuse medical treatment, and stand trial as adults after committing a violent crime. Ultimately, understanding cognitive development and decision-making will help us understand how best to educate youth overall, and especially specific populations of youth such as those from urban environments. These youth often do not have the financial or social support necessary to fully appreciate the importance of their decisions. Further, urban youth often have more opportunities to engage in risk behavior, and have fewer positive role models to deter such engagement.

The results from the numerous studies on adolescent decision-making, cognitive and psychosocial maturity, and perceptions of risks and benefits have important implications. Research on the relationship between perceptions and behavior supports efforts to reduce adolescents' engagement in risk behaviors through providing them with information about risks. It has been recognized that rather than solely focus efforts on disseminating information about the health implications of risky behavior, we need to broaden our discussions to include aspects of decision-making most relevant and immediate to youth. For example, we need to acknowledge potential benefits of various risky behaviors and discuss safer ways of obtaining similar benefits, or help adolescents learn how to delay the need, or acknowledge and defer the desire for such benefits. This is especially true given research showing that adolescents with greater desire for sensation-seeking perceive greater benefits associated with risk behavior. We also need to include in the discussion social consequences that adolescents highly value in their decision-making process. For example, studies have shown that adolescents care greatly about whether they are popular or look more grown up, and such desire to gain positive social feedback and avoid negative social consequences influences their decisions. Program curricula have also focused on developing adolescents' skills, such as skills to resist peer pressure. Adolescents' greater attention to beneficial over harmful outcomes suggests that interventions should emphasize the benefits of abstaining from behavior rather than just focusing on risks (Cauffman et al., 2010; Halpern-Felsher et al., 2001). Changing attitudes and knowledge and providing social skills, however, may not be enough to deter engagement in risk behavior.

In addition, we need to reduce opportunities for engagement in risk behavior, thus reducing the likelihood that adolescents will be able to impulsively take risks (e.g., Steinberg, 2007). Indeed, some interventions aimed at changing the context have been effective (Larson & Hansen, 2005). Unfortunately, there are few studies on the role of culture in the link between perceptions and behavior. It is possible that the level of perceived risk (and benefit) may differ across groups of individuals, possibly as a factor of culture, socioeconomic status (SES), or differences in exposure to behavior-related outcomes. This is particularly relevant for urban adolescents, as they tend to represent minority populations. For example, studies have found that substance use among urban Latino adolescents is generally shaped by complex cultural (e.g., acculturation) and social environmental influences (e.g., poverty, gang violence, crime) (De La Rosa, 2002; Martinez Jr, 2006; McCoy et al., 2010; Wahl & Eitle, 2010) that may influence their perceived risk and benefits of engaging in substance use. In addition, there are significant cultural differences in sexual perceptions. For example, Asian and, to a certain extent, Hispanic youth generally perceive greater risk and fewer benefits of sex compared to their European American counterparts. However, the relationship between these perceptions and sexual behavior does not appear to vary across racial groups. There is a need for further research on the role of culture in adolescent decision-making.

There is a large increase in risk of experiencing academic difficulties and school failure during adolescence, especially for youth from urban and low SES families (Murray, 2009), which may have an impact on an adolescent's cognitive development, thus influencing their decision-making abilities. Studies have shown that Latino and African American youth are more likely than their White counterparts to report poor grades, drop out of school, and suffer disengagement from school (McLoyd,

1998). In addition, urban minority youth may also be more likely to experience racial discrimination. Previous research has indicated that urban African American and Latino youth perceive discriminatory treatment from adults, including teachers, police, and shopkeepers (Rosenbloom & Way, 2004). The school environment may be an important factor, particularly for youth who are minorities and from disadvantaged families, because there may be fewer resources available to these youth or, indeed, to the community at large (Li & Lerner, 2011). Minority youth and youth from low SES families disproportionately attend schools that are crowded, understaffed, dysfunctional, and inadequately funded (Li & Lerner, 2011).

There are also important implications for current health messages aimed at reducing adolescent risk. Typically, health educators attempt to deter adolescents from engaging in health risk behaviors by conveying messages about risks, with the goal being that providing such information will inform their decision-making. However, these messages tend to focus mostly on long-term health risks, such as getting lung cancer from smoking. For an adolescent who is more concerned about immediate gratification, in addition to peer acceptance and approval, health messages that focus on long-term negative consequences are less likely to deter behavior, especially when such negative consequences are rarely experienced by them or their friends. Instead, communicating more realistic messages about short-term health risks, demystifying benefits, and providing a more balanced message will have a greater impact on adolescents' behavioral decisions.

In sum, adolescence is defined by extensive, rapid and simultaneous physical, cognitive, emotional, and psychosocial maturation. These combined changes shape adolescents' ability to think and reason. Theory and some research discuss adolescents' ability to make decisions, reason, and judge risks. What has been less studied is whether and how cognitive development varies by context and neighborhood, including whether development and judgment differ among adolescents from urban, rural and suburban environments. Understanding decision-making abilities and development amongst urban youth is critical, since there are disproportionately more adolescents from urban neighborhoods participating in certain risk behaviors. Thus, understanding the role of cognitive development on risk behavior among urban youth, and potential predictors and moderators of such relationship, will have strong implications for the development of more appropriate and effective interventions with urban youth that take into account the various physical, social, psychological, and environmental factors influencing these youth.

References

Albert, D., & Steinberg, L. (2011). Judgment and decision making in adolescence. *Journal of Research on Adolescence, 21*(1), 211–224.

Borland, R. (1997). What do people's estimates of smoking related risk mean? *Psychology and Health, 12*(4), 513–521.

Brady, S. S., & Halpern-Felsher, B. L. (2007). Adolescents' reported consequences of having oral sex versus vaginal sex. *Pediatrics, 119*(2), 229–236.

Cauffman, E., Shulman, E. P., Steinberg, L., Claus, E., Banich, M. T., Graham, S., . . . & Woolard, J. (2010). Age differences in affective decision making as indexed by performance on the Iowa Gambling Task. *Developmental Psychology, 46*(1), 193–207.

Cobbina, J. E., Miller, J., & Brunson, R. K. (2008). Gender, neighborhood danger, and risk avoidance strategies among urban African American youths. *Criminology, 46*(3), 673–709.

De La Rosa, M. (2002). Acculturation and Latino adolescents' substance use: A research agenda for the future. *Substance Use & Misuse, 37*(4), 429–456.

Dearing, E. (2008). Psychological costs of growing up poor. *Annals of the New York Academy of Sciences, 1136*(1), 324–332.

Fischhoff, B., Bruine de Bruin, W., Parker, A. M., Millstein, S. G., & Halpern-Felsher, B. L. (2010). Adolescents' perceived risk of dying. *Journal of Adolescent Health, 46*(3), 265–269.

Gerrard, M., Gibbons, F. X., Houlihan, A. E., Stock, M. L., & Pomery, E. A. (2008). A dual-process approach to health risk decision making: The prototype willingness model. *Developmental Review, 28*(1), 29–61.

Gutnik, L. A., Hakimzada, A. F., Yoskowitz, N. A., & Patel, V. L. (2006). The role of emotion in decision-making: a cognitive neuroeconomic approach towards understanding sexual risk behavior. *Journal of Biomedical Informatics, 39*(6), 720–736.

Halpern-Felsher, B. L., & Cauffman, E. (2001). Costs and benefits of a decision: Decision-making competence in adolescents and adults. *Journal of Applied Developmental Psychology, 22*(3), 257–273.

Halpern-Felsher, B. L., Millstein, S. G., Ellen, J. M., Adler, N. E., Tschann, J. M., & Biehl, M. (2001). The role of behavioral experience in judging risks. *Health Psychology, 20*(2), 120–126.

Kristiansen, C. M., Harding, C. M., & Eiser, J. R. (1983). Beliefs about the relationship between smoking and causes of death. *Basic and Applied Social Psychology, 4*(3), 253–261.

Larson, R., & Hansen, D. (2005). The development of strategic thinking: Learning to impact human systems in a youth activism program. *Human Development, 48*(6), 327–349.

Li, Y., & Lerner, R. M. (2011). Trajectories of school engagement during adolescence: Implications for grades, depression, delinquency, and substance use. *Developmental Psychology, 47*(1), 233–247.

Martinez Jr, C. R. (2006). Effects of Differential Family Acculturation on Latino Adolescent Substance Use. *Family Relations, 55*(3), 306–317.

Maslowsky, J., Buvinger, E., Keating, D. P., Steinberg, L., & Cauffman, E. (2011). Cost-benefit analysis mediation of the relationship between sensation seeking and risk behavior among adolescents. *Personality and Individual Differences, 51*(7), 802–806.

Matsueda, R. L., Kreager, D. A., & Huizinga, D. (2006). Deterring delinquents: A rational choice model of theft and violence. *American Sociological Review, 71*(1), 95–122.

McCoy, S. I., Jewell, N. P., Hubbard, A., Gerdts, C. E., Doherty, I. A., Padian, N. S., et al. (2010). A trajectory analysis of alcohol and marijuana use among Latino adolescents in San Francisco, California. *Journal of Adolescent Health, 47*(6), 564–574.

McLoyd, V. C. (1998). Socioeconomic disadvantage and child development. *American Psychologist, 53*(2), 185–204.

Murray, C. (2009). Parent and teacher relationships as predictors of school engagement and functioning among low-income urban youth. *The Journal of Early Adolescence, 29*(3), 376–404.

Prochaska, J. O., & Velicer, W. F. (1997a). Introduction: The transtheoretical model. *American Journal of Health Promotion, 12*(1), 6–7.

Prochaska, J. O., & Velicer, W. F. (1997b). The transtheoretical model of health behavior change. *American Journal of Health Promotion, 12*(1), 38–48.

Reyna, V. F., & Farley, F. (2006). Risk and rationality in adolescent decision making: Implications for theory, practice, and public policy. *Psychological Science in the Public Interest, 7*(1), 1–44.

Rosenbloom, S. R., & Way, N. (2004). Experiences of discrimination among African American, Asian American, and Latino adolescents in an urban high school. *Youth & Society, 35*(4), 420–451.

Schoenbaum, M. (1997). Do smokers understand the mortality effects of smoking? Evidence from the Health and Retirement Survey. *American Journal of Public Health, 87*(5), 755–759.

Song, A. V., Morrell, H. E. R., Cornell, J. L., Ramos, M. E., Biehl, M., Kropp, R. Y., . . . & Halpern-Felsher, B. L. (2009). Perceptions of smoking-related risks and benefits as predictors of adolescent smoking initiation. *American Journal of Public Health, 99*(3), 487–492.

Steinberg, L. (2007). Risk taking in adolescence. *Current Directions in Psychological Science, 16*(2), 55–59.

Steinberg, L., Albert, D., Cauffman, E., Banich, M., Graham, S., & Woolard, J. (2008). Age differences in sensation seeking and impulsivity as indexed by behavior and self-report: Evidence for a dual systems model. *Developmental Psychology, 44*(6), 1764–1778.

Steinberg, L., Cauffman, E., Woolard, J., Graham, S., & Banich, M. (2009). Are adolescents less mature than adults?: Minors' access to abortion, the juvenile death penalty, and the alleged APA "flip-flop." *American Psychologist, 64*(7), 583–594.

Sutton, S. R. (1999). How accurate are smokers' perceptions of risk? *Health, Risk & Society, 1*(2), 223–230.

Viscusi, W. K. (1990). Do smokers underestimate risks? *Journal of Political Economy, 98*(6), 1253–1269.

Viscusi, W. K. (1991). Age variations in risk perceptions and smoking decisions. *The Review of Economics and Statistics, 73*(4), 577–588.

Viscusi, W. K. (1992). *Smoking: Making the risky decision.* Oxford University Press, USA.

Viscusi, W. K., Carvalho, I., Antoñanzas, F., Rovira, J., Brana, F. J., & Portillo, F. (2000). Smoking risks in Spain: Part III—Determinants of smoking behavior. *Journal of Risk and Uncertainty, 21*(2), 213–234.

Wahl, A. M. G., & Eitle, T. M. N. (2010). Gender, acculturation and alcohol use among Latina/o adolescents: A multi-ethnic comparison. *Journal of Immigrant and Minority Health, 12*(2), 153–165.

7

ADOLESCENT SOCIAL CHANGES

Role Transitions from Childhood to Adolescence

Gabriel P. Kuperminc and Michelle A. DiMeo-Ediger

What does developmental theory tell us about the normative role transitions that occur from childhood to adolescence? Research has emphasized that youth undergo changes in the nature and quality of their relationships with parents, peers, and nonparental adults as they seek a greater sense of behavioral and emotional autonomy, and strive toward developing an adult identity. New relationships and activities, including dating and getting a first job, serve both as markers of role transitions and foundations from which youth seek to explore adult-like roles. This chapter reviews extant research on role transitions from childhood to adolescence and explores the interplay of gender, culture, and social class with these normative processes as they relate to urban youth. We begin with a broad definition of social roles and consider the developmental and interpersonal context in which children begin to experience changes in their roles through the transition to adolescence. Guided by an ecological framework (Bronfenbrenner & Morris, 1998), we next consider role transitions occurring in three key developmental contexts: family, school, and peers. The ecological framework further leads us to consider the interplay of role transitions across these settings. We conclude with a consideration of implications for working with youth and the adults that help shape these transitions along with directions for future research.

Roles and Role Transitions

Peterson (1987) defined social roles as interaction processes that are assigned to different social positions and provide meaning, direction, and organization to behavior. Roles are interdependent; that is, the "members" of interpersonal associations have mutual expectations to perform roles within a range of acceptable behaviors. The role of "student" has little meaning in the absence of a "teacher" role.

Research has emphasized the interplay of biological, cognitive, and social processes (Lerner & Steinberg, 2009) as underlying developmental transitions from childhood through adolescence. The onset of puberty engenders sexual feelings and new expectations about dating and relationships on the part of children, parents, peers, teachers, and others (Harold, Colarossi, & Mercier, 2007). Cognitive changes also bring about shifts in social roles; when advances in abstract reasoning abilities and emotion regulation enable youth to develop increasingly mutual relationships that balance their own perspectives with those of others (Levitt, Selman, & Richmond, 1991). While acknowledging the importance of biological and cognitive changes, this chapter focuses on social changes involved in role transitions from childhood to adolescence.

A paramount consideration is that *autonomy* is a fundamental developmental task of adolescent development, and that growth in autonomy is facilitated by, rather than antithetical to, maintaining strong positive relationships with parents and other important people (Allen, 2010). Autonomy is most often studied in western contexts that emphasize individualism; however, the conception of development toward "autonomous-relatedness" that we espouse is consistent with cross-cultural perspectives (Kagitcibasi, 2005). Whereas some role transitions (e.g., the onset of dating or getting a first job) can be viewed as discontinuities in development, those new roles do not necessarily supplant existing roles. Instead, new roles most often come about through a continuous process of *renegotiating* rather than relinquishing ongoing relationships. Key settings in which renegotiation processes occur include the family, school, and peer settings.

Family

Research largely confirms that changes in relationships with parents, including increased conflict and less intimate contact, accompany the transition to adolescence (Shanahan, McHale, Osgood, & Crouter, 2007). Research indicates youth and their parents experience these changes as difficult (Harold et al., 2007) but not necessarily bringing about long-term difficulties for the relationship. Instead, this process seems to mark a period in which adolescents and their parents begin to renegotiate their relationship in a way that fosters increasing adolescent autonomy while confirming the importance of the parent–adolescent relationship (Allen, 2010).

One of the primary challenges facing urban families involves constraints on parents' ability to foster independence in their children who are undergoing the transition into adolescence. An extensive body of research documents that an *authoritative* parenting style that emphasizes children's autonomy and self-control brings about more positive outcomes across most domains of development than either an *authoritarian* style that emphasizes parental authority and power, or other parenting styles (Steinberg, 2001). However, a major concern for many urban families involves dangerous neighborhood conditions, in which letting down one's guard risks exposing children to violence and negative influences, such as gangs and drug trafficking. Cultural factors, including traditional beliefs that parents should engage in higher levels of control of their children's behavior, may further contribute to the prominence of authoritarian parenting among ethnic minority families (Fuligni, Hughes, & Way, 2009).

Sources of cultural and ethnic variations in parenting styles include socioeconomic disadvantage and variations in cultural beliefs about parenting and children's roles. Socioeconomic disadvantage is not a single risk factor—families living in poverty also are likely to experience multiple risks, including high community disorder, low community efficacy, and lack of institutional resources (Roche & Leventhal, 2009). These conditions of risk can affect parenting in a number of ways. Parents may have limited time available to spend with their children due to working in low-status occupations that afford little flexibility in work schedules, or working multiple low-wage jobs to make ends meet. The stress of unemployment or underemployment can further limit parents' ability to be at their best in raising their children. Among immigrant families, which currently comprise about 20% of the U.S. population and represent a concentrated and rapidly growing sector of many urban areas (Fuligni et al., 2009), parents may have limited English proficiency and limited understanding of how to navigate the social institutions of American society, leaving them little choice but to rely on their children for assistance (Fuligni et al., 2009).

Despite these constraints, research shows that urban youth are successfully navigating the transition to adolescence, in no small part due to parental efforts to identify and support their children's connections to positive influences at home, at school, and in the community. Ethnographic studies of African American urban parents (Jarrett, 1999) and qualitative interviews with 10–12-year-old African American youth (Outley & Floyd, 2002) provide converging evidence of strategies used by parents to insulate their children from neighborhood dangers: youth monitoring, resource seeking, and in-home learning strategies. Parents monitor their children's activities by screening peers to discourage friendships with children viewed as negative influences while encouraging friendships with prosocial youth. Other monitoring strategies include having adult relatives, family friends, or older siblings accompany children in daily activities outside the home and sending youth to live with relatives in a less risky environment. Parents seek resources by identifying well-functioning local organizations that offer positive activities and supports for their children (e.g., after-school programs), and relying on kinship networks to access resources in other communities.

Paradoxically, perhaps, an emphasis on family obligation may represent one of the pathways to autonomy for urban adolescents (Fuligni et al., 2009; Kuperminc, Jurkovic, & Casey, 2009; Pomerantz, Qin, Wang, & Chen, 2011). Research has documented that adolescents from many minority groups hold a stronger sense of obligation to support their families than European American peers, and that youth who value roles such as caring for younger siblings or "language brokering" for parents with limited English proficiency often report positive psychosocial functioning and high academic achievement (Fuligni et al., 2009; Kuperminc et al., 2009). Much of the clinical literature on constructs such as *parentification, role-reversal,* and *caregiver burden* has focused on concerns that such responsibilities might overburden young adolescents, particularly in highly stressed circumstances, such as poverty, parental disability, or immigrant acculturation. However, recent research suggests that families that value, acknowledge, and reciprocate youth's contributions may facilitate the positive psychosocial development of young adolescents (Kuperminc et al., 2009).

Indeed, youth may derive a sense of autonomy through maintaining a belief in the importance of respect for parents and family loyalty (Phinney, Kim-Jo, Osorio, & Vilhjalmsdottir, 2005; Pomerantz et al., 2011).

School

School transitions

The transition to middle or junior high school typically demands that youth adapt to having multiple teachers, larger class sizes, more challenging work, new behavior expectations, and new peers (Grills-Taquechel, Norton, & Ollendick, 2010). This challenge is exacerbated by the co-occurring transition to adolescence (Simmons, Burgeson, Carlton-Ford, & Blyth, 1987). Not surprisingly, youth report high levels of anxiety during this transition (Grills-Taquechel et al., 2010). The transition may be especially challenging for urban, rather than suburban youth, who are more likely to live in poverty (U.S. Census Bureau, 2010), have poorer health (Contoyannis & Li, 2011), and face environmental stressors (Allison et al., 1999). Compared to other settings, urban schools are often underfunded, larger, and have fewer resources. Such schools also tend to have higher teacher turnover, teacher shortages, and rely more on substitute teachers due to higher absenteeism (e.g., Lankford, Loeb, & Wyckoff, 2002). The co-occurring transitions to adolescence and to middle school may place youth at increased risk for cascading developmental challenges. Seidman and Allen's (1994) study of ethnically diverse urban youth following the transition to a middle school found declines in self-esteem, preparation for class, academic grades, perceptions of social support from school personnel, and participation in extracurricular activities. Comparing the transition to middle school among urban and suburban youth, Wenz-Gross and Parker (1999) found that urban youth experienced more stress and less social support from family, friends, and school personnel. Roeser, Eccles, and Sameroff (2000) showed that 7th-graders who were emotionally distressed earned lower grades in 8th grade than others and were consequently more likely to have lower academic confidence by 9th grade. These findings point to the importance of enhancing supports provided to middle school students, given that academic success in middle school is strongly predictive of high school graduation (United Way, 2008).

Unfortunately, many schools in 2012 are failing to meet youth's developmental needs during the transition to adolescence. Despite strong evidence that support from teachers and school personnel is more strongly associated with youth well-being than support from family or friends (Chu, Saucier, & Hafner, 2010), research indicates that students in middle school experience reduced opportunities to develop connections with their teachers (Seidman & Allen, 1994). Furthermore, youth may find fewer opportunities to fulfill their developmental needs for autonomy and independence as teachers' objectives shift towards maintaining control of the classroom (Eccles & Roeser, 2009) and incessant test preparation.

Eccles and colleagues' stage–environment fit perspective purports that school systems should support the developmental needs of youth transitioning to adolescence. Promoting a supportive school climate is an example of one way to support youth during this transitional time. Middle school students' perceptions of a supportive school climate have been associated with fewer internalizing and externalizing problems and may be particularly important for youth who are most vulnerable to difficulties in psychosocial functioning (Kuperminc, Leadbeater, & Blatt, 2001). Additional ways to provide youth support at school include facilitating positive achievement expectations among teachers, promoting positive teacher–student relationships, providing interesting and cognitively appropriate curriculums, providing after-school programs, and creating predictable classroom environments which foster autonomy (Eccles, 2004). Teacher looping, in which a teacher remains with youth over more than one academic year, can also support youth transitioning to adolescence by allowing teachers time to develop relationships with students and facilitate youth trust in their teacher (Franz et al., 2010). Team teaching, in which teachers work together to integrate curriculum, increases middle school students' social bonding with peers, school, and teachers (Wallace, 2007).

Urban teachers not only must rise to the challenge of meeting youth developmental needs during the transition to adolescence, but they must do so while also addressing the unique needs of urban youth and families. Professional training of urban teachers should emphasize a strong commitment to social justice, a belief in the value of diversity, and a grounding of teaching practices within the moral, cultural, and political environment of the school (Quartz, 2003). Such training will prepare urban teachers to meet the needs of their students. Both ongoing professional training for current teachers, and pre-service training in graduate programs, are needed. Some graduate teacher training programs offer opportunities to work in the urban communities they will eventually teach in—providing important experiences in real-life contexts while also being afforded ongoing consultation and supervision from their graduate program. In sum, the co-occurring transitions to adolescence and middle school can be challenging, especially among urban youth; however, providing school-level supports to address these needs may be an important first step in promoting positive youth development (PYD) and preventing poor mental health trajectories.

Peers

Peer relationships change in many ways during the transition to adolescence. Peer groups undergo significant changes resulting from the transition to middle school (Hardy, Bukowski, & Sippola, 2002). Youth spend more time with peers, peer groups are less likely to be monitored by adults, peer groups are more likely to involve mixed-genders, and youth begin to engage in romantic relationships (McElhaney, Antonishak, & Allen, 2008). Peer acceptance becomes increasingly important and can have significant influences on youth well-being. Youth are at increased risk for internalizing, externalizing, and social problems if they lack peer acceptance, lack high-quality friendships, or have few friends (Waldrip, Malcolm, & Jensen-Campbell, 2008). Further, peer stressors, such as the pressure to party, can lead to depression or social withdrawal (Hankin, Mermelstein, & Roesch, 2007; McElhaney et al., 2008).

Peer influences may be particularly salient for urban youth, given that a greater likelihood of living in poverty (U.S. Census Bureau, 2010) may limit the extent to which their caregivers are available to supervise them during after-school hours (e.g., due to long work hours or holding multiple jobs) (Deardorff, Gonzales, & Sandler, 2003). Urban youth are likely to experience unique peer stressors, such as the pressure to learn and follow "street codes" to earn and maintain "respect" from peers (Allison et al., 1999). Urban youth are more likely to be exposed to peer violence and to experience peer pressure to join a gang and to use drugs (Farrell & White, 1998; Walker-Barnes & Mason, 2001; Walton et al., 2009). These factors may lead to greater peer stress among urban youth, which is associated with depressive symptoms (Deardorff et al., 2003).

Positive peer interactions provide opportunities for emerging adolescents to gain interpersonal skills (Zimmer-Gembeck, Geiger, & Crick, 2005) which can predict successful social development. Social confidence and popularity at age 13 predicts social adjustment at age 14 (McElhaney et al., 2008). Feeling socially connected among even small peer groups can promote socio-emotional adjustment. Thus, providing spaces— such as after-school programs—where youth feel socially accepted and empowered may be an important way to promote positive youth development (PYD).

Although peers can have strong positive influences, they can also be a source of negative influence. During the transition to adolescence, urban youth are more likely to associate with deviant peers and thus are at increased risk for externalizing behaviors (Roosa et al., 2011). Additionally, as a part of their initiation into adolescent peer groups, transitioning youth may feel pressured to participate in gangs, substance use, and sexual behaviors (Delaney, 1995). This is especially true given that having older friends is associated with participating in more risky behaviors (Velazquez, Pasch, Perry, & Komro, 2011) and the likelihood of having older peers increases with the transition to middle school (Seidman & Allen, 1994). Emotion regulatory capacities in the brain change during adolescence and predict youth susceptibility to peer influences (Pfeifer et al., 2011). Emotion regulation training for youth transitioning to adolescence (and perhaps targeting such interventions to youth who have older friends) may bolster their ability to resist peer pressure.

During the transition to adolescence, youth are more likely to participate in or be the victim of aggressive behaviors (Pellegrini, 2002). Whereas *nationally* representative data on youth in the US suggest that few youth are involved in aggressive behaviors (Nansel et al., 2001), studies indicate that most *urban* youth are both victims and perpetrators of peer aggression during the transition to adolescence (Williford, Brisson, Bender, Jenson, & Forrest-Bank, 2011). The good news is that having supportive friendships can buffer the negative effects of peer victimization (Waldrip et al., 2008). Although aggressive behavior and victimization are shared experiences among most urban early adolescents, this pattern does not persist over time (Williford et al., 2011). It may be that this increase in peer aggression during the transition to adolescence is due in large part to youth's desires to impress peers and climb social ladders (Pellegrini, 2002).

The transition to adolescence typically marks the start of romantic relationships. The rate that youth progress into romantic relationships differs among cultures, with some evidence suggesting that African American youth begin to engage in mixed-gender groups and sexual behaviors at an earlier age than White youth (Paikoff, 1995). In 2002, 20% of youth who were a part of a nationally representative sample reported sexual behavior before age 14 (Abma, Martinez, Mosher, & Dawson, 2004). Youth who associate with deviant peers and who are seen as "popular" are more likely to have engaged in sexual behaviors (Prinstein, Meade, & Cohen, 2003). Thus, peer pressure is likely a large factor in youth decisions to engage in sexual behavior. In fact, 27% of females who had sexual intercourse before the age of 14 years reported that they "didn't really want it to happen at that time" (Abma et al., 2004). PYD programs providing sex education can facilitate healthy sexual outcomes such as the prevention of teen pregnancy (Gavin, Catalano, David-Ferdon, Gloppen, & Markham, 2010). PYD programs may work by helping youth learn to resist peer pressures and by providing youth with the knowledge and skills needed to make healthy decisions.

In sum, peer relationships undergo significant changes during the transition to adolescence, including the emergence of romantic relationships. Peers can serve as an important protective factor and lay necessary groundwork toward the development of socialization skills that will be necessary for future relationships in adulthood. However, peer relationships with deviant peers can also pose risks, through acts of aggression and by increasing the likelihood of youth engagement in risky behaviors.

Conclusion and Future Directions: Bridging Developmental Contexts

We conclude by returning to the conceptual frameworks that have guided our discussion of role transitions from childhood to adolescence. First, the ecological perspective highlights the need to consider the family, school, and peer contexts that youth interact with. Second, our developmental framework focused on autonomy, which develops optimally within the context of strong relationships with parents. This focus on contexts and the role of human connections leads to considering how the varied settings in which youth spend their everyday lives can work in concert to promote or hinder successful role transitions.

Across the family, school, and peer contexts, this chapter has considered some of the salient risks and opportunities that can contribute to the success urban youth have in navigating those transitions. Cultural or ethnic factors, such as immigration, and socioeconomic factors, such as poverty, can isolate parents from many community resources. Schools may fail to afford students the opportunities they seek to make independent decisions. Peer groups can influence youth in the direction of prosocial or antisocial activities.

The ecological perspective does not stop at identifying the various contexts of development, but emphasizes the need to study how linkages across these contexts can influence the possibilities for youth to experience successful role transitions. Increasing the systematic study of these linkages is critical to advancing understanding of, and strategies for, promoting successful social transitions in early adolescence. Parents play important direct and indirect roles in promoting their children's school success. Parents who encourage in-home learning and rewarding children's effort and achievement (Jarrett, 1999) seek directly to influence their children's academic motivation and persistence. Without face-to-face interactions with teachers and school administrators, however, those efforts may not be acknowledged in the school setting. These findings suggest that efforts to connect parents to their children's schools might contribute indirectly to academic achievement by building youth's access to social capital in the school setting (Kuperminc, Darnell, & Alvarez-Jimenez, 2008).

Another promising approach to bridging the family, school, and peer contexts can be found in structured after-school and youth development programs. In addition to providing safe spaces in which youth can interact with prosocial peers and adults, such programs typically reinforce academic skills (e.g., by providing tutoring and homework help) and emphasize the teaching of socio-emotional skills (Hirsch, 2005). Indeed, Fredricks, Hackett, and Bregman (2010) report that youth who attend Boys and Girls clubs perceive the setting as a safe place, where they can engage in fun activities with friends and where they can get homework help. Larson and Angus (2011) showed that participating in arts and youth leadership programs contributes to identity development and gains in strategic thinking skills necessary for working through adult-like challenges.

In addition to the direct effects on youth development, community-based youth programs may also strengthen features of youth's ecologies. Parents may derive a range of benefits from their children's participation, including decreased parenting and work-related stress, improved parenting skills, and increases in supportive social networks. In our research, for example, parents of girls in the Cool Girls, Inc. program reported reduced worry about their daughters' safety after school, improved communication with their daughters, and greater access to information about community resources (Kuperminc et al., 2012). Such benefits to parents, in turn, may indirectly contribute to youth development goals (DiMeo, 2011). Participation in such programs also may engage youth in prosocial peer networks, and increase the time spent in structured, adult-led activities that have been shown to increase the likelihood of high school graduation (Mahoney & Cairns, 1997). However, not all youth programs afford such benefits, and much remains to be learned about how to design and implement effective programs. Nevertheless, ecologically grounded research is increasingly showing that multi-faceted initiatives that engage the collaboration of parents, youth, schools, and community organizations have the potential to enhance youth's access to the resources that facilitate positive role transitions.

References

Abma, J., Martinez, G., Mosher, W., & Dawson, B. (2004). Teenagers in the United States: Sexual activity, contraceptive use and childbearing 2002. *Vital Health Statistics, 23*(34), 1–48.

Allen, J. P. (2010). Experience, development, and resilience: The legacy of Stuart Hauser's explorations of the transition from adolescence into early adulthood. *Research in Human Development, 7(4),* 241–256.

Allison, K. W., Burton, L., Marshall, S., Perez-Febles, A., Yarrington, J., Kirsh, L. B., & Merriwether-DeVries, C. (1999). Life experiences among urban adolescents: Examining the role of context. *Child Development, 70*(4), 1017–1029.

Bronfenbrenner, U., & Morris, P. A. (1998). The ecology of developmental processes. In W. Damon, & R. M. Lerner (Eds.), *Handbook of child psychology: Volume 1: Theoretical models of human development (5th ed.).* (pp. 993–1028). Hoboken, NJ: John Wiley & Sons Inc.

Chu, P. S., Saucier, D. A., & Hafner, E. (2010). Meta-analysis of the relationships between social support and well-being in children and adolescents. *Journal of Social and Clinical Psychology, 29*(6), 624–645.

Contoyannis, P., & Li, J. (2011). The evolution of health outcomes from childhood to adolescence. *Journal of Health Economics, 30*(1), 11–32.

Deardorff, J., Gonzales, N. A., & Sandler, I. N. (2003). Control beliefs as a mediator of the relation between stress and depressive symptoms among inner-city adolescents. *Journal of Abnormal Child Psychology: An official publication of the International Society for Research in Child and Adolescent Psychopathology, 31*(2), 205–217.

Delaney, C. H. (1995). Rites of passage in adolescence. *Adolescence, 30*(120), 891–897.

DiMeo, M. (2011). After-school programs: Do parents matter? (Doctoral dissertation), from http://digitalarchive.gsu.edu/psych_diss/96/.

Eccles, J. S. (2004). Schools, academic motivation, and stage-environment fit. In R. M. Lerner, & L. Steinberg (Eds.), *Handbook of adolescent psychology (2nd ed.).* (pp. 125–153). Hoboken, NJ: John Wiley & Sons Inc.

Eccles, J. S., & Roeser, R. W. (2009). Schools, academic motivation, and stage-environment fit. In J. V. Lerner, & L. Steinberg (Eds.), *Handbook of adolescent psychology (Vol. 1,* pp. 404–434). Hoboken, NJ: John Wiley & Sons, Inc.

Farrell, A. D., & White, K. S. (1998). Peer influences and drug use among urban adolescents: Family structure and parent–adolescent relationship as protective factors. *Journal of Consulting and Clinical Psychology, 66*(2), 248–258.

Franz, D. P., Thompson, N. L., Fuller, B., Hare, R. D., Miller, N. C., & Walker, J. (2010). Evaluating mathematics achievement of middle school students in a looping environment. *School Science and Mathematics, 110*(6), 298–308.

Fredricks, J. A., Hackett, K., & Bregman, A. (2010). Participation in Boys and Girls Clubs: motivation and stage environment fit. *Journal of Community Psychology, 38*(3), 369–385.

Fuligni, A. J., Hughes, D. L., & Way, N. (2009). Ethnicity and immigration. In R. M. Lerner, & L. Steinberg (Eds.), *Handbook of adolescent psychology, Vol 2: Contextual influences on adolescent development (3rd ed.).* (pp. 527–569). Hoboken, NJ: John Wiley & Sons Inc.

Gavin, L. E., Catalano, R. F., David-Ferdon, C., Gloppen, K. M., & Markham, C. M. (2010). A review of positive youth development programs that promote adolescent sexual and reproductive health. *Journal of Adolescent Health, 46*(3, Suppl), S75-S91.

Grills-Taquechel, A. E., Norton, P., & Ollendick, T. H. (2010). A longitudinal examination of factors predicting anxiety during the transition to middle school. *Anxiety, Stress & Coping, 23*(5), 493–513.

Hankin, B. L., Mermelstein, R., & Roesch, L. (2007). Sex differences in adolescent depression: Stress exposure and reactivity models. *Child Development, 78*(1), 279–295.

Hardy, C. L., Bukowski, W. M., & Sippola, L. K. (2002). Stability and change in peer relationships during the transition to middle level school. *Journal of Early Adolescence, 22*(2), 117.

Harold, R. D., Colarossi, L. G., & Mercier, L. R. (2007). *Smooth sailing or stormy waters? Family transitions through adolescence and their implications for practice and policy.* Mahwah, NJ: Lawrence Erlbaum Associates Publishers.

Hirsch, B. J. (2005). *A place to call home: After-school programs for urban youth.* Washington, DC: American Psychological Association.

Jarrett, R. L. (1999). Successful parenting in high-risk neighborhoods. *The Future of Children, 9*(2), 45–50. doi: 10.2307/1602704

Kagitcibasi, C. (2005). Autonomy and relatedness in cultural context: Implications for self and family. *Journal of Cross-Cultural Psychology, 36*(4), 403–422.

Kuperminc, G. P., Darnell, A. J., & Alvarez-Jimenez, A. (2008). Parent involvement in the academic adjustment of Latino middle and high school youth: Teacher expectations and school belonging as mediators. *Journal of Adolescence, 31*(4), 469–483.

Kuperminc, G. P., Jurkovic, G. J., & Casey, S. (2009). Relation of filial responsibility to the personal and social adjustment of Latino adolescents from immigrant families. *Journal of Family Psychology, 23*(1), 14–22.

Kuperminc, G. P., Leadbeater, B. J., & Blatt, S. J. (2001). School social climate and individual differences in vulnerability to psychopathology among middle school students. *Journal of School Psychology, 39*(2), 141–159.

Kuperminc, G. P., Thompson, J., Fromelt, K., Duggins, S., Germain, N., Faust, L., & DiMeo, M. (2012). *Evaluation Report to Cool Girls, Inc. Data from 2010–2011 School Year.* Atlanta, GA: Georgia State University.

Lankford, H., Loeb, S., & Wyckoff, J. (2002). Teacher sorting and the plight of urban schools: A descriptive analysis. *Educational Evaluation and Policy Analysis, 24*(1), 37–62.

Larson, R. W., & Angus, R. M. (2011). Adolescents' development of skills for agency in youth programs: Learning to think strategically. *Child Development, 82*(1), 277–294.

Lerner, R. M., & Steinberg, L. (2009). The scientific study of adolescent development: Historical and contemporary perspectives. In R. M. Lerner, & L. Steinberg (Eds.), *Handbook of adolescent psychology, Vol 1: Individual bases of adolescent development (3rd ed.).* (pp. 3–14). Hoboken, NJ: John Wiley & Sons Inc.

Levitt, M. Z., Selman, R. L., & Richmond, J. B. (1991). The psychosocial foundations of early adolescents' high-risk behavior: Implications for research and practice. *Journal of Research on Adolescence, 1*(4), 349–378.

Mahoney, J., & Cairns, R. B. (1997). Do extracurricular activities protect against early school dropout? *Developmental Psychology, 33*(2), 241–253.

McElhaney, K. B., Antonishak, J., & Allen, J. P. (2008). "They like me, they like me not": Popularity and adolescents' perceptions of acceptance predicting social functioning over time. *Child Development, 79*(3), 720–731.

Nansel, T. R., Overpeck, M., Pilla, R. S., Ruan, W. J., Simons-Morton, B., & Scheidt, P. (2001). Bullying behaviors among US youth: Prevalence and association with psychosocial adjustment. *JAMA: Journal of the American Medical Association, 285*(16), 2094–2100.

Outley, C. W., & Floyd, M. F. (2002). The home they live in: Inner city children's views on the influence of parenting strategies on their leisure behavior. *Leisure Sciences, 24*(2), 161–179.

Paikoff, R. L. (1995). Early heterosexual debut: Situations of sexual possibility during the transition to adolescence. *American Journal of Orthopsychiatry, 65*(3), 389.

Pellegrini, A. D. (2002). Bullying, victimization, and sexual harassment during the transition to middle school. *Educational Psychologist, 37*(3), 151–163.

Peterson, G. W. (1987). Role transitions and role identities during adolescence: A symbolic interactionist view. *Journal of Adolescent Research, 2*(3), 237–254.

Pfeifer, J. H., Masten, C. L., Moore, W. E., Oswald, T. M., Mazziotta, J. C., Iacoboni, M., & Dapretto, M. (2011). Entering adolescence: Resistance to peer influence, risky behavior, and neural changes in emotion reactivity. *Neuron, 69*(5), 1029–1036.

Phinney, J. S., Kim-Jo, T., Osorio, S., & Vilhjalmsdottir, P. (2005). Autonomy and relatedness in adolescent-parent disagreements: Ethnic and developmental factors. *Journal of Adolescent Research, 20*(1), 8–39.

Pomerantz, E. M., Qin, L., Wang, Q., & Chen, H. (2011). Changes in early adolescents' sense of responsibility to their parents in the United States and China: Implications for academic functioning. *Child Development, 82*(4), 1136–1151.

Prinstein, M. J., Meade, C. S., & Cohen, G. L. (2003). Adolescent oral sex, peer popularity, and perceptions of best friends' sexual behavior. *Journal of Pediatric Psychology, 28*(4), 243–249.

Quartz, K. H. (2003). "Too angry to leave": Supporting new teachers' commitment to transform urban schools. *Journal of Teacher Education, 54*(2), 99–111.

Roche, K. M., & Leventhal, T. (2009). Beyond neighborhood poverty: Family management, neighborhood disorder, and adolescents' early sexual onset. *Journal of Family Psychology, 23*(6), 819–827.

Roeser, R. W., Eccles, J. S., & Sameroff, A. J. (2000). School as a context of early adolescents' academic and social-emotional development: A summary of research findings. *The Elementary School Journal, 100*(5), 443–471.

Roosa, M. W., Zeiders, K. H., Knight, G. P., Gonzales, N. A., Jenn-Yun, T., Saenz, D., . . . & Berkel, C. (2011). A test of the social development model during the transition to junior high with Mexican American adolescents. *Developmental Psychology, 47*(2), 527–537.

Seidman, E., & Allen, L. (1994). The impact of school transitions in early adolescence on the self-system and perceived social context of poor urban youth. *Child Development, 65*(2), 507–522.

Shanahan, L., McHale, S. M., Osgood, D. W., & Crouter, A. C. (2007). Conflict frequency with mothers and fathers from middle childhood to late adolescence: within- and between-families comparisons. *Developmental Psychology, 43*(3), 539–550.

Simmons, R. G., Burgeson, R., Carlton-Ford, S., & Blyth, D. A. (1987). The impact of cumulative change in early adolescence. *Child Development, 58*(5), 1220–1234.

Steinberg, L. (2001). We know some things: Parent–adolescent relationships in retrospect and prospect. *Journal of Research on Adolescence, 11*(1), 1–19.

U.S. Census Bureau. (2010). 2005–2009 American Community Survey 5-Year Estimates. Retrieved from http://factfinder.census.gov/servlet/GCTTable?_bm=y&-geo_id=&-ds_name=ACS_2009_5YR_G00_&-_lang=en&-mt_name=ACS_2009_5YR_G00_GCT1701_US37F&-format=US-37F&-CONTEXT=gct.

United Way. (2008). Seizing the middle ground: Why middle school creates the pathway to college and the workforce. Los Angeles, CA: United Ways of Greater Los Angeles. Retrieved from http://69.65.15.147/QOL08edufull.pdf.

Velazquez, C. E., Pasch, K. E., Perry, C. L., & Komro, K. A. (2011). Do high-risk urban youth also have older friends? *Journal of Adolescent Health, 48*(5), 467–472.

Waldrip, A. M., Malcolm, K. T., & Jensen-Campbell, L. A. (2008). With a little help from your friends: The importance of high-quality friendships on early adolescent adjustment. *Social Development, 17*(4), 832–852.

Walker-Barnes, C. J., & Mason, C. A. (2001). Perceptions of risk factors for female gang involvement among African American and Hispanic women. *Youth & Society, 32*(3), 303–336.

Wallace, J. J. (2007). Effects of interdisciplinary teaching team configuration upon the social bonding of middle school students. *RMLE Online: Research in Middle Level Education, 30*(5), 1–18.

Walton, M. A., Cunningham, R. M., Goldstein, A. L., Chermack, S. T., Zimmerman, M. A., Bingham, . . . & Blow, F. C. (2009). Rates and correlates of violent behaviors among adolescents treated in an urban emergency department. *Journal of Adolescent Health, 45*(1), 77–83.

Wenz-Gross, M., & Parker, R. (1999). Differences in stress and social support among students entering urban, urban fringe, or suburban middle schools. Presented at the Biennial Meeting of the Society for Research in Child Development, Albuquerque, NM.

Williford, A. P., Brisson, D., Bender, K. A., Jenson, J. M., & Forrest-Bank, S. (2011). Patterns of aggressive behavior and peer victimization from childhood to early adolescence: A latent class analysis. *Journal of Youth & Adolescence, 40*(6), 644–655.

Zimmer-Gembeck, M. J., Geiger, T. C., & Crick, N. R. (2005). Relational and physical aggression, prosocial behavior, and peer relations: Gender moderation and bidirectional associations. *Journal of Early Adolescence, 25*(4), 421–452.

PART III

Immediate Contexts for Adolescent Development

8

THE URBAN FAMILY

Wendy Kliewer, Kimberly Goodman,
and Kathryn Reid-Quiñones

The Other Wes Moore (Moore, 2010) is an interesting and dramatic account of two young men with the same name, who grew up in the same under-resourced, urban neighborhood, and whose lives took dramatically different turns. One Wes Moore became a Rhodes scholar; the other Wes Moore is serving a life term for murder. How did the lives of these two young men turn out to be so different? What can their experiences, along with research on thousands of other adolescents living in under-resourced, urban neighborhoods, tell us about resilience and the role of the family in this context?

This chapter addresses those questions by reviewing the challenges facing youth and families in urban communities, noting the negative outcomes associated with these challenges with a focus on academic outcomes influenced by the family. We then describe a set of family processes that are associated with good adjustment and school achievement in urban contexts. Finally, we review family-focused interventions associated with improved academic achievement among urban youth.

Stressors in the Urban Environment

Adolescents living in under-resourced, urban environments face a host of stressors. Although there has been a surge of interest in urban living in the past decade (Kilgore, 2010), the economic revitalization that has accompanied return to the inner city has not extended to all communities. The most under-resourced, urban environments are replete with environmental stressors including community violence, elevated noise levels, crowded housing and poor housing quality (Allison et al., 1999; Attar, Guerra, & Tolan, 1994; Evans, 2004). Psychosocial risk factors include family discord, familial substance abuse, parental mental health problems, and health issues of family members (Tolan, Guerra, & Montaini-Klovdahl, 1997). High rates of sociodemographic risk factors such as low parental education, single-parent status and poverty also are present in these environments (Furstenberg, Cook, Eccles, Elder, & Sameroff, 1999).

Environmental Stressors

Families living in urban settings face a number of stressors which impact the family unit and the individual. Studies have reported that approximately 80% of urban youth have experienced some form of community violence in their lifetime (see Fowler, Tompsett, Braciszewski, Jacques-Tiura, & Baltes, 2009). Concerns about safety due to exposure to community violence and other crimes often prompt parents to restrict their offspring from spending much time outside of the home and in the neighborhood, one of several "preventive management strategies" mentioned by Furstenberg and colleagues (1999). Furthermore, this preventive management strategy, while reducing adolescents' exposure to dangers in the community, does little to steer youth *toward* activities, such as after-school or community youth development programs, that could promote positive development (e.g., social competence, self-efficacy, civic commitment).

In spite of the efforts of many parents, youth continue to be exposed to violence within their communities. Research consistently has revealed the damaging consequences of children's repeated exposure to community violence, including greater distress symptoms, aggressive behavior, depression, anxiety, academic problems, social maladjustment, and substance use (see Fowler et al., 2009 for a review). Post-traumatic Stress Disorder (PTSD) is the most commonly cited internalizing disorder associated with community violence exposure (Fowler et al., 2009) and is important to study because symptoms of PTSD can interfere with academic performance. While parental efforts to shield their children from exposure to community violence are not always successful, certain family factors have linked youths' psychological and academic outcomes in response to community violence exposure (e.g., family conflict; Overstreet & Braun, 2000).

Family Stressors

On top of environmental problems associated with living in urban environments, adolescents are also affected by family stressors. For instance, parents may experience employment stressors such as nonflexible work schedules, lack of paid time off, and transportation difficulties. Such barriers may prevent parents from being actively involved with their youths' school activities (Heymann & Earle, 2000). Additionally, severe economic difficulties resulting in foreclosure and eviction may create disruptions that make consistent parental involvement in school problematic. Parents of low socioeconomic status (SES) also tend to have less education and may feel unprepared to assist their adolescents with schoolwork. Parental mental health conditions related to poverty, such as depression, may also impact adolescent functioning (Goosby, 2007).

Some family characteristics have been identified as influencing adolescent academic achievement. While previous research has demonstrated that family disruption is linked to negative behavioral and psychological outcomes for youth (Evans & Wachs, 2010), relatively little research has examined the relation between family disruption and adolescent academic functioning. Additionally, the few studies that have been performed define family disruption in a variety of ways. For example, Marcynyszyn,

Evans, and Eckenrode (2008) demonstrated that family instability—defined as changes in parents' intimate partners, parents' work hours, residences lived in, and children's schools—was associated with lower English and math grades on top of higher risk of internalizing and externalizing behaviors.

Extending this literature, Somers and colleagues (2011) conducted a 15-year longitudinal examination of the impact of a wide range of family disruptions on academic functioning in urban, African American adolescents. In their investigation, caregiver marital status and paternal involvement emerged as the most substantial family disruption variables influencing teen academic achievement. Specifically, adolescents whose caregiver was unmarried and who reported lower father involvement demonstrated lower scores on study-administered achievement testing.

In contrast to family disruption, family routine has been conceptualized as the degree to which parents provide structure, consistency, and organization within the home environment (Lanza & Taylor, 2010) and has been linked with adolescents' positive adjustment (Taylor, 1996; Taylor & Lopez, 2005). Lanza and Taylor (2010) examined family routine as a moderator of the relation between school disengagement and delinquent behaviors in urban, African American, low SES adolescents. Their findings revealed that for adolescents displaying higher levels of school disengagement, lower levels of family routine were related to higher levels of delinquent behaviors. In contrast, higher levels of family routine were not associated with lower levels of delinquent behaviors, but were independently linked to lower levels of school disengagement. Lower levels of family routine have also been associated with higher re-experiencing and avoidance symptoms for children and early adolescents exposed to trauma in low-income, urban communities (Kiser, Medoff, & Black, 2010). The absence of consistent family routines places urban adolescents at greater risk for experiencing the negative sequalae of living in an urban neighborhood.

Urban Stressors and Minority Status

Minority youth are over-represented in disadvantaged, urban neighborhoods, and Hispanic youth comprise the largest and fastest growing minority group in the United States (Pew Hispanic Center, 2010). However, to date, much of the research on challenges of urban, minority youth has focused largely on African American youth and relatively little is known in regard to stressors specific to Latino adolescents (Cervantes & Cordova, 2011). In addition to enduring many of the same stressors as other minority adolescents, including discrimination, increased poverty, and health disparities, Latino adolescents also experience acculturation-related stressors including language barriers, immigration, and sometimes parental separation during the immigration process. These stressors impact adolescents' academic performance, particularly given that some research has suggested that the majority of discrimination experienced by minority adolescents occurs at school (e.g., Cordova & Cervantes, 2010). Furthermore, language barriers significantly reduce the ability of recent immigrant parents to take an active role in their youths' education (Cervantes & Cordova, 2011).

Summarizing, youth living in under-resourced, urban neighborhoods experience high levels of stressors, yet, *many such adolescents do succeed and thrive*. Apart from refraining from risk-taking behavior and displaying low levels of depression or anxiety, these youth have a positive outlook on life and do well academically. Protective factors in the family associated with good adjustment include family cohesion, family routines, and genuine love among family members. However, more research is needed to identify pathways that contribute to adolescent success in spite of risk and adversity and to understand how those pathways can be enhanced.

Family Processes Associated with Positive Adjustment

Kliewer and colleagues (Kliewer, 2010; Kliewer et al., 2006) tested a model of parental socialization that is embedded within a stress and coping framework and that can be applied to a wide range of adolescent outcomes. In this model, caregivers— who may not be the adolescent's biological parent—influence adolescent outcomes in three primary ways. First, caregivers influence adolescent coping and adjustment via *coaching*. Coaching involves messages parents relay to their children about how to think about a stressful situation or actions to take to reduce the source of the problem or the adolescent's distress about it. *Modeling*, a second path of influence, concerns parents' own stress management practices and other behaviors youth observe directly. Parents may or may not be conscious of their actions. The third pathway through which parents influence adolescent coping and adjustment is via the *family context*. In our perspective, parents are the architects of the family environment, and as such shape the patterns of conflict, communication, and cohesion embedded in family life. Coping behaviors are learned, reinforced, or discouraged within the family environment. These paths of influence are affected by caregivers' personalities, values, experiences, and socioeconomic level.

Coaching

Within urban families, we know relatively little about coaching processes associated with good adjustment and academic achievement. We conducted a prospective study of urban youth and caregivers focused on socialization of coping with violence (Kliewer et al., 2006) in which we examined a range of outcomes including academic performance. We found that caregiver suggestions to cope actively with violence, that were coded from a video-taped parent–child discussion, predicted adolescents' use of active coping. Active coping, in turn, was associated with improvements in grades six months later.

Strom and Boster (2007) echoed the importance of supportive communication in a meta-analysis of the associations between supportive messages from parents concerning educational attainment and high school drop-out. Supportive messages were defined as expectations about school success (e.g., messages conveying the importance of graduating and doing well in courses). Overall, the relation between supportive parental messages and lower drop-out rates was fairly robust. Interestingly, communication regarding educational aspirations and expectations more strongly predicted school drop-out than general parent–child interaction. The results of the meta-analysis were similar across different regions in the United States.

Modeling

In terms of modeling and urban adolescents' outcomes, researchers have shown that parental education is positively associated with children's achievement (Davis-Kean, 2005). However, this relationship is not straightforward. Rather, parental education exerts an influence on youth achievement largely through the transmission of expectations and beliefs (e.g., Zhang, Haddad, Torres, & Chen, 2011). For example, well-educated parents are more likely than less well-educated parents to relay the importance of education to their children, the belief that education is a key to getting ahead, and the expectation that their children will receive an education. These data suggest that coaching and modeling processes work in concert to influence adolescent achievement.

Family Context

The vast amount of research related to adolescent adjustment broadly, and academic achievement specifically, addresses the family environment. Within this framework we will discuss several protective processes including (a) monitoring-related processes, (b) parental warmth and the quality of the parent–adolescent relationship, and (c) parental involvement in youth's education.

Monitoring-related Processes and Adolescent Adjustment

Although the definition of parental monitoring has fueled some debate in the literature, many researchers conceptualize monitoring as encompassing parent-driven processes (e.g., soliciting information, setting boundaries for adolescents' behavior) as well as youth-driven processes (e.g., disclosure of information) (e.g., Kerr & Stattin, 2000). Interestingly, monitoring is often operationalized as parental knowledge. In the context of academic socialization, this knowledge might pertain to school-related activities such as courses the adolescent is taking, required homework and other class assignments, and any difficulties the adolescent is having at school. A large literature has demonstrated the benefits of parental monitoring on outcomes such as aggressive behavior and delinquency, including substance use (Kerr & Stattin, 2000; Kliewer, 2010). With respect to studies of parental monitoring and school-related outcomes, several studies have shown that parental monitoring is associated with increased indicators of school engagement. For example, in a study of 848 Latino middle school students recruited from schools in seven states, Woolley, Kol, and Bowen (2009) found that "parent education monitoring" which included items such as "school activities or events that interest you" and "attendance, homework, or problems with a teacher," was associated with greater levels of teacher support and school satisfaction, which in turn was associated with higher grades. Notably, middle school interventions designed to reduce homework-related difficulties are promising. Toney, Kelley, and Lanclos (2003) found support for one intervention that involved parental monitoring and structuring of homework and for another intervention that focused on adolescent self-management. Such interventions are important in middle school because as homework and other school assignments become more difficult, adolescents' desire for autonomy may fuel a reluctance to seek parental support in this area.

Quality of the Parent-adolescent Relationship and Adolescent Adjustment

Myriad research projects have shown that a warm and loving relationship between adolescents and their parents, accompanied by appropriate boundaries, is associated with good adjustment, including academic achievement (Baumrind, 1991). A recent article focused on connectedness, which includes feelings of belonging, attachment, and engagement in specific contexts among 437 urban ethnically diverse adolescents, illustrates this point. Witherspoon, Schotland, Way, and Hughes (2009) examined adolescent connectedness to family, school, and neighborhood contexts in relation to academic adjustment. After accounting for demographic and contextual variables and classroom-level effects, analyses showed that adolescents with high connectedness in multiple contexts, including connectedness to the family, had higher grades than adolescents with low connectedness across contexts. Our work with urban youth exposed to violence consistently finds that felt acceptance from caregivers—a form of connectedness—is the strongest predictor of good adjustment in youth (Kliewer et al., 2004).

Parental Involvement and Adolescent Adjustment

Parental involvement (also referred to as "family engagement") in youths' education may be one modifiable protective factor for reducing youth problem behavior and increasing academic achievement (see Hill & Taylor, 2004). Meta-analytic work consistently finds that parental involvement is linked to academic achievement (Fan & Chen, 2001; Jeynes, 2005). Parental involvement improves students' grades (Aeby, Manning, Thyer, & Carpenter-Aeby, 1999; Keith et al., 1998; van Voorhis, 2003), and locus of control (Aeby et al., 1999), while decreasing absenteeism (Sheldon & Epstein, 2004) and drop-out rates (Anguiano, 2004).

Within the field of education, parental engagement is often conceptualized as a multi-dimensional construct, comprised of caretaker participation in volunteering, communicating, learning at home, parenting, community collaboration, and decision-making (Epstein, 1996). Below, we will further explore some important conceptual and definitional issues, and we will review findings to illustrate how parental involvement is a key protective factor for adolescents.

Types of Involvement and Adolescent Adjustment

Parental involvement often has been operationalized in behavioral terms such as volunteering at school, communicating with teachers and other school personnel, and attending school events, meetings of parent–teacher associations (PTAs), and parent–teacher conferences. These behaviors reflect *school-based involvement strategies*. However, these behavioral indicators overlook parental engagement with children outside of school, or *home-based involvement strategies* (e.g., engaging in educational activities at home, and parent training programs). Grolnick and Slowiaczek (1994) conceptualized parental involvement along three dimensions: behavioral, cognitive-intellectual, and personal. *Behavioral involvement* includes home-based and school-based involvement strategies. *Cognitive-intellectual involvement* includes parents' efforts to expose children to educationally stimulating activities and experiences. *Personal involvement* includes attitudes and expectations around the value and utility of education. This "personal involvement" is also referred to as *academic socialization* (Hill & Tyson, 2009).

With a focus on urban school children, Jeynes (2005) found overall parental involvement improved academic achievement and these findings held up across ethnic groups. Interestingly, the type of parent involvement most strongly related to academic achievement was *parental expectations*, conceptualized above as *personal involvement* by Grolnick and Slowiaczek (1994) or *academic socialization* by Hill and Tyson (2009). Similarly, a meta-analysis by Hill and Tyson (2009) focused on middle school students found that academic *socialization* showed the strongest positive relationship with academic achievement. School-based involvement was also positively related to academic achievement (although less strongly) and the results for home-based involvement were mixed. Specifically, parents' efforts to assist with homework were not consistently associated with achievement. The results of this meta-analytic work are consistent with findings related to coaching and modeling processes and suggest that parents should focus on communication of expectations for achievement and value for education, foster educational and occupational aspirations, discuss learning strategies with children, and make preparations and plans for the future. Hill and Tyson (2009) also emphasized that academic socialization may be especially important in adolescence, because these strategies support adolescents' autonomy and independence while helping to shape goals, beliefs, and motivations. This type of involvement builds on the relationship between the parent and adolescent but is not necessarily dependent on parents' developing a deep, high-quality relationship with teachers (Hill & Tyson, 2009). There likely are, however, reciprocal relations between socialization and achievement and thus the direction of effects for much of this work are unclear.

Although parental involvement is strongly associated with youth's academic achievement, it is precisely during the transition from elementary to middle school when parental involvement dramatically decreases and the role of parents and caregivers in their children's education becomes less established (Brough & Irvin, 2001). Research is needed to identify strategies that enhance parental involvement in adolescents' education without simultaneously thwarting their need for autonomy.

Social Capital and Social Control

Hill and Taylor (2004) posit a theoretical framework for understanding *how* parents/caregivers and schools can facilitate educational outcomes. According to this framework, *social capital* and *social control* are two mechanisms through which parental involvement increases academic achievement. Social capital refers to parents' skills and information that leave them empowered to facilitate their children's learning at home. Social control occurs when families and schools work together to build a consensus about appropriate behavior so that consistent messages are communicated to children. These messages in turn strengthen children's motivation and engagement in school (Grolnick & Slowiaczek, 1994).

Parents of higher SES may be more likely to be involved in children's education than parents with a lower SES for a variety of reasons. First, there are practical barriers to involvement. Parents of low SES may face several challenges such as nonflexible work schedules, lack of resources, and transportation problems. Second, there may be psychological and experiential barriers to involvement. Parents lower in SES may have fewer years of education and therefore may be less likely to model academic achievement for their children relative to higher SES families. Parents lower in SES may lack self-efficacy around school interactions, as work by Eccles and Harold (1996) suggests. Experientially, parents of low SES may have experienced more negative interactions with schools, and thus may not feel empowered to work collaboratively with the teacher and school (Lareau, 1996). Finally, parents' own experiences as students can shape how they become involved in children's education, as positive experiences will likely enhance parents' sense of trust and comfort interacting with the school (Hill & Taylor, 2004; Taylor, Clayton, & Rowley, 2004).

Interestingly, Wes Moore, the Rhodes scholar, had a mother who was very involved in his education and who took steps to make sure he had appropriate academic opportunities, especially when his performance at school declined. In contrast, the mother of the other Wes Moore apparently was relatively disengaged where her son's academic performance was concerned. While other factors undoubtedly contributed to the divergent paths in the lives of these two men, parental involvement appeared to play a role in the success of Wes Moore, the Rhodes scholar.

Family-focused Interventions

Most family-focused interventions with urban adolescents have not been designed to affect academic achievement specifically, but rather to prevent problems such as aggression, delinquency, and substance use that co-vary with academic performance. However, some of these programs do address academics in the context of the program. We illustrate this idea below with a few select programs.

One example of such a program is the *Coping Power* program, designed for youth and families at the middle school transition (Lochman, Wells, & Murray, 2007). Coping Power includes a 34-session group intervention for adolescents, and a 16-session parent component. One specific parent session focuses on skills for academic success and deals extensively with issues surrounding homework completion. Evaluations of the Coping Power program indicate that the program improved adolescent school bonding, improved behavior at school, and increased perceptions of academic competence (Lochman et al., 2007). One mechanism through which the program works is to increase parental consistency in their parenting practices.

A second example of a program that targets problem behavior but also addresses academic performance is *Familias Unidas*, a parent-centered intervention designed to prevent problem behavior in Hispanic adolescents (Pantin et al., 2007). One major component of the program is to work on improving parental investment in adolescents' school performance as well as peer relationships. The intervention teaches parents to create connections with their child's school that should result in better supervision of the adolescent's academic progress. The intervention also facilitates meetings between parents and their adolescent's school counselor. Evaluations of the intervention to date show improvements in parental investment, but not in school bonding or academic achievement (Pantin et al., 2007). Further refinement and assessment of this intervention may reveal the components needed to affect change in adolescent academic performance.

A final example of a family-focused intervention is the *Strengthening Families Program*, one of the most widely adopted prevention programs in the United States (Kumpfer, Molgaard, & Spoth, 1996). Designed for parents and youth, there are several versions of the Strengthening Families Program, including versions for early teens and high school students, and a version for high-risk adolescents. The program is comprised of three components: parent skills training, children's life skills training, and family skills training and has been used in urban, suburban, and rural communities. The program works by improving parent competencies and strengthening parental bonds with their children. The parenting skills sessions review appropriate developmental outcomes, encourage praise, positive family communication, effective and consistent discipline, and teach parents how to engage in child-directed play. While the program does not directly target academic functioning, outcome research indicates that the Strengthening Families Program does have a positive impact on adolescents' academic success. In a recent evaluation of the Iowa Strengthening Families Program (ISFP) on school success, Spoth, Randall, and Shin (2008) found that the intervention delivered when youth were in the 6th grade had significant effects on 8th-grade school engagement and on 12th-grade academic performance.

Thus, family-focused interventions targeting problem behavior and psychosocial outcomes show considerable promise for improving adolescents' academic achievement. These interventions may exert their effects through increasing parent efficacy and competence in two domains: (1) monitoring and communicating with their adolescents, and (2) interacting with the school system. The literature on family involvement provides empirical foundation for further testing the mechanisms through which these programs exert their effects.

Conclusions

Urban families in under-resourced communities face numerous challenges. However, even in these contexts, parents can manage well and can facilitate adaptive coping and adjustment, including school achievement, in their adolescent offspring. Key pathways of parental influence include coaching, modeling, and family context, which work in concert to impact adolescent coping and adjustment. This work illustrates that when parents communicate their educational expectations, monitor carefully, enact family routines consistently, and engage with schools with a sense of self-efficacy, their adolescents are better equipped to demonstrate positive academic outcomes; they are more bonded with school and do better academically.

In addition to providing us with the knowledge of family characteristics required to promote favorable academic outcomes for urban youth, the field of positive youth development offers several evidenced-based interventions that have been proven effective in fostering these qualities among parents who do not inherently parent in these optimal styles. Widespread dissemination and implementation of these family-focused interventions should be pursued to stimulate the strengthening of the urban family and the academic achievement of urban youth. Public policy advocates highlight the long-term economic benefits of improving academic outcomes for adolescents growing up in under-resourced communities—higher educational attainment will enable these youth to obtain better paying jobs and improve the future success of their neighborhoods.

References

Aeby, V. G., Manning, B. H., Thyer, B. A., Carpenter-Aeby, T. (1999). Comparing outcomes of an alternative school program offered with and without intensive family involvement. *The School Community Journal, 9*, 17–32.

Allison, K. W., Burton, L., Marshall, S., Perez-Febles, A., Yarrington, J., & Kirsh, L. B. (1999). Life experiences among urban adolescents: Examining the role of context. *Child Development, 70*, 1017–1029.

Anguiano, R. P. V. (2004). Families and schools: The effect of parental involvement on high school completion. *Journal of Family Issues, 25*, 61–85.

Attar, B. K., Guerra, N. G., & Tolan, P. H. (1994). Neighborhood disadvantage, stressful life events, and adjustment in urban elementary-school children. *Journal of Clinical Child Psychology, 23*, 391–400.

Baumrind, D. (1991). Effective parenting during the adolescent transition. In P. A. Cowan, & E. M. Hetherington (Eds.), *Family transitions: Advances in family research series* (pp. 111–163). Hillsdale, NJ: Lawrence Erlbaum.

Brough, J. A., & Irvin, J. L. (2001). Parental involvement supports academic improvement among middle schoolers: What research says. *Middle School Journal, 32*, 56–61.

Cervantes, R. C., & Cordova, D. (2011). Life experiences of Hispanic adolescents: Developmental and language considerations in acculturation stress. *Journal of Community Psychology, 39*, 336–352.

Cordova, D., Jr., & Cervantes, R. C. (2010). Intergroup and within-group perceived discrimination among U.S.-born and foreign-born Latino youth. *Hispanic Journal of Behavioral Sciences, 32*, 259–274.

Davis-Kean, P. E. (2005). The influence of parent education and family income on child achievement: The indirect role of parental expectations and the home environment. *Journal of Family Psychology, 19*, 294–304.

Eccles, J. S., & Harold, R. D. (1996). Family involvement in children's and adolescents' schooling. In A. Booth, & J. F. Dunn (Eds.), *Family-school links: How do they affect educational outcomes?* (pp. 3–34). Hillsdale, NJ: Lawrence Erlbaum.

Epstein, J. L. (1996). Perspectives and previews on research and policy for school, family, and community partnerships. In A. Booth, & J. F. Dunn (Eds.), *Family-school links: How do they affect educational outcomes?* (pp. 209–246). Hillsdale, NJ: Lawrence Erlbaum Associates, Inc.

Evans, G. W. (2004). The environment of childhood poverty. *American Psychologist, 59*, 77–92.

Evans, G. W., & Wachs, T. D. (Eds.) (2010). *Chaos and its influence on children's development. An ecological perspective.* Washington, DC: American Psychological Association.

Fan, X., & Chen, M. (2001). Parental involvement and students' academic achievement: A meta-analysis. *Educational Psychology Review, 13*, 1–22.

Fowler, P. J., Tompsett, C. J., Braciszewski, J. M., Jacques-Tiura, A. J., & Baltes, B. B. (2009). Community violence: A meta-analysis of the effect of exposure and mental health outcomes of children and adolescents. *Development and Psychopathology, 21*, 227–259.

Furstenberg, F. F., Cook, T. D., Eccles, J., Elder, G. H., & Sameroff, A. (1999). *Managing to make it. Urban families and adolescent success*. Chicago, IL: The University of Chicago Press.

Goosby, B. J. (2007). Poverty duration, maternal psychological resources, and adolescent socioemotional outcomes. *Journal of Family Issues, 28*, 1113–1134.

Grolnick, W. S., & Slowiaczek, M. L. (1994). Parents' involvement in children's schooling: A multidimensional conceptualization and motivational model. *Child Development, 65*, 237–252.

Heymann, S. J., & Earle, A. (2000). Low-income parents: How do working conditions affect their opportunity to help school-age children at risk? *American Educational Research Journal, 37*, 833–848.

Hill, N. E., & Taylor, L. C. (2004). Parental school involvement and children's academic achievement: Pragmatics and issues. *Current Directions in Psychological Science, 13*, 161–164.

Hill, N. E., & Tyson, D. F. (2009). Parental involvement in middle school: A meta-analytic assessment of the strategies that promote achievement. *Developmental Psychology, 45*, 740–763.

Jeynes, W. H. (2005). A meta-analysis of the relation of parental involvement to urban elementary school student academic achievement. *Urban Education, 40*, 237–269.

Keith, T. Z., Keith, P. B., Quirk, K. J., Sperduto, J., Santillo, S., & Killings, S. (1998). Longitudinal effects of parent involvement on high school grades: Similarities and differences across gender and ethnic groups. *Journal of School Psychology, 36*, 335–363.

Kerr, M., & Stattin, H. (2000). What parents know, how they know it, and several forms of adolescent adjustment: Further support for a reinterpretation of monitoring. *Developmental Psychology, 36*, 366–380.

Kiser, L. J., Medoff, D. R., & Black, M. M. (2010). The role of family processes in childhood traumatic stress reactions for youths living in urban poverty. *Traumatology, 16*, 33–42.

Kilgore, A. (2010). http://www.housingwire.com/2010/03/08/inner-city-housing-alternatives-grow-attractive-for-young-professionals.

Kliewer, W. (2010). Family processes in drug use etiology. In L. M. Scheier (Ed.), *Handbook of drug use etiology: Theory, methods, and empirical findings* (pp. 365–381). Washington, DC: American Psychological Association.

Kliewer, W., Adams Parrish, K., Taylor, K. W., Jackson, K., Walker, J. M., & Shivy, V. A. (2006). Socialization of coping with community violence: Influences of caregiver coaching, modeling, and family context. *Child Development, 77*, 605–623.

Kliewer, W., Nelson Cunningham, J., Diehl, R., Adams Parrish, K., Walker, J. M., Atiyeh, C., . . . & Mejia, R. (2004). Violence exposure and adjustment in inner-city youth: Child and caregiver emotion regulation skill, caregiver-child relationship quality, and neighborhood cohesion as protective factors. *Journal of Clinical Child and Adolescent Psychology, 33*, 477–487.

Kumpfer, K. L., Molgaard, V., & Spoth, R. (1996). The Strengthening Families Program for the prevention of delinquency and drug use. In R. D. Peters, & R. J. McMahon (Eds.), *Preventing childhood disorders, substance abuse, and delinquency, Banff international behavioral science series, Vol. 3* (pp. 241–267). Thousand Oaks, CA: Sage Publications.

Lanza, H. I., & Taylor, R. D. (2010). Parenting in moderation: Family routine moderates the relation between school disengagement and delinquent behaviors among African American adolescents. *Cultural Diversity and Ethnic Minority Psychology, 16*, 540–547.

Lareau, A. (1996). Assessing parent involvement in schooling: A critical analysis. In A. Booth, & J. F. Dunn (Eds.), *Family-school links: How do they affect educational outcomes?* (pp. 57–64). Mahwah, NJ: Lawrence Erlbaum Associates.

Lochman, J. E., Wells, K. C., & Murray, M. (2007). The Coping Power program: Preventive intervention at the middle school transition. In P. Tolan, J. Szapocznik, & S. Sambrano

(Eds.), *Preventing youth substance abuse. Science-based programs for children and adolescents* (pp. 185–210). Washington, DC: American Psychological Association.

Marcynyszyn, L. A., Evans, G. W., & Eckenrode, J. (2008). Family instability during early and middle adolescence. *Journal of Applied Developmental Psychology, 29,* 380–392.

Moore, W. (2010). *The Other Wes Moore.* New York: Random House.

Overstreet, S., & Braun, S. (2000). Exposure to community violence and post-traumatic stress symptoms: Mediating factors. *American Journal of Orthopsychiatry, 70,* 263–271.

Pantin, H., Schwartz, S. J., Coatsworth, J. D., Sullivan, S., Briones, E., & Szapocznik, J. (2007). Familias Unidas: A systemic, parent-centered approach to preventing problem behavior in Hispanic adolescents. In P. Tolan, J. Szapocznik, & S. Sambrano (Eds.), *Preventing youth substance abuse. Science-based programs for children and adolescents* (pp. 185–210). Washington, DC: American Psychological Association.

Pew Hispanic Center. (2011). *Statistical portrait of Hispanics in the United States, 2009.* Retrieved August 20, 2011, from http://pewhispanic.org/factsheets/factsheet.php?Fact sheetID=70.

Sheldon, S. B., & Epstein, J. L. (2004). Getting students to school: Using family and community involvement to reduce chronic absenteeism. *The School Community Journal, 14,* 39–56.

Somers, C. L., Chiodo, L. M., Yoon, J., Ratner, H., Barton, E., & Delaney-Black, V. (2011). Family disruption and academic functioning in urban, Black youth. *Psychology in the Schools, 48,* 357–370.

Spoth, R., Randall, G. K., & Shin, C. (2008). Increasing school success through partnership-based family competency training: Experimental study of long-term outcomes. *School Psychology Quarterly, 23,* 70–89.

Strom, R. E., & Boster, F. J. (2007). Dropping out of high school: A meta-analysis assessing the effect of messages in the home and in school. *Communication Education, 56,* 433–452.

Taylor, L. C., Clayton, J. D., & Rowley, S. J. (2004). Academic socialization: Understanding parental influences on children's school-related development in the early years. *Review of General Psychology, 8,* 163–178.

Taylor, R. D. (1996). Adolescents' perceptions of kinship support and family management practices: Association with adolescent adjustment in African American families. *Developmental Psychology, 32,* 687–695.

Taylor, R. D., & Lopez, E. I. (2005). Family management practice, school achievement, and problem behavior in African American adolescents: Mediating processes. *Journal of Applied Developmental Psychology, 26,* 39–49.

Tolan, P. H., Guerra, N. G., & Montaini-Klovdahl, L. R. (1997). Staying out of harm's way: Coping and the development of inner-city children. In S. A. Wolchik, & I. N. Sandler (Eds.), *Handbook of children's coping: Linking theory and intervention* (pp. 453–479). New York: Plenum.

Toney, L. P., Kelley, M. L., & Lanclos, N. F. (2003). Self- and parental monitoring of homework in adolescents: Comparative effects on parents' perceptions of homework behavior problems. *Child and Family Behavior Therapy, 25,* 35–51.

van Voorhis, F. L. (2003). Interactive homework in middle school: Effects on family involvement and science achievement. *Journal of Educational Research, 96,* 323–338.

Witherspoon, D., Schotland, M., Way, N., & Hughes, D. (2009). Connecting the dots: How connectedness to multiple contexts influences the psychological and academic adjustment of urban youth. *Applied Developmental Science, 13,* 199–216.

Woolley, M. E., Kol, K. L., & Bowen, G. L. (2009). The social context of school success for Latino middle school students: Direct and indirect influences of teachers, family, and friends. *The Journal of Early Adolescence, 29,* 43–70.

Zhang, Y., Haddad, E., Torres, B., & Chen, C. (2011). The reciprocal relationships among parents' expectations, adolescents' expectations, and adolescents' achievement: A two-wave longitudinal analysis of the NELS data. *Journal of Youth and Adolescence, 40,* 479–489.

9

PEERS AND ACADEMIC ADJUSTMENT IN URBAN CONTEXTS

Heather A. Bouchey and Amy Bellmore

After nearly a century of focus on student-level factors that explain academic outcomes, achievement motivation, and related educational constructs, recent research has turned to the contextual factors that underlie adolescents' beliefs, plans, and decision-making with respect to the scholastic domain (Wigfield, Eccles, Schiefele, Roeser, & Davis-Kean, 2006). Given the increased salience of peers during adolescence (Brown & Larson, 2009), the field has begun to explore the role of the peer context in influencing individual adolescents' academic outcomes. Longstanding achievement and performance gaps associated with adolescents' ethnic or racial minority status are widely acknowledged, but less is known about the role of peers in this arena for urban low-income adolescents. The bulk of the literature on urban peers has instead focused on delinquent behavior, drug and alcohol use, and other maladaptive behavioral patterns.

We will meld both developmental and educational perspectives to discuss conceptions of how peers may influence academic adjustment in urban underserved contexts. In contrast to the deficit model approach often employed when conceptualizing urban low-income youth, the potential *positive* aspects of urban adolescents' peer groups are highlighted here. We first introduce normative peer group structural changes that occur during adolescence, illustrating how each structural change may be linked to different facets of adolescents' academic functioning. Next, potential underlying mechanisms by which peers may influence educational outcomes are unpacked. Social support provision from peers, peers serving as role models with respect to educational values, and peer tutoring are some of the most comprehensively investigated areas. The unique features of urban schools and how they jointly interface with the peer context and students' academic outcomes are discussed next. The chapter concludes by discussing how current knowledge can help inform academic interventions with underserved urban youth both within and outside traditional academic settings, as well as delineating areas in need of further study.[1]

---

1   Although romantic relationships are an important component of adolescent peer contexts, this chapter focuses solely on non-romantic relationships and interactions.

Peer Group Structures in Adolescence

During adolescence, peer groups undergo several substantial transformations. The amount of time that adolescents spend with their peers increases (Brown & Larson, 2009), the composition of the peer group changes (Eckert, 1989), and the attainment of a high status within the peer hierarchy takes on great importance (LaFontana & Cillessen, 2010). These transformations are not unique to urban underserved settings, but the manner in which they influence adolescents likely depends on features that are unique to urban low-income contexts. In this section we consider how normative features of the peer group can support urban adolescents' academic functioning.

Crowds

Peer crowds, social categories that identify adolescents based on an image or reputation (e.g., ethnic background, activity participation) that is shared among the group members (Brown & Klute, 2003), emerge in adolescence. An adolescent's crowd assignment is determined by the larger peer group in which he or she resides (e.g., a high school). Thus, an adolescent may be affiliated with a certain crowd despite having no significant social interactions with other members of that same crowd. Crowds are hypothesized to promote identity development (Newman & Newman, 2001) and facilitate the negotiation of the social structure of secondary school settings (Brown, Mory, & Kinney, 1994). These functions may be even more critical within urban schools that serve large student populations.

Crowd structures have been identified in most U.S. school settings, although the particular social categories that are present differ from school to school. Many schools contain a crowd related to academic functioning, "brains" (Prinstein & La Greca, 2002) or "nerds" (Kinney, 1993), and adolescents in these school-oriented crowds demonstrate higher academic achievement (Steinberg, Dornbusch, & Brown, 1992). However, because the overall social hierarchy of crowds is contextually defined, the status associated with membership in these academically inclined crowds may differ substantially across schools. This has implications for the academic performance of youth in urban underserved settings; students in schools where academic crowd membership co-occurs with low peer status will be encouraged to adopt anti-school behaviors.

Cliques

A second peer group structure that emerges in adolescence is the clique. Cliques, or friendship groups, contain approximately 3–9 members and are formed on the basis of shared social interactions (Dunphy, 1963). Because clique membership is derived from mutual liking among members and participation in shared activities, cliques play a strong role in the promotion of academic values. Urban adolescents who are members of the same clique are similar on a host of academic outcomes. Students who perceive positive school-related peer norms and values within their peer network (e.g., the importance of homework) are more engaged in school, and expect more success in school (Goodenow & Grady, 1993; Shin, Daly, & Vera, 2007).

Several processes may explain similarities between clique members. Adolescents may self-select into groups with similar academic orientations, and clique members may be socializing agents that either facilitate or inhibit academic success. Wentzel (2009) described several processes through which clique membership may promote academic achievement—clique members may communicate expectations for its members, may provide help to one another, and may provide mutual emotional support. We further explore the evidence on these potential mechanisms in a subsequent section.

Social Status

A third transformation of adolescent peer groups is the increased importance that adolescents ascribe to peer status. Social status is a characteristic of an individual that is determined by the peer group (Rubin, Bukowski, & Parker, 2006). Both preference-based status such as acceptance, and prominence-based status such as perceived popularity are valued, but popularity takes on particular importance (Cillessen, Schwartz, & Mayeux, 2011). In general, high levels of perceived popularity are associated with lower academic performance (Gorman, Kim, & Schimmelbusch, 2002); even strivings toward popularity predict poor academic engagement (Kiefer & Ryan, 2008). However, Schwartz, Gorman, Nakamoto, and McKay (2006) found that the association between perceived popularity and poor academic performance is present only in aggressive adolescents. They argue that aggressive adolescents may disengage from academics to increase their social standing. Unlike crowd and clique membership that may promote academic achievement, then, perceived popularity seems to be consistently associated with low achievement. Youth may reap social rewards that come with popular status but simultaneously face greater risk for poor academic outcomes.

Gang Membership

Gangs, self-formed collectives of individuals that are usually involved in delinquent activities (Petersen, 2000) are not unique to urban school settings (Evans, Fitzgerald, Weigel, & Chvilicek, 1999), but their ubiquity within urban environments makes them an essential peer group structure to consider. Gang activity is a highly salient aspect of urban neighborhoods and schools; large percentages of urban adolescents report awareness of where gang members associate, and knowing or being friends with gang members (Arfániarromo, 2001; Bursik & Grasmick, 1993; Cadwallader & Cairns, 2002). From a functional standpoint, gangs encapsulate each of the three peer group structures. They share features of crowds in that adolescents can adopt displays such as clothing, language, and locations to associate that are indicative of membership within a certain gang. Gangs also share features of cliques in that localized gangs are determined by shared activities and close connections between the members (Taylor, 1990). Finally, adolescents in underserved urban environments identify acceptance by their peers as a strong motivation for gang membership (Walker-Barnes & Mason, 2001).

Numerous studies have found concurrent associations between gang involvement and academic functioning including low degrees of school engagement, lower standardized test scores, and greater risk of dropping out (Hill, Howell, Hawkins, & Battin-Pearson, 1999; Bowker & Klein, 1983; Maxson, Whitlock, & Klein, 1998). Compared to low achievers, high achievers are also less likely to have close friends who are gang members (Lopez, Wishard, Gallimore, & Rivera, 2006). Further, poor academic functioning often is a gateway to gang participation (Dukes, Martinez, & Stein, 1997). Moreover, an adolescent's status within the gang is also associated with achievement—youth with high status within violent groups are at much greater risk of high school dropout than others (Staff & Kreager, 2008).

Given that academic failure precedes gang membership, an opportunity to prevent adolescents' initiation into gangs is present within schools. Special emphasis could be given to promote the achievement of youth who are at risk of gang membership. Given the social provisions offered by gangs, it would be important to also promote feelings of social acceptance with the school. Any approach should recognize the importance of the urban public school ecology to adolescents' social and academic adjustment.

Mechanisms of Peer Influence

In addition to detailing how different aspects of normative peer structures may play a role in students' academic functioning, scholars have also delineated specific mechanisms of peer influence with respect to academics. Much of this work, however, has omitted salient peer structural changes in the underlying conceptual model. Instead, researchers have typically reasoned that peers, like parents and teachers, are an important socialization entity that accordingly warrants further inclusion in broader studies of risk and protection factors for urban underserved populations.

Support

One frequently studied mechanism of peer influence on student academic adjustment is perceived or actual social support from peers. "Peers" in this work are typically considered friends of the respondent, linking this body of literature most closely with the work on adolescent cliques discussed earlier. Broadly, peer social support is conceptualized as the adolescent's sense of caring from, connection to, and instrumental aid from the friend in question (Malecki & Demaray, 2006).

With respect to underserved urban students, peer support is positively linked with their academic adjustment, although the literature has not been entirely consistent. For instance, high achieving youth in Walker's (2006) qualitative study of math success in urban teens indicated high levels of both instrumental and emotional support from peers for doing well. Classmate support has been linked with both math/science scholastic behavior and GPA in low-income middle school students (Bouchey, 2004; Malecki & Demaray, 2006). Students' educational aspirations have also been consistently linked with high levels of perceived peer support (Berzin, 2010; Strand & Winston, 2008). Conversely, other studies with urban low-income middle school students reported that social support from friends was *not* strongly linked to school engagement or academic behavior (Bouchey & Harter, 2007; Shin et al., 2007). Given these disparate findings additional investigation is warranted. Systematizing the assessment of peer support in future studies would be beneficial, as differences in the way that peer support is conceptualized or measured across studies could account for these inconsistent findings.

An emergent strength of research on peer support is the care that investigators have taken to control for similar sources of influence from both parents and significant others in adolescents' lives (see Turner, 2007). Accordingly, accumulating evidence regarding the extent to which peers are "unique" influences on academic adjustment, independent of support from others in the adolescent's life, is an important future direction for this work.

Peers as Role Models

Aligning most closely with normative reference group theory and role theory (Hallinan & Williams, 1990), a comprehensive literature has documented linkages among peer behavior with academic adjustment and long-term educational plans in youth. Urban adolescents who report more positive peer behaviors regarding school and community engagement, as well as a stronger sense of their own ethnic identity, have higher levels of academic engagement (Shin et al., 2007). Conversely, negative peer norms in the form of high levels of peer delinquency, maladaptive scholastic behavior, and peer discouragement of academics, have been negatively related to students' own academic performance (Azmitia & Cooper, 2001; Jessor, Turbin, & Costa, 1998). Peer norms also play a central role, at least theoretically, in the links between urban neighborhood features and low-income adolescents' ultimate academic adjustment (see Levanthal, Dupéré, & Brooks-Gunn, 2009), with low levels of collective efficacy in the neighborhood increasing adolescents' peer deviant affiliation, which is itself linked with less optimal school engagement and success. In sum, the norms and behaviors of low-income adolescents' peers may exert a powerful influence on their own academic-relevant behavior.

The belief systems held by one's peers also predict individual students' academic adjustment. For instance, the extent to which classmates were perceived to value math/science coursework has been linked with low-income urban early adolescents' own self-perceived importance of math/science (Bouchey & Harter, 2007). Moreover, the educational values and aspirations held by the peer group had a positive impact, both directly and indirectly through educational outcomes such as academic proficiency, on high school students' plans for college and career aspirations (Ma & Wang, 2001). These findings are consistent with Ryan's (2001) work indicating that peer group valuing of school has a long-term, positive change on individual group members' intrinsic valuing of school and academic performance. In addition to normative behavior, then, the values and beliefs that are embedded within one's peer network appear to shape the individual adolescent's academic outcomes.

Peer Tutoring

From a different theoretical perspective, namely the educational and pedagogical practice literature, a large body of work demonstrates the effects of peer tutoring, or peer-assisted learning (PAL), with respect to individual students' academic performance and associated academic self-perceptions. Notably, much of this research has relied on experimental or quasi-experimental designs within formal educational settings, allowing for the detection of causal effects due to peer tutoring (Ginsburg-Block, Rohrbeck, & Fantuzzo, 2006; McMaster, Fuchs, & Fuchs, 2006). There are many different peer tutoring models employed in the classroom, but each typically involves the selection of dyads wherein one peer is the tutor and one is the tutee; provision of a structured set of activities, assignments, or curricula for the dyad to work on or complete; and frequent use of this pedagogical practice in the classroom. In sum, peer tutoring appears to have consistent, small to moderate effects on students' academic performance, academic self-concept, and task-oriented behavior (see Robinson, Schofield, & Steers-Wentzel, 2005). In addition, evidence indicates that peer-mediated educational practices such as tutoring work most effectively for low-income and ethnic minority youth (Ginsburg-Block et al., 2006).

Although the large majority of work on peer tutoring has been conducted with elementary aged children (i.e., 4th–6th graders), evidence suggests that the practice is effective for high school students provided they are able to frequently switch tutoring partners and engage in material that is relevant to their daily lives (Fuchs, Fuchs, & Kazdan, 1999). Further, a range of academic outcomes should be considered. Based on the findings with early elementary students (Ginsburg-Block et al., 2006), the strongest impact of peer tutoring is likely on students' classroom behavior, a critical predictor of actual performance. Although empirical study has begun to disentangle the components of peer tutoring—including how it might be similar to collaborative writing and group-based work—more work in this area is needed.

Urban School Features and their Impact on Peers

To best understand which mechanisms (peer support, role-modeling, and tutoring) will be most influential, it is critical to consider urban school structural and compositional characteristics. Urban secondary schools serve more disadvantaged students than their suburban and rural counterparts (Jacob, 2007). With increased school size, students report lower attachment to school and less involvement in extracurricular activities (Crosnoe, Johnson, & Elder, 2004). As a result, students may be unable to create social connections and friendships. Students in urban settings are also quite mobile (Jacob, 2007), creating a peer group that is in constant flux. This instability hinders the formation of close friendship networks (South & Haynie, 2004) and it may disrupt peer crowd or individual status hierarchies.

Ethnic segregation is also a prominent characteristic of urban secondary schools. Adolescents not only find themselves in schools that are ethnically segregated from each other (Orfield & Lee, 2006), within-school ethnic segregation is prevalent. Many schools rely on ability groupings/tracking that effectively divides the school population into racially segregated units (Khmelkov & Hallinan, 1999). This limits opportunities for relationships with peers of all ethnicities and for visibility among all peers. High achieving youth also lose opportunities to maintain friendships with low achievers, even if they have longstanding connections to them (Horvat & Lewis, 2003; Mickelson & Greene, 2006). Flores-González (2005) explored how tracking practices within one underserved urban high school resulted in the separation of "school kids" and "street kids" and concluded that the segregation promoted distinct academic and social spheres for high and low achievers where popularity among the high achievers was maintained through academic, social, and athletic abilities and popularity among the low achievers was sought through intimidation.

A final characteristic of urban schools that is important to students' peer relationships is ethnic composition: the number or proportion of students within a school who are from a particular ethnic group (e.g., the proportion of White and Black students in a school). Though often presented as a risk factor for students (e.g., "percentage of ethnic minority students in a school"), the impact of school ethnic composition is actually not so clear cut. Social benefits, such as greater peer acceptance and lower peer ethnic discrimination, come with being in the numerical ethnic majority (Bellmore, Nishina, Witkow, Graham, & Juvonen, 2007; Bellmore, Nishina, You, & Ma, 2012; Hallinan & Smith, 1985). There are also social benefits to numerical minority group membership. The unbalanced representation of students from different ethnic groups in the peer group may enable self-preserving attributions among minority students who are not well-accepted by out-group peers (Graham, Bellmore, Nishina, & Juvonen, 2009). Majority and minority group status also interact with specific ethnic group membership. Fuller-Rowell and Doan (2010) found that there were social costs of academic achievement for Black adolescents attending high achieving schools; however, these costs were highest when Blacks were in the numerical minority within the school population.

In contrast to minority and majority group status, ethnic diversity accounts for the number of groups that are present and their relative representation in a school. For example, a school with two ethnic groups that are equally balanced represents a moderately ethnically diverse setting whereas a school with four ethnic groups that are equally balanced is even more ethnically diverse. Research on the benefits of ethnic diversity has shown that in ethnically diverse schools, adolescents have many cross-ethnic friendships (Moody, 2001) and are rarely victimized by peers (Juvonen, Nishina, & Graham, 2006). Students attending these schools also report relatively low levels of loneliness and social anxiety (Bellmore, Witkow, Graham, & Juvonen, 2004). Greater ethnic heterogeneity of cliques is more possible in ethnically diverse schools; a key benefit here is that students' social capital increases (Haynie & Payne, 2006).

Some research describes how the normative features of peers in concert with the benefits of ethnically diverse contexts can promote the academic success of youth. One exemplar is the program described by Conchas and Noguera (2004) where small school communities were particularly effective in promoting a strong pro-academic ideology in African American boys within a large ethnically diverse urban high school. Among the factors that the boys noted as critical to their success were the changes that participation brought to their peer relations. These changes included the development of peer networks that stressed high achievement while providing encouragement and help, and opportunities to interact with peers from different ethnic backgrounds that contrasted with the extreme peer ethnic segregation present in the larger school context. Community-based organizations can also capitalize on the importance of peers in adolescence to reinforce positive attitudes toward school. After-school centers and youth clubs are most effective when they promote peer-bonding and fun while providing academic support (Anderson, Sabatelli, & Kosutic, 2007; Loder & Hirsch, 2003; Quane & Rankin, 2006). Recognition of the developmental significance of peers across settings is important to note and can serve as a guide for the development of similar programs in the future.

Conclusions

What can we conclude about the likely strategies involving peers that should be used to enhance urban underserved adolescents' academic adjustment? First, given our review, a promising approach might be for adults to actively engage the peer context in both the learning of core academic content and in the formative shaping of collective values and aspirations or goals. In addition to enhancing academic achievement, PAL interventions such as peer tutoring might be used fruitfully to shape students' academic self-perceptions and aspirations, given the natural linkage between the existing values of the peer group and students' own value systems. Second, better integration is necessary to meld the developmental literature concerning our understanding of normative peer structural changes with the more focused mechanisms and interventions that have been typically investigated by the educational community. For instance, peer tutoring may work particularly well when tutors are close friends or clique members of the tutee, or at least come from the same crowd within the school.

Additionally, the normative establishment of crowd identities could be used to design school-wide interventions that address and change divergent educational pathways for separate groups of students, perhaps capitalizing on their identity with respect to ethnic minority or majority status. Employing cross-crowd student perspectives in such intervention designs might be particularly beneficial, given that adults may learn just as much information from students as students can learn from educational personnel.

In addition, we must rectify seemingly inconsistent sets of findings, such as (1) the reported negative links between perceived popularity and academic success with (2) positive links between more local, clique-based valuing of school and students' academic adjustment. We should also better understand how peer contexts outside of the educational and friendship arenas play a role in academic development. For instance, we know little about how gang presence in one's school or neighborhood (even if one is not a member of such a group) or broader peer networks such as those established via on-line social networks have an impact on urban underserved adolescents' beliefs, behavior, and performance with respect to school. Ideally, discussion of the potential unique influence of peers with respect to urban youths' academic adjustment should be incorporated into pre-service teacher training or within in-service professional development activities. The literature on peer-based interventions for enhancing urban low-income adolescents' academic adjustment remains relatively understudied but the information reviewed in this chapter can hopefully serve as a springboard for designing empirically and contextually validated interventions.

References

Arfániarromo, A. (2001). Toward a psychosocial and sociocultural understanding of achievement motivation among Latino gang members in U.S. schools. *Journal of Instructional Psychology, 28*, 123–136.

Anderson, S., Sabatelli, R., & Kosutic, I. (2007). Families, urban neighborhood youth centers, and peers as contexts for development, *Family Relations, 56*, 346–357.

Azmitia, M., & Cooper, C. R. (2001). Good or bad? Peer influences on Latino and European American adolescents' pathways through school. *Journal of Education for Students Placed at Risk, 6*, 45–71.

Bellmore, A. D., Nishina, A., Witkow, M. R., Graham, S., & Juvonen, J. (2007). The influence of classroom ethnic composition on same- and other-ethnicity peer nominations in middle school. *Social Development, 16*, 720–740.

Bellmore, A., Nishina, A., You, J., & Ma, T. (2012). School context protective factors against peer ethnic discrimination across the high school years. *American Journal of Community Psychology, 49*, 98–111.

Bellmore, A. D., Witkow, M. R., Graham, S., & Juvonen, J. (2004). Beyond the individual: The impact of ethnic context and classroom behavioral norms on victims' adjustment. *Developmental Psychology, 40*, 1159–1172.

Berzin, S. C. (2010). Educational aspirations among low-income youths: Examining multiple conceptual models. *Children and Schools, 32*, 112–124.

Bouchey, H. A. (2004). Parents, teachers, and peers: Discrepant or complementary achievement socializers? In H. A. Bouchey, & C. E. Winston (Eds.), *Social and self-processes underlying math and science achievement. New directions in child and adolescent development*, Vol. 106 (pp. 35–53). San Francisco, CA: Jossey-Bass.

Bouchey, H. A., & Harter, S. (2007). Reflected appraisals, academic self-perceptions, and math/science performance during early adolescence. *Journal of Educational Psychology, 97*, 673–686.

Bowker, L. H., & Klein, M. W. (1983). The etiology of female juvenile delinquency and gang membership: A test of psychological and social structural explanations. *Adolescence, 18*, 739–751.

Brown, B., & Klute, C. (2003). Friendships, cliques, and crowds. In G. R. Adams, & M. D. Berzonsky (Eds.), *Blackwell handbook of adolescence* (pp. 330–348). Malden, MA: Blackwell Publishing.

Brown, B., & Larson, J. (2009). Peer relationships in adolescence. In R. M. Lerner, & L. Steinberg (Eds.), *Handbook of adolescent psychology (3rd ed.). Volume 2: Contextual influences on adolescent development* (pp. 74–103). Hoboken, NJ: Wiley.

Brown, B., Mory, M. S., & Kinney, D. (1994). Casting adolescent crowds in a relational perspective: Caricature, channel, and context. In R. Montemayor, G. R. Adams, & T. P. Gullotta (Eds.), *Personal relationships during adolescence* (pp. 123–167). Thousand Oaks, CA: Sage Publications, Inc.

Bursik, R. J., & Grasmick, H. G. (1993). *Neighborhoods and crime: The dimension of effective community control*. New York: Lexington Books.

Cadwallader, T. W., & Cairns, R. B. (2002). Developmental influences and gang awareness among African-American inner city youth. *Social Development, 11*, 245–265.

Cillessen, A. H. N., Schwartz, D., & Mayeux, L. (2011). *Popularity in the peer system*. New York: Guilford.

Conchas, G. Q., & Noguera, P. A. (2004). Understanding the exceptions: How small schools support the achievement of academically successful black boys. In N. Way, & J. Y. Chu (Eds.), *Adolescent boys: Exploring diverse cultures of boyhood* (pp. 317–337). New York: New York University Press.

Crosnoe, R., Johnson, M., & Elder, G. R. (2004). School size and the interpersonal side of education: An examination of race/ethnicity and organizational context. *Social Science Quarterly, 85*, 1259–1274.

Dukes, R. L., Martinez, R. O., & Stein, J. A. (1997). Precursors and consequences of membership in youth gangs. *Youth & Society, 29*(2), 139–165.

Dunphy, D. C. (1963). The social structure of urban adolescent peer groups. *Sociometry, 26*, 230–246.

Eckert, P. (1989). *Jocks and Burnouts: Social identity in the high school.* New York: Teachers College Press.

Evans, W. P., Fitzgerald, C., Weigel, D., & Chvilicek, S. (1999). Are rural gang members similar to their urban peers? Implications for rural communities. *Youth & Society, 30*, 267–282.

Flores Gonzáles, N. (2005). Popularity versus respect: School structure, peer groups and Latino academic achievement. *International Journal of Qualitative Studies in Education, 18*, 625–642.

Fuchs, L. S., Fuchs, D., & Kazdan, S. (1999). Effects of peer-assisted learning strategies on high school students with serious reading problems. *Remedial and Special Education, 20*, 309–318.

Fuller-Rowell, T. E., & Doan, S. N. (2010). The social costs of academic success across ethnic groups. *Child Development, 81*, 1696–1713.

Ginsburg-Block, M. D., Rohrbeck, C. A., & Fantuzzo, J. W. (2006). A meta-analytic review of social, self-concept, and behavioral outcomes of peer-assisted learning. *Journal of Educational Psychology, 98*, 732–749.

Goodenow, C., & Grady, K. E. (1993). The relationship of school belonging and friends' values to academic motivation among urban adolescent students. *Journal of Experimental Education, 62*, 60–71.

Gorman, A., Kim, J., & Schimmelbusch, A. (2002). The attributes adolescents associate with peer popularity and teacher preference. *Journal of School Psychology, 40*, 143–165.

Graham, S., Bellmore, A., Nishina, A., & Juvonen, J. (2009). "It must be me": Ethnic diversity and attributions for peer victimization in middle school. *Journal of Youth and Adolescence, 38*, 487–499.

Hallinan, M. T., & Smith, S. S. (1985). The effects of classroom racial composition on students' interracial friendliness. *Social Psychology Quarterly, 48*, 3–16.

Hallinan, M. T., & Williams, R. A. (1990). Students' characteristics and the peer-influence process. *Sociology of Education, 63*, 122–132.

Haynie, D. L., & Payne, D. C. (2006). Race, friendship networks, and violent delinquency. *Criminology: An Interdisciplinary Journal, 44*, 775–805.

Hill, K. G., Howell, J. C., Hawkins, J., & Battin-Pearson, S. R. (1999). Childhood risk factors for adolescent gang membership: Results from the Seattle Social Development Project. *Journal of Research in Crime and Delinquency, 36*, 300–322.

Horvat, E., & Lewis, K. S. (2003). Reassessing the "Burden of 'Acting White'": The importance of peer groups in managing academic success. *Sociology of Education, 76*, 265–280.

Jacob, B. (2007). The challenges of staffing urban schools with effective teachers. *The Future of Children: Excellence in the classroom, 17*, 129–153.

Jessor, R., Turbin, M. S., & Costa, F. M. (1998). Risk and protection in successful outcomes among disadvantaged adolescents. *Applied Developmental Science, 2*, 194–208.

Juvonen, J., Nishina, A., & Graham, S. (2006). Ethnic diversity and perceptions of safety in urban middle schools. *Psychological Science, 17*, 393–400.

Khmelkov, V. T., & Hallinan, M. T. (1999). Organizational effects on race relations in schools. *Journal of Social Issues, 55*, 627–645.

Kiefer, S. M., & Ryan, A. M. (2008). Striving for social dominance over peers: The implications for academic adjustment during early adolescence. *Journal of Educational Psychology, 100,* 417–428.

Kinney, D. A. (1993). From nerds to normals: The recovery of identity among adolescents from middle school to high school. *Sociology of Education, 66,* 21–40.

LaFontana, K., & Cillessen, A. (2010). Developmental changes in the priority of perceived status in childhood and adolescence. *Social Development, 19,* 130–147.

Leventhal, T., Dupéré, V., & Brooks-Gunn, J. (2009). Neighborhood influences on adolescent development. In R. M. Lerner, & L. Steinberg (Eds.), *Handbook of adolescent psychology (3rd ed.). Volume 2: Contextual influences on adolescent development* (pp. 411–443). Hoboken, NJ: Wiley.

Loder, T. L., & Hirsch, B. J. (2003). Inner-city youth development organizations: The salience of peer ties among early adolescent girls. *Applied Developmental Science, 7,* 2–12.

Lopez, E. M., Wishard, A., Gallimore, R., & Rivera, W. (2006). Latino high school students' perceptions of gangs and crews. *Journal of Adolescent Research, 21,* 299–318.

Ma, X., & Wang, J. (2001). A confirmatory examination of Walberg's model of educational productivity in student career aspiration. *Educational Psychology, 21,* 443–453.

Malecki, C. K., & Demaray, M. K. (2006). Social support as a buffer in the relationship between socioeconomic status and academic performance. *School Psychology Quarterly, 21,* 375–395.

Maxson, C. L., Whitlock, M. L., & Klein, M. W. (1998). Vulnerability to street gang membership: Implications for practice. *Social Service Review, 72,* 70–91.

McMaster, K. L., Fuchs, D., & Fuchs, L. S. (2006). Research on peer-assisted learning strategies: The promise and limitations of peer-mediated instruction. *Reading and Writing Quarterly, 22,* 5–25.

Mickelson, R., & Greene, A. D. (2006). Connecting pieces of the puzzle: Gender differences in black middle school students' achievement. *The Journal of Negro Education, 75,* 34–48.

Moody, J. (2001). Race, school integration, and friendship segregation in America. *American Journal of Sociology, 107*(3), 679–716.

Newman, B. M., & Newman, P. R. (2001). Group identity and alienation: Giving the We its due. *Journal of Youth and Adolescence, 30,* 515–538.

Orfield, G., & Lee, C. (2006). *Racial transformation and the changing nature of segregation.* Cambridge, MA: Civil Rights Project at Harvard University.

Petersen, R. D. (2000). Definitions of a gang and impact on public policy. *Journal of Criminal Justice, 28,* 139–149.

Prinstein, M. J., & La Greca, A. M. (2002). Peer crowd affiliation and internalizing distress in childhood and adolescence: A longitudinal follow-back study. *Journal of Research on Adolescence, 12,* 325–351.

Quane, J., & Rankin, B. (2006). Does it pay to participate? Neighborhood-based organizations and the social development of urban adolescents. *Children and Youth Services Review, 28,* 1229–1250.

Robinson, D. R., Schofield, J. W., & Steers-Wentzel, K. L. (2005). Peer and cross-age tutoring in math: Outcomes and their design implications. *Educational Psychology Review, 17,* 327–362.

Rubin, K. H., Bukowski, W. M., & Parker, J. G. (2006). Peer interactions, relationships, and groups. In N. Eisenberg, W. Damon, & R. M. Lerner (Eds.), *Handbook of child psychology: Vol. 3, Social, emotional, and personality development (6th ed.)* (pp. 571–645). Hoboken, NJ: John Wiley & Sons Inc.

Ryan, A. M. (2001). The peer group as a context for the development of young adolescents' motivation and achievement. *Child Development, 72,* 1135–1150.

Schwartz, D., Gorman, A., Nakamoto, J., & McKay, T. (2006). Popularity, social acceptance, and aggression in adolescent peer groups: Links with academic performance and school attendance. *Developmental Psychology, 42,* 1116–1127.

Shin, R., Daly, B., & Vera, E. (2007). The relationships of peer norms, ethnic identity, and peer support to school engagement in urban youth. *Professional School Counseling, 10,* 379–388.

South, S. J., & Haynie, D. L. (2004). Friendship networks of mobile adolescents. *Social Forces, 83,* 315–350.

Staff, J., & Kreager, D. A. (2008). Too cool for school?: Violence peer status and high school dropout. *Social Forces, 87,* 445–471.

Steinberg, L., Dornbusch, S. M., & Brown, B. (1992). Ethnic differences in adolescent achievement: An ecological perspective. *American Psychologist, 47,* 723–729.

Strand, S., & Winston, J. (2008). Educational aspirations in inner city schools. *Educational Studies, 34,* 249–267.

Taylor, C. (1990). *Dangerous society.* Michigan: Michigan State University Press.

Turner, S. L. (2007). Preparing inner-city adolescents to transition into high school. *Professional School Counseling, 10,* 245–252.

Walker, E. (2006). Urban high school students' academic communities and their effects on mathematics success. *American Educational Research Journal, 43,* 43–73.

Walker-Barnes, C. J., & Mason, C. A. (2001). Perceptions of risk factors for female gang involvement among African American and Hispanic women. *Youth & Society, 32*(3), 303–336.

Wentzel, K. R. (2009). Peers and academic functioning at school. In K. H. Rubin, W. M. Bukowski, & B. Laursen (Eds.), *Handbook of peer interactions, relationships, and groups* (pp. 531–547). New York: Guilford Press.

Wigfield, A., Eccles, J. S., Schiefele, U., Roeser, R., & Davis-Kean, P. (2006). Development of achievement motivation. In N. Eisenberg, W. Damon, & R. M. Lerner (Eds.), *Handbook of child psychology: Volume 3, Social, emotional, and personality development (6th ed.)* (pp. 933–1002). New York: Wiley.

10

URBAN SCHOOLS AND ADOLESCENT DEVELOPMENT

Cynthia Hudley and Richard Durán

American education is a contested topic in arenas as local as the family and as broad as national policy. Much has been written about the poor academic environments of "urban," "disadvantaged," and otherwise coded schools over the past decades and the dysfunctional adolescent outcomes accruing in these schools. The picture of what is "wrong" emerges from across the disciplinary and political spectra, from Jonathon Kozol to Bill Bennett. The National Education Association weighed in over five years ago on the need for "improving the quality of teaching, increasing student achievement, and making schools safer" (NEA, 2006).

The term "urban American schools" has been a code word for schools serving a metropolitan area experiencing social problems, including a lack of employment and commercial services, frequent criminal activity, substandard housing, and poor and disadvantaged residents most of whom are members of ethnic minority groups (i.e., Black, Latino, and Southeast Asian). Students in urban schools typically are defined as low-income, low achieving, and "at risk" for school and social failure. However, urban schools are defined more often by racial/ethnic and socioeconomic characteristics than by geographic location, and the populations and social and economic challenges in some suburban areas and small cities are similar to those in metropolitan areas (Foster, 2007).

Demographic data (Council of the Great City Schools, 2008) further clarify the term *urban schools*. Schools in cities with populations over 250,000 or districts with student enrollment over 35,000 represent 12% of the schools, 14% of the teachers, and 15% of the students in public school in the United States. Yet they enroll 32% of African American students and 29% of English language learners. An average of 64% of all students receive free or reduced price lunches, indicating that their families are near or below the Federal poverty level. Our selective review will examine characteristics of school environments that may impact adolescent development. We conclude with a discussion of efforts to improve developmental outcomes for these adolescents.

Academic Motivation and Consequences for Achievement

Students in urban schools are often presumed to be poorly motivated. However, we begin with the reality that urban students who struggle academically are often seen as unmotivated or conduct-disordered, while struggling affluent, White children receive services (e.g., counseling, tutoring) to improve learning (Bowles & Gintis, 1976). Such services are less often freely or economically available in urban schools and communities.

The Physical Plant

Deteriorating facilities, often a characteristic of urban schools, can diminish student achievement and engagement. More than a decade ago, physical conditions in urban schools predicted academic engagement and performance (Lewis et al., 1999) but basic materials—including textbooks, science equipment, and desks—were generally in disrepair or absent. Thus, the condition of urban schools too often renders them sites of developmental risk rather than assets that would enhance student developmental outcomes.

Theories of stress and coping define structural conditions such as dirty bathrooms, physical decay, and overcrowding that are rampant in many urban schools, as stressors that undermine students' ability to concentrate (Lepore & Evans, 1996), and lack of concentration, or poor "on-task behavior," is a core indicator of low motivation and disengagement in students. However, when school facilities provide intellectual and technological resources, students can develop motivation as they explore their own intellectual abilities. Providing laptops for urban adolescents, for example, has increased motivation, engagement, and achievement when computer use moves beyond rote skill practice (Penuel, 2006). A reform initiative that provided laptops and wireless access in an urban high school (Project Hiller) increased standardized test scores, engagement and motivation, and technological literacy for adolescents in grades 8 and 9 (Light, McDermott, & Honey, 2002). An innovative project to teach physics concepts to urban high school students using video technology developed student motivation, engagement, and sense of agency for subject matter that is too often closed to urban minority students (Elmesky, 2005). The addition of technology is no substitute for clean, well-maintained schools, but the investment in physical infrastructure and equipment can support the development of student motivation and increase achievement.

The School Climate

School climate influences the development of academic motivation and achievement. One construct, variously labeled "school belonging" or "school bonding," refers to students' feelings of trust, acceptance, safety, and personal connection at school. In urban middle schools (Goodenow & Grady, 1993), a sense of belonging in school significantly related to students' valuing of education, (i.e., "schoolwork is worthwhile and important"), a belief that is important to the development of achievement motivation. Some extracurricular activities (sports and youth groups) have been positively related to school belonging and are thus an indirect influence on academic motivation (Brown & Evans, 2002). Other data from urban schools revealed that a feeling of school belonging mediated the relationship between motivation and achievement (Faircloth & Hamm, 2005). Feelings of belonging may amplify motivation and academic success for urban students. Perceived school safety, an element of school belonging, also makes a unique contribution to adolescents' achievement and motivation in urban schools that disproportionately suffer from community violence (Hudley & Novak, 2007).

A school's academic climate has also been implicated in the development of motivation and achievement in urban schools. *Academic press* is defined as an emphasis on achievement, rigorous standards and expectations, and the agreement among the entire school community that academics are the priority. A strong press for academic achievement has long been identified as an important characteristic of effective schools (Edmonds, 1979).

A reform known as "nativity schools," parochial middle schools that provide low-income urban students a low cost, elite education, has demonstrated the combined power of academic press and social support. Students in nine nativity schools across the United States (Fenzel & Monteith, 2008) reported a significantly stronger sense of belonging than students in traditional parochial schools and increased their standardized achievement test scores at rates double those of comparison students. Unfortunately, students in the poorest, largest, and lowest-achieving public schools are the least likely to enjoy high levels of academic press and social support (Lewis et al., 1999), although they are most in need of such a school climate. Recent research finds that urban teachers are less highly qualified than their suburban counterparts in experience, educational background, and teaching certification (Shen & Poppink, 2003), although not all researchers agree that these qualities make them less effective teachers (Jacob, 2007).

Another innovation in public education has been the "school within a school" model, in which large secondary schools are subdivided into smaller learning communities. Each comprises a smaller number of students and teachers but still benefits from the physical resources of a larger campus. Often these groupings are organized around specific themes (e.g., medical professions, technology), and students self-select learning communities to pursue personal goals and talents. When the structure works successfully, teachers and students develop more personalized relationships; teachers are able to more closely monitor student progress and adjustment; and students experience significantly greater feelings of belonging to school, increased achievement motivation, and higher future aspirations (Conchas, 2006). Stated simply, the best developmental contexts to support academic achievement for low-income, urban students are schools that demonstrate both a strong sense of belonging and a strong academic press. Understanding how specific school and classroom practices affect student development requires a more fine-grained examination of urban schools, a topic to which we now turn.

Student–Teacher Relationships

Research has established connections between adult–student relationships at school and academic motivation and achievement (Martin & Dowson, 2009). However, interactions among students and the adults in urban schools may not support student motivation and engagement. Low-income Korean high school students in inner city New York perceived teachers to hold low expectations and counselors to be hostile to students' aspirations (Lew, 2006). Perhaps unsurprisingly, participants, typically considered a model minority, left schools that they perceived to be warehouses. Data from Latino and African American students also reveal that urban minority students want teachers, counselors, and other adults in school to support their aspirations, recognize their abilities, and care about them as individuals (Martin & Dowson, 2009).

The classroom environment has also been persuasively linked to motivation. A comparison of classroom structures in urban middle schools enrolling low-income minority students, for example, revealed that student ratings of intrinsic motivation for academics were significantly influenced by specific classroom features (Hudley, 1997). Classrooms in which teachers held high expectations, provided choice in selecting individualized and hands-on activities, and were governed by a minimum of behaviorally stated rules had more positive motivational consequences than remedial classrooms emphasizing lecture, memorization, and discipline that relied on individual reprimands. Findings concerning supportive classroom structures are consistent with cognitive evaluation theory (Deci & Ryan, 1987), which specifies that intrinsic motivation is supported in contexts perceived as supportive of personal autonomy, interpersonal relatedness, and personal competence. Conversely, contexts experienced as controlling, uncaring, or signaling personal incompetence tend to diminish intrinsic motivation.

Similarly, an experimental urban middle school classroom grounded in self-worth theory examined change in student motivation over time (Teel, Debruin-Parecki, & Covington, 1998). The theory posits that academic motivation and engagement are related to a sense of academic self-worth, and motivation is suppressed when students anticipate failure, defined as a threat to academic self-worth. In the experimental classroom, grading was based on effort, students had more responsibility and choice in determining the curriculum, and specific attention was paid to each student's cultural heritage. Over time, these strategies produced increased school engagement and effort, more time on task, and greater cooperation among students and with the teacher. This intervention demonstrated a causal relationship between classroom pedagogy and the development of student behavioral engagement and motivation in urban classrooms.

This selective review generally points to school effects as significant influences on the development of motivation and school engagement, and motivational variables significantly predicting academic achievement. As well, the physical environment influences school climate in complex ways, and the relationship between these two variables predicts student achievement (Uline & Tschannen-Moran, 2008). Urban schools that provide an academically demanding, emotionally supportive environment in a clean, well-resourced physical plant support the development of optimal academic motivation and achievement, as with any school. Having examined characteristics that support the development of motivation and achievement, we now turn to a consideration of the impact of urban schools on adolescents' cognitive development.

Cognitive Development

To understand how cognitive development is related to positive youth development and academic success in urban schools, we begin by considering the role of how fundamental cognitive processes underlie learning. We then consider how contextual factors and culture deepen our understanding of adolescent cognitive development in urban schools.

Subject Matter Knowledge and Cognitive Development

We follow Byrnes (2006), drawing on Kosslyn and Koenig (1994) to define cognition as mental functioning related to the acquisition, modification, and manipulation of knowledge in particular contexts. Psychological approaches to adolescent development consider mental abilities, including reasoning, representation of abstract concepts and their interrelationships, and solving conceptually complex problems. Subject matter reasoning is of fundamental importance to schooling, as the development of subject matter expertise in adolescence is foundational to academic success and preparation for higher education.

Research in the learning sciences (Bransford, Brown, & Cocking, 2000) shows that subject matter expertise requires a deep understanding of how subject matter knowledge (e.g., algebra, history) is organized into bodies of interconnected concepts to represent knowledge of the field. Students are expected to learn to reason about knowledge and apply or extend knowledge to novel situations through classroom assignments, projects, or real-world circumstances. Urban adolescents' development of expertise and deep understanding through classroom instruction requires teachers who are sensitive to students' cultural and linguistic knowledge. Teachers must possess deep knowledge of any subject matter they instruct and also be expert in assisting urban students in acquiring knowledge that generalizes beyond past experiences and ameliorates misconceptions. Students must develop an understanding of how their subject matter knowledge benefits from reformulation and alignment with expert conceptual knowledge and reasoning skills in a given area.

Recent learning sciences research that probes these concerns with urban youths has involved close-in observational research. Wolfe and Goldman (2005) conducted a qualitative discourse analysis examining how urban adolescents with guidance from a teacher can learn to critically compare various historical texts about the same historical events through discussion of similarities and differences in the text content, and learn to reason about differences. Similarly, discourse analysis and inferential statistics were used to study how urban adolescent middle school students (mostly African American and Hispanic) learned to create scientific hypotheses in an earth science curriculum by discussing how they knew that their hypotheses were reasonable (Kuhn, Black, Keselman, & Kaplan, 2010).

An examination of science learning and development among urban middle school students, who were predominantly of an ethnic minority status, used mixed methods procedures to assess implementation of the *ThinkerTools* Inquiry Curriculum that focused on helping students learn to learn (i.e., metacognition) through project-based learning (White & Frederiksen, 1998). The curriculum included reflective assessment strategies that required students to evaluate the quality of their work and learning against standards for content mastery and scientific reasoning established by the curriculum and teachers. Findings indicated that low achieving students benefited significantly from exposure to the *ThinkerTools* curriculum and subsequently compared positively to higher achieving students. Importantly, the curriculum was designed as a *learning community* that socialized students to become partners in learning, as opposed to believing they are individual students in a hierarchy of better and poorer learners.

A Cultural Models Approach to Cognitive Development

Recent work has also connected cognitive development and learning to adolescents' understanding of the social and cultural contexts (including classrooms) within which skills are introduced, mastered, and used as tools for expression of personal and social agency (Rogoff, 2003). Ethnographic research on Haitian immigrant middle school students' biology learning in schools connected their cultural beliefs to their classroom learning community (Rosebery, Warren, & Conant, 1992). This research showed how the Haitian cultural theme *Chèche Konnen* ("search for knowledge") helped students appreciate the notion that scientific ways of knowing were part of their cultural heritage. The research also traced how students were able to translate their classroom learning into scientific investigations conducted in field settings in the community.

Lee's (2000) work on *cultural models* and urban adolescents' learning and literacy development is also relevant here. From a learning sciences perspective, cultural models are memory schemata or chunks of declarative and procedural knowledge that represent our understanding of the world of everyday events and their perceived organization into recognizable activities. Lee's work draws on a Vygotskian notion of cognitive development, in that cultural models arise through extended social-ization processes rather than just brain maturation and isolated exposure to precursor skills and knowledge at the microgenetic level of development studied by many early learning scientists (Siegler & Crowley, 1991). Her ethnographic work shows how urban adolescent youths' cultural models for understanding and doing school tasks, and preferred ways of using language while doing tasks, can be at variance with teachers' cultural models. Urban African Americans' folk notions of "signifying," socialized through their community experiences, display complex forms of reason-ing and intentional communication not unlike what is expected in learning to argue and reason in school-based tasks, but for different reasons with different social outcomes. A cultural models approach seeks to understand how urban students from diverse backgrounds develop an understanding of the value and the demands of acquiring knowledge and expertise in problem solving as characterized by a school curriculum.

What emerges from the foregoing perspectives is that learning is a cultural process (Nasir, Rosebery, Warren, & Lee, 2006). But much research needs to be done on how the social processes that underlie interventions that support urban students, such as those cited in the first section of this chapter, actually support the acquisition of particular cognitive and problem solving skills and knowledge. Research attention is needed to examine how interventions enable students to develop an ongoing repertoire of cultural models, supporting students' development of identities and a sense of agency as they transition from school to the workforce or higher education.

A cultural modeling approach to adolescent cognitive development in urban schools demonstrates the need to view the development of cognitive skills and acquisition of knowledge as social and cultural processes. Optimal cognitive development requires the alignment of students' background knowledge with the demands of academic learning and ways of thinking. Clear links are evident from urban students' cultural knowledge and identities as social beings in and out of school settings to the skills required in classroom learning activities.

Social Development

Schools are inherently social places. Secondary schools in particular are important social settings in which adolescents are able at various points during the day to interact with little direct adult supervision. This social setting, unsurprisingly, is an important site of social development for all students and in all schools. As this chapter is specifically interested in adolescents in urban schools, we will concentrate on two topics that are particularly relevant to the social development of students of color in urban settings: racial/ethnic identity and peer influences.

Racial/Ethnic Identity

Urban schools are social settings that typically comprise a majority of students who represent a broad range of Black, Latino, and Asian ethnic groups. Adolescents in urban schools thus often have more opportunities and a greater need to interact across cultural and ethnic borders than students enrolled in more advantaged, suburban, and racially restricted school settings (Sohoni & Saporito, 2009). The diversity typical of the student body in urban schools is an important school influence on the development of racial/ethnic identity, as this dimension of identity serves as a marker that distinguishes an individual in contrast to other groups.

The development of a positive racial/ethnic identity influences psychological and social adjustment of adolescents of color. Adolescents with a more positive racial/ethnic identity are less likely to use illegal substances, engage in violent and antisocial behavior (Choi, Harachi, Gillmore, & Catalano, 2006), or endorse beliefs supporting antisocial behavior (e.g., "It is acceptable to 'get around' the law to get what you want") and more likely to hold positive attitudes toward outgroup members (Virta, Sam, & Westin, 2004). Although true for all adolescents of color, the benefits of a positive racial/ethnic identity are particularly strong for adolescents living in urban poverty. Thus, a well-developed ethnic identity may be a valuable characteristic to support positive youth development for students in urban schools.

We conclude this section with the recognition of a unique benefit of a positive racial/ethnic identity for students in urban American schools. Adolescents from a variety of racial and ethnic groups, both native born and immigrant, report experiences of discrimination (Szalacha et al., 2003), and these experiences are related to negative behavior and general psychological distress (Wakefield & Hudley, 2007). A positive ethnic identity seems to buffer adolescents in the face of inequitable treatment, leading them to endorse more socially skillful rather than aggressive behavior (Wakefield & Hudley, 2005). Given the reality that students of color in urban schools, particularly Black and Latino students, can experience discrimination in the community and in the school from the adults around them (Way, Santos, Niwa, & Kim-Gervey, 2008), including some teachers (Sleeter, 1992), a positive racial/ethnic identity is an important domain of social development in the urban school context.

Peer Relationships

The influence of peers represents another dimension of social development in urban school contexts (also see Chapter 9 in this volume). Peers may exert negative pressure on high achieving ethnic minority students, who may be labeled "acting white" for being engaged, cooperative, and motivated in school (Fordham & Ogbu, 1986; Lew, 2006). However, more recent research has found that successful African American middle and high school students do not consistently suffer from "acting white" taunts (Tyson, Darity, & Castellino, 2005). High achieving, urban early adolescents were more likely to consider the opinions of their high achieving peers before adopting inappropriate social behaviors (Wentzel & Caldwell, 1997). A strong peer social network is characteristic of very high achieving and gifted urban students, irrespective of student ethnicity (Chhuon, Hudley, Brenner, & Macias, 2010; Hébert & Reis, 1999). The benefits of peer influences are explained by the principle of homophily (Berndt, 1982). Youth seek out peers who are like themselves (i.e., selective association), and once affiliated, peer group members become more similar to one another due to repeated interactions (i.e., reciprocal socialization). Thus, high achieving or highly motivated youth are more likely to seek out similar peers, creating a peer group that reinforces and supports high achievement and motivation. However, we also must acknowledge, in a similar process, antisocial peers can create negative socialization (Dishon, McCord, & Poulin, 1999), in a reciprocal spiral of negative social development. The troubling reality in urban schools is that school and community violence are significant problems, and antisocial peers are a significant presence (Bowen & Bowen, 1999). In sum, although the attention given to negative influences from peers on the development of social competence in urban settings is unsurprising, given that urban youth are more often exposed to antisocial peer groups, peer support can also serve as a powerful agent of positive social development.

Conclusions

This chapter has considered specific characteristics of urban schools that might influence several dimensions of adolescent development. Research findings may have important implications for school practice. Our discussion of academic achievement and motivation pointed to three specific characteristics of schools that have demonstrated impacts on students: the physical plant, the school climate, and teacher–student relationships. Ageing, substandard physical plants and facilities are undeniable stressors sometimes found in urban schools. But as plants age, replacing them with well-equipped, technologically sophisticated facilities provides demonstrated benefits for the development of motivation and achievement. This is a challenging prescription in an era of declining public resources and contested political priorities, but the evidence is clear that a substandard school environment, like substandard housing, yields troublesome academic and developmental sequelae.

Our earlier consideration of school climate variables showed that school belonging is an important psychosocial dimension that supports successful adolescent development. A growing body of evidence indicates that schools can successfully develop school bonding through the use of targeted life skills programs. As defined by the World Health Organization (1997), life skills are a group of competencies that help people think critically and cope with and manage their lives in a healthy and productive manner. Life skills programs that vary from after-school cultural heritage programs (Hanlon, Simon, O'Grady, Carswell, & Callaman, 2009) to comprehensive, multicomponent, longitudinal programs (Catalano, Haggerty, Oesterle, Fleming, & Hawkins, 2004) have all demonstrated the ability to enhance feelings of school bonding in adolescence. Schools, beyond providing programs for students, must also adjust their own environments to promote bonding. Academic communities that provide concrete social and emotional support through caring counselors, school nurses, social workers, parent volunteers, and other interested adults can provide an environment of trust, encouragement, and academic support (Hudley, 2008). Authentic, developmental opportunities for student involvement can promote positive attitudes toward school and reduce problem behavior. Opportunities such as student organized assemblies or media projects, service learning opportunities for community involvement, or family and community history programs may have both educational and psychosocial benefits for urban adolescents (Hudley, 2008).

The evidence is also clear that careful attention to adolescents' racial, ethnic, and cultural backgrounds yields positive benefits for achievement motivation, cognitive development, and students' mental health. For example, perceived cultural sensitivity on campus, i.e., school racial climate, has been positively related to ethnic minority adolescents' achievement and engagement (Hudley & Daoud, 2007). Thus, schools that include positive attention to students' cultural heritage and provide opportunities for students to explore their own ethnic identity (e.g., ethnic studies classes) more effectively support positive youth development.

Finally student–teacher relationships can be promoted through a variety of avenues. As a single example, schools that promote diverse extracurricular activities (e.g., chess, photography, drama productions, debate teams) draw both students and teachers cooperatively into tasks that they find personally interesting and rewarding. A shared commitment to, and enjoyment of, activities that are more flexible and egalitarian than traditional classroom activities benefits student–teacher relations (Fredricks & Eccles, 2006). Teachers gain important knowledge about students' interests and ideas that can be translated into more effective and engaging classroom instruction. As well, positive, interest-driven activities also help teachers sustain positive attitudes about schools and students and allow teachers to pursue their own interests and avocations alongside their students.

Educators and policymakers will do well to remember that every school identified as underperforming or not making adequate yearly progress has students who demonstrate positive learning and developmental outcomes. Therefore, the goal of school reform must be to create urban centers of learning that lead to effective schooling, maximize adolescents' developmental assets, and meet the developmental needs of adolescents and the teachers who serve them.

References

Berndt, T. J. (1982). The features and effects of friendship in early adolescence. *Child Development, 53*, 1447–1460.

Bowen, N., & Bowen, G. (1999). Effects of crime and violence in neighborhoods and schools on the school behavior and performance of adolescents. *Journal of Adolescent Research, 14*, 319–342.

Bowles, S., & Gintis, H. (1976). *Schooling in capitalist America*. New York: Basic Books.

Bransford, J., Brown. A., & Cocking, R. (Eds.) (2000). *How people learn. Expanded edition.* Washington, DC: National Academy Press.

Brown, R., & Evans, W. (2002). Extracurricular activity and ethnicity: Creating greater school connection among diverse student populations. *Urban Education, 37*, 41–58.

Byrnes, J. (2006). Cognitive development during adolescence. In G. Adams, & M. Berzonsky (Eds.), *Blackwell handbook of adolescence* (pp. 227–246). Malden, MA: Blackwell Publishing Ltd.

Catalano, R., Haggerty, K., Oesterle, S., Fleming, C., & Hawkins, J. (2004). The importance of bonding to school for healthy development: Findings from the Social Development Research Group. *Journal of School Health, 74*, 252–261.

Chhuon, V., Hudley, C., Brenner, M., & Macias, R. (2010). The multiple worlds of successful Cambodian American students. *Urban Education, 45*, 30–57.

Choi, Y., Harachi, T., Gillmore, M., & Catalano, R. (2006). Are multiracial adolescents at greater risk? Comparisons of rates, patterns, and correlates of substance use and violence between monoracial and multiracial adolescents. *American Journal of Orthopsychiatry, 76*, 86–97.

Conchas, G. (2006). *The color of success: Race and high-achieving urban youth*. New York: Teachers College Press.

Council of the Great City Schools (2008). *Urban School Statistics*. Retrieved December 15, 2010, from http://www.cgcs.org/about/statistics.aspx.

Deci, E., & Ryan, R. (1987). The support of autonomy and the control of behavior. *Journal of Personality and Social Psychology, 53*, 1024–1037.

Dishon, T. J., McCord, J., & Poulin, F. (1999). When interventions harm: Peer groups and problem behavior. *American Psychologist, 54*, 755–764.

Edmonds, R. (1979). Effective schools for the urban poor. *Educational Leadership, 37*, 15–18.

Elmesky, R. (2005). "I am science and the world is mine": Embodied practices as resources for empowerment. *School Science & Mathematics, 105*, 335–342.

Faircloth, B., & Hamm, J. (2005). Sense of belonging among high school students representing four ethnic groups. *Journal of Youth and Adolescence, 34*, 293–309.

Fenzel, L. M. & Monteith, R. (2008). Successful alternative middle schools for urban minority children: A study of nativity schools. *Journal of Education for Students Placed at Risk, 13*, 381–401.

Fordham, S., & Ogbu, J. U. (1986). Black students' school success: Coping with the "burden of acting white." *The Urban Review, 18*, 176–206.

Foster, M. (2007). Urban education in North America: Section editor's introduction. In W. T. Pink, & G. W. Noblit (Eds.), *International handbook of urban education* (pp. 765–778). New York: Springer.

Fredricks, J., & Eccles, J. (2006). Extracurricular involvement and adolescent adjustment: Impact of duration, number of activities, and breadth of participation. *Applied Developmental Science, 10*, 132–146.

Goodenow, C., & Grady, K. (1993). The relationship of school belonging and friends' values to academic motivation among urban adolescent students. *Journal of Experimental Education, 62*, 60–71.

Hanlon, T., Simon, B., O'Grady, K., Carswell, S., & Callaman, J. (2009). The effectiveness of an after-school program targeting urban African American youth. *Education and Urban Society, 42*, 96–118.

Hébert, T., & Reis, S. (1999). Culturally diverse high-achieving students in an urban high school. *Urban Education, 34*, 428–457.

Hudley, C. (1997). Teacher practices and student motivation in a middle school program for African American males. *Urban Education, 32*, 304–319.

Hudley, C. (2008). *You did that on purpose: Understanding and changing children's aggression.* New Haven, CT: Yale University Press.

Hudley, C., & Daoud, A. (2007). High school students' engagement in school: Understanding the relationship to school context and student expectations. In F. Salili, & R. Hoosain (Eds.), *Culture, motivation and learning: A multicultural perspective* (pp. 365–389). New York: Information Age.

Hudley, C., & Novak, A. (2007). Environmental influences, the developing brain, and aggressive behavior. *Theory into Practice, 46*, 121–129.

Jacob, B. (2007). The challenges of staffing urban schools with effective teachers. *Future of Children, 17*, 129–153.

Kosslyn, S., & Koenig, O. (1994) *Wet mind: The new cognitive neuroscience.* New York: Free Press.

Kuhn, D., Black, J., Keselman, A., & Kaplan, D. (2010). The development of cognitive skills to support inquiry learning. *Cognition and Instruction, 18*(4), 495–523.

Lee, C. (2000). Signifying in the Zone of Proximal Development. In Carol D. Lee, & Peter Smagorinsky (Eds.), *Vygotskian Perspectives on Literacy Research* (pp. 191–225). New York: Cambridge University Press.

Lepore, S., & Evans, G. (1996). Coping with multiple stressors in the environment. In M. Zeidner, & N. Endler, *Handbook of coping: Theory, research, applications* (pp. 350–377). Oxford: John Wiley.

Lew, J. (2006). *Asian Americans in class: Charting the achievement gap among Korean American youth.* New York: Teachers College Press.

Lewis, L., Snow, K., Farris, E., Smerdon, B., Cronen, S., & Kaplan, J. (1999). Condition of America's public school facilities. *Education Statistics Quarterly, 2*, 42–46.

Light, D., McDermott, M., & Honey, M. (2002). *The impact of ubiquitous portable technology on an urban school: Project Hiller.* New York: Education Development Center/Center for Children & Technology.

Martin, A., & Dowson, M. (2009). Interpersonal relationships, motivation, engagement, and achievement. *Review of Educational Research, 79*, 327–365.

Nasir, S., Rosebery, A., Warren, B., & Lee, C. (2006). Learning as a cultural process: Achieving equity through diversity. In R. Sawyer (Ed.), *The Cambridge handbook of the learning sciences* (pp. 489–504). New York: Cambridge University Press.

National Education Association (2006). *NEA's vision, mission, and values.* Retrieved June 9, 2011 from http://www.nea.org/home/19583.htm.

Penuel, W. R. (2006). Implementation and effects of one-to-one computing initiatives: A research synthesis. *Journal of Research on Technology in Education, 38,* 329–348.

Rogoff, B. (2003). *The cultural nature of human development.* New York: Oxford University Press.

Rosebery, A., Warren, B., & Conant, F. (1992). Appropriating scientific discourse: Findings from language minority classrooms. *The Journal of the Learning Sciences, 2,* 61–94.

Shen, J., & Poppink, S. (2003). The certification characteristics of the public school teaching force: National, longitudinal, and comparative perspectives. *Educational Horizons, 57,* 130–137.

Siegler, R. S., & Crowley, K. (1991). The microgenetic method: A direct means for studying cognitive development. *American Psychologist, 46,* 606–620.

Sleeter, C. (1992). Resisting racial awareness: How teachers understand the social order from their racial, gender, and social class locations. *Educational Foundations, 6,* 7–32.

Sohoni, D., & Saporito, S. (2009). Mapping school segregation: Using GIS to explore racial segregation between schools and their corresponding attendance areas. *American Journal of Education, 115,* 569–600.

Szalacha, L., Erkut, S., García Coll, C., Fields, J., Alarcón, O., & Ceder, I. (2003). Perceived discrimination and resilience. In S. Luthar (Ed.), *Resilience and vulnerability: Adaptation in the context of childhood adversities* (pp. 414–435). New York: Cambridge.

Teel, K., Debruin-Parecki, A., & Covington, M. (1998). Teaching strategies that honor and motivate inner-city African-American students: A school/university collaboration. *Teaching and Teacher Education, 14,* 479–495.

Tyson, K., Darity, W., & Castellino, D. (2005). It's not "a black thing": Understanding the burden of acting White and other dilemmas of high achievement. *American Sociological Review, 70,* 582–605.

Uline, C., & Tschannen-Moran, M. (2008). The walls speak: The interplay of quality facilities, school climate, and student achievement. *Journal of Educational Administration, 46,* 55–73.

Virta, E., Sam, D., & Westin, C. (2004). Adolescents with Turkish background in Norway and Sweden: A comparative study of their psychological adaptation. *Scandinavian Journal of Psychology, 45,* 15–25.

Wakefield, W. D., & Hudley, C. (2005). African American male adolescents' preferences in responding to racial discrimination: Effects of ethnic identity and situational influences. *Adolescence, 40,* 237–256.

Wakefield, W. D., & Hudley, C. (2007). Ethnic and racial identity and adolescent well-being. *Theory into Practice, 46,* 147–154.

Way, N., Santos, C., Niwa, E., & Kim-Gervey, C. (2008). To be or not to be: An exploration of ethnic identity development in context. *New Directions for Child and Adolescent Development, 120,* 61–79.

Wentzel, K., & Caldwell, K. (1997). Friendships, peer acceptance, and group membership: Relations to academic achievement in middle school. *Child Development, 68,* 1198–1209.

White, B., & Frederiksen, J. (1998). Inquiry, modeling, and metacognition: Making science accessible to all students. *Cognition and Instruction, 16,* 3–118.

Wolfe, M., & Goldman, S. (2005). Relations between adolescents' text processing and reasoning. *Cognition and Instruction, 23,* 467–502.

World Health Organization (1997). *Life skills education in schools.* Geneva: WHO.

11

PHYSICAL ACTIVITY AND MEDIA USE[1]

Daheia J. Barr-Anderson and Sofiya Alhassan

Low levels of physical activity (PA) and heavy media use (TV, computer, video games) are related to health concerns, psychological distress, and cognitive impairment in urban youth. Such activity (or rather inactivity) may be associated with a complex interplay of lifestyle factors. Individual, behavioral, and social factors play a large role in predicting adolescent behavior and, subsequently, health in urban youth.

Urban youth, particularly in disordered communities, face clear challenges that limit their ability to participate in leisure PA, but promote sedentary behavior. The goal of this chapter is to describe adolescents' PA and media use behavior in the context of urban settings. We begin by presenting the current prevalence of adolescents' leisure PA and media use. Next, we link how broader economic and cultural factors within urban settings impact adolescents' opportunities to engage in these behaviors. This chapter concludes with challenges and solutions to implementing interventions to increase PA and decrease media use in urban settings.

Rates of Physical Activity

School-age children (above 5 years) should engage in 60 minutes of moderate-to-vigorous physical activity (MVPA) daily that include aerobic, muscle-strengthening and bone-strengthening movements (Table 11.1) (Physical Activity Guidelines Advisory Committee, 2008).

However, as evidenced in Table 11.2, less than 20% of adolescents report meeting the recommended level of PA. One out of five students do not report participating in any form of weekly PA. The reported prevalence of PA is higher in boys and greater in non–Hispanic White students compared to their minority counterparts.

The prevalence of youth meeting PA recommendations (Figure 11.1) and engaging in total daily MVPA (Table 11.3) is lower (Troiano et al., 2008) compared to values reported in Table 11.1, as accuracy is reduced because of the reliance on youth self-report (Sirard & Pate, 2001). However, similar to YRBSS (Youth Risk

[1] The authors would like to thank Sally Weinrich, PhD, FAAN, for her review of the manuscript and the following colleagues for their various input: Monica Baskin, PhD, Andrea Williams, MEd, Gwen Preston, MEd, Sonya Dinizulu, PhD, Kristin Reitz, MSW, Mamie Tisue, MSW, Eduardo Bustamante, PhD(c), and Christine Pietrich, MA.

TABLE 11.1 Recommendations for physical activity and media use in youth

Physical Activity[1]	Sixty minutes or more of physical activity every day of the week. • Aerobic: Most of the 60 or more minutes a day should be either moderate- or vigorous-intensity aerobic physical activity, and should include vigorous-intensity physical activity at least 3 days a week. • Muscle-strengthening: As part of their 60 or more minutes of daily physical activity, children and adolescents should include muscle-strengthening physical activity on at least 3 days of the week. • Bone-strengthening: As part of their 60 or more minutes of daily physical activity, children and adolescents should include bone-strengthening physical activity on at least 3 days of the week.
Media Use[2]	Parents should limit their children's total screen time to less than 2 hours of non-educational programming per day with children age 0–2 years discouraged from any screen exposure.

[1] Physical Activity Guidelines Advisory Committee, 2008, p. 16.
[2] Strasburger et al., 2011, p. 204.

TABLE 11.2 Prevalence of self-reported physical activity and media use in youth

	Total	Race/ethnicity			Sex	
		NH White	NH Black	Hispanic	Boys	Girls
Physical activity (% of youth)[1]						
At least 60 min for last 7 days	18.4	19.7	17.2	15.6	24.8	11.4
At least 60 min for 5+ days	37.0	39.6	32.6	33.1	45.6	27.7
No activity in last 7 days	23.1	20.3	32.1	23.9	17.0	29.9
Media Use[2] (daily hr:min)						
TV & movies	4:29	3:36	5:54	5:21	4:40	4:18
Video games	1:13	0:56	1:25	1:35	1:37	0:49
Computers	1:29	1:17	1:24	1:49	1:37	1:22
Cell phones[3]	2:08	1:47	2:49	2:19	1:42	2:36
Music	2:31	1:48	2:42	2:52	2:18	2:45

[1] Youth Risk Behavior Surveillance Summaries—United States, 2010, pp. 117–119.
[2] Rideout et al., 2010, pp. 16–28.
[3] Cell phone use includes talking and texting and excludes listening to music, playing games, and watching TV.

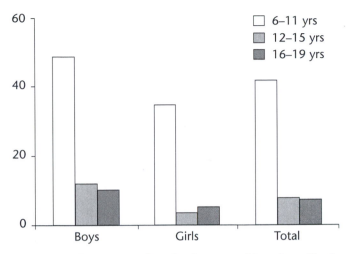

FIGURE 11.1 Percentage of youth who engaged in at least 60 minutes of MVPA in five out of seven days: objectively measured. (Troiano, et al., 2008, 181–188.)

TABLE 11.3 Prevalence of objectively-collected moderate-to-vigorous physical activity in youth (mean min/day)[1]

	Total	NH White	NH Black	Hispanic
6–11 year olds				
Boys	95.4	92.3	114.0	97.0
Girls	75.2	73.1	87.4	70.8
12–15 year olds				
Boys	45.3	41.0	54.1	50.6
Girls	24.6	22.4	26.4	26.9
16–19 year olds				
Boys	32.7	29.3	42.5	41.0
Girls	19.6	19.1	18.1	25.7

[1]Troiano et al., 2008, pp. 181–188.

Behavior Surveillance System) data, as age increases, the recorded minutes/day of MVPA decreases and boys report more PA than girls.

Geographical differences in PA also exist. Children from urban areas engage in greater amounts of PA then their rural counterparts (Singh, Kogan, Siahpush, & van Dyck, 2009; Springer, Hoelscher, Castrucci, Perez, & Kelder, 2009). The rationale behind this is not exactly clear. However, it is possible that the greater amount reported could be due to PA as a result of transportation (i.e., walking or biking to school/stores/other locations).

Rates of Media Use in Youth

Historically, television viewing, video game play, and computer use represent the types of media most commonly studied in youth. However, there is a growing interest in cell phones and music as media outlets; these two types of media will occasionally be referenced in this chapter. The American Academy of Pediatrics' (AAP) recommendation of less than two hours of non-educational programming per day (Table 11.1) provides a media framework for parents (Strasburger et al., 2011). However, despite these recommendations, youth are using more media than ever before. Youth spend more than 7.5 hours/day using some type of media (Rideout, Foehr, & Roberts, 2010); an hour increase over a five-year period (Roberts, Foehr, & Rideout, 2005). Multitasking is very common among youth and contributes to almost 11 hours/day of concomitant media exposure with the most exposure resulting from TV, music, computer, and video game involvement (Table 11.2) (Rideout et al., 2010). Children aged 8–10 years are exposed to less than 8 hours/day of media while 11–14 and 15–18 year olds report almost 12 and 11.5 hours, respectively. Similar significant differences for media exposure exist by race/ethnicity and sex (Table 11.2).

Benefits of Physical Activity

The health benefits of a physically active lifestyle in preventing metabolic risk factors (i.e., obesity), are widely documented in adults. The available data for youth are inconsistent but a physically active lifestyle does appear to have positive influences (Alhassan & Robinson, 2008; Ku, Gower, Hunter, & Goran, 2000). Studies report associations between PA with improvements in measures of obesity (body mass index (BMI) and percent body fat), hypertension, total cholesterol, triglyceride, high-density lipoprotein cholesterol (HDL-C), fasting insulin and glucose in children (Alhassan & Robinson, 2008; Durant, Linder, Harkess, & Gray, 1983; Eaton et al., 1995). Further, PA could be an effective intervention in improving academic performance (Donnelly et al., 2009) and psychological health (i.e., improvement in depressive symptoms, self-esteem, and body dissatisfaction) (Calfas & Taylor, 1994; Johnson et al., 2008).

Media Influences

Media can serve as a powerful educational tool or have potentially harmful effects on youth. Exposure to varied types of media (i.e., TV, music, internet) can encourage language and reading skills (Linebarger & Walker, 2005), make information about safe health practices accessible to youth, enhance social connectedness, and promote diversity through modeling of positive behaviors (Hogan & Strasburger, 2008; Strasburger, Jordan, & Donnerstein, 2010).

Despite positive educational effects of media, the AAP has long recognized negative aspects related to some types of media (Bar-on et al., 2001a; Bar-on et al., 2001b; Fuld et al., 2009). Positive associations have been found between some media use and increased aggressive behavior, heightened desensitization to violence, lower quality sleep, poorer academic performance, unhealthier dietary habits, riskier sexual behavior, and increased substance use (Strasburger, Wilson, & Jordan, 2009). The popularity of multitasking and rapid introduction of new technologies raises concern about possible negative impacts on brain development (Small & Vorgen, 2008).

These negative associations may be exacerbated because instead of studying or sleeping, youth spend more time using media, which may be related to their sexual and violence-related behaviors and beliefs (Strasburger et al., 2010). Media violence might have a long-lasting impact on youth because during childhood and adolescence, frequent exposure to media violence may promote negative behavior (e.g., risky sex, smoking, drug use, aggression) (Bushman & Huesmann, 2006; Strasburger et al., 2010).

Media-related sedentary activities are cited as possible contributors to excessive weight gain. During the time spent engaging in media use, especially TV viewing, not only do youth expend little energy (Klesges, Shelton, & Klesges, 1993), but they are exposed to numerous advertisements for unhealthy foods, and sugar-sweetened beverages (IOM, 2005) that can influence the type and amount of food desired and consumed (IOM, 2006). These factors may foster unhealthy perceptions about food and nutrition (Byrd-Bredbenner & Grasso, 2000) and promote weight gain (IOM, 2006).

Factors that Contribute to Physical Activity

There are many physiological, psychological, ecological, and sociocultural factors that predict physical activity (Kohl & Hobbs, 1998). Several studies of racially diverse youth highlight the importance of physiological (e.g., gender, BMI) and psychological (e.g., self-efficacy, motivation, PA attitude) variables as important determinants in PA levels (Lemmon, Ludwig, Howe, Ferguson-Smith, & Barbeau, 2007; Lown & Braunschweig, 2008). For example, sociocultural factors such as parental social support for PA, role modeling, socioeconomic status, and parenting style are identified as important determinants of PA levels (Gordon-Larsen, McMurray, & Popkin, 2000; Lindquist, Reynolds, & Goran, 1999). One of the major categories for the impact of sociocultural aspects on PA is attributed to peer and/or parental social support for PA (Beets, Cardinal, & Alderman, 2010; Neumark-Sztainer, Story, Hannan, Tharp, & Rex, 2003). There are strong associations between parenting practices and children's PA (Gustafson & Rhodes, 2006), as parents can model (or not model) healthy eating habits and PA, and provide a home environment that is either conducive (or not conducive) to these activities (e.g., types of foods purchased; presence of home gym) (Beets et al., 2010). Unfortunately, the aforementioned findings are more prevalent in children from middle/high socioeconomic environments compared to their low socioeconomic counterparts (Brockman et al., 2009).

Several studies of racially diverse children highlight ecological factors such as availability of school facilities, home PA environment facilities, and neighborhood safety as important determinants in PA levels (Gordon-Larsen et al., 2000; Lindquist et al., 1999; Sallis, Prochaska, & Taylor, 2000). Factors such as school policy (Fernandes & Sturm, 2011), play equipment (Nielsen, Taylor, Williams, & Mann, 2010), and school safety issues (Zhu & Lee, 2009) are school environmental factors positively associated with PA in youth. Also, PA levels are associated with the availability of commercial PA facilities (Evenson, Scott, Cohen, & Voorhees, 2007; Tucker et al., 2009) and neighborhood factors such as well-lit streets, less dense neighborhood traffic, and bicycle/walking trails (Evenson et al., 2007).

When examining perceived facilitators of PA in urban and rural youth and their parents, both report facility access as the primary facilitator of increasing PA (Moore et al., 2010). Additionally, parents report distance, cost, and crime rate as primary barriers to such access, while youth consider school policies related to PA and crime as primary barriers. Also, high concern about neighborhood safety is associated with lower PA levels (Molnar, Gortmaker, Bull, & Buka, 2004; Weir, Etelson, & Brand, 2006). Thus, promoting neighborhood safety, community efficacy, and access to PA facilities could be used as an effective strategy to increase PA.

Factors that Contribute to Media Use

There are myriad individual, psychological, and environmental factors that influence youth's media use. Among adolescents, psychological factors (i.e., perceived barriers to changing sedentary behavior, low self-efficacy and family support) are associated with media use (Norman, Schmid, Sallis, Calfas, & Patrick, 2005).When examining TV use exclusively, access to TV within the home environment, the number of TVs within the home, and frequency of eating meals while watching TV were associated with increased daily TV viewing time (Granich, Rosenberg, Knuiman, & Timperio, 2011; Saelens et al., 2002).

Further, a review of 30 studies including youth age 4–18 years found that sex, low parental education, and emotional distress are associated with video game use; while parental education, single-parent household, and parental TV viewing behavior are associated with TV viewing; and BMI is associated with all screen-time media use (Uijtdewilligen et al., 2011). Hinkley and colleagues found that permissive parenting was associated with high media use (TV viewing, electronic games, computer use) (Hinkley, Salmon, Okely, & Trost, 2010). Thus, as stated before, the manner in which parents model or encourage media use, physical activities and healthy eating habits plays a major role in the manner in which adolescents engage in similar behavior.

Increasing Physical Activity and Decreasing Media Use: Challenges and Solutions

Despite the wealth of knowledge on the benefits of increased PA and reduced media use, PA in youth is declining while media use is expansively increasing. Researchers have proposed the utilization of interventions as a viable method to increase PA (Pate & O'Neill, 2009) and decrease media use in youth (Leung, Agaronov, Grytsenko, & Yeh, 2012). Urban youth are a vulnerable population faced with many challenges that have been outlined throughout this volume. The next section identifies some of the key challenges present in implementing interventions to increase PA and decrease media use and possible solutions in addressing these challenges (see Table 11.4).

TABLE 11.4 Challenges and possible solutions for increasing physical activity and decreasing media use in urban youth[1]

Challenges	Solutions
Challenge #1: Utilization of one-size fits all intervention model	*Solution #1*: Create age-appropriate, culturally relevant interventions *Solution #2*: Collect additional data on urban youth
Challenge #2: Recruitment and enrollment	*Solution #1*: Involve familiar social network (i.e., peers) *Solution #2*: Involve family members *Solution #3*: Select convenient, familiar locations to conduct interventions
Challenge #3: Keeping urban youth engaged	*Solution #1*: Utilize technology *Solution #2*: Make healthy living relevant in the context of their lives

[1]Challenges and solutions generated from community-based experts who have extensive experience working with urban youth.

Challenge #1: Utilization of "One-Size Fits" All Intervention Model

Current interventions designed to alter PA and media use report small, if any, significant effects on behavior (Leung et al., 2012; Pate & O'Neill, 2009). Various reasons cited for less than stellar results include the utilization of a "one-size fits all" intervention model (Kamath et al., 2008), which entails replicating the principles and strategies of an intervention in another population without making modifications to address the needs of this "new" population. An example is designing a TV watching reduction program for preschoolers and implementing the same program (without any adaptations) in a sample of high school students.

Solution #1: Create Age-Appropriate, Culturally Relevant Interventions

In trying to increase PA and decrease media use, particularly among ethnic minorities and those from urban environments, a "one-size fits all" intervention model must be discarded and replaced with a culturally relevant intervention that introduces age-appropriate activities and strategies which infuse aspects of their generational and racial/ethnic culture. For example, a PA after-school program for African American teens living in an urban area may include hip hop dance and the use of parallel musical lyrics, which reflects pieces of their culture.

Solution #2: Collect Additional Data on Urban Youth

Although a fair amount of PA and media use interventions focusing on youth have been conducted, it is not clear that the targeted population have been youth in urban areas, especially for media use. Various forms of media are widely available and increasingly affordable, which makes TV, video games, and computers accessible to many urban youth. Much of the research focused on media primarily targets TV watching only. In order to effectively address decreasing the use of media among youth, more research needs to be conducted on factors that contribute to the use of other types of media, especially the internet and handheld electronic devices, such as smartphones and tablets, which make the internet available virtually anywhere.

There is a fair amount of understanding of the prevalence of media use, but gaps exist related to the link of health outcomes with sedentary behavior, valid and reliable measures to assess sedentary behavior, and interventions' effects on reducing sedentary behavior (Salmon, Tremblay, Marshall, & Hume, 2011). Additionally, practical translation of research findings to real-world scenarios must be addressed to begin to pragmatically answer the question of how to reduce media use in youth. This is especially critical for youth who live in urban areas and are exposed to other life situations that may interact with sedentary lifestyles and media use.

Challenge #2: Recruitment and Enrollment

Even with a good programmatic idea, issues usually arise with recruiting and enrolling youth, since they may already have full schedules or face transportation and financial barriers in accessing activities that require physical exertion. Additionally, the unfamiliarity and inexperience of the interventionists with the lives of the youth can cause a cultural discord. This can prevent keeping the youth interested and engaged and negatively impact recruitment, enrollment, and retention.

Solution #1: Involve Familiar Social Network (i.e., Peers)

A successful tactic to keep urban youth engaged that has been used in other fields is to utilize important people in their lives. The use of a peer leadership model is one such example (Barr-Anderson et al., 2011). Peer leadership, which involves similar-age peers motivating others to start, continue, and maintain a positive behavior, is successful in interventions targeting healthy eating, alcohol, and tobacco use, and is a feasible method for increasing PA and media use.

All youth, including those living in urban areas, are influenced by their peers. The involvement of a peer leadership model allows an urban youth to be positively influenced by a peer in ways such as substituting time usually spent indoors watching TV or playing video games with joining an active program at the local community center. In addition, peer leaders can be used as youth advisors during the development of the intervention, which allows for ideas, thoughts, and preferences directly from those who understand and are a part of the targeted intervention group.

Solution #2: Involve Family Members

The less than stellar results of PA and media use interventions can also be partially attributed to the lack of familial involvement (Kamath et al., 2008). Family members, particularly parents, play an important role in the overall development of children's health behavior (Taylor, Baranowski, & Sallis, 1994). The family provides a social and learning environment for youth because similar health behaviors are shared by members of the same family rather than members of a different family (Patterson et al., 1989). Involvement of family members allows the intervention to account for their personal values and traditions and include adults important to the youth, thus allowing for the reinforcement of knowledge and behavior. It creates an instantaneous support system and lower probability of the youth receiving contradictory information from their family members because the family members are receiving the same information as the youth.

Solution #3: Select Convenient, Familiar Locations to Conduct Intervention

All youth are comfortable in areas in which they are familiar. When choosing a location to conduct any intervention, especially a PA intervention, picking a familiar location (i.e., school, local recreational/community center) can help with attracting the youth as well as create a platform of sustainability. This allows the intervention to be rooted in the community that is being served and an investment in the youth and the community.

Challenge #3: Keeping Urban Youth Engaged and Participating

As outlined in other chapters of this volume, urban youth are faced with external forces that are out of their control. Addressing PA and media use may not be their top priority, so it is important for interventionists to be creative to get the youth involved and keep them engaged.

Solution #1: Utilize Technology

The current generation is very technologically savvy, hence the increase in media use. Strategies that utilize social media (i.e., PA tracking apps) or physically active video games or DVDs should be included as a means to increase PA. This may mean an increase of media use to increase PA, but this use of media is not sedentary and may be a practical way to increase PA (Barr-Anderson et al., 2011).

Solution #2: Make Healthy Living Relevant in the Context of their Lives

Urban youth may have pressing challenges (i.e., violence, gangs, poverty) that may supersede healthy living related to PA and media use. Interventions should be holistic and not only address those two behaviors, but incorporate aspects of the youth's lives (i.e., academic achievement, bullying, risky sexual and drug-related behaviors) to address healthy living and other important issues and concerns.

Conclusions

Addressing increasing PA and reducing media use are not easy tasks to achieve in any youth, let alone among urban youth, a group who is presented with unique challenges specific to their environment. However, solutions are available if urban youth advocates are willing to utilize strategies that truly address the needs of urban youth by incorporating into interventions what is most important in the youth's lives. These interventions would entail not applying what usually works in other populations to urban youth, but considering all aspects of these youth's lives (i.e., developmental, psychological, environmental, relational) and tailoring the program to address those issues.

References

Alhassan, S., & Robinson, T. N. (2008). Objectively measured physical activity and cardiovascular disease risk factors in African American girls. *Ethnicity and Disease, 18*(4), 421–426.

Bar-on, M. E., Broughton, D. D., Buttross, S., Corrigan, S., Gedissman, A., Gonzalez de Rivas, M. R., . . . & Shifrin, D. L. (2001a). Children, adolescents, and television. *Pediatrics, 107*(2), 423–426.

Bar-on, M. E., Broughton, D. D., Buttross, S., Corrigan, S., Gedissman, A., Gonzalez de Rivas, M. R., . . . & Shifrin, D. L. (2001b). Media violence. *Pediatrics, 108*(5), 1222–1226.

Barr-Anderson, D. J., Laska, M. N., Veblen-Mortenson, S., Farbakhsh, K., Dudovitz, B., & Story, M. (2011). A school-based, peer leadership physical activity intervention for 6th graders: Feasibility and results of a pilot study. *Journal of Physical Activity and Health, 9*(4), 492–499.

Beets, M. W., Cardinal, B. J., & Alderman, B. L. (2010). Parental social support and the physical activity-related behaviors of youth: A review. *Health Education and Behavior, 37*(5), 621–644.

Brockman, R., Jago, R., Fox, K. R., Thompson, J. L., Cartwright, K., & Page, A. S. (2009). "Get off the sofa and go and play": Family and socioeconomic influences on the physical activity of 10–11 year old children. *BMC Public Health, 9*, 253.

Bushman, B. J., & Huesmann, L. R. (2006). Short-term and long-term effects of violent media on aggression in children and adults. *Archives of Pediatrics & Adolescent Medicine, 160*(4), 348–352.

Byrd-Bredbenner, C., & Grasso, D. (2000). Health, medicine, and food messages in television commercials during 1992 and 1998. *Journal of School Health, 70*(2), 61–65.

Calfas, J. J., & Taylor, W. C. (1994). Effects of physical activity on psychological variables in adolescents. *Pediatric Exercise Science, 6*, 406–423.

Donnelly, J. E., Greene, J. L., Gibson, C. A., Smith, B. K., Washburn, R. A., Sullivan, D. K., . . . & Williams, S. L. (2009). Physical Activity Across the Curriculum (PAAC): A randomized controlled trial to promote physical activity and diminish overweight and obesity in elementary school children. *Preventive Medicine, 49*(4), 336–341.

Durant, R. H., Linder, C. W., Harkess, J. W., & Gray, R. G. (1983). The relationship between physical activity and serum lipids and lipoproteins in black children and adolescents. *Journal of Adolescent Health Care, 4*(1), 55–60.

Eaton, C. B., Lapane, K. L., Garber, C. E., Assaf, A. R., Lasater, T. M., & Carleton, R. A. (1995). Physical activity, physical fitness, and coronary heart disease risk factors. *Medicine & Science in Sports and Exercise, 27*(3), 340–346.

Evenson, K. R., Scott, M. M., Cohen, D. A., & Voorhees, C. C. (2007). Girls' perception of neighborhood factors on physical activity, sedentary behavior, and BMI. *Obesity (Silver Spring), 15*(2), 430–445.

Fernandes, M. M., & Sturm, R. (2011). The role of school physical activity programs in child body mass trajectory. *Journal of Physical Activity and Health, 8*(2), 174–181.

Fuld, G. L., Mulligan, D. A., Altmann, T. R., Brown, A., Christakis, D. A., Clarke-Pearson, K., . . . & Strasburger, V. C. (2009). Impact of music, music lyrics, and music videos on children and youth. *Pediatrics, 124*(5), 1488–1494.

Gordon-Larsen, P., McMurray, R. G., & Popkin, B. M. (2000). Determinants of adolescent physical activity and inactivity patterns. *Pediatrics, 105*(6), E83.

Granich, J., Rosenberg, M., Knuiman, M. W., & Timperio, A. (2011). Individual, social, and physical environment factors associated with electronic media use among children: Sedentary behavior at home. *Journal of Physical Activity and Health, 8*(5), 613–625.

Gustafson, S. L., & Rhodes, R. E. (2006). Parental correlates of physical activity in children and early adolescents. *Sports Medicine, 36*(1), 79–97.

Hinkley, T., Salmon, J., Okely, A. D., & Trost, S. G. (2010). Correlates of sedentary behaviours in preschool children: A review. *International Journal of Behavioral Nutrition and Physical Activity, 7*, 66.

Hogan, M. J., & Strasburger, V. C. (Eds.). (2008). *Media and prosocial behavior in children and adolescents*. Mahwah, NJ: Lawrence Erlbaum.

IOM. (2005). *Preventing childhood obesity: Health in the balance*. Washington, DC: The National Academies Press.

IOM. (2006). *Food marketing to children and youth: threat or opportunity?* Washington, DC: The National Academies Press.

Johnson, C. C., Murray, D. M., Elder, J. P., Jobe, J. B., Dunn, A. L., Kubik, M., . . . & Schachter, K. (2008). Depressive symptoms and physical activity in adolescent girls. *Medicine and Science in Sports and Exercise, 40*(5), 818–826.

Kamath, C. C., Vickers, K. S., Ehrlich, A., McGovern, L., Johnson, J., Singhal, V., . . . & Montori, V. M. (2008). Clinical review: Behavioral interventions to prevent childhood obesity: a systematic review and metaanalyses of randomized trials. *Journal of Clinical Endocrinology and Metabolism, 93*(12), 4606–4615.

Klesges, R. C., Shelton, M. L., & Klesges, L. M. (1993). Effects of television on metabolic rate: Potential implications for childhood obesity. *Pediatrics, 91*(2), 281–286.

Kohl, H., & Hobbs, K. (1998). Development of physical activity behaviors among children and adolescents. *Pediatrics, 101*(3), 549–554.

Ku, C. Y., Gower, B. A., Hunter, G. R., & Goran, M. I. (2000). Racial differences in insulin secretion and sensitivity in prepubertal children: Role of physical fitness and physical activity. *Obesity Research, 8*(7), 506–515.

Lemmon, C. R., Ludwig, D. A., Howe, C. A., Ferguson-Smith, A., & Barbeau, P. (2007). Correlates of adherence to a physical activity program in young African-American girls. *Obesity (Silver Spring), 15*(3), 695–703.

Leung, M. M., Agaronov, A., Grytsenko, K., & Yeh, M. C. (2012). Intervening to reduce sedentary behaviors and childhood obesity among school-age youth: A systematic review of randomized trials. *Journal of Obesity, 2012*, 685430.

Lindquist, C. H., Reynolds, K. D., & Goran, M. I. (1999). Sociocultural determinants of physical activity among children. *Preventive Medicine, 29*(4), 305–312.

Linebarger, D. H., & Walker, D. (2005). Infants' and toddlers' television viewing and language outcomes. *American Behavioral Scientist, 48*(5), 624–645.

Lown, D. A., & Braunschweig, C. L. (2008). Determinants of physical activity in low-income, overweight African American girls. *American Journal of Health Behavior, 32*(3), 253–259.

Molnar, B. E., Gortmaker, S. L., Bull, F. C., & Buka, S. L. (2004). Unsafe to play? Neighborhood disorder and lack of safety predict reduced physical activity among urban children and adolescents. [Research Support, Non-U.S. Gov't Research Support, U.S. Gov't, P.H.S.]. *American Journal of Health Promotion, 18*(5), 378–386.

Moore, J. B., Jilcott, S. B., Shores, K. A., Evenson, K. R., Brownson, R. C., & Novick, L. F. (2010). A qualitative examination of perceived barriers and facilitators of physical activity for urban and rural youth. *Health Education Research, 25*(2), 355–367.

Neumark-Sztainer, D., Story, M., Hannan, P. J., Tharp, T., & Rex, J. (2003). Factors associated with changes in physical activity: A cohort study of inactive adolescent girls. *Archives of Pediatrics & Adolescent Medicine, 157*(8), 803–810.

Nielsen, G., Taylor, R., Williams, S., & Mann, J. (2010). Permanent play facilities in school playgrounds as a determinant of children's activity. *Journal of Physical Activity & Health, 7*(4), 490–496.

Norman, G. J., Schmid, B. A., Sallis, J. F., Calfas, K. J., & Patrick, K. (2005). Psychosocial and environmental correlates of adolescent sedentary behaviors. *Pediatrics, 116*(4), 908–916.

Pate, R. R., & O'Neill, J. R. (2009). After-school interventions to increase physical activity among youth. *British Journal of Sports Medicine, 43*(1), 14–18.

Patterson, T. L., Sallis, J. F., Nader, P. R., Kaplan, R. M., Rupp, J. W., Atkins, C. J., & Seen, K. L. (1989). Familial similarities of changes in cognitive, behavioral, and physiological variables in a cardiovascular health promotion program. *Journal of Pediatric Psychology, 14*(2), 277–292.

Physical Activity Guidelines Advisory Committee. (2008). *Physical Activity Guidelines Advisory Committee Report.* Washington, DC: Department of Health and Human Services.

Rideout, V. J., Foehr, U. G., & Roberts, D. F. (2010). *Generation M2: Media in the lives of 8- to 18-year olds.* Menlo Park, CA: Kaiser Family Foundation.

Roberts, D., Foehr, U. G., & Rideout, V. (2005). *Generation M: Media in the lives of 8–18 Year-Olds.* Menlo Park, CA: Kaiser Family Foundation.

Saelens, B. E., Sallis, J. F., Nader, P. R., Broyles, S. L., Berry, C. C., & Taras, H. L. (2002). Home environmental influences on children's television watching from early to middle childhood. *Journal of Developmental & Behavioral Pediatrics, 23*(3), 127.

Sallis, J. F., Prochaska, J. J., & Taylor, W. C. (2000). A review of correlates of physical activity of children and adolescents. *Medicine & Science in Sports and Exercise, 32*(5), 963–975.

Salmon, J., Tremblay, M. S., Marshall, S. J., & Hume, C. (2011). Health risks, correlates, and interventions to reduce sedentary behavior in young people. *American Journal of Preventive Medicine, 41*(2), 197–206.

Singh, G. K., Kogan, M. D., Siahpush, M., & van Dyck, P. C. (2009). Prevalence and correlates of state and regional disparities in vigorous physical activity levels among US children and adolescents. *Journal of Physical Activity & Health, 6*(1), 73–87.

Sirard, J. R., & Pate, R. R. (2001). Physical activity assessment in children and adolescents. *Sports Medicine, 31*(6), 439–454.

Small, G., & Vorgen, G. (2008). *iBrain: Surviving the technology alteration of the modern mind.* New York: Harper Collins.

Springer, A. E., Hoelscher, D. M., Castrucci, B., Perez, A., & Kelder, S. H. (2009). Prevalence of physical activity and sedentary behaviors by metropolitan status in 4th-, 8th-, and 11th-grade students in Texas, 2004–2005. *Preventing Chronic Disease, 6*(1), A21.

Strasburger, V. C., Jordan, A. B., & Donnerstein, E. (2010). Health effects of media on children and adolescents. *Pediatrics, 125*(4), 756–767.

Strasburger, V. C., Mulligan, D. A., Altmann, T. R., Brown, A., Christakis, D. A., Clarke-Pearson, K., . . . & O'Keeffe, G. S. (2011). Children, adolescents, obesity, and the media. *Pediatrics, 128*(1), 201–208.

Strasburger, V. C., Wilson, B. J., & Jordan, A. B. (2009). *Children, adolescents, and the media* (2nd ed.). Thousand Oaks, CA: Sage.

Taylor, W. C., Baranowski, T., & Sallis, J. F. (1994). Family determinants of childhood physical activity: A social cognitive model. In R. K. Dishman (Ed.), *Advances in exercise adherence* (pp. 319–342). Champaign, IL: Human Kinetics.

Troiano, R. P., Berrigan, D., Dodd, K. W., Masse, L. C., Tilert, T., & McDowell, M. (2008). Physical activity in the United States measured by accelerometer. *Medicine and Science in Sports and Exercise, 40*(1), 181–188.

Tucker, P., Irwin, J. D., Gilliland, J., He, M., Larsen, K., & Hess, P. (2009). Environmental influences on physical activity levels in youth. *Health & Place, 15*(1), 357–363.

Uijtdewilligen, L., Nauta, J., Singh, A. S., van Mechelen, W., Twisk, J. W. R., van der Horst, K., & Chinapaw, M. J. M. (2011). Determinants of physical activity and sedentary behaviour in young people: A review and quality synthesis of prospective studies. *British Journal of Sports Medicine, 45*(11), 896–905.

Weir, L. A., Etelson, D., & Brand, D. A. (2006). Parents' perceptions of neighborhood safety and children's physical activity. [Research Support, U.S. Gov't, P.H.S.]. *Preventive Medicine, 43*(3), 212–217.

Youth Risk Behavior Surveillance Summaries—United States. (2010). Vol. 59 (No. SS-5). Atlanta, GA: Centers for Disease Control and Prevention.

Zhu, X., & Lee, C. (2009). Correlates of walking to school and implications for public policies: Survey results from parents of elementary school children in Austin, Texas. *Journal of Public Health Policy, 30 Suppl. 1*, S177–202.

12

CIVIC ENGAGEMENT

Volunteerism, Community Involvement, and Political Action

David M. Hansen, Nadia Jessop, and Michael J. Crawford

The focus of this chapter is on *urban* adolescents' (ages 12–18) civic engagement that includes not only political involvement but also the myriad ways for individuals to express their civic interests, including volunteering or participating in community organizations. Adolescence is a key period during which individuals begin to consolidate ideas of the self in relation to others and larger society; thus, understanding how civic engagement develops represents an important research topic. Adolescent civic engagement, however, occurs within the contexts of ethnicity, race, socio-economic status (SES), poverty, institutional discrimination, etc. (Bronfrenbrenner, 1979; Evans & English, 2002; Halpern, 2005; Kraus, Piff, & Keltner, 2011; Lerner 2004; McLoyd, 1998; Sherrod, 2008). Living in high-poverty, urban environments can lead to a growing sense of skepticism, self-doubt, and mistrust among adolescents, as well as diminished agency and belief in their ability to influence their environment (Halpern, 2005), which translates into less civic engagement (Jankowski, 1992, 2002; Sherrod, 2003). Yet, because civic engagement provides tangible and powerful means to address problems of poverty, social injustice, etc., it is an especially important developmental task for urban adolescents. The aim of this chapter, then, is to provide a concise synthesis of existing research on the distinct opportunities, challenges, and development of urban adolescents' civic engagement.

Although there are numerous definitions and dimensions of civic engagement, (Sherrod, Torney-Purta, & Flanagan, 2010), we focus on three concepts that together comprise our ideas of civic engagement. *Civic literacy* concerns needed political knowledge and understanding of polity (e.g., government structure and functions; Flanagan & Faison, 2001). It is difficult to imagine meaningful civic engagement without a minimum of requisite knowledge. *Civic competence* includes a host of skills (e.g., social skills, leadership) for using civic knowledge and conveys the idea of practice or application of knowledge (Flanagan & Faison, 2001; Youniss et al., 2002). *Civic development* concerns how adolescents learn and become engaged citizens; it is process-oriented and addresses questions of how and why adolescents engage in civic matters.

Chapter Overview

Deeply embedded in scholarship on civic engagement both across and within disciplines are distinct views or assumptions about how adolescents learn and, by extension, society's role in civic education. These views are sometimes stated explicitly but more often they surface in the form of particular research questions being asked. In this chapter, we chose to organize this review of the research literature around four common views of adolescent learning about civic engagement, which will provide valuable, fresh insights.

An *instructional* learning approach represents traditional teacher–learner relationships in which the adult is the expert with requisite knowledge or skill to impart to the student. The purpose of this approach is the transmission of information, rather than the practical application of the information. A *relational* learning approach emphasizes performing a civic service (e.g., neighborhood cleanup day), commonly with others who convene to work on projects or events. Learning occurs through interacting with both other providers as well as recipients of the civic service. *Didactic* learning approaches involve an instructor who intentionally creates the conditions (e.g., project) through which adolescents learn civic-related and non-civic-related (e.g., social skills) skills. The role of the instructor focuses not on imparting knowledge per se, but on creating conditions conducive to skill development. With *facilitative* learning approaches, the adolescent and adult operate as relative equals, and both co-determine the work or project as well as co-partner to accomplish the tasks. Facilitative learning occurs in the context of doing *real* work (i.e., work that has a real-world, tangible, social impact), which *is* the primary purpose. Learning occurs because it is required in order to complete the work.

Instructional Civic Learning Approaches

Dewey (1916) theorized that schools could be a place for children to develop dispositions and capacities for citizenship in the United States, and schools are typically where adolescents develop civic literacy, including knowledge about politics and democracy (Chapman, Nolin, & Kline, 1997; Niemi & Junn, 1998; Torney-Purta, Lehmann, Oswald, & Schulz, 2001). The school's role in students' civic development, however, has not been without controversy: philosophical arguments and empirical research have raised concerns about its efficacy. Controversies aside, many contend that the quality of classroom instruction impacts civic engagement—especially civic literacy—among a diverse range of students (CIRCLE, 2003; Galston, 2007; Gould et al., 2011; Kahne & Sporte, 2008; Langton & Jennings, 1968; Niemi & Junn, 1998; Torney-Purta, 2002). Research literature explicitly evaluating civic education among urban adolescents is relatively limited. Thus, it was necessary to broaden the focus of this section to include research from samples including non-urban adolescents.

Niemi and Junn (1998) reported on their analysis of data from the 1988 National Assessment of Educational Progress (NAEP) Civics Assessment—using scores from 4,275 students in grade 12. Controlling for several demographic variables, the researchers concluded that taking civics courses significantly influences political knowledge among adolescents, bolstering the *very weak* associations found between civic classes and civic outcomes in earlier work (e.g., Jennings & Niemi, 1974; Langton & Jennings, 1968). Moreover, students who took Civics or American government in grade 12 scored significantly higher on the NAEP Civics Assessment than students who did not take such courses. These patterns were relatively consistent across races, although minority students scored lower than White students overall. Although some scholars raise questions about the methodology and interpretation of Niemi and Junn (see Torney-Purta, 1999, and Greene, 2000, for critiques), this influential book suggested classrooms can play a role in increasing civic literacy.

In light of the research by Niemi and Junn (1998), an alternative instructional method, the "open classroom environment" (e.g., Campbell, 2008), was proposed to more effectively teach civic literacy. An open classroom environment encourages discussion of controversial or contemporary issues, leading to increased interest and engagement (Ehman, 1980). It also encourages students to recognize that people have different opinions about issues, that issues may have many solutions, and that "finding the most appropriate solution requires time, effort, and conflict" (Hibbing & Theiss-Morse, 2002). Research suggests that most students view such discussions positively, and, over time, students' affinity for discussion and their ability to participate in the discussion increases (Hess & Posselt, 2002; Torney-Purta, 2002). However, one study found that a large majority of students in the United States (90%) reported that reading textbooks and studying worksheets were still the most frequent form of civic instruction (Torney-Purta, 2002). Given the curtailed emphasis on civics education in the No Child Left Behind Act, the frequency with which civics topics are engaged in classrooms—open or not—has been more limited (Hinde, 2008).

Using a subsample of the IEA Civic Education Study, Campbell (2008) evaluated the impact of open classrooms on students' civic literacy and competencies. Results indicated that open classroom environments were significantly related to civic knowledge, appreciation of conflict, and voting expectations. Importantly, Campbell also found that the association between classroom openness and appreciation of conflict and future voting was stronger for students who had low educational expectations (i.e., educational aspirations) than for those with higher expectations. This finding is noteworthy because educational attainment is positively correlated with political engagement (Nie, Junn, & Stehlik-Berry, 1996). Campbell's (2008) finding is consistent with other research (e.g., Langton & Jennings, 1968; Torney-Purta, Barber, & Wilkenfeld, 2007), suggesting that gains made through civic education are greater for youth from low-SES backgrounds than for youth from high-SES backgrounds.

Relational Civic Learning Approaches

The relational learning approach emphasizes performance of civic service and learning that occurs through interactions with others (e.g., peers or community residents). We include most of the research on service learning in the relational approach. Service learning has become a common component of many schools' civic curriculum, and many high schools include service as a requirement for graduation (Chapin, 1998; Yates, 1999). According to the National Student Service-Learning and Community

Service Survey by the National Center for Educational Statistics (NCES; Skinner & Chapman, 1999), 64% of all public schools and 83% of all public high schools recognize and/or arrange students' participation in community service activities. A recent national study by Kielsmeier, Scales, Roehlkepartain, and Neal (2004) estimated that approximately 15 million students in roughly 56,000 public K-12 schools engage in community service. Community-based organizations (CBOs) and faith-based programs are another means through which adolescents engage in service (Hart & Atkins, 2002; Youniss et al., 2002). Findings based on 10 years of research on 120 CBOs in 34 different urban communities suggested that youth involved in CBOs placed greater value on community service and volunteering, as well as gaining a sense of community that encourages social trust and endears social responsibility (McLaughlin, 2000).

Overall, research suggests a positive association between participation in service activities and adolescents' civic literacy and competency (Atkins & Hart, 2003; Billig, Root, & Jesse, 2005; Hart & Atkins, 2002; Hart, Atkins, & Ford, 1998; Yates & Youniss, 1996; Youniss, McLellan, Su, & Yates, 1999; Youniss, McLellan, & Yates, 1997). Using data from the Monitoring the Future survey, Youniss and colleagues (1999) found that community service was significantly associated with—and was one of the strongest predictors of—both conventional (e.g., voting) and unconventional (e.g., boycotting) political behaviors; additionally, minority status was significantly associated with unconventional political behaviors, but not conventional ones. Across all adolescents, service activities appear to increase adolescents' positive attitudes toward service itself (Walker, 2002), although most of these findings emanate from studies using evaluations of programs and/or studies that indiscriminately mixed adolescents and older participants (Astin, Sax, & Avalos, 1999; Markus, Howard, & King, 1993; Melchior, 1997; Newmann & Rutter, 1983).

The value of service as a method for adolescent civic engagement, however, has been questioned (Hunter & Brisbin, 2000; Niemi, Hepburn, & Chapman, 2000; Walker, 2000b). Some purport that linking service with formal education strengthens the relationships between adolescents, schools, and communities (Skinner & Chapman, 1999), though others express concern that service learning encourages a conceptualization of citizenship as individual efforts, possibly to the detriment of group or collective efforts to influence social institutions (Walker, 2000a, 2000b). Research also suggests that the "civic" impact of service activities depends how closely the service activities align with those that are civic (e.g., political) in nature. In a report on a study of 1,000, mostly minority (> 50% Latino) high school adolescents from across the U.S., adolescents in service activities more closely linked to political or social action (e.g., organizing a community forum) had higher scores on civic knowledge and civic dispositions compared to adolescents in other types of service activities (Billig et al., 2005). It is important to note that a major hypothesis of the Billig et al. (2005) study—that there would be a significant difference in civic outcomes between adolescents in service activities and those not in service activities—was not supported.

For urban adolescents, the relation between service activities and civic engagement is not always clear. For example, Zeldin and Topitzes (2002) looked at the relationship between urban youth volunteering, sense of community, and positive youth outcomes but found little support for an association among the variables. In addition, a qualitative study by Raskoff and Sundeen (1999) found that service activities took away from urban adolescents' conscious civic development and feelings of community connectedness. Similarly, using a national sample of 8,000 adolescents in 6th through 12th grade, Atkins and Hart (2003) reported that urban youth living in concentrated poverty communities were less likely to volunteer for community service and scored lower on measures of civic knowledge and political tolerance compared to non-urban peers from higher income communities. Parallel findings have been reported with other samples (e.g., Nolin, Chaney, & Chapman, 1997). Interestingly, Quane and Rankin (2006) found that the difference between urban and non-urban adolescents was moderated by the number and availability of organizations through which adolescents could volunteer; once controlling for availability, researchers found that African American urban adolescents actually had higher rates of participation.

Didactic Civic Learning Approaches

Didactic learning approaches emphasize providing experiences through which adolescents will learn civic-related and non-civic-related competencies (e.g., social skills) that can be used in the future. The role of the instructor focuses, not on imparting knowledge as it is with an educational approach, or on relational learning that occurs through service, but on fostering specific competencies.

Youth community action research emerged as a way for CBOs to involve youth in the locating, recording, and evaluating of opportunities for youth development within the community (McLaughlin, 2000); it allows adolescents to become agents for the amelioration of identified deficits in their neighborhoods' resources. Qualitative studies have found positive associations between urban adolescents' civic development using action research. In two studies of early adolescents (ages 11–14), the findings suggest that through participating in activities designed to systematically identify and address issues in their communities, urban adolescents developed a greater personal critical civic consciousness/awareness (Kirshner, Strobel, & Fernandez, 2003; McIntyre, 2000). In another qualitative study, Camino (2005) examined a youth-led research initiative in two urban community programs over a 2½-year period and found that youth gained greater voice in the execution of civic duties and developed collective resources among community members.

Internships and apprenticeships may also foster the development of adolescents' civic engagement. Based on their research on 59 high school student interns at local government offices in four counties in central New York State, Hamilton and Zeldin (1987) found that youth appeared to increase their political efficacy and knowledge about politics, governance, and other civic affairs but did not appear to increase favorable attitudes toward local government. In a qualitative study of an urban community work apprenticeship program, adolescents appeared to learn executive thinking skills, interpersonal skills, as well as self-initiative for interacting with their communities (Halpern, 2006).

Facilitative Civic Learning Approaches

Facilitative civic learning emphasizes practicing civic involvement by co-partnering with other youth and adults to accomplish real, tangible work that aims to have a social impact. Learning is driven by the need to solve problems and overcome challenges that arise in the process of working towards social change. Meaningful civic objectives can cover a wide range of topics, from attempts to change communities through influencing political officials to directly working on neighborhood improvement projects. The co-partnerships are characterized by relative equality in the relationship(s) between members. We found four studies, all qualitative research, that fit a facilitative approach, that we will discuss next.

A consistent finding across studies in this category was a linkage between engaging in civic activities through youth–adult partnerships and urban adolescents' self-efficacy/confidence. In a qualitative study of community organizations that included adolescents and young adults (ages 16–20) in the governance structure of the organization, Zeldin (2004) reported that these adolescents and young adults developed a sense of personal agency and confidence through interacting with adults both on the organizational board and in the community. Ginwright and Cammarota (2007) reported that as urban adolescents and young adults interacted with intergenerational networks of caring adults, they were exposed to meaningful political ideas through a variety of activities and discussions intended to surface the structural realities and personal choices behind the identified issues, and they developed "critical civic praxis" (Ginwright & Cammarota, 2007). In another qualitative study, Larson and Hansen (2005) reported findings on how a group of urban high school adolescents became motivated and interested in addressing school and community issues they identified; in partnership with a skillful adult youth worker, they enacted plans to influence the Chicago school board to abide by its own policies regarding student suspensions. As a result of their civic actions, the adolescents reported gaining confidence and a sense of power in working to influence adult-controlled institutions.

Urban adolescents in facilitative learning approaches also appear to begin forging their own civic identities. In the study by Zeldin (2004), 75% of the adolescents and young adults discussed their "future selves" in the community, which the author suggested helped these urban adolescents begin to think of themselves as "change agents" in their communities. Adolescents and young adults in Ginwright and Cammarota's (2007) study also began to perceive and talk about themselves as "civic problem-solvers."

Intergenerational relationships are a common component of facilitative learning approaches. Establishing connections to adults in community organizations and neighborhoods was a common finding across several of the research studies; urban adolescents discussed how they were coming to know key adults in their communities and, for some, how these key adults were also getting to know them (Ginwright & Cammarota, 2007; Larson & Hansen, 2005; Zeldin, 2004). The authors suggest that these new connections provide adolescents access and power to operate in civic worlds previously unavailable.

Part of the goal of facilitative learning is to support the growth of civic competencies. In a study of community organizations across the United States that were implementing youth–adult partnerships, Camino (2000) reported that both youth (ages not specified) and adults learned essential communication, teamwork, and coaching skills. Adolescents in the youth-activism program in Chicago appeared to learn pragmatic, strategic thinking skills in the realm of human systems/social institutions (Larson & Hansen, 2005).

Conclusions

Based on our review of the research literature, we offer several "lessons learned" that suggest ways to support urban adolescents' development of civic engagement. First, and foremost, an understanding of adolescent civic socialization and learning is filtered through one's fundamental beliefs about human development. Rarely were these beliefs explicitly stated in the research. Instructional approaches to adolescent civic learning, and subsequent research from this approach, are rooted in a belief that the adolescent is shaped by external forces, a relatively passive recipient of incoming information. We agree with Haste (2010) that such an approach to and understanding of human development and learning is outmoded; contemporary models of human development (e.g., Lerner, 2004; Vygotsky, 1978) in which the individual is an interactive agent with the environment more accurately reflect civic learning processes. The remaining three learning approaches (relational, dialectic, facilitative) view the adolescent as an active agent in the civic learning process, although some more so than others.

The second lesson learned from the research literature is that adolescent civic engagement, the type that will endure into adulthood, develops most fully when there is meaningful, real-world civic practice. Relational civic learning approaches provide adolescents with much needed "on-the-ground" interaction with people, neighborhoods, and communities, typically in the form of service projects. These interactions have the potential to meet adolescent's desire for meaningful civic practice, but there is a very real danger that such interactions will lead to a service-perpetuating civic engagement—service becomes normative and a primary definition of civic engagement. Scholars, such as Walker (2000a, 2000b), warn that service alone can usurp political and other forms of civic engagement, and we echo this warning. We do not, however, propose eliminating traditional service activities; they provide an important affective connection between adolescents and society. Instead, we suggest service activities follow the example given in Larson and Hansen (2005). High school students in that qualitative study began participating in the civic activism youth program in Chicago because it fulfilled their service hour requirement for graduation. The adult youth worker, who was well trained and adept at social activism methods, used this opportunity to guide these students in becoming active agents in influencing Chicago public school policy. We suggest then that service learning as a whole could support adolescents' civic engagement if adult youth workers, trained to support civic development, are integral to the service learning activities.

The final lesson learned concerns the role of adults in the development of urban adolescents' civic engagement. Within a facilitative learning approach, adults and adolescents co-partner to accomplish work that has a more immediate social impact—

the aim is to address a present need or issue. By contrast, adults within a didactic approach primarily lend their expertise to adolescents in order to promote the development of adolescents' skills or competencies for future application. Co-partnering with adults to accomplish co-determined, meaningful civic objectives we suggest more fully integrates adolescents into "adult worlds" and, no less importantly, vice versa. It is this unique co-partnering dimension that, we propose, provides the greatest potential for sustainability because civic engagement occurs in present-tense—it occurs in real time and not as part of a future disposition—alongside other individuals from a range of ages who are civically engaged. Such facilitative approaches to civic learning are consonant with contemporary theories of human development previously mentioned (e.g., Vygotsky, 1978) because adolescents (and adults) gain access to thinking and norms that they can then use to construct civic meaning and skills. Although there is a limited base of research, the extant research suggests that a facilitative approach not only supports civic literacy, competency, and development, but that it has the greatest potential for sustained civic engagement over time. This is a promising finding as it suggests that such youth may eventually "serve," rather than "flee," their urban community.

We offer final comments on differentiating urban and non-urban adolescent civic engagement. At a fundamental level, urban adolescent learning is no different from non-urban adolescent learning; basic principles of human development apply equally. However, urban adolescents experience a wide range of challenges (e.g., poverty, institutional discrimination) that their non-urban counterparts typically do not, which as noted in the introduction can lead to less civic engagement (Sherrod, 2003; Jankowski, 1992, 2002). For this reason, we think facilitating (i.e., facilitative learning approaches) civic engagement among urban adolescents is especially salient—it offers a powerful means with which to address social issues and exert a measure of control over one's environment.

References

Astin, A. W., Sax, L. J., & Avalos, J. (1999). The long-term effects of volunteerism during the undergraduate years. *Review of Higher Education, 21*(2): 187–202.

Atkins, R., & Hart, D. (2003). Neighborhoods, adults, and the development of civic identity in urban youth. *Applied Developmental Science, 7*, 156–165.

Billig, S., Root, S., & Jesse, D. (2005). The impact of participation in service-learning on high school students' civic engagement. CIRCLE Working Paper 33.

Bronfenbrenner, U. (1979). *The ecology of human development.* Cambridge, MA: Harvard University Press.

Camino, L. A. (2000). Youth-adult partnerships: Entering new territory in community work and research. *Applied Developmental Science, 4*, 11–20.

Camino, L. (2005). Youth-led community building: Promising practices from two communities using community-based service-learning. *Journal of Extension, 43*(1).

Campbell, D. E. (2008). Voice in the classroom: How an open classroom climate fosters political engagement among adolescents. *Political Behavior, 30*(4), 437–454.

Center for Information & Research on Civic Learning & Engagement (CIRCLE). (2003). *The civic mission of schools.* New York, NY: CIRCLE and Carnegie Corporation of New York.

Chapin, J. R. (1998). Is service learning a good idea? Data from the National Longitudinal Study of 1988. *The Social Studies, 89*(5), 205–211.

Chapman, C., Nolin, M. J., & Kline, K. (1997). *Student interest in national news and its relation to school courses.* Washington, DC: National Center for Education Statistics, Office of Educational Research and Improvement, U.S. Department of Education.

Dewey, J. (1916). *Democracy and education: An introduction to the philosophy of education.* New York: Free Press.

Ehman, L. H. (1980). Change in high school students' political attitudes as a function of social studies classroom climate. *American Educational Research Journal, 17,* 253–265.

Evans, G. W., & English, K. (2002). The environment of poverty: Multiple stressor exposure, psychophysiological stress, and socioemotional adjustment. *Child Development, 73,* 1238–1248.

Flanagan, C., & Faison, N. (2001). Youth civic development: Implications of research for social policy and programs. *Social Policy Reports,* no. 1.

Galston, W. A. (2007). Civic knowledge, civic education, and civic engagement: A summary of recent research. *International Journal of Public Administration, 30,* 623–642.

Ginwright, S., & Cammarota, J. (2007). Youth activism in the urban community: Learning critical civic praxis within community organizations. *International Journal of Qualitative Studies in Education (QSE), 20*(6), 18.

Gould, J., Jamieson, K. H., Levine, P., McConnell, T., Smith, D. B., McKinney-Browning, M., & Cambell, K. (2011). *Guardian of democracy: The civic mission of schools.* The Leonore Annenberg Institute for Civics of the Annenberg Public Policy Center at the University of Pennsylvania and the Campaign for the Civic Mission of Schools.

Greene, J. P. (2000). Review of R. G. Niemi and J. Junn, *Civic education. Social Science Quarterly, 81,* 696–697.

Halpern, R. (2005). Instrumental relationships: A potential relational model for inner-city youth programs. *Journal of Community Psychology, 33*(1), 11–20.

Halpern, R. (2006). After-school matters in Chicago. *Youth & Society, 38*(2), 203–235.

Hamilton, S. F., & Zeldin, R. S. (1987). Learning civics in the community. *Curriculum Inquiry, 17*(4), 407–420.

Hart, D., & Atkins, R. (2002). Civic competence in urban youth. *Applied Developmental Science, 6*(4), 227–236.

Hart, D., Atkins, R., & Ford, D. (1998). Urban America as a context for the development of moral identity in adolescence. *Journal of Social Issues, 54*(3), 513–530.

Haste, H. (2010). Citizenship education: A critical look at a contested field. In L. Sherrod, J. Torney-Purta, & C. Flanagan (Eds.), *Handbook of research on civic engagement in youth* (pp. 161–188). Hoboken, NJ: Wiley.

Hess, D. E., & Posselt, J. (2002). How high school students experience and learn from the discussion of controversial public issues. *Journal of Curriculum and Supervision, 17*(4), 283–314.

Hibbing, J. R., & Theiss-Morse, E. (2002). *Stealth democracy: Americans' belief about how government should work.* New York: Cambridge University Press.

Hinde, E. R. (2008). Civic education in the NCLB era: The contested mission of elementary and middle schools. *Journal of Curriculum and Instruction, 2*(1), 74–86.

Hunter, S., & Brisbin, R. A. (2000). The impact of service learning on democratic and civic values. *PS: Political Science and Politics, 33*(3), 623–626.

Jankowski, M. (1992). Ethnic identity and political consciousness in different social orders. *New Directions for Child Development, 56,* 79–93.

Jankowski, M. (2002). Minority youth and civic engagement: The impact of group relations. *Applied Developmental Science, 6*(4), 237–245.

Jennings, M. K., & Niemi, R. G. (1974). *The political character of adolescence.* Princeton, NJ: Princeton University Press.

Kahne, J. E., & Sporte, S. E. (2008). Developing citizens: The impact of civic learning opportunities on students' commitment to civic participation. *American Educational Research Journal, 45*(3), 738–766.

Kielsmeier, J. C., Scales, P. C., Roehlkepartain, E. C., & Neal, M. (2004). Community service and service-learning in public schools. *Reclaiming Children & Youth, 13*(3), 138–143.

Kirshner, B., Strobel, K., & Fernandez, M. (2003). Critical civic engagement among urban youth. *Penn GSE Perspectives on Urban Education, 2*(1).

Kraus, M. W., Piff, P. K., & Keltner, D. (2011). Social class as culture: The convergence of resources and rank in the social realm. *Current Directions in Psychological Science, 20,* 246–250.

Larson, R., & Hansen, D. (2005). The development of strategic thinking: Learning to impact human systems in a Youth Activism program. *Human Development, 48,* 327–349.

Langton, K. P., & Jennings, M. K. (1968). Political socialization and the high school civics curriculum in the United States. *American Political Science Review, 62*(3), 852–867.

Lerner, R. M. (2004). *Liberty: Thriving and civic engagement among America's youth.* Thousand Oaks, CA: Sage Publications.

Markus, G., Howard, J., & King, D. (1993). Integrating community service and classroom instruction enhances learning: Results from an experiment. *Educational Evaluation and Policy Analysis, 15,* 410–419.

McIntyre, A. (2000). Constructing meaning about violence, school, and community: Participatory action research with urban youth. *The Urban Review, 32*(2), 123–154.

McLaughlin, M. W. (2000). *Community counts: How youth organizations matter for youth development* (37 pp.). Washington, DC: Public Education Network.

McLoyd, V. C. (1998). Socioeconomic disadvantage and child development. *American Psychologist, 53,* 185–204.

Melchior, A. (1997). National evaluation of Learn and Serve America school and community-based programs. Interim Report, April.

Newmann, F. M., & Rutter, R. A. (1983). *The effects of high school and community service programs on students' social development.* Madison: Wisconsin Center for Education Research.

Nie, N. H., Junn, J., & Stehlik-Berry, K. (1996). *Education and democratic citizenship in America.* Chicago, IL: University of Chicago Press.

Niemi, R. G., Hepburn, M. A., & Chapman, C. (2000). Community service by high school students: A cure for civic ills? *Political Behavior, 22*(1), 45–69.

Niemi, R. G., & Junn, J. (1998). *Civic education: What makes students learn.* New Haven, CT: Yale University Press.

Nolin, M. J., Chaney, B., & Chapman, C. (1997). *Student participation in community service activity.* Retrieved October 12, 2011 from National Center for Education Statistics Web site: http://nces.ed.gov/pubs97/97331.pdf.

Quane, J. M., & Rankin, B. H. (2006). Does it pay to participate? Neighborhood-based organizations and the social development of urban adolescents. *Children and Youth Services Review, 28*(10), 1229–1250.

Raskoff, S. A., & Sundeen, R. A. (1999). Community service programs in high schools. *Law and Contemporary Problems, 62,* 73–111.

Sherrod, L. R. (2003). Promoting the development of citizenship in diverse youth. *PS: Political Science and Politics, 36*(2), 287–292.

Sherrod, L. R. (2008). Youth's perceptions of citizenship. In M. Ruck, & S. Horn (Eds.), *Young people's perspectives on the rights of the child. Journal of Social Issues, 64,* 771–790.

Sherrod, L., Torney-Purta, J., & Flanagan, C. (2010). Research on the development of citizenship: A field comes of age. In L. Sherrod, J. Torney-Purta, & C. Flanagan (Eds.), *Handbook of research on civic engagement in youth* (pp. 1–22). Hoboken, NJ: Wiley.

Skinner, R., & Chapman, C. (1999). Service-learning and community service in K-12 public schools. Statistics in Brief. *Education Statistics Quarterly, 1*(4), 51–59.

Torney-Purta, J. V. (1999). Review of R. G. Niemi and J. Junn, *Civic Education. American Journal of Education, 107,* 256–260.

Torney-Purta, J. (2002). The school's role in developing civic engagement: A study of adolescents in twenty-eight countries. *Applied Developmental Science, 6,* 203–212.

Torney-Purta, J., Barber, C. H., & Wilkenfeld, B. (2007). Latino adolescents' civic development in the United States: Research results from the IEA Civic Education Study. *Journal of Youth and Adolescence, 32*, 111–125.

Torney-Purta, J., Lehmann, R., Oswald, H., & Schulz, W. (2001). *Citizenship and education in twenty-eight countries: Civic knowledge and engagement at age fourteen.* Amsterdam: IEA.

Vygotsky, L. (1978). *Mind in society.* Cambridge, MA: Harvard University Press.

Walker, T. (2000a). The service/politics split: Rethinking service to teach political engagement. *PS: Political Science and Politics, 33*(3), 647–649.

Walker, T. (2000b). A feminist challenge to community service: A call to politicize service-learning. In B. Balliet, & K. Heffeman (Eds.), *Service learning in women's studies* (pp. 25–45). Washington, DC: American Association for Higher Education.

Walker, T. (2002). Service as a pathway to political participation: What research tells us. *Applied Developmental Science, 6*(4), 183–188.

Yates, M. (1999). Community service and political-moral discussions among adolescents: A study of a mandatory school-based program in the United States. In M. Yates, & J. Youniss (Eds.), *Roots of civic identity: International perspectives on community service and activism in youth* (pp. 16–31). New York: Cambridge University Press.

Yates, M., & Youniss, J. (1996). Community service and political-moral identity in adolescents. *Journal of Research on Adolescence, 6*, 271–284.

Youniss, J., Bales, S., Christmas-Best, V., Diversi, M., McLaughlin, M., & Silbereisen, R. (2002). Youth civic engagement in the twenty-first century. *Journal of Research on Adolescence, 22*(1), 121–148.

Youniss, J., McLellan, J. A., Su, Y., Yates, M. (1999). The role of community service in identity development: Normative, unconventional, and deviant orientations. *Journal of Adolescent Research, 14*, 249–262.

Youniss, J., McLellan, J. A., & Yates, M. (1997). What we know about engendering civic identity. *American Behavioral Scientist, 40*(5), 620–631.

Zeldin, S. (2004). Youth as agents of adult and community development: Mapping the processes and outcomes of youth engaged in organizational governance. *Applied Developmental Science, 8*, 75–90.

Zeldin, S., & Topitzes, D. (2002). Neighborhood experiences, community connection, and positive beliefs about adolescents among urban adults and youth. *Journal of Community Psychology, 30*(6), 647–669.

13

RELIGION AND AMERICA'S URBAN YOUTH

Korie L. Edwards and Brad Christerson

A renewed interest in urban youth has emerged as economic decline has produced a concentration of poverty in many urban neighborhoods (Leventhal, Dupéré, & Brooks-Gunn, 2009), and subsequently a decline in institutional resources that are important to adolescent development, including, for example, health services (Newacheck, Hughes, & Stoddard, 1996), after-school programs (Eccles & Gootman, 2002), and employment opportunities (Wilson, 1996; Pattillo-McCoy, 1999). However, there is one institution that has proven to help youth thrive in spite of these kinds of structural limitations: religion.

A chapter focus on religion and urban youth is warranted for two main reasons. The first is that poverty and the institutional divestment that follows precipitates other challenges that affect youth (Levanthal et al., 2009), such as family conflict (Brooks-Gunn & Duncan, 1997), early sexual activity, low mental and physical health (Bianchi, 1999), gangs, drugs, violence (Teitelman et al., 2010; Maimon & Browning, 2010; Conchas & Vigil, 2010) and underperforming schools (Lleras, 2008). Invariably, the protective power of religion may be uniquely vital to the quality of life for urban youth who live in these kinds of settings. The second reason is that poor urban neighborhoods are often highly segregated and are home to large populations of Black and Latino families (Massey & Denton, 1993). Urban religious organizations are especially important for the protection and development of youth of color. Outside of the family, religious organizations are perceived as the *primary* vehicle through which youth of color are protected (Christerson, Edwards, & Flory, 2010).

We discuss key findings on the protective power of religion for urban youth. We then take a look at results from the first wave of the National Study of Youth and Religion survey to explore the role of religion in the lives of urban youth. We end by sketching out a theoretical framework to understand the protective potential of religion in the lives of urban youth.

Key Findings on Religion of American Youth

There are several lines of research on the role of religion in the lives of youths. One examines how religion impacts positive youth development, which includes qualities such as a positive sense of self and high self-esteem (Wagener, Furrow, King, Leffert, & Benson, 2003; Furrow, King, & White, 2004). More religious youth have strong positive youth development (Smith & Faris, 2002; Furrow et al., 2004). Demographic factors, such as gender and age, however, mediate the effect of religion on this growth. Positive youth development more consistently matters for males. It is also more positively impactful for older youth, presumably because older youth have more autonomy in deciding to participate in religious activities (Wagener et al., 2003).

Another research thread examines the role that religion plays in deterring adolescent substance use (Chu, 2007; Longest & Vaisey, 2008). However, which *dimension* of religion matters more and under what circumstances religion matters is less clear. For instance, evidence suggests that religious participation (i.e., the type and frequency of religious activities in which a person participates) is most important for *desistance* from substance use (Chu, 2007). When it comes to deterring *initial* substance use, some argue that religious salience (i.e., the extent to which a person sees their religion as critically important) matters (Longest & Vaisey 2008) while others find that religious participation (Chu, 2007) is a more powerful deterrent. Religious identity also affects social outcomes for youth. Youth affiliated with more fundamentalist religions are less likely than their peers affiliated with more liberal religions to participate in heavy drug use because, it is suggested, more fundamentalist religions have higher levels of social control. Still, religion is not universally protective against substance use. Religion, regardless of how it is measured, is less protective against the use of hard drugs (i.e., cocaine, heroine, etc.) as compared to the use of soft drugs (i.e., tobacco and alcohol) (McIntosh, Fitch, Wilson, & Nyberg, 1981). This may be because religion is the primary source of social control for less serious forms of substance use. Other institutions actively participate in deterring the use of more serious substances making religion less consequential for serious substance use deterrence (Hadaway, Elifson, & Petersen, 1984).

A third area of research looks at the relationship between religion and mental health among youth. Religion is associated with lower levels of psychological distress among youth (Dowling et al., 2004). Religious participation appears to be the most important dimension of religion when it comes to protection against psychological distress (Wong, Rew, & Slaikeu, 2006). However, demographic factors—in this case race and gender—mediate the effect of religion on psychological distress among youth (Petts & Joliff, 2008; Wong et al., 2006). Again, religion is most consistently protective against psychological distress among males (Wong et al., 2006). Then, ethno-racial background has some interesting effects on psychological distress. For both White and Black youth (of both genders) and Latino males, religious participation is associated with lower levels of psychological distress. However, religion actually increases psychological distress among Asian youth of both genders. And more moderate religiosity is more effective against psychological distress for Latina youth than low or high levels of religiosity (Petts & Joliff, 2008).

The story that emerges from the broader literature on religion in the lives of American youth is that although all measures of religion have an impact on social outcomes for youth, religious participation, compared to religious identification and religious salience, is more consistently linked to positive social outcomes for adolescents. Further, we see that sociodemographic characteristics, particularly age, gender and ethno-racial identity, intervene on the effect of religion on social outcomes for youth. Age has a greater impact on social outcomes among younger youth. Religion is more protective for males. This is somewhat surprising since, in America, religion is more common among females. Finally, race and ethnicity are relevant intervening factors to consider when aiming to understand the relationship between religion and social outcomes among adolescents. Considering that most of the studies on religion and social outcomes among youth are based upon survey data, it is difficult to ascertain the reasons behind the effects of gender and race.

In the following section, we focus on how religion matters for urban American youth in particular. The findings are, in some ways, consistent with the general literature in this area, but they also highlight how urbanicity might intervene on the way in which religion plays a role in the lives of youth.

The Role of Religion in the Lives of Urban American Youth

There is a focus in this body of work on how religion protects urban youth against the psychological stresses of living in socioeconomically disadvantaged urban communities. Studies reveal that religion, particularly the social support that it offers, helps socioeconomically disadvantaged urban youth manage psychological distress (Van Dyke, Glenwick, Cecero, & Kim, 2009; Carleton, Esparza, Thaxter, & Grant, 2008).[1] Yet, religion is shown to have a minimal effect on urban youth who are dealing with high levels of stress (Carleton et al., 2008). Sociodemographic factors mediate the effect of religion on psychological distress for urban youth as well. Gender is a factor, but reports on the effect of gender on psychological distress of urban youth are inconsistent. Some say that religion helps socioeconomically disadvantaged urban female youth, but not males (Carleton et al., 2008). Others say that religion is more helpful for males but not females (Van Dyke et al., 2009).[2] The seemingly contradictory effects of gender could be due to differences in how religion is measured as well as differences in sampling. Another mediating factor in the role of religion for psychological distress of urban youth is age. As with more inclusive studies, there is no association found between religion and psychological distress among older urban youth, but there is among younger youth (Van Dyke et al., 2009). Furthermore,

---

1   The mediating effect of age for religion and psychological distress is not consistently found (see Huebner, Suldo, Valois, Drane, & Zullig, 2004).

2   While religiosity measures do not demonstrate a strong association with psychological distress among urban female adolescents, there is a strong negative association between spiritual experiences and psychological distress among urban female adolescents relative to their male counterparts (Van Dyke et al., 2009).

urban, socioeconomically disadvantaged youth of color are more inclined to rely upon religion to cope with psychological distress than White youth and more socioeconomically advantaged youth (Pargament, 1997; Van Dyke et al., 2009). Scholars suggest that urban youth of color may rely on religion more to cope with psychological distress because they experience greater exposure to stress-inducing environments.

Another area of inquiry is how religion affects urban youth's involvement in drug-related activities. One study looks at urban black male teens and their involvement in drug-related activities, including the use and selling of drugs (Johnson, Larson, Li, & Jang, 2000). The sample is drawn from poor urban neighborhoods. The results reveal that religious practice, specifically church attendance, protects against involvement in drug-related activities, but religious salience does not. Interestingly, in one of the few studies that looked at urban White middle-class youth, findings show almost the reverse. Religious participation and religious salience *both* negatively affect substance use as well as attitudes towards substance use among urban, White middle-class youth. But religious salience matters more (Hadaway et al., 1984). Also, similar to other work, the effect of religion on drug-related activities varies depending on the kind of substance used. Religion is more protective against less serious substance use, such as marijuana and alcohol.

Religion can protect urban youth from violent activities as well (Powell, 1997). A study examining urban disadvantaged youth of both genders and different races, examines the effect of religious salience on nonviolence among urban youth. Youth who consider religion to be important and who have greater adult support are more likely to be nonviolent. Additionally, youth who are younger or female are more likely to be nonviolent than other youth (Powell, 1997).

Religion is in some ways protective for urban youth. But, it matters differently for urban youth than for youth generally. Religious participation matters, particularly when it leads to greater social support and connection for urban youth. However, although the evidence is far from conclusive, religious salience appears to be more important than religious participation. More research that examines why religious salience is so important for urban youth is needed. We also see the limits of religion for urban youth. When the pressures of urban life are too challenging, religion has no effect on social outcomes, and thus no longer acts as a protective force for urban adolescents.

As mentioned, the literature on the role of religion in the lives of urban youth is limited. In the following section, we explore urban youth religion using the National Survey of Youth and Religion (NSYR). We look at a variety of results to provide a broader, more inclusive view, of what religion means for urban American youth, and to point to areas where future research might examine the role of religion in the lives of urban youth.

Exploring Religion among Urban Youth

The NSYR includes survey data generated from a nationally representative telephone survey of 3,290 U.S. English- and Spanish-speaking teenagers between the ages of 13 and 17 and their parents, as well as 267 in-depth interviews from a sub-sample of the adolescents who participated in the survey. About 27% of the total sample (910) is classified as urban.[3]

Religiosity, Social and Cultural Capital among Urban Teens

Analyses comparing religiosity of youth across geographic area (i.e., urban, suburban, or rural) reveal that despite the differences in religiosity across urban, suburban, and rural youth, geographic area alone does not mediate the effects of religion on social outcomes among youth. Thus, urban youth are no more or less religious than their suburban or rural counterparts. So, we instead take a look at the religiosity of just urban youth and examine several indicators of religiosity, and social and cultural capital, to explore: (1) Are there signs that religion can protect urban youth from social deviance?; and (2) Do religious urban youth have certain advantages compared to those urban youth who are not particularly religious?

The results in Table 13.1 show that there are clear differences between urban teens who regularly attend religious services (participation) and report that religion is "extremely" or "very" important to their daily lives (salience) and urban teens who do not. We see that more religious youth are significantly more likely than their less religious counterparts to not only have aspirations for college, but also to have the confidence that they can actually complete a degree. They are more likely to have volunteered in their communities, planned an event or led a meeting, and participated in organized extracurricular activities. They are more likely to feel loved, accepted, and understood. And they are less likely to engage in risky behaviors such as sexual intercourse and substance use.

These data suggest that the positive benefits associated with religion among urban teens are quite similar to those found among teens more broadly. Religion appears to provide a moral framework, which casts a vision for future achievement, as well as motivation to avoid risky behavior. Religion also fosters learned competencies that come from interacting with adults and encourages a moral responsibility for the well-being of society. Lastly, religion provides social support from adults in the form of love and understanding.

Ethno-racial Identity and Religiosity among Urban Teens

Our research has documented that ethno-racial identity affects the religiosity of youth (Christerson et al., 2010). In fact, ethno-racial identity matters more than geographic

---

3 An urban area is defined as a Census Block Group with a density greater than or equal to 2,000 people per square mile, a place that has a total population greater than or equal to 100,000 people and a density greater than or equal to 2,000 people per square mile, or a place that has a total population greater than or equal to 200,000 people.

TABLE 13.1 Indicators of social and cultural capital formation of urban teens (age 13–17) by religious participation and religious salience ($N = 910$).

Percentage of urban teens who . . .	Does teen attend church more than once a month?		Is religion extremely or very important to daily life of teen?	
	Yes	No	Yes	No
Think they will graduate from college	78★	66	80★	72
"Regularly" or "occasionally" do organized volunteer work/ community service	38★	26	36★	27
Have planned an event or led a meeting	34★	24	34★	24
Spend two or more weeknights in organized extracurricular activities	76★	61	42★	33
Feel loved and accepted for who they are "a lot"	78★	64	77★	66
Feel alone and misunderstood "some" or "a lot"	26★	41	32	35
Have had sexual intercourse	17★	27	19★	26
Have been drunk in the past year	17★	29	14★	33

Source: National Study of Youth and Religion Survey 2003.
Note: ★*differences* between all ethno-racial groups are significant at $p < .01$ (Pearson's Chi Square Test)

area, and we argue that ethno-racial background conditions how youth experience and live out their religion.

Data that include urban, suburban, and rural youth show that African American youth are by far the most religious. They express the most commitment and connection to their religion when compared to White, Latino, and Asian youth. Further, we propose that differences that emerge in the survey data are manifestations of something more fundamental to how youth of different ethno-racial backgrounds experience religion, and present four archetypes that represent how youth of different ethno-racial backgrounds understand and experience religion. We hypothesize that African American youth present a religious orientation best explained as a "personalistic absolutism." They perceive God as both an authoritarian figure and a loving, involved personality. White youth's religious orientation is more likely to be one of "therapeutic individualism." Religion is about their happiness and meeting their personal needs. God supports them but demands nothing, or very little, from them in return. Latino youth's religion tends to follow a pattern of "religious familialism." Religion tends to be embedded in, and acts as a source of support for, family. Finally, many Asian youth express religion as "relativistic pragmatism."

Religion tends to be far more fluid and optional for these youth compared to other groups.

Thus, when we consider religion among urban youth, it is important to account for the ways in which ethno-racial identity might condition how urban youth express their religion and, further, how religion and ethno-racial identity together affect social outcomes of urban adolescents. We focus our analyses here then on how ethno-racial identity affects the religiosity of urban youth and the extent to which the more general patterns of religiosity by ethno-racial background are supported for urban youth particularly.

Table 13.2 shows descriptive statistics for a variety of religious indicators for urban youth by ethno-racial background. For urban teens, religion plays a more salient role in the lives of African American teens. This is despite their church attendance rates being similar to those of White and Latino urban teens—again highlighting the importance of examining multiple dimensions of religion. The moral directives and spiritual experiences that religion provides are particularly important for urban African American teens. African American urban teens are more likely than other urban teens to report that religion is very or extremely important in shaping their daily life. They

TABLE 13.2 Religious beliefs, practices, and experiences of urban teens by race ($N = 910$).

Percentage of urban teens who . . .	*White*	*African American*	*Latino*	*Asian American*
Religion is very or extremely important in shaping daily life	37	64	48	25
Religion is very or extremely important in shaping life decisions	39	58	50	32
Have experienced a miracle	41	63	46	13
Have committed their lives to god	49	67	44	12
Pray alone at least once a day	33	50	44	13
Talk with their families about religion at least once a week	35	67	52	14
Read scripture alone at least once a week	23	33	33	22
Feel very or extremely close to god	32	48	35	19
Attend religious services more than once a month	49	45	49	25
Attend youth group more than once a month	38	29	25	25
Think it's OK to "pick and choose" from a number of religious beliefs	50	41	51	63
Agree that morals are based on fixed standards	46	53	49	31

Source: National Study of Youth and Religion Survey 2003.
Note: All differences between racial/ethnic groups statistically significant at $p < .01$.

are also more likely than the other ethno-racial groups to report that they have experienced a miracle, committed their lives to God, prayed alone every day, talked to their families about religion, and feel very close to God. Thus, religion is important to the lives of urban African American teens.

Urban Latino teens are second only to urban African American teens and significantly more likely than White and Asian urban teens to report that religion shapes their decisions and daily life. They are also second only to urban African American teens in their likelihood to report that they have experienced a miracle, committed their lives to God, talked to their families about religion, and feel very or extremely close to God. Similar to African American urban youth, religion appears to be integral to the lives of a majority of urban Latino teens.

Urban White teens are the most likely ethno-racial group to attend a religious youth group, which may reflect the greater resource base of predominantly White churches. Predominately White churches are more easily able to afford to pay a youth pastor and offer organized youth activities.[4] This targeted investment in their youth reflects a greater degree of expectation at predominantly White churches that the youth should have their individual needs met by organized programs (Christerson, Edwards, & Emerson, 2005; Christerson et al., 2010). This pattern also suggests that urban White youth are more actively involved in religion as an institution. That is, they attend worship services as regularly as other youth and are more likely to participate in organized activities tailored to their unique needs. Coupled with their lower levels of religious salience, religion then, for many urban White youth, appears to be less about who they are and more about something they do or belong to.

Asian American urban teens are the least overtly religious among all racial/ethnic groups. They tend to be less committed to a set of fixed moral and religious beliefs. They are significantly more likely than the other ethno-racial groups to think it is acceptable to "pick and choose" from a number of religious beliefs and are significantly less likely to agree that morals are based on fixed standards.

These aforementioned analyses might be indicative of the persistent religious racial and ethnic segregation in America. Over 90% of congregations are racially and ethnically segregated in the U.S. It is not surprising then that religion is practiced differently across racial and ethnic lines (Edwards, 2008; Christerson et al., 2005). This division in American religious life likely manifests in the lives of urban youth. Additionally, when we consider the results from Table 13.1 and Table 13.2 together, African American urban youth, followed closely by Latino urban youth, may receive the greatest protection from religion. It could be that because of the limited resources of the African American and Latino urban population, religion is necessarily more important for African American and Latino youth. More research that explores why and how urban youth draw upon religion as a protective source would improve our understanding of this social phenomenon.

---

4 This does not mean that churches of color are not actively investing in the lives of their youth. The interview data of the NSYR suggests that African American and Latino youth in particular are well integrated into the lives of their congregations.

Conclusions

We argue that religion contributes to three important resources for urban adolescents becoming successful as adults: social capital, cultural capital, and coping skills. As such, religious belief and participation can partially compensate in various ways for neighborhood deficits in these resources and can thus expand the life chances of teens growing up in disadvantaged urban neighborhoods. We agree with Smith (2003) who argues that religion uniquely offers deeply historical moral orders, beliefs and spiritual experiences that can aid people and society in ways other institutions cannot.

Religion and Three Key Resources for Adolescent Development

Social Capital refers to the ability to gain access to resources by virtue of membership in social networks and other social structures (Bourdieu, 1986). In urban areas with high concentrations of poverty, young residents lack connections to resources and formal organizations that can lead to upward mobility (Rankin and Quane, 2000). Religious organizations, however, can potentially offer youth the opportunity to connect to adults outside of their families on a consistent basis (Smith, 2003). To the extent that urban congregations are welcoming to neighborhood teens and are socioeconomically diverse, urban religious organizations can open opportunities for youth to acquire "bonding" social capital—relational ties that provide advice and support, and "bridging" social capital—from connections with people and organizations outside of one's own context and community (Putnam, 2000). Bonding capital can translate into employment opportunities, career advice, help in practical matters, or simply an understanding adult who is not a family member to process emotions and life problems.

Moreover, most urban congregations have ties to larger organizations outside of the communities and have opportunities for youth to participate in citywide, regional, national, or even international conferences, service trips, and camps (Smith, 2003). The social connections built through these external activities can be accessed later in life to connect youth to opportunities for jobs, resources, and career advice.

Cultural Capital refers to the verbal skills, knowledge base, and ways of interacting that help a person advance in society (Bourdieu, 1984). The cultural capital affirmed by dominant society is more difficult to obtain in segregated poor neighborhoods because schools are often poorly resourced and low-performing, and the language patterns, ways of interacting socially, and informal knowledge base are often different from those in the dominant mainstream culture (Farkas, 1996; Wilson, 1996). In addition, opportunities to gain knowledge from participation in formal organizations such as employers' or after-school programs are limited. Thus, the ability to connect with and advance in formal organizations outside of their communities as adults is compromised in urban areas (Wilson, 1996).

In many urban neighborhoods, religious organizations are often among the strongest and most resourced institutions (Farnsley, 2003). They provides teens in resource-poor environments an important opportunity to learn how to take on leadership roles in a formal organization, which then can build organizational competencies that are important for non-religious settings.

Religious organizations also provide exposure to a rich intellectual tradition, developing and dispensing theological, philosophical, historical, and cultural knowledge. They provide opportunities for learning and performing music, dance, and drama, for example, as well as an organizational context where public speaking, organizational leadership, and professional skills can be developed (Smith, 2003). Lastly, they provide motivation to avoid risky behavior and to achieve academically. These resources are crucial in neighborhoods where schools are low-performing and under resourced; opportunities to access knowledge and skills from outside of the neighborhood context are limited; and the chances for engagement in risky behavior are plentiful.

Coping Abilities. Poor urban neighborhoods expose adolescents to stressful, violent, and difficult situations (Kiser, Donohue, Hodgkinson, Medoff, & Black, 2010). The lack of institutional investment in many urban neighborhoods also means that counseling and mental health services are difficult to obtain (Gonzalez, 2005).

Religion provides a number of coping mechanisms that are not typically available to youth in non-religious contexts (Smith, 2003). Religion fosters the belief that there is a powerful deity who is looking out for them and that suffering can be redemptive. It also includes specific practices, such as prayer, forgiveness, and reconciliation, that aid in coping with stress (Smith, 2003). These powerful coping mechanisms are particularly important in neighborhoods where life is stressful, difficult, and often marked by tragedy.

Religion also promotes strict behavioral codes and moral directives that youth often internalize to guide them in making personal life decisions (Smith, 2003). In communities where risky and destructive behavior among youth is common (which includes both urban and suburban communities), the internal moral convictions that come from religion are particularly important resources for coping with these temptations. To the extent that teens internalize moral directives, religious youth can avoid some exposure to some difficult and risky settings.

There have been few studies that comprehensively examine urban teens of all socioeconomic and ethno-racial backgrounds to assess the effects of religious belief, participation, and salience on their lives. More research is needed to examine the types of religious organizations that produce the most benefits for urban teens of various backgrounds and life circumstances. Particularly urgent is the need for understanding what types of religious activity are most effective in protecting the most vulnerable of our urban youth.

In summary, religious belief and participation provide resources that can serve as a countervailing force to many of the negative social effects of living in poor, divested urban neighborhoods. As religion is not helpful for all teens, religious organizations should be seen as a key resource in developing the potential of adolescents in urban areas. As poverty and inequality grow in our urban areas, and government continues to divest in the well-being of urban youth, religious organizations will only grow in importance for supporting these adolescents.

References

Bianchi, S. M. (1999). Feminization and juvenilization of poverty: Trends, relative risks, causes, and consequences. *Annual Review of Sociology, 25,* 307–33.

Bourdieu, P. (1984). *Distinction: A social critique of the judgment of taste.* Cambridge: Harvard University Press.

Bourdieu, P. (1986). The forms of capital. In J. Richardson (Ed.), *Handbook of theory and research for the sociology of education* (pp. 241–258). New York: Greenwood.

Brooks-Gunn, J., & Duncan, G. J. (1997). The effects of poverty on children. *Future of Children, 7,* 55–71.

Carleton, R. A., Esparza, P., Thaxter, P. J., & Grant, K. E. (2008). Stress, religious coping resources, and depressive symptoms in an urban adolescent sample. *Journal for the Scientific Study of Religion, 47, 113–121.*

Christerson, B., Edwards, K. L., & Emerson, M. O. (2005). *Against all odds: The struggle for racial integration in religious organizations.* New York: New York University Press.

Christerson, B., Edwards, K. L., & Flory, R. (2010). *Growing up in America: The power of race in the lives of teens.* Stanford, CA: Stanford University Press.

Chu, D. (2007). Religiosity and desistance from drug use. *Criminal Justice and Behavior, 34,* 661–679.

Conchas, G. Q., & Vigil, J. D. (2010). Multiple marginality and urban education: Community and school socialization among low-income Mexican descent youth. *Journal of Education for Students Placed at Risk, 15,* 51–65.

Dowling, E. M., Gestsdottir, S., Anderson, P. M., von Eye, A., Almerigi, J., & Lerner, R. M. (2004). Structural relations among spirituality, religiosity, and thriving in adolescence. *Applied Developmental Science, 8,* 7–16.

Eccles, J., & Gootman, J. A. (2002). *Community programs to promote youth development.* Washington, DC: National Research Council.

Edwards, K. L. (2008). *The elusive dream: The power of race in interracial churches.* New York: Oxford University Press.

Farkas, G. (1996). *Human capital or cultural capital? Ethnicity and poverty groups in an urban school district.* New York: Aldine De Gruyter.

Farnsley, A. E. (2003). *Rising expectations: Urban congregations, welfare reform, and civic life.* Bloomington: Indiana University Press.

Furrow, J. L., King, P. E., & White, K. (2004). Religion and positive youth development: identity, meaning, and prosocial concerns. *Applied Developmental Science, 8,* 17–26.

González, M. J. (2005). Access to mental health services: The struggle of poverty affected urban children of color. *Child & Adolescent Social Work Journal, 22,* 245–256.

Hadaway, C., Elifson, K. W., & Petersen, D. M. (1984). Religious involvement and drug use among urban adolescents. *Journal for the Scientific Study of Religion, 23,* 109–128.

Huebner, E. S., Suldo, S., Valois, R. F., Drane, J. W., & Zullig, K. (2004). Brief multidimensional students' life satisfaction scale: Sex, race, and grade effects for a high school sample. *Psychological Reports, 94,* 351–356.

Johnson, B. R., Larson, D. B., Li, S. D., & Jang, S. J. (2000). Escaping from the crime of inner cities: Church attendance and religious salience among disadvantaged youth. *Justice Quarterly, 17,* 377–391.

Kiser, L. J., Donohue, A., Hodgkinson, S., Medoff, D., & Black, M. M. (2010). Strengthening family coping resources: The feasibility of a multifamily group intervention for families exposed to trauma. *Journal of Traumatic Stress, 23,* 802–806.

Leventhal, T., Dupéré, V., and Brooks-Gunn, J. (2009). Neighborhood influences on adolescent development. In R. M. Lerner, & L. D. Steinberg (Eds.), *Handbook of adolescent psychology: Contextual influences on adolescent development* (pp. 524–558). Hoboken, NJ: John Wiley & Sons.

Lleras, C. (2008). Race, racial concentration, and the dynamics of educational inequality across urban and suburban schools. *American Educational Research Journal, 45,* 886–912.

Longest, K. C., & Vaisey, S. (2008). Control or conviction: Religion and adolescent initiation of marijuana use. *Journal of Drug Issues, 38*, 689–715.

Maimon, D., & Browning, C. R. (2010). Unstructured socializing, collective efficacy and violent behavior among urban youth. *Criminology, 48*, 443–474.

Massey, D. S., & Denton, N. A. (1993). *American apartheid: Segregation and the making of the underclass*. Cambridge: Harvard University Press.

McIntosh, W. A., Fitch, S. D., Wilson, J. B., & Nyberg, K. L. (1981). The effect of mainstream religious social controls on adolescent drug use in rural areas. *Review of Religious Research, 23*, 54–75.

Newacheck, P. W., Hughes, D. C., & Stoddard, J. J. (1996). Children's access to primary care: Differences by race, income, and insurance status. *Pediatrics, 97*, 26–32.

Pattillo-McCoy, M. (1999). *Black picket fences: Privilege and peril among the black middle class*. Chicago: University of Chicago.

Pargament, K. I. (1997). *The psychology of religion and coping*. New York: Guilford.

Petts, R. J., & Jolliff, A. (2008). Religion and adolescent depression: The impact of race and gender. *Review of Religious Research, 49*, 395–414.

Powell, K. B. (1997). Correlates of violent and nonviolent behavior among vulnerable inner-city youths. *Family & Community Health, 20*, 38–47.

Putnam, R. (2000). *Bowling alone*. New York: Simon and Schuster.

Rankin, B. H., & Quane, J. M. (2000). Neighborhood poverty and the social isolation of inner-city African Americans. *Social Forces, 79*, 139–164.

Smith, C. (2003). Theorizing religious affects among American adolescents. *Journal of the Society for the Scientific Study of Religion, 42*, 17–30.

Smith, C., & Faris, R. (2002). *Religion and the life attitudes and self-images of American adolescents*. Chapel Hill: University of North Carolina, National Study of Youth & Religion.

Teitelman, A., McDonald, C. C., Wiebe, D. J., Thomas, N., Guerra, T., Kassam-Adams, N., & Richmond, T. S. (2010). Youth's strategies for staying safe and coping. *Journal of Community Psychology, 38*, 874–885.

Van Dyke, C. J., Glenwick, D. S., Cecero, J. J. and Kim, S. (2009). The relationship of religious coping and spirituality to adjustment and psychological distress in urban early adolescents. *Mental Health, Religion & Culture, 12*, 369–383.

Wagener, L. M., Furrow, J. L., King, P. E., Leffert, N., & Benson, P. (2003). Religious involvement and developmental resources in youth. *Review of Religious Research, 44*, 271–284.

Wilson, W. J. (1996). *When work disappears: The world of the new urban poor*. New York: Knopf.

Wong, Y. J., Rew, L., & Slaikeu, K. (2006). A systematic review of recent research on adolescent religiosity/spirituality and mental health. *Issues in Mental Health Nursing, 27*, 161–183.

14

ADOLESCENTS AND ADULTS IN THE URBAN CONTEXT

Mentorship Relationships

Justin Perry, Eric W. Wallace, and Lisa Barto

Mentoring is a popular approach to promoting youth development (Walker, 2007). The sheer volume of publications on mentoring though is extremely difficult to systematically interpret. Thus, researchers have pointed to the discrepancy between public enthusiasm for youth mentoring and the supply of evidence to bolster the anecdotal rhetoric (Karcher, Kuperminc, Portwood, Siple, & Taylor, 2006). Rhodes and Lowe (2008), for example, described the hyperbolic claims about the effectiveness of mentoring as lending a "patina of superficiality to the field that discourages investigators from pursuing serious studies" (p. 10). With the heightened call for more rigorous impact studies and a deeper, contextualized understanding of the active mechanisms of change in mentoring, there is a concomitant demand for all youth service programs to show that they can improve academic achievement. As such, youth mentoring has come under scrutiny as a potential solution to high-stakes problems in K–12 education. If it can reduce risky behaviors, boost self-esteem, and increase social skills, can it also change school performance? If so, how does it happen, why does it happen, and under what conditions? Moreover, for whom does it work best and delivered by whom? With these questions in mind, the purpose of this chapter is to offer a scientifically minded approach to practice.

Youth Mentoring

What is Mentoring?

Because mentoring entails a host of principles and practices that naturally overlap with other youth experiences (e.g., coaching, tutoring, after-school clubs), it is difficult to distinguish what constitutes mentoring and differentiates it within the broader system of educational, mental health, and human services. Interventions or activities that might be called project-based learning, career education, college advising, workplace apprenticeships, academic support, cultural enrichment, or social skills building, might also be described as mentoring. In essence, the meaning of the word may be in danger of becoming "all things to all people."

Mentoring is an experience in which a non-parental/extra-familial adult engages in a supportive, caring relationship with a young person (persons) that consists of activities that can occur across multiple settings and modes of communication (e.g., school, face-to-face, online) and in different formats (e.g., individual, group, cross-age peers). According to Karcher and Nakkula (2010), a basic distinction is made between *developmental* and *instrumental* mentoring relationships. While all mentoring contains a mixture of developmental and instrumental activities, mentoring differs on emphasis and the degree to which one approach dominates the initial activities. In the developmental style, establishing a close, trusting bond with the mentee is central to the relationship, and goal-directed activities are often ancillary to the focus on the relationship. On the other hand, instrumental mentoring tends to focus on concrete goals (e.g., applying to college) before relational activities, such as "hanging out" or playing recreational games.

In the developmental camp, Spencer (2006) proposed using relational concepts from feminist theory: authenticity, empathy, companionship, and collaboration. Likewise, Rhodes, Spencer, Keller, Liang, and Noam (2006) suggest that effective mentoring is driven by three processes: (a) enhancing social relationships, (b) improving cognitive skills, and (c) promoting positive identity development. Since these processes may be driven by the centrality of the relationship, psychotherapeutic language, then, is often used to describe them, such as forging a "working alliance" between mentor and mentee or providing positive regard and emotional support.

Hamilton and Hamilton (2004, 2010) exemplify the instrumental camp, suggesting that while the relationship is important, it does not exist in the absence of goal-directed activities. Mentors and mentees meeting without goals will struggle to form a relationship. Hamilton et al. (2006) contend that "being able to do something that matters is a motivation to participate and a stimulus to forming a relationship naturally" (p. 728). Preparing for future careers is viewed as being highly salient to adolescent development, and thus stands as a natural aspect of mentoring activities during this period.

Does Youth Mentoring Work?

Unfortunately, the evidence does not paint an equally glowing portrait of results. As summarized in Table 14.1, three randomized controlled trials (RCTs) published after Rhodes and Lowe (2008) provide a sobering assessment. Across all studies, null or minimal effects for school-based mentoring (SBM) were found for a wide range of outcomes and none of the RCTs revealed sustained influences.

The summary of community-based mentoring (CBM) programs in Table 14.2 offers similar conclusions, yet, provides implications for the underlying processes and practices of CBM. In the Grossman and Rhodes (2002) RCT, the findings pertaining to the duration of the mentoring relationship and types of volunteers who were most likely to terminate make intuitive sense. But regardless of duration, grades were not improved by CBM. What is noteworthy in the DuBois, Holloway, Valentine, and

TABLE 14.1 Summary of randomized controlled trials for school-based mentoring programs

Authors	Intervention	Design	Mean Age	Youth Demographics	Main Impact Results
Bernstein et al. (2009)	Student Mentoring Program funded by U.S. Department of Education Average length of mentoring was 5.8 months; majority of mentors met on 1:1 basis	RCT of 32 programs	11.2 years Grades 4 to 8 (N = 2,573) Control group received no mentoring	47% male 41% Black 31% Hispanic 86% free/reduced lunch	• No significant impact on any of the three domains for total sample: academic achievement, interpersonal relationships and personal responsibility, and high-risk or delinquent behavior • Small positive effect size on academic outcomes for girls • Small negative effect size on pro-social behavior for boys (treatment group fared worse than the control group) • Medium positive effect size for decrease in truancy among students below age 12
Karcher (2008)	"SMILE" (School-Based Mentoring Program) Average dosage was 8 sessions	RCT of 19 schools (N = 516) Control group was supportive services alone	Not reported Grades 5 to 12	% of gender not reported % of race/ethnicity not reported, although author reported it was predominately Latino % of SES not reported	• Small positive effect size for connectedness to peers, self-esteem, and social support • No significant impact on grades or social skills • Elementary school boys and high school girls benefited the most
Herrera et al. (2011)	Big Brothers Big Sisters School-Based Mentoring Program Average length of mentoring was 4.9 months by 9-month assessment; average of 3.1 sessions per month	RCT of 1,139 youth in 10 cities Control group received no mentoring	11.23 years Grades 4 to 9	54% female 63% "minority" 69% free/reduced lunch	• No significant impact on classroom effort, self-worth, relationships with parents, teachers or peers, or problem behaviors • Small effect size on teacher-report school performance, attitudes, and youth-reported perceptions of academic abilities • Gains in academic outcomes were not sustained into the second school year

TABLE 14.2 Summary of community–based mentoring programs studies

Authors	Intervention	Design	Mean Age	Youth Demographics	Main Impact Results
Grossman and Rhodes (2002)	Big Brothers Big Sisters Mentoring Programs	RCT of 1,138 urban youth at 8 agencies	12.25 years Grade levels not reported	62.4% male 57.5% "minority" 40% lived in homes receiving food stamps or public assistance	• Relationships that lasted a year or longer reported largest number of improvements • Relationships that terminated in a short period of time reported decrements in functioning • Older youth, youth referred for services, or youth with history of abuse were most likely to be in early terminations • Married volunteers between ages 26 to 30 and volunteers with lower incomes were most likely to terminate early • Regardless of length of relationship, no significant impact on grades • Small positive treatment effect sizes, Even for outcomes analyzed for relationships that lasted a year
DuBois et al. (2002a)	Not applicable	Meta-analysis of 55 studies of mentoring programs	Not reported Grade levels not reported	22 studies were majority female; 20 studies were majority male 20 studies late childhood or early adolescence; 21 studies middle or late adolescence 37 studies had no low–SES; 22 studies did	• Small average positive treatment effects • Effects are significantly enhanced when more theory–based and empirically–based best practices are utilized and when strong mentoring relationships are formed • At–risk or disadvantaged youth are most likely to benefit from mentoring programs • Poor implementation can have adverse effects on at–risk youth

Cooper (2002a) meta-analysis is that program effects were enhanced when theory-based practices (i.e., > 6 versus < than 6) and empirically based practices (i.e., > 4 versus < 4) were utilized more frequently, and when strong mentoring relationships were formed. Conversely, DuBois et al. (2002a) found that poor implementation led to adverse consequences for at-risk and environmentally disadvantaged youth. While speculative, it is reasonable to infer that "poor implementation" coincides with poor fidelity of program implementation and/or lack of competent services, thus resulting in a lower quality of mentoring.

Overall, the literature supports the benefits that mentoring can provide with respect to socioemotional or psychological outcomes (e.g., self-esteem) and alleviating high-risk behaviors (e.g., delinquency). The strength of this evidence, however, is modest at best, typically showing small to moderate effect sizes. Moreover, as illustrated in Table 14.1, the consistency of the evidence is poor and perhaps the most pertinent conclusion is that mentoring does not seem to be effective in terms of improving academic outcomes such as grades, attendance, school engagement, or motivation.

Ingredients of Change

Above any other mechanism of change thought to explain the varying effects of mentoring, the duration of the mentoring relationship has received an extensive amount of attention. In general, studies reveal that relationship quality, as reported by the mentee, is linked with duration, such that a more positive experience that youth feel in the relationship tends to lead to a longer amount of contact (e.g., DuBois, Neville, Parra, & Pugh-Lilly, 2002b). Unfortunately, about half of all mentoring relationships terminate early after only a few months (Styles & Morrow, 1992), which can be highly detrimental, possibly leading to significant declines in self-worth or increases in alcohol use (Grossman & Rhodes, 2002).

Thus, it would follow that when mentors meet for longer periods of time, mentees may enjoy greater benefits. Yet, there is still no evidence to indicate that meeting, say, for two years, produces better results than meeting for one year. In our view, the realities governing youth mentoring programs are multi-faceted and cannot be reduced to how much time is spent between mentor and mentee. The characteristics of the mentee and mentor, as well as all of the factors that can build and strengthen the quality of the relationship (e.g., ongoing supervision, parent involvement) are more likely candidates that can explain variations in the potency of mentoring.

Matching characteristics based on the race of mentors and mentees have also received considerable attention, but this has been met with inconclusive results. According to Jucovy's (2002) review, race, in itself, does not seem to play a significant role in determining the quality of mentoring relationships. Dubois et al.'s (2002a) meta-analysis reinforces this conclusion, as same-race matching was not a significant moderator of mentoring program outcomes. However, neither was same-gender nor the matching of youth and mentor interests, which is inconsistent with standard matching practices in many programs.

Aside from duration, race, and gender, Karcher, Nakkula, and Harris (2005), examined a broader array of factors that influenced mentoring relationships among high school students mentoring elementary school mentees. Relationship quality was measured from the mentor perspective; the authors found that mentors' self-efficacy and mentees' support-seeking behaviors at six months were the significant predictors in the final model, which also included program quality (amount of training mentors received), parental involvement of the mentee (how supportive parents were on mentee participation), mentee disposition (mental health characteristics and risk status of the mentee), and mentor motivation (degree to which mentors were motivated to grow and to have a positive experience for themselves). While limited by a small sample size, these findings are consistent with a previous study (Parra, DuBois, Neville, & Pugh-Lilly, 2002).

Summary

To date, the benefits of youth mentoring appear to be modest, mixed, and short-lived. A major void in the field is the lack of generalizability, for the vast majority of research has been confined to children, with mean ages typically falling between 11 and 13 years. With the possible exception of elementary girls (Bernstein, Dun Rappaport, Olsho, Hunt, & Levin, 2009), there is no evidence of gains in academic achievement. And though attitudes such as a sense of school connectedness may be increased, these changes do not gain traction powerful enough to translate into improvements in achievement. Despite these shortcomings, the potential for youth mentoring to assume an important role in educational reform remains strong.

Charting a Course for Future Directions

Many points summarized in Table 14.3 are hard to dispute. Indeed, it is difficult to propose how a mentoring program can maximize its impact in the absence of high-quality training and ongoing support, monitoring, and supervision. While these are useful guidelines, the question still remains as to what type of mentoring practices work best for whom, delivered by whom, and under what conditions. Equally crucial to future inquiry is explaining why such practices bring about change in the ways that they do, and how to maximize their effects.

Because adolescence requires different developmental changes and psychosocial tasks of adjustment, what may be effective for mentoring programs among children, even those at 12 or 13 years of age, is not necessarily transferrable to this population, especially as they enter upper grades of high school. In the remaining sections, we discuss future directions in research and practice that focus on targeting academic achievement.

Work-Based Mentoring

Adolescents may prefer instrumental mentoring relationships that emphasize goal-directed activities (e.g., learning an occupational skill) rather than developmental mentoring relationships that stress relational activities seeking to establish a close emotional connection. The Hamiltons and colleagues (Hamilton & Hamilton, 2002;

TABLE 14.3 Summary of recommendations for best practices in mentoring programs

Authors	*Recommendations*
Karcher and Herrera (2007)	• Mentor support and training, staff support, and school support on an ongoing basis is essential
	• In order to lengthen the duration of school-based matches, it is crucial to match youth as early in the school year as possible
	• Establish programs or connections with feeder schools to help ensure that youth continue to receive mentoring despite school transitions
	• Programs should establish procedures for closure, train mentors on its importance, and help mentors implement termination procedures
	• Maintaining summer contact may help increase match longevity and quality, which does not have to involve face-to-face meetings
Rhodes and Lowe (2008)	• Develop and empirically validate training protocols
	• To reduce volunteer attrition, set reasonable goals for number of youth to be served and seek out technical assistance when needed
	• Connect mentoring with other youth settings, such as after-school programs, summer camps, or church youth groups
Deutsch and Spencer (2009)	• Select mentors with some experience working with youth
	• Provide support for parent involvement
	• Provide systematic monitoring of the implementation of program practices
	• Use community settings rather than relying solely on in-school contact
	• Set up clear expectations for frequency of contact between mentors and youth

Hamilton et al., 2006) have created a compelling argument for this perspective. The rationale is *not* that instrumental mentoring should strictly consist of concrete activities that are somehow anti-relational, but that such activities are the appropriate starting point to build an emotional connection in the first place, especially for adolescents in high school who are more invested in the school-to-work transition, or college and career readiness. The findings indicating superior effects of work-based mentoring (DuBois et al., 2002a; Rhodes, 2008) over school- and community-based mentoring seem to implicitly support this argument.

To illustrate, Hamilton and Hamilton (2002) interviewed 42 mentors and 26 mentees in a work-based program. The most typical behavior in their study was for mentors to work with their mentees on developing job-specific competence. Outside of this core activity, however, half of the mentors worked with their mentees on what might be called "relational" outcomes of well-being (i.e., self-confidence), while 74% of the mentors assisted mentees on exploring career pathways. These finding are consistent with other qualitative studies on work-based mentoring. Noonan, Hall, and Blustein (2007) found that work-based mentors encouraged mentees from low-income urban high schools to consider how future careers are relevant to their performance in school.

Linnehan (2001, 2003) conducted two studies on work-based mentoring with regard to their effect on academic outcomes and perceptions of school relevance. In 2001, he looked at 202 African American youth who wanted to be involved in a work-based mentoring program, and a control group. Linnehan found that participation alone did not lead to improvements in grade-point-average or attendance; however, duration of participation had significant impact on both outcomes. At follow-up in 2003, Linnehan included a question in his survey to identify students who had "informal" workplace mentors during the period in question. All of the students who worked had higher levels of self-esteem, but students with mentors (whether formal or informal) had elevated attitudes of endorsing the relevance of school compared to those who worked without a mentor.

The utility of work-based mentoring makes developmental sense given that career exploration is inextricable from the process of identity exploration during adolescence (Malanchuk, Messersmith, & Eccles, 2010). More specifically, helping adolescents participate in a meaningful, purposeful approach to vocational exploration can improve school engagement and, in turn, lead to improvements in academic performance (Perry, Liu, & Pabian, 2010). Indeed, the more adolescents are invested in the process of preparing for their future careers, the better they will do in school. A number of psychologists have argued that youth become unmotivated to succeed in school because they do not perceive a meaningful connection between what they are learning and what they value in terms of their future goals (Perry, 2008). Thus, work-based mentoring can help counteract the boredom and eventual withdrawal from school efforts that often characterize youth in urban schools.

School-Based Mentoring

School-based mentoring (SBM) has witnessed an unprecedented expansion over the past decade. Its growth has been so rapid that it has surpassed CBM as the most common practice. Despite the drawbacks that are commonly cited, such as having less time in a "school year" (6 to 7 months) to meet, or being constrained by class schedules, there are many advantages that appeal to agencies and schools, such as that SBM:

- offers a structured, predictable, supervised environment to mentor youth;
- circumvents the complications of having to coordinate transportation to meet;
- can reach underserved youth with serious academic, social, or behavioral problems; and
- allows for greater control over supervision of staff.

Among adolescents, even the stated disadvantages of SBM may not be so problematic. For example, not having access to places in the school to congregate is an unlikely burden for most adolescents who would prefer to sit down and engage in specific goals, work independently on problem-solving tasks, or participate in social conversation with peers. Indeed, a key merit of SBM is the opportunity it affords for youth to engage in peer interactions, which can provide mentors valuable insight into the adolescent's social skills and relationships. Because peers figure prominently in adolescence, peer relationships, support, and connectedness are appropriate outcomes for SBM. Previous research suggests that SBM improves connection to and engagement with school, as well as connectedness to peers (Herrera, Grossman, Kauh, & McMaken, 2011; Karcher, 2008).

According to Karcher and Herrera (2007), SBM mentors report engaging in academic activities more frequently than CBM mentors. When targeting older adolescents, a ratio favoring academic activities over non-academic activities may be expected. While such an imbalance may deter adolescents from participating due to fears of being seen as under-achievers, there is no evidence to support this idea. Moreover, it remains unclear whether or not a session of SBM is less effective than CBM. The presumed constraints of SBM may actually create ideal conditions for mentors and mentees to be more engaged. As Karcher and Herrera noted, it is possible "that an hour in SBM is much more focused and productive than a given hour in CBM, simply because the mentor and youth know that they have very little time together, so they use it more wisely" (p. 5). Based on a survey in three Big Brothers Big Sisters programs, Herrera (2004) did not confirm speculations that SBM takes away "fun time" or developmental activities. On the contrary, 85% of the mentors spent time on social activities, and about 33% attended school activities like sports or assemblies. The sample was restricted to children in the 3rd to 5th grades, so the findings cannot be generalized to adolescents.

Given that our review did not find evidence that SBM improves academic achievement, we cannot assert that there are any promising SBM programs. Because most research has been in elementary schools, it would also be premature to suggest that if existing SBM programs, or any other type of mentoring program, were implemented with better quality and fidelity we would see positive gains for adolescents. The more plausible scenario is that what we currently know about best practices in the field will need to be modified and tailored to fit the tasks of adolescence and the conditions of urban high schools. In our view, SBM may function as a viable alternative for youth who do not have access to work-based mentoring, or attend schools that are not linked to such services. We anticipate that part of the future of SBM research among urban adolescents will involve experimenting with innovative formats such as group mentoring.

Group Mentoring in Schools

From both a developmental and a practical standpoint, this relatively untested model of mentoring deserves greater attention among programs that target adolescents in school settings. Instead of the conventional dyad, group mentoring is, according to Herrera, Vang, and Gale (2002), "based on the idea that volunteers who interact regularly with small groups of youth can fulfill the role of a mentor—to be a trusted counselor or guide—by developing a number of successful and productive relationships simultaneously" (p. ii). As such, not only does group mentoring have the power to reach more youth, but naturally aligns with the adolescent sense of social self that forms in relation to peers. Without question, part of adolescent development and the school-to-work transition is to acquire 21st-century skills that enable individuals to effectively work/cooperate in groups and collaborate on achieving common goals. Similar to the practice of group counseling or psychotherapy, group mentoring requires parallel processes to occur in creating a "culture" or "cohesiveness" that not only fosters a connection between the mentor and each person, but among the group as a whole.

In one study, Herrera et al. (2002) found that group mentors reported the central goals being aimed at helping youth get along with others and teaching them behavioral skills. In their study, the average size of groups was ten mentees; activities spanned a wide range of topics (e.g., health, leadership, science, music), with an average meeting time of 21 hours per month. Moreover, 56% of mentors reported meeting in a school, with the rest meeting in multiple locations (e.g., church, community center). Consistent with the most often reported goal, the most frequently reported benefit cited by mentors and mentees was improvement in social skills; improvements in relationships with teachers, parents, and friends were also reported. Consistent with much of the research reported so far in this chapter, in terms of academic gains, results were less impressive.

School–University Urban Partnerships

We submit that a wealth of opportunities exists for joining with educational stakeholders in reducing dropout rates and improving academic achievement through urban school–university partnerships. In this arrangement, which is still far from commonplace in mentoring programs, the resources and facilities of each institution are brought together to achieve common goals and serve mutual interests. One example of how to carry such a vision out is the usage of university faculty and students (undergraduate or graduate) to collaboratively design, implement, evaluate, and sustain a comprehensive approach, with youth mentoring serving as only one of multiple interventions that are coordinated. This scenario could involve university students, for example, entering an urban school (during school or after school) and working with teachers or school staff to provide mentoring activities in conjunction with other services. In theory, this would be highly cost-effective because the services provided would count as part of a student's academic or training requirements, such as service learning, practicum, or a form of student-teaching.

Aside from being cost-effective, aligning mentoring programs with universities can become sustainable because they directly benefit the learning and training needs of higher education. Students in teacher education programs, school counseling, or social work, to name just a few professions, would gain useful competencies from learning how to develop mentoring relationships under the supervision of faculty. Through the relationship, teacher candidates and other students would be able to understand the mentee's experience, school, and culture. Joining mentoring programs with universities also provides a mechanism for getting faculty, with much needed theoretical and empirical skills, involved in every stage of a mentoring program.

A Framework for Guiding Future Research

It is a tenuous proposition to think that any single mentoring program could make a long-lasting impact on an outcome as difficult to change as achievement. Even the most potent mentoring program, or package of programs, could not swing the tides of achievement alone. As such, we concur with other scholars (Karcher et al., 2006) who advocate to investigate ways in which mentors can connect youth to resources (e.g., after-school programs, youth groups) and to examine how effective mentoring is when delivered in a multi-service package.

In Figure 14.1, we visually summarize the detailed and intricate process of "capturing the magic," as Deutsch & Spencer (2009) coined it, involved in the mentoring relationship. At the same time, researchers should also pay attention to systematically testing the manipulation or natural occurrence of independent variables that exist at the program level. While achievement tests are important indicators, they should not be evaluated at the expense of other academic outcomes (e.g., attendance, grades, dropout rates) that matter to stakeholders, and perhaps represent even greater threats to the educational success and future quality of life among adolescents. As we portray in Figure 14.1, examining these many avenues of research would ideally occur within an experimental or quasi-experimental design so that threats to internal validity are minimized.

We propose that a second and third strategy are required in order to accumulate the most persuasive body of evidence. In a *comparative approach*, mentoring programs of different type, setting, format, or model (as well as any combination) would be tested for their relative impact. Scholars would want to know whether one program is superior to another program(s), and if combining more than one program yields greater impact than a single program. In an *additive approach*, the attachment of a mentoring program to a non-mentoring program, or package of non-mentoring programs, would enable researchers to evaluate the "added value" of mentoring in the context of co-occurring interventions. This is perhaps the most exciting approach because it places mentoring programs within the broader system of services (e.g., tutoring, counseling, after-school programming, family outreach) that many urban youth, especially those identified as at-risk for academic failure or dropping out, will probably be receiving in most situations.

Conclusions

It is difficult to speculate how mentoring programs would compare, or add value, to the impact of other academic and social service programs that are well-known and well-researched. Despite these uncertainties, we believe that the future of youth mentoring must break out of its normal delivery systems and paradigms; otherwise, it will become perceived as an unfulfilled panacea that cannot be taken seriously as an answer to the major academic problems urban youth face.

The evidence for the benefits of youth mentoring is still, overall, positive for a number of important psychosocial and behavioral outcomes, even if the benefits are often modest. Many leading scholars are doing outstanding work in raising the

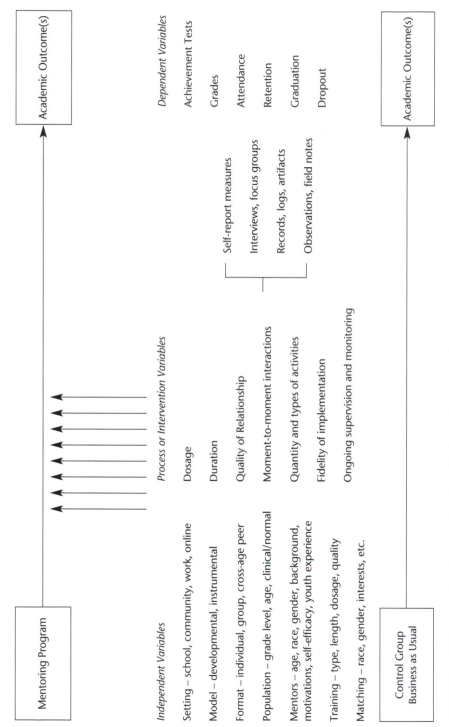

FIGURE 14.1 A Process-oriented approach to investigating a single mentoring program.

scientific rigor of youth mentoring so that it can be used with a greater level of confidence and specificity. Guided by a balanced perspective, we hope that the directions we discussed will build on these contributions, generate critical dialogue, and take youth mentoring programs to the next level of theoretical and scientific maturation.

References

Bernstein, L., Dun Rappaport, C., Olsho, L., Hunt, D., & Levin, M. (2009). *Impact evaluation of the U.S. Department of Education's student mentoring program: Final report.* Washington, DC: U.S. Department of Education, Institute of Education Sciences, National Center for Education Evaluation and Regional Assistance.

Deutsch, N. L., & Spencer, R. (2009). Capturing the magic: Assessing the quality of youth mentoring relationships. *New Directions for Youth Development, 121,* 47–70.

Dubois, D. L., Holloway, B. E., Valentine, J. C., & Cooper, H. (2002a). Effectiveness of mentoring programs for youth: A meta-analytic review. *American Journal of Community Psychology, 30,* 157–197.

DuBois, D. L., Neville, H. A., Parra, G. R., & Pugh-Lilly, A. O. (2002b). Testing a new model of mentoring. *New Directions for Youth Development, 93,* 21–57.

Grossman, J. B., & Rhodes, J. E. (2002). The test of time: Predictors and effects of duration in youth mentoring relationships. *American Journal of Community Psychology, 30,* 199–219.

Hamilton, M. A., & Hamilton, S. F. (2002). Why mentoring in the workplace works. *New Directions for Youth Development, 93,* 59–89.

Hamilton, S. F., & Hamilton, M. A. (2004). Contexts for mentoring: Adolescent-adult relationships in workplaces and communities. In R. M. Lerner, & L. Steinberg (Eds.), *Handbook of adolescent psychology* (pp. 395–428). New York: Wiley.

Hamilton, S. F., & Hamilton, M. A. (2010). Building mentoring relationships. *New Directions for Youth Development, 126,* 141–144.

Hamilton, S. F., Hamilton, M. A., Hirsch, B. J., Hughes, J., King, J., & Maton, K. (2006). Community contexts for mentoring. *Journal of Community Psychology, 34,* 727–746.

Herrera, C. (2004). *School-based mentoring: A closer look.* Philadelphia: Public/Private Ventures.

Herrera, C., Grossman, J. B., Kauh, T. J., & McMaken, J. (2011). Mentoring in schools: An impact study of Big Brothers Big Sisters School-Based Mentoring. *Child Development, 82,* 346–361.

Herrera, C., Vang, Z., & Gale, L.Y. (2002). *Group mentoring: A study of mentoring groups in three programs.* Philadelphia: Public/Private Ventures.

Jucovy, L. (2002). *Same-race and cross-race matching.* Philadelphia: Public/Private Ventures.

Karcher, M. J. (2008). The Study of Mentoring in the Learning Environment (SMILE): A randomized evaluation of the effectiveness of school-based mentoring. *Prevention Science, 9,* 99–113.

Karcher, M. J., & Herrera, C. (2007). School-based mentoring. *Youth mentoring: Research in action, 1,* 3–16.

Karcher, M. J., Kuperminc, G. P., Portwood, S. G., Sipe, C. L., & Taylor, A. S. (2006). Mentoring programs: A framework to inform program development, research, and evaluation. *Journal of Community Psychology, 34,* 709–725.

Karcher, M. J., & Nakkula, M. J. (2010). Youth mentoring with a balanced focus, shared purpose, and collaborative interactions. *New Directions for Youth Development, 126,* 13–32.

Karcher, M. J., Nakkula, M. J., & Harris, J. (2005). Developmental mentoring match characteristics: Correspondence between mentors' and mentees' assessments of relationship quality. *Journal of Primary Prevention, 26,* 93–110.

Linnehan, F. (2001). The relation of a work-based mentoring program to the academic performance and behavior of African-American students. *Journal of Vocational Behavior, 59,* 310–325.

Linnehan, F. (2003). A longitudinal study of work-based adult-youth mentoring. *Journal of Vocational Behavior, 63,* 40–54.

Malanchuk, M., Messersmith, E. E., & Eccles, J. S. (2010). The ontogeny of career identities in adolescence. In S. Schulman, & J. E. Nurmi (Eds.), *The role of goals in navigating individual lives during emerging adulthood. New Directions for Child and Adolescent Development, 130,* 97–110.

Noonan, A. E., Hall, G., & Blustein, D. L. (2007). Urban adolescents experience of social class in relationships at work. *Journal of Vocational Behavior, 70,* 542–560.

Parra, G. R., DuBois, D. L., Neville, H. A., & Pugh-Lilly, A. O. (2002). Mentoring relationships for youth: Investigation of a process-oriented model. *Journal of Community Psychology, 30,* 367–388.

Perry, J. C. (2008). School engagement among urban youth of color: Criterion pattern effects of vocational exploration and racial identity. *Journal of Career Development, 34,* 397–422.

Perry, J. C., Liu, X., & Pabian, Y. (2010). School engagement as a mediator of academic performance among urban youth: The role of career preparation, parental career support, and teacher support. *The Counseling Psychologist, 38,* 269–295.

Rhodes, J. E. (2008). Improving youth mentoring interventions through research-based practice. *American Journal of Community Psychology, 41,* 35–42.

Rhodes, J., & Lowe, S. R. (2008). Youth mentoring and resilience: Implications for practice. *Child Care in Practice, 14,* 9–17.

Rhodes, J. E., Spencer, R., Keller, T. E., Liang, B., & Noam, G. (2006). A model for the influence of mentoring relationships on youth development. *Journal of Community Psychology, 34,* 691–707.

Spencer, R. (2006). Understanding the mentoring process between adolescents and adults. *Youth and Society, 37,* 287–315.

Styles, M. B., & Morrow, K. V. (1992). *Understanding how youth and elders form relationships: A study of four Linking Lifetimes programs.* Philadelphia: Public/Private Ventures.

Walker, G. (2007). *Mentoring, policy, and politics.* Philadelphia: Public/Private Ventures.

15

PARTNERSHIPS BETWEEN SCHOOLS, TEACHERS, CHILDREN, FAMILIES, AND COMMUNITIES

Robert E. Lee, Cristina Pacione-Zayas, Sara Bosch,
Keri Blackwell, and Dakota M. Pawlicki

Public schools are pushed beyond their means to provide high-quality education. It is every administrator's mission to raise student achievement while providing a well-rounded education in a nurturing environment. However, this is no easy task in urban schools serving communities marked by chronic poverty, violence and high percentages of students with socio-emotional needs. In these cases, the path to student achievement must come through the school working in partnership with the community it serves. A school that makes use of such resources extends its walls into the community to expand academic supports.

This chapter will specify how community-based partnerships that are strategically aligned help reclaim public schools, and positively impact adolescent development, as well as encourage meaningful engagement in education with residents in the neighborhood. Organizationally, we will focus each thematic area around one partner stakeholder and highlight exemplary cases that provide experiences in situ to each author's respective effort in Chicago while working to develop what we term a "community of choice," or, previously neglected and disenfranchised neighborhoods that are engaging in strategic and genuine transformative development led by the community in the best interest of all stakeholders. In other contexts, community renewal has been synonymous with gentrification and pushing out residents to make way for more economically stable and upwardly mobile households and businesses. Conversely, our notion of communities of choice places those who are typically undermined, marginalized or ignored as leaders and change agents in their neighborhood. While the work described is based in Chicago neighborhoods, the themes resonate nationally across other urban communities.

Community-based Organizations

Community-based organizations come in various forms and lead multiple initiatives usually from a "grassroots" or bottom-up approach. While some focus on campaigns to address community-identified social justice issues, others provide direct services. Community members perceive these organizations as valuable hubs that bridge the gap between neighbors, families, schools, universities, businesses and social services. The work spans from connecting residents to public resources, offering educational classes to policy advocacy in local government.

A comprehensive community-based organization engages stakeholders in a myriad of ways such as participant, member, partner and/or employer. Although organizations represent an entity, the heartbeat lies in the collective vision and action of the organization's leaders, participants, members and its external partners. By convening community stakeholders to identify and address issues, the power of community-based organizations amplifies the clamor of community residents who are not always poised to take on social issues alone.

> *Case Study:* The Logan Square Neighborhood Association (LSNA) provides one example of what can be accomplished through intensive organizing within one neighborhood. Historically, LSNA has fostered affordable housing, improved neighborhood safety, and enhanced economic development in a largely immigrant Chicago community.
>
> LSNA launched its education organizing work in the early 1990s when it spearheaded a community effort to end school overcrowding. LSNA played a crucial role in bringing together schools to address this common problem. The campaign resulted in five new annexes and two new middle schools. Just as important, the campaign both demonstrated LSNA's power as a community organization and built a foundation of mutual trust among the principals, teachers, parent leaders and LSNA staff who had been involved in the campaign and witnessed the results.
>
> From this groundwork arose other programs that have affirmed immigrant families, particularly mothers, as crucial contributors to the life and success of public schools. LSNA enjoys close working relationships with nine schools in its service area (five of which are community learning centers), sponsoring several programs that provide critical opportunities to engage in school culture.

While all schools have the potential, transforming into a community learning center or "community school" is essential to start the process. The Coalition for Community Schools (2003) defines a community school as a school where partnerships between the school and community resources integrate academics, health and social services, youth and community development to improve the quality of academic learning, build stronger families, and develop healthier communities. Thus, the community school strategy repurposes the role of a neighborhood school as a community hub for resources, services, and classes that support holistic youth, family, and community development, including keeping their doors open beyond school hours for students, as well as parents/community members at large. Overall, the community school model boasts improvement in four general areas: student learning, family engagement, school effectiveness, and community vitality (Walen, 2007).

As a national movement, Chicago boasts over 150 community schools. Grown out of the successful model developed by the Children's Aid Society in New York City, Chicago's community schools initiative unites each school with one lead-partner agency (LPA) that collaborates with a site-based team of school personnel and parents to craft services that address an array of issues: Academic achievement, health and social services, violence prevention, post-secondary preparation, and civic engagement. The role of the LPA in this collaboration is to not only provide direct services, but also act as an umbrella for out-of-school programming, parent/guardian resources, and extended learning options. Schools, children, families, and neighborhood residents alike come to view its surrounding community from an asset-based lens, inviting existing resources into the building to meet student and family needs and enhance learning.

Furthermore, the community school model also redefines the community as a whole. Densely populated urban settings tend to rely on neighborhood schools as the only educational option. Thus, neighborhood schools are poised to become a natural space for community services. However, across the nation, neighborhood schools have fallen under criticism for not meeting national benchmarks on standardized tests. Conversely, the privatized models of charter schools have been championed as a viable alternative to underperforming public schools. While politicians sway popular opinion toward these education alternatives, such neighborhood schools are often left behind. Unfortunately, they are painted as a place for students and families who have no other options. In order to turn this negative perception into one that represents a community's school of choice, a school must offer success in student achievement, and resources to support both the family and whole child. When schools partner with community-based organizations to tackle these issues, they are engaged in community development that reaffirms the original notion of schools as centralized locations to provide support to all community members.

Case Study: Madero Middle School is a prime example of the community schools model, especially because of their partnership with the local community-based organization, Enlace Chicago. The partnership between Madero and Enlace has raised student achievement over a two-year period. Since Enlace began offering programs at Madero, standardized test scores in reading and science have risen by 8.1% and math scores have increased by 6.1%. While these gains are modest, they reflect the most significant improvement the school has seen in the past 10 years and have taken the school from not meeting Adequate Yearly Progress on several national benchmarks to reaching more of them.

In addition to academic support, the school has increased the social-emotional support given to students through mentorship and counseling services. Students identified as "high risk" were able to make significant personal growth while they improved attendance, behavior, and levels of self-control. Other students showed dramatic increases in self-esteem, building confidence and creating friendships through enrichment classes.

Parent involvement has also increased. Parents can further their own education while also participating in workshops, seminars, and adult education classes [e.g., GED,[1] ESL (English as a second language), computer literacy]. Because these opportunities are not limited to community members who currently have students enrolled at Madero, the benefits help create a positive view of the school from the vantage point of the community at large.

The community school staff is a go-to resource for students, families, and school staff alike. Because Enlace is a widespread community-based organization, they also have outreach initiatives happening in several areas. This has allowed the school to provide violence prevention, economic development, and other resources to the families and students in need. Altogether, the school is beginning to change in the eyes of the community. Both students and parents are more satisfied with the services provided and community members look to the school as a resource and a pillar for the neighborhood.

In reality, neighborhood schools are better equipped to serve local students than organizations that are not neighborhood-based as they can tailor their programs to meet the unique needs of the community. Schools of choice within a community not only have a high record of student achievement, but they offer programs for families that are convenient and relevant.

For example, Chicago Public Schools (CPS) continues to strive for accelerated student achievement while having one of the shortest school days in the nation. According to the National Center for Education Statistics (2006) the average school day is 6.7 hours while CPS students attend classes for 5.75 hours. This shortened day puts students at a fundamental disadvantage as shown through standardized test scores.

As Chicago students fall farther behind, they have the greatest need for individualized assistance through differentiated instruction, a type of instruction that meets the needs of all students in a developmentally appropriate way (Wormeli, 2006). Differentiated instruction is necessary to ensure a learning environment that is safe for students to seek challenges and risks, and allow students to construct their own meanings of content (Tomlinson & Kalbfleisch, 1998). However, in shortened days, teachers have difficulty finding time to implement this differentiation. Similar challenges arise with fine arts. Proponents of whole-child education stress the importance of arts in the learning process, but there are continuous barriers to achieving this in most schools. Time, budget, and high pressure on standardized tests eliminate art, sports, and other programs considered not to be critical to student achievement. In a community of choice, however, schools can overcome these obstacles by offering a multitude of programs after school that address the need for differentiated instruction and enrichment courses. This also fits well within the middle school philosophy that highlights the importance of providing integrated topics and programs for students to explore. Adolescents should explore different aspects of academics, express themselves through various creative outlets, and engage in activities that help them learn about the world and themselves (National Middle School Association, 2003).

---

1   GED: General Equivalency Degree (or diploma); certifies that passing score means the test taker has American or Canadian high school level academic skills.

Case Study: Madero Middle School compensates for short school days by becoming a community school and offering two types of academic classes after school. Students who are not meeting standards on benchmark tests are targeted for remedial instruction, while students who are achieving are offered classes in enrichment. School staff from the regular school day work in conjunction with the instructors from the after-school program to complete a seamless transition from one part of the instructional day to the other.

The Community School program at Madero adds an average of 17 hours of learning a week. During the 2010–2011 school year, almost 100% of the activities offered included reading and/or math enrichment. Of these same activities, 69% focused on cultural enrichment, 21% on art and music, and 11% offered physical education and health programming.

To track the success, several measures including standardized test data, student grades, teacher and student surveys, and attendance are used. Forty two percent of students increased their math and reading grades within one academic year. Teacher surveys on student participation and achievement show even more significant improvement. After the program's second year, 73% of students showed improvement in homework completion and 69% were more likely to come to school motivated to learn. Teachers reported that 51% of the students showed improved behavior and 63% got along better with their peers.

Bridging the Gap to Higher Education

According to the Bureau of Labor Statistics (2003), substantial gaps in educational attainment across income groups are reported. In Little Village where Madero Middle School is located, approximately 15,000 K-8 students attend 17 public schools in the community and Madero students feed into an overcrowded David G. Farragut Career Academy, which has a graduation rate of 55% and a yearly dropout rate of 17%. These gaps in the local community statistics are representative of similar statistics found in other under-resourced communities and demonstrate the need to address access to higher education for underrepresented groups.

Research (Blanco, 2003) has identified several factors as possible culprits for the lower college enrollment and graduation rates of underrepresented groups, such as: Quality and accessibility (i.e., school facilities, academic counselors); individual setbacks (i.e., family obligations, neighborhood conditions, financial hardship); and cultural differences (i.e., language barriers). Due to such variables, underrepresented adolescents are not only more likely to be academically unprepared to meet the challenges of college-level work, but also less likely to prepare for these opportunities in the first place. Furthermore, even if they are aware of the options, they may not have the familial guidance necessary to successfully navigate the college entrance and financial aid application process, as many of these students often are first generation college-goers in the family.

To help equip more parents with accurate information, community schools can partner with local institutions of higher education to offer workshops that explain the benefits, attainability and pathways to a college education. These workshops relieve some of the intimidation that parents often feel regarding the financing of a college education.

For students who enroll in college, many face cultural, academic, and financial difficulties. Many of these students transition from high schools where most of the student population has dissimilar demographics to the higher education institutions where they are an isolated minority. This isolation causes detrimental reactions that impede success, such as: Lack of self-confidence and inappropriate expectations about college; lack of connection to the college community; unfamiliar cultural contexts; and limited support from family members who also do not understand college requirements (Garcia, 2001). These types of attitudinal factors and college experiences relate to student success.

The attainment of a college education has been linked to positive outcomes. College graduates have higher levels of civic engagement, such as volunteering or voting and are less likely to be unemployed or incarcerated (College Board, 2005). According to the Bureau of Labor Statistics (2003), college graduates earned substantially more than high school graduates and high school dropouts, earning $982 per week, $551 per week, and $379 per week, respectively. Due to the benefits associated with higher education, it is not surprising that college is viewed as one fundamental pathway to social justice.

However, not all sectors of society have or are able to take advantage of this pathway. In fact, ample evidence shows a significant difference in college access and persistence between different demographic groups, with lower-income and minority college-aged adolescents disproportionally affected (College Board, 2005).

Case Study: The Chicago Teacher Education Pipeline™ at Illinois State University has been working to recruit more students from Chicago public schools to pursue higher education with a specific focus on studying teacher education. Partnership efforts that started in 2004 led to the creation of the Teacher Education and Access to College for Highschoolers (TEACH) Program in 2005 to support an early intervention paradigm designed to increase college attendance of adolescents in urban communities. Promoting early college preparation through comprehensive mentoring, counseling, outreach and supportive services [e.g., college campus visits, ACT (American College Testing Program) prep courses, scholarship application writing workshops, and financial literacy/planning workshops] for participating students and parents has been a critical step in bridging the gap to higher education.

Thus far, a concentrated number of students attending Chicago neighborhood high schools with an established TEACH chapter have applied and been accepted to attend the university. In one example, students from the aforementioned David G. Farragut Career Academy, a local public high school with chronically endemic low graduation rates had three applications and one acceptance to the university in 2006. Each year since, applications and relative acceptance rates have steadily increased. To date, 78 students from Farragut have applied and 24% have been accepted to attend.

While the TEACH program's main goal is to increase its members' awareness of and matriculation into universities, TEACH also illustrates different post-secondary options that students can choose once they have graduated from high school. Whether they decide to attend one of the city's community colleges, a vocational school or, later, transition to a four-year college, students are supported to take the necessary steps to continue their education.

Identifying Barriers to Family Engagement

Family engagement is an important component for creating a supportive foundation for learning in schools (Ferguson, Ramos, Rudo, & Wood, 2008). In fact, CPS (2010) identifies "Family and Community Involvement" as one of the "five fundamentals for school success." However, some schools admit that family engagement is an afterthought when designing supports to ensure its materialization. In order to overcome the shortsightedness, factors that limit family engagement must be identified to better plan for realized outcomes that encourage consistent parent/guardian participation. These barriers include, but are not limited to, three major categories: Historical, social/emotional and logistical (Ferguson et al., 2008).

The first barrier is historical and can be attributed to parents' own aversion to schools. Sometimes this stems from a negative experience they personally had while in school that may contribute to discomfort when summoned to the school building. This hesitancy of parents/guardians who are not visibly involved is often wrongly perceived by school personnel to be apathy or negligence about their child's education (Payne, 2008), but should rather be identified as skepticism due to the historical barriers.

Additionally, social-emotional factors can compound the feeling if school personnel do not actively welcome parents/guardians into the building as valuable stakeholders. This single factor arguably has the most direct effect on family involvement (Ferguson et al., 2008). In the most extreme cases, school personnel contribute to the escalation of conflict and anger expressed by guardians when school invitations to parents largely revolve around negative behavior issues related to their child (Resto & Alston, 2006).

Another challenge relates to the feeling of inferiority parents potentially have when they are undereducated. Some parents/guardians may be forced to confront literacy barriers to understand the basic elements of their child's progress (i.e., grade reports, written teacher feedback). In cases involving parents of English-language learners, lack of translation services or bilingual staff may contribute to feelings of inadequacy for parents who are non-English speakers (Quiocho & Daoud, 2006). Sometimes, this inferiority complex can be connected to real or perceived divisions as it relates to educational attainment, race, and class differences among staff/faculty and parents/guardians (Baker, Denessen, & Brus-Laven, 2007).

Yet another social-emotional barrier arises when communication between stakeholders breaks down. For instance, when communication from schools to families primarily consists of informing "bad" news, the underlying message can be interpreted as schools only reach out to condemn parents. This type of interaction can encourage parents to develop a defensive attitude and deflect blame back onto the school to rationalize the predicament, citing that teachers are "racist," and/or "don't like" their child (Ferguson et al., 2008). Unfortunately, the cycle of blame and shame just breathes life into the aforementioned barriers.

The last barrier, a logistical one, exists when schools fail to consider the daily responsibilities of families. Many families in urban, underserviced areas may be classified as lower-income: Parents/guardians often work full-time, limiting the time they have available to partake in school functions. Luckily, this barrier can be improved with some creativity from the school. For example, in community schools of choice, family involvement activities are scheduled at convenient times for working parents, communicated far in advance, giving the family ample time to secure time off work, transportation, and childcare. In the most effective schools of choice, childcare and transportation are even offered, alleviating the burden altogether. Schools of choice further extend their considerations by anticipating that some students do not derive from the typical nuclear family structure. In the event that a child is raised by a grandparent, for example, schools can offer home visits as an outreach initiative instead of a customary parent/guardian event at the school. These collective efforts help parents overcome logistical barriers and maximize their participation in the schools.

The aforementioned barriers can be overcome with open communication. Despite this seemingly simple solution, though, many educators struggle to connect with all educational stakeholders since most teachers are traditionally trained to perform their function within their particular classrooms, limiting their experience in communicating with other staff or parents. To help bridge this gap for educators, communities of choice build partnerships with institutions of higher education to help incorporate such an understanding within their preparation modules.

University Partnerships to Train Community-engaged Teachers

Just as family engagement is crucial to creating a supportive foundation for learning in schools, contextual preparation of urban teachers is a critical component of creating systemic change in public schools (Lee, Eckrich, Lackey, & Showalter, 2010). Institutions of higher education (IHE) such as Illinois State University aggressively recruit and retain underrepresented minority students in hopes that these graduates will return to their communities and reinvest their expertise to make positive local-level impact. While those efforts represent a longer-term solution, the fact remains that the majority of graduates from universities are not reflective of the populations that comprise our urban public schools. This disconnect between the cultural identities of the professionals working in our schools and the stakeholders that the school serves often results in culturally irrelevant curriculum and cognitive barriers to meaningful family and community engagement (Lee, Creasey, Showalter, & D'Santiago, 2010). School environments also suffer greatly from this cultural divide resulting in disproportionate referral rates and expulsions along racial lines (Raffaele-Mendez & Knoff, 2003).

Partnerships that include IHEs, neighborhood schools, and community-based organizations provide authentic contextual preparation for professionals working in a partner community. While IHEs provide specific career training, they often lack the ability to tie skills and knowledge to the local context in which these factors will be applied. By involving community organizations and neighborhood schools in the development of the future workforce, more culturally relevant professionals are able to make a meaningful impact in the community (Lee, Nelson, Auffant, & Perveiler, 2012).

Case Study: The Chicago Teacher Education Pipeline™ at Illinois State University has implemented a summer internship for pre-service teachers to contextualize urban teacher training for community schools, called the Summer Teacher Education Partnership for Urban Preparation (STEP-UP) Program. STEP-UP is a four-week immersion program where Fellows co-teach alongside a veteran teacher in a CPS summer school, complete a project-based service-learning internship with a community-based organization, and participate in seminars including English language learner teaching strategies, response to intervention, restorative justice, introspective teaching, and community contextualization. Fellows also live with a host family, fully immersed in the community in which they are working. Throughout the program, community youth, school personnel, community organizations, host families, and university faculty and staff provide insight, skill development, and perspective to Fellows, resulting in significant improvement of community commitment and multicultural attitudes (Lee et al., 2012). Subsequently, 63% of Fellows find employment in these community schools with an additional 20% employed in other high-need urban schools immediately upon graduation, compared to a national average of 41% (National Center for Education Statistics, 2010).

Broader Organization of Communities to Influence Development

Neighborhoods are complex systems with finely integrated components and agents, whose overall interactions produce the neighborhood's identity. In communities with harsh circumstances, strategic interactions and partnerships that support comprehensive neighborhood development are critical. One model of community development that seeks to support that agenda is the Local Initiatives Support Corporation (LISC)/Chicago's New Communities Program (NCP), which offers a strategic framework for capturing neighborhood resources and focusing them through community planning processes. NCP is an urban development initiative that combines community planning with facilitated involvement of community residents and local organizations to develop quality-of-life plans for improving the community conditions.

NCP planning processes provide a vehicle for bringing together diverse individuals and organizations where relationships and programs can be built around a common vision. The planning sets into motion a dynamic cycle of neighborhood improvement, one that is further propelled by the program's operating principles. To date, NCP has fostered the development of 14 neighborhood "quality-of-life plans" for 16 Chicago community areas.

Across the board, NCP participants have called for smaller class size, after-hours community use of schools, foreign language training, math-science centers, better teachers, and more responsive principals. As a result, community networks are integrating existing partnerships and resources to improve the broader learning environment by improving safety, providing in-classroom help, and connecting teachers with students and families.

> *Case Study*: Elev8, an initiative that grew out of NCP planning is one example of how a broad-based organization of communities can have great impact at the local level. Five Chicago-based community organizations are currently partnering with a middle school in each respective community to transform the educational achievement and life outcomes of disadvantaged students.
>
> Elev8 Chicago established networks of relationships among school and community partners to: Extend the school day to connect programs to regular, school-day learning; create on-site, adolescent-focused health centers; mobilize parent and community leaders to accelerate change and promote advocacy while engaging them in the daily life of the school; and advocate for policies that support similar comprehensive programs city-, state-, and nationwide.

LISC/Chicago has mobilized residents to take a fresh look at their neighborhoods. Residents have worked collectively to prioritize community concerns, and the resulting plans have engaged hundreds of institutions in projects that are transforming their communities. In 2012, LISC/Chicago's neighborhood platform ties together a vibrant network of community organizations across Chicago and connects them with citywide public and private institutions.

In order to achieve a community of choice, professionals working with youth need to not only be aware of these other institutions, but be active in exploring and collaborating with the various pieces of the partnership that compete for students' attention. When a school leaves its doors open beyond school hours for community organizations, parent groups, and other stakeholders to utilize, it allows the community and school to become even more connected and provides even greater opportunity for the adolescents.

And, while it may be difficult for individual teachers or the school to know of the resources and services of the surrounding institutions, working with a broader organization can help keep all parties informed. In doing so, each institution is able to fulfill the needs of its constituents. For example, the staff and administration at Madero recognize the importance of addressing both the academic and social-emotional needs of adolescents. The school makes use of several outside organizations to meet these needs. Students that have a high risk of leading a violent lifestyle are mentored by social workers that are employed through a community safety initiative, while girls who are at high risk for teen pregnancy are involved with a community program that provides sex education. Obesity is addressed through nutrition and fitness classes for both parents and students. Parents and community members are a daily presence in the school as they attend ESL or GED classes. Student teachers from its IHE partner work as tutors to help teachers reach their students. Programs are run to help parents support their children's academic careers, from college application processes to homework and financial aid support. Annually, the school partners with local businesses to help students develop career awareness and goals. Working together, rather than in silos, the broader partnerships at Madero allow for a holistic community school of choice.

Conclusions

Stronger families equal a stronger community, and a strong community demands a school of choice. By promoting engaged problem solving and connecting learning to the experiences of students, parents, residents, and teachers as partnered stakeholders, we collectively move beyond media-generated, deficit-model stereotypes to a better understanding of the representative culture in situ. Providing families this reflective opportunity underscores the importance of investing in our own communities.

As adolescent achievement improves, a concerted effort must be made to provide youth the next step to developing a model of civic engagement and reinvestment in their communities. Such positions connect students to communities and prepare residents to be engaged citizens who will promote the collective goals of society. As the reinvestment continues, each member promotes active learning experiences through which students begin to gain an understanding of civic engagement as a lifelong responsibility with the motivation to improve their communities. And, as adolescents mature toward young adults they serve as engaged leaders and role models to the next generation, promoting the quality of life for all citizens through collaborative and individual action.

Through the promotion of public neighborhood schools, the community at large is lifted as well. School success will attract families into a community and support those that already reside there. The goal in creating a community of choice is to change the paradigm where residents view education as an opportunity to leave their neighborhood to one where residents view their education as a way to improve the community. A school's role in creating a community of choice is to support student achievement while encouraging students to return to, and serve, the community. Thus, a cycle is started where not only are youth connected with the community, but they are starting on the path to contributing their own influence to the betterment of the community.

As we collectively develop a new generation of "citizen" who has strong academic content knowledge, grounded in theory and contextually practiced in high-need areas, communities can see dramatic transformations. As a result, students and their families actualize social justice for social change within their philosophy as working professionals. In partnership, community-based organizations, universities, local schools, and social service agencies can organize around mutually identified community needs. Such cyclical action bridges curricular and co-curricular experiences to continuously deliver activities focused on assisting adolescents in their development of civic skills and engage the community at large in meaningful ways. By supporting adolescents as they build transferable civic skills that will benefit their future communities, each has the potential to apply skills to develop real-world experiences in leadership and service. This long-term approach holds promise for a bright future for community and its continued renewal.

References

Baker, J., Denessen, E., & Brus-Laven, M. (2007). Socio-economic background, parental involvement and teacher perceptions of these in relation to pupil achievement. *Educational Studies, 33*(2), 177–192.

Blanco, C. (2003). *Knocking at the college door: Projections of high school graduates by state, income and race/ethnicity.* ACT, College Board and Western Interstate Commission for Higher Education.

Bureau of Labor Statistics (2003). *Occupational employment and wages.* U.S. Department of Labor. Washington, DC: U.S. Government Printing Office.

Chicago Public Schools (CPS). (2010). *Five fundamentals of school success.* School Improvement Planning for Advancing Academic Achievement, Office of Strategy & Planning. Retrieved July 6, 2011, from http://www.stratplan.cps.k12.il.us/school_success.shtml.

Coalition for Community Schools. (2003). *Making the difference: Research and practice in community schools.* Washington, DC: Institute for Educational Leadership.

College Board. (2005). Education pays 2004 update: The benefits of higher education for individuals and society. *Trends in Higher Education Series.*

Ferguson, C., Ramos, M., Rudo, Z., & Wood, L. (2008). *The school–family connection: Looking at the larger picture.* Austin, TX: National Center for Family and Community Connections with Schools.

Garcia, P. (2001). Summer bridge: Improving retention rates for underprepared students. *Journal of Freshman Year Experiences, 3*(2), 91–105.

Lee, R. E., Creasey, G., Showalter, B. D., & D'Santiago, V. (2010). Cognitive development of social justice through re-designed courses and community-based partnerships: An initial investigation. *Perspectives on Urban Education, 8*(1), 29–34.

Lee, R. E., Eckrich, L. T., Lackey, C., & Showalter, B. D. (2010). Pre-service teacher pathways to urban teaching: A partnership model for nurturing community-based urban teacher preparation. *Teacher Education Quarterly,* Special Issue on "Moving Teaching Education in Urban Schools and Communities," *37*(3), 101–122.

Lee, R. E., Nelson, C., Auffant, P., & Perveiler, R. (2012). Transforming teacher education: A community- and school-based "residency" model of urban teacher preparation. In National Evaluation Systems (Ed.), *Preparing Effective Teachers for Tomorrow's Schools.* Amherst, MA: National Evaluation Systems.

National Center for Education Statistics. (2006). *School and staffing survey.* U.S. Department of Education. Washington, DC: U.S. Government Printing Office.

National Center for Education Statistics. (2010) *The condition of education 2010, Indicator 28: Newly hired teachers.* U.S. Department of Education. Washington, DC: Institute of Education Sciences.

National Middle School Association. (2003). *This we believe: Successful schools for young adolescents.* Westerville, OH: National Middle School Association.

Payne, C. M. (2008). *So much reform, so little change: The persistence of failure in urban schools.* Cambridge, MA: Harvard Education Press.

Quiocho, A. M. L., & Daoud, A. M. (2006). Dispelling myths about Latino parent participation in schools. *The Educational Forum, 70*, 255–267.

Raffaele-Mendez. L. M. & Knoff, H. M. (2003). Who gets suspended from school and why: A demographic analysis of schools and disciplinary infractions in a large school district. *Education and Treatment of Children, 26*(1), 30–51.

Resto, W., & Alston, A. (2006). *Parent involvement at selected ready schools.* Washington, DC: Council of Chief State School Officers.

Tomlinson, C. A., & Kalbfleisch, M. L. (1998). Teach me, teach my brain: A call for differentiated classrooms. *Educational Leadership, 56*(3), 52–55.

Walen, S. (2007). *Three years into Chicago's Community Schools Initiative: Progress, challenges and emerging lessons.* Chicago: University of Illinois Press.

Wormeli, R. (2006). *Fair isn't always equal: Assessing and grading in the differentiated classroom.* Westerville, OH: National Middle School Association.

PART IV

Positive Outcomes Associated with Adolescence

16

TRANSFORMATIONS IN RELATIONSHIPS, INDEPENDENCE, AND INTERDEPENDENCE

Nina S. Mounts, Laura Pittman, Jennifer K. Karre, and Tracy Walters

The physical, cognitive, and social changes that occur during the adolescence period set the stage for adolescents to become increasingly autonomous (Zimmer-Gembeck & Collins, 2003). Autonomy development is an essential aspect of healthy psychosocial development (Hill & Holmbeck, 1986). For adolescents growing up in urban environments, there are significant challenges to establishing autonomy. In this chapter, we consider autonomy development within the context of the urban environment. First, we consider the major dimensions of adolescent autonomy development and changes that occur during adolescence. Second, we consider autonomy development in the parent–child context generally and, more specifically, for adolescents in low-income urban environments. Finally, we consider the school context generally and, more specifically, in impoverished urban areas. Throughout the chapter our focus is on identifying the ways in which practitioners might facilitate autonomy development for urban adolescents in underserved communities.

Two broad definitions of adolescent autonomy derived from different theoretical orientations are noted in the literature and tap different aspects of autonomy (Beyers, Goossens, Vansant, & Moors, 2003). The first definition, found in the psychodynamic approach, is a relational definition and defines autonomy as changes in the relationship between adolescents and parents. Psychoanalytic theory emphasizes detachment in which normative adolescent development includes severing ties with parents through high levels of conflict (Freud, 1958) and low levels of conflict are viewed as indicative of abnormal adolescent development (McElhaney, Allen, Stephenson, & Hare, 2009). In contrast, neoanalytic theories suggest that high levels of parent–adolescent conflict are not normative and autonomy is not characterized by detachment. Rather, the relationship between adolescents and their parents is gradually transformed into a more egalitarian relationship through the process of individuation (Blos, 1967). Embedded in the process of individuation is the notion of maintenance of connectedness or interdependence with parents (Yu, 2011). The second definition of autonomy has an emphasis on the individual. The focus, here, is on self-governance, or feelings of agency, with little emphasis on adolescents' connections to parents (Beyers et al., 2003). Researchers have examined adolescents' decision-making, which is likely related to their sense of agency (Qin, Pomerantz, & Wang, 2009). In this chapter we focus on the two broad dimensions of autonomy support while maintaining interdependence and agency as a way for practitioners to easily conceptualize the autonomy development of poor urban adolescents.

Autonomy Development during Adolescence

The substantial changes in autonomy during the adolescence period are expressed in a variety of ways (McElhaney et al., 2009). For instance, adolescents are likely to be less accepting of parental control throughout the period, less likely to agree with their parents' opinions, and, as they mature, more likely to make their own decisions (Gutman & Eccles, 2007; Romich, Lundberg, & Tsang, 2009; Wray-Lake, Crouter, & McHale, 2010). In addition, adolescents are increasingly able to see their parents' positive as well as negative features through a process of deidealization (Blos, 1979) and the relationship between adolescents and parents becomes more egalitarian over time (De Goede, Branje, & Meeus, 2009). For adolescents growing up in poor urban environments, these changes occur in a context that might not be as forgiving or supportive, as adolescents make choices leading to more autonomous functioning. The degree to which parents maintain control of adolescent decision-making may vary based on the neighborhood context. Despite the dangers inherent in coming of age in the urban environment, the parent context and the school context can facilitate autonomy development through supporting changes in adolescents' relationships with adults, while maintaining interdependence, and through supporting a sense of agency in the adolescent.

Challenges to Healthy Autonomy in Urban Environments

Research on adolescents in urban communities has focused on minority youth living in low-income, inner-city neighborhoods that are noted for multiple disadvantages including higher rates of poverty, unemployment, and crime (e.g., Leventhal & Brooks-Gunn, 2000; Li, Nussbaum, & Richards, 2007). Because of this, adolescents growing up in inner cities are faced with both family and neighborhood factors that are different from their middle-class counterparts. Parents in these settings must often make decisions related to allowing increased adolescent autonomy or ensuring adolescents' safety in a dangerous neighborhood. Adolescents might also live in situations where adults in their lives grant them autonomy prematurely (Farrell et al., 2007) because parents are working to support the family, are single parents, or have mental health or physical issues that limit their capacity to grant autonomy in a more measured way (Burton, 2007). Thus, in some cases, adolescents in urban areas might function with less autonomy than their peers; in other cases, they might function with considerably more autonomy than their peers.

Similar to the parent–child context, the school context experienced by youth in urban settings may be quite different from their suburban or rural counterparts. About

50% of the nation's low-performing high schools are found in urban areas that are composed of neighborhoods with concentrated and intergenerational poverty (Balfanz, Legters, West, & Weber, 2007). Students who are functioning at or above grade level often leave neighborhood high schools to attend more selective high school programs. As a result, neighborhood high schools often have students with below grade level academic skills, poor attachment to school, attendance problems, and who often fail to graduate (Balfanz et al., 2007). In addition, urban school districts have fewer qualified teachers (Lankford, Loeb, & Wyckoff, 2002), fewer resources available for supporting learning in disadvantaged adolescents (Kozol, 1991), and adolescents may be less likely to find teachers who provide support for autonomy development. Thus, there are numerous challenges to healthy autonomy development for urban adolescents.

Parents and Autonomy Development

Parental Support of Autonomy

Parental autonomy support is linked to more positive perceptions of cognitive competence, better grades, greater sense of school membership, use of better learning strategies, more intrinsic motivation (Bronstein, Ginsburg, & Herrera, 2005; Farkas & Grolnick, 2010; Gray & Steinberg, 1999; Isakson & Jarvis, 1999; Wang, Pomerantz, & Chen, 2007), and lower declines in reading scores over time (Grolnick, Kurowski, Dunlap, & Hevey, 2000) in ethnically homogeneous and heterogeneous middle school and high school samples. Parental autonomy support may also influence academic outcomes through its influence on other factors. In a year-long longitudinal study of adolescents, Steinberg, Elmen, and Mounts (1989) demonstrated that parental autonomy-granting was related to psychosocial maturity one year later, which, in turn, was related to grade point average. Likewise, in a longitudinal study of early adolescents, Bronstein and colleagues (2005) found that autonomy support in 5th grade was related to better 5th-grade academic performance which, in turn, was related to higher intrinsic motivation in 7th grade. In another investigation, self-regulation of academic work was a mediator between parental autonomy support and academic performance in adolescents (Wong, 2008).

The positive effects of autonomy support are not limited to academic performance. Indeed, autonomy support from parents has been consistently shown to be related to positive psychosocial development across diverse groups of adolescents. Across ethnically diverse samples, higher levels of autonomy support by parents is related to higher levels of self-reliance, self-esteem, work orientation, internal locus of control, and life satisfaction for adolescents (Bean & Northrup, 2009; Farkas & Grolnick, 2010; Gray & Steinberg, 1999; Wang et al., 2007). Similar to psychosocial development, parental autonomy-granting is linked to more positive feelings of well-being, fewer feelings of negative emotion, and smaller increases in externalizing behavior (Grolnick et al., 2000; Wang et al., 2007). Overall, parental autonomy support has been linked with positive adolescent outcomes in both the academic and psychological domains.

Parental Autonomy Support and Urban Youth

Few investigations examine parental autonomy support among urban youth. In addition, it is difficult to disentangle differences from studies in suburban communities because of ethnic and socioeconomic differences in these samples. Within ethnically diverse families, especially Latino and Asian families, the degree of interdependence between parents and adolescent (i.e., the desire to maintain connection with the family even when becoming more autonomous) is likely to be another important autonomy construct (Leyendecker & Lamb, 1999). In an observational study of 10- to 15-year-old African American and Latino boys living in the inner city, more externalizing behaviors and drug use were reported when parental autonomy support was higher and family interdependence was lower (Florsheim, Tolan, & Gorman-Smith, 1998). Furthermore, this was found to hold even when controlling for ethnicity, single- versus two-parent household, and other parenting variables such as warmth and monitoring. In another investigation of inner-city, ethnic minority adolescents in treatment for a substance abuse problem, less undermining of autonomy on the part of parents was related to lower levels of drug use (Samuolis, Hogue, Dauber, & Liddle, 2005). However, like the study by Florsheim and colleagues, higher levels of autonomy support were related to higher levels of externalizing behavior, perhaps reflecting parents' attempts to change their behavior toward their children who were already engaging in problem behaviors.

In an investigation of urban, lower income, ethnically diverse college students, African American, Asian, and Latino adolescents were more likely to report family interdependence (i.e., help family) as a reason for attending college than were White adolescents after controlling for socioeconomic status (Phinney, Dennis, & Osorio, 2006). These results are at least suggestive that the motivation for higher education among minority adolescents might include consideration of interdependence as opposed to solely focusing on autonomy as is more normative among White middle-class adolescents. Similarly, Fuligni and Witkow (2004) found evidence of inter-dependence in the form of feelings of obligation and provision of assistance to family members (particularly financial support) in their sample of East Asian, Filipino, Latino, and White adolescents. The provision of assistance to family members was also associated with a small but significant negative relationship with educational progress. Interdependence may be particularly important in specific family situations including when adolescents become pregnant. For example, Spanish-speaking Latina adolescent girls reported more positive feelings about their pregnancy and fewer fears about parenting when their mothers emphasized both interdependence and autonomy in their discussions with their daughters (Nadeem & Romo, 2008).

One important idea that emerges in the literature on autonomy and the development of urban adolescents is that parental autonomy support is often balanced with the needs of the parents to keep the adolescent safe in a risky environment. In a large study of inner-city families, Furstenberg, Cook, Eccles, Elder, and Sameroff (1999) found that parental support for autonomy was linked to fewer problem behaviors and more positive outcomes, including academic competence, psycho-logical adjustment, and self-competence. Interestingly, it was noted that parents in these contexts provided a level of control appropriate for the environment in which their child was being raised, but that their use of control needed to be balanced so that it did not undermine their adolescents' growing sense of autonomy. Similarly, in a qualitative study of African American mothers and their adolescent daughters, mothers reflected that they were concerned about supporting their daughters' growing autonomy while balancing the need to keep them safe (Cauce, Hiraga, Graves, & Gonzales, 1996). To that end, daughters were given more freedom about personal decisions as they related to their identity (e.g., clothing, hairstyles), but were given less freedom in other regards (e.g., at what age they can start dating or have friends over alone). Thus, this balance of autonomy support and safety is salient to the parents in more disadvantaged communities.

Parental Support of Adolescent Agency

One of the ways in which parents support the development of the sense of agency and competence is by allowing adolescents to participate in decision-making or by engaging in autonomy-granting (Noom, Dekovic, & Meeus, 2001). African American and White adolescents who were given more decision-making opportunities had higher self-esteem and lower levels of depression than their peers (Bynum & Kotchick, 2006; Gutman & Eccles, 2007). Similar to autonomy support, some investigations suggest that a balance is needed in terms of providing opportunities for decision-making. In a longitudinal study that followed adolescents from 7th grade through graduation from high school, Gutman and Eccles (2007) reported that, although decision-making opportunities increased from ages 13 through 19, White adolescents reported more decision-making opportunities given by their parents than African American adolescents. However, higher levels of decision-making opportunities were related to higher levels of depression for White, but not African American adolescents. Results suggest that too many decision-making opportunities may have provided inappropriate levels of autonomy for the White adolescents. Similarly, higher levels of decisional autonomy by the adolescent when paired with lower levels of parental involvement were related to increases in externalizing problem behaviors over time (Reitz, Dekovic, & Meijer, 2006). Taken together, these results suggest that allowing adolescents to engage in joint decision-making in dialogue with parents, while at the same time maintaining connectedness with parents, might be an appropriate way to facilitate autonomy development.

Developing a Sense of Agency in Urban Adolescents

In considering autonomy and the development of urban adolescents, it is important to consider neighborhood, particularly when the focus is on adolescent decision-making. The impact of neighborhood may vary based on ethnicity and neighborhood context. For example, in one investigation among a diverse sample of middle school students, unilateral parental decision-making was associated with a lower likelihood of sexual initiation for adolescents in disadvantaged neighborhoods, but a greater likelihood of sexual initiation among adolescents in advantaged neighborhoods (Roche et al., 2005). Roche and colleagues suggest that this pattern of results might reflect that adolescents in disadvantaged neighborhoods might view parental unilateral decision-making as more legitimate because of safety concerns than would adolescents in more advantaged neighborhoods where safety is not as much a concern. Again, this reflects the necessity of parents to balance autonomy support with keeping the adolescent safe.

Among a diverse high school sample, in general, lower levels of unilateral decision-making by adolescents and higher levels of joint parent–adolescent decision-making were related to more positive outcomes including higher feelings of self-reliance, higher self-esteem, more positive work orientation, lower levels of problem behaviors, and more positive academic outcomes (Lamborn, Dornbusch, & Steinberg, 1996). However, these associations were not consistently found among African American adolescents. Furthermore, these effects were moderated by community context such that the negative impacts of unilateral adolescent decision-making as well as the positive effects of joint decision-making were more pronounced for Latino adolescents when they lived in ethnically mixed, more disadvantaged neighborhoods.

As noted earlier, one of the challenges for urban adolescents is that their living situations, where parents might be less available because of work obligations or mental health or substance abuse issues, may not allow for joint decision-making with parents and instead may lead to increased unilateral decision-making by such adolescents at a far earlier age than peers (Burton, 2007; Farrell et al., 2007). In some cases, adolescents take on adult decision-making roles because of a short-term issue, such as parental illness, and might receive some guidance from adults during this time period; in other cases, these roles might be permanent and adolescents might receive little assistance in their decision-making (Burton, 2007). In cases where adolescents assume these adult decision-making responsibilities, they report higher levels of stress and forego normative academic and social pursuits because of the responsibilities being placed on them (Burton, 2007; Farrell et al. 2007). Nonetheless, Burton (2007) argues that adolescents who assume adult decision-making responsibilities might also benefit from these responsibilities in terms of acquiring developmental assets such as leadership skills, social awareness, and responsibility.

How Parents Might Support Autonomy in Urban Adolescents

Taken together, the results suggest that parents who are raising adolescents in urban areas must balance the adolescents' growing need for autonomy with the need to keep the adolescent safe. In cases where adolescents have been prematurely required to assume adult responsibilities at home, practitioners might work with parents or other family members so that they gradually assume these adult responsibilities.

Teachers and Autonomy Development

Despite the fact that autonomy development is an important developmental task during adolescence, the school classroom is one place where autonomy support typically declines. The theory of stage-environment fit is particularly useful for understanding autonomy development within the school context. Specifically, children's development may be impeded if the context they are in does not fit with their developmental stage (Eccles et al., 1993). Indeed, Eccles and colleagues suggested that the junior high school context is not developmentally appropriate for young adolescents because it often provides fewer opportunities for autonomy than does the elementary school context. Further support for this notion was found in a socio-economically and ethnically diverse sample where the average trajectory of opportunities for autonomy in the classroom declined across the middle school period (Way, Reddy, & Rhodes, 2007). Although the literature on adolescent autonomy development, particularly decision-making, and school contexts is more limited than the literature on adolescent autonomy development and parent–child relationships, in this section we examine the way in which schools can facilitate autonomy development.

Importance of Teacher Support of Autonomy

Teacher autonomy support might include allowing adolescents an opportunity to lead the class, allowing adolescents choice in completing course requirements, and providing material relevant to adolescents' experiences (Hafen et al., 2012). In his review, Reeve (2009) reported that teacher autonomy support in the classroom was related to five types of outcomes including motivation, development, learning, performance, and psychological well-being. Other researchers reported that autonomy support was related to higher preference for challenge, increases in intrinsic motivation, increases in self-esteem, increases in internal control, and higher levels of academic engagement (Deci, Nezlek, and Sheinman, 1981; Hafen et al., 2012; Jang, Reeve, & Deci, 2010; Van Ryzin, Gravely, & Roseth, 2009; Wong, Wiest, & Cusick, 2002).

According to Kozol (1991), adolescents living in poverty experience systemic inequities that could undermine their motivation. These students may not believe their academic efforts will pay off or that their academic achievement is important, either to their teachers or for their future (Kozol, 1991).

Kenney, Walsh-Blair, Bluestein, Bempechat, and Seltzer (2010) investigated the contributions of support and autonomy in the school and workplace to specific achievement-related beliefs in a sample of students in an urban Catholic high school with a work-based learning program. Results revealed a positive relationship between teachers' autonomy support and adolescents' sense of self-efficacy and mastery goal orientation. In addition, higher levels of teachers' autonomy support were related to lower skepticism about the relevance of school. These findings are consistent with self-determination theory (Ryan & Deci, 2000).

Decision-making in the Classroom

Similar to parenting, another aspect of autonomy that is relevant in the school context is adolescent decision-making. In one investigation that examined trajectories across the middle school years, Way and colleagues (2007) found that more opportunities for decision-making in the 6th-grade classroom were not only related to fewer depressive symptoms, fewer behavior problems, and higher self-esteem concurrently, but also were related to fewer behavior problems later during middle school. Using a demographically stratified sample in regards to age, race, and geographic locations, Lohman, Kaura, and Newman (2007) reported that higher levels of adolescent differentiation (which included decision-making in school) were related to higher grade point averages and lower numbers of absences, disciplinary problems, internalizing, and externalizing behaviors in a sample of adolescents.

As described above, Kenney and colleagues (2010) conducted a study investigating the contributions of "work hope" and career planning to specific achievement-related beliefs in a sample of students enrolled in an urban Catholic high school. Work hope included decision-making regarding careers and adolescents' sense of agency in regard to a career. Results revealed that adolescents who were engaged in decision-making regarding careers and who had a positive sense of agency in regard to their future careers reported higher levels of academic efficacy and mastery goal orientation. In addition, they reported lower levels of skepticism about the relevance of school.

Burton (2007) raises the issue that teachers in urban schools should be aware that adolescents who are given adult decision-making responsibilities might have obligations that interfere with completion of school work or attendance at school. These adolescents might be balancing school and family obligations in the same way that many adults are balancing work and family obligations. In addition, the relatively equal status that the adolescent has with the parents in the household might set the stage for conflicts, feelings of ambiguity, and anxiety in regard to appropriate behavior. All of these might have implications for adolescents' experiences within the school environment.

How Might Teachers Support Autonomy in Urban Adolescents

Taken together, the results suggest that teachers who work with adolescents in urban areas might provide a safe context for supporting adolescents' growing need for autonomy. Reeve (2009) suggests three ways that teachers can develop their autonomy support skills. First, teachers may strive to become less controlling. Teachers might control students for a variety of reasons including pressure from administrators or because they view their role as a teacher as being someone in power (see Reeve (2009) for more details). This might be especially challenging for teachers in urban areas where issues such as school violence might encourage teachers to exert relatively high levels of control in their classrooms. Second, teachers need to develop a desire to be autonomy supportive in the classroom context and create classroom contexts that allow autonomy support. There are also benefits to teachers when they encourage autonomy in the classroom that might be highlighted in working with teachers, including enhanced well-being and greater positive affect. Third, teachers need to develop specific autonomy supporting skills that they can use in the classroom, such as nurturing adolescents' inner motivational resources and offering rationales for particular classroom requirements (see Reeve, 2009). The lack of resources and support available for teachers in urban schools in combination with the great needs of the students attending urban schools might make it challenging for teachers to adopt autonomy supportive strategies. Nevertheless, the rewards for implementing autonomy supportive strategies in urban classrooms are potentially far greater for urban adolescents than for more advantaged adolescents.

For adolescents who prematurely are required to assume adult responsibilities at home, teachers might recognize their assets in the classroom in terms of leadership or planning skills. Teachers should be prepared to accommodate the special needs of adolescents trying to balance familial obligations with meeting personal academic goals. As outlined above, this is particularly the case with minority adolescents where there may be more emphasis placed on familial interdependence than in White families (Leyendecker & Lamb, 1999).

Thus far, most of the research on teachers and adolescent autonomy development focuses on classroom activities. Yet, many teachers are actively involved in advising the extracurricular activities of students. It could be that extracurricular activities, by their nature, lend themselves more readily to autonomy supportive activities than classroom activities because students are asked to take ownership over many extracurricular activities (Larson & Angus, 2011). Indeed, Larson and Angus suggest that youth advisors in urban and rural out-of-school activities allow students the freedom to control their projects, provide nondirective suggestions for their projects, and provide assistance only when adolescents are feeling unsure of how to proceed with their projects. These autonomy supportive behaviors are likely to facilitate adolescents' sense of agency. More research is needed to examine whether teachers employ similar strategies when working with adolescents who are participating in extracurricular activities and the effects of these autonomy supportive strategies on adolescents' adjustment.

Conclusions

In sum, in urban areas, one of the greatest challenges facing parents and teachers in supporting autonomy development is balancing the adolescents' growing need for autonomy with the need to keep them safe in an often violent environment. Parents and teachers can learn how to facilitate autonomy development, while maintaining connections with youth, through parenting training and teacher development workshops. Parents and teachers who can successfully navigate this challenge find that they can have a positive impact on urban adolescents' academic achievement, positive feelings about the self, and involvement in problem behaviors.

References

Balfanz, R., Legters, N., West, T. C., & Weber, L. (2007). Are NCLB's measures, incentives, and improvement strategies the right ones for the nation's low-performing high schools? *American Educational Research Journal, 44*, 559–593.

Bean, R. A., & Northrup, J. C. (2009). Parental psychological control, psychological autonomy, and acceptance as predictors of self-esteem in Latino adolescents. *Journal of Family Issues, 30*, 1486–1504.

Beyers, W., Goossens, L., Vansant, I., & Moors, E. (2003). A structural model of autonomy in middle and late adolescence: Connectedness, separation, detachment, and agency. *Journal of Youth and Adolescence, 32*, 351–365.

Blos, P. (1967). The second individuation process of adolescence. *Psychoanalytic Study of the Child, 22,* 162–186.

Blos, P. (1979). *The adolescent passage: Developmental issues.* New York: International Universities Press.

Bronstein, P., Ginsburg, G. S., & Herrera, I. S. (2005). Parental predictors of motivation orientation in early adolescence: A longitudinal study. *Journal of Youth and Adolescence, 34,* 559–575.

Burton, L. (2007). Childhood adultification in economically disadvantaged families: A conceptual model. *Family Relations, 56,* 329–345.

Bynum, M. S., & Kotchick, B. A. (2006). Mother-adolescent relationship quality and autonomy as predictors of psychosocial adjustment among African American adolescents. *Journal of Child and Family Studies, 15,* 529–549.

Cauce, A. M., Hiraga, Y., Graves, D., & Gonzales, N. (1996). African American mothers and their adolescent daughters: Closeness, conflict, and control. In B. J. R. Leadbeater, & N. Way (Eds.), *Urban girls. Resisting stereotypes, creating identities* (pp. 100–116). New York: New York University Press.

Deci, E. L., Nezlek, J., & Sheinman, L. (1981). Characteristics of the rewarder and intrinsic motivation of the rewardee. *Journal of Personality and Social Psychology, 40,* 1–10.

De Goede, I. H. A., Branje, S. J. T., & Meeus, W. H. J. (2009). Developmental changes in adolescents' perceptions of relationships with their parents. *Journal of Youth and Adolescence, 38,* 75–88.

Eccles, J. S., Midgley, C., Wigfield, A., Buchanan, C. M., Reuman, D., Flanagan, C., . . . & MacIver, D. (1993). Development during adolescence: The impact of stage-environment fit on young adolescents' experiences in schools and in families. *American Psychologist, 48,* 90–101.

Farkas, M. S., & Grolnick, W. S. (2010). Examining the components and concomitants of parental structure in the academic domains. *Motivation and Emotion, 34,* 266–279.

Farrell, A. D., Erwin, E. H., Allsino, K. W., Meyer, A., Sullivan, T., Camou, S., . . . & Esposito, L. (2007). Problematic situations in the lives of urban African American middle school students: A qualitative study. *Journal of Research on Adolescence, 17,* 413–454.

Florsheim, P., Tolan, P., & Gorman-Smith, D. (1998). Family relationships, parenting practices, the availability of male family members, and the behavior of inner-city boys in single-mother and two-parent families. *Child Development, 69*(5), 1437–1447.

Freud, A. (1958). *Psychoanalytic study of the child, 13,* 255–278.

Fuligni, A. J., & Witkow, M. (2004). The postsecondary educational progress of youth from immigrant families. *Journal of Research on Adolescence, 14,* 159–183.

Furstenberg, F. F., Cook, T. D., Eccles, J., Elder, G. H., & Sameroff, A. (1999). *Managing to make it: Urban families and adolescent success.* Chicago: University of Chicago Press.

Gray, M. R., & Steinberg, L. (1999). Unpacking authoritative parenting: Reassessing a multidimensional construct. *Journal of Marriage and the Family, 61,* 574–587.

Grolnick, W. S., Kurowski, C. O., Dunlap, K. G., & Hevey, C. (2000). Parental resources and the transition to junior high. *Journal of Research on Adolescence, 10,* 465–488.

Gutman, L. M., & Eccles, J. S. (2007). Stage-environment fit during adolescence: Trajectories of family relations and adolescent outcomes. *Developmental Psychology, 43,* 522–537.

Hafen, C. A., Allen, J. P., Mikami, A. Y., Gregory, A., Hamre, B., & Pianta, R. C. (2012). The pivotal role of adolescent autonomy in secondary school classrooms. *Journal of Youth and Adolescence, 41,* 245–255.

Hill, J., & Holmbeck, G. (1986). Attachment and autonomy during adolescence. *Annals of Child Development, 3,* 145–189.

Isakson, K., & Jarvis, P. (1999). The adjustment of adolescents during the transition into high school: A short-term longitudinal study. *Journal of Youth and Adolescence, 28,* 1–26.

Jang, H., Reeve, J., & Deci, E. (2010). Engaging students in learning activities: It is not autonomy support or structure but autonomy support and structure. *Journal of Educational Psychology, 102,* 588–600.

Kenney, M. E., Walsh-Blair, L. Y., Blustein, D. L., Bempechat, J., & Seltzer, J. (2010). Achievement motivation among urban adolescents: Work hope, autonomy support, and achievement-related beliefs. *Journal of Vocational Behavior, 77*, 205–212.

Kozol, J. (1991). *Savage inequalities: Children in America's schools.* New York: Crown.

Lamborn, S. D., Dornbusch, S. M., & Steinberg, L. (1996). Ethnicity and community context as moderators of the relations between family decision making and adolescent adjustment. *Child Development, 67*, 283–301.

Lankford, H., Loeb, S., & Wyckoff, J. (2002). Teacher sorting and the plight of urban schools: A descriptive analysis. *Educational Evaluation and Policy Analysis, 24*, 37–62.

Larson, R. W., & Angus, R. M. (2011). Adolescents' development of skills for agency in youth programs: Learning to think strategically. *Child Development, 82*, 277–294.

Leventhal, T., & Brooks-Gunn, J. (2000). The neighborhoods they live in: The effects of neighborhood residence on child and adolescent outcomes. *Psychological Bulletin, 126*(2), 309–337.

Leyendecker, B., & Lamb, M. E. (1999). Latino families. In M. E. Lamb (Ed.), *Parenting and child development in "nontraditional" families* (pp. 247–262). Mahwah, NJ: Lawrence Erlbaum.

Li, S. T., Nussbaum, K. M., & Richards, M. H. (2007). Risk and protective factors for urban African American youth. *American Journal of Community Psychology, 39*(1–2), 21–35.

Lohman, B. J., Kaura, S. A., & Newman, B. (2007). Matched or mismatched environments? The relationship of family and school differentiation to adolescents' psychosocial adjustment. *Youth & Society, 39*, 3–32.

McElhaney, K. B., Allen, J. P., Stephenson, J. C., & Hare, A. L. (2009). Attachment and autonomy during adolescence. In R. M. Lerner, & L. Steinberg (Eds.), *Handbook of adolescent psychology: Volume 1: Individual bases of adolescent development (3rd ed.)* (pp. 358–403). Hoboken, NJ: Wiley.

Nadeem, E., & Romo, L. F. (2008). Low-income Latina mothers' expectations for their pregnant daughters' autonomy and interdependence. *Journal of Research on Adolescence, 18*, 215–238.

Noom, M. J., Dekovic, M., & Meeus, W. (2001). Conceptual analysis and measurement of adolescent autonomy. *Journal of Youth & Adolescence, 30*, 577–595.

Phinney, J. S., Dennis, J., & Osorio, S. (2006). Reasons to attend college among ethnically diverse college students. *Cultural Diversity and Ethnic Minority Psychology, 12*, 347–366.

Qin, L., Pomerantz, E., & Wang, Q. (2009). Are gains in decision-making autonomy during early adolescence beneficial for emotional functioning? The case of the United States and China. *Child Development, 80*, 1705–1721.

Reeve, J. (2009). Why teachers adopt a controlling motivating style toward students and how they can become more autonomy supportive. *Educational Psychologist, 44*, 159–175.

Reitz, E., Deković, M., & Meijer, A. M. (2006). Relations between parenting and externalizing and internalizing problem behavior in early adolescence: Child behavior as moderator and predictor. *Journal of Adolescence, 29*, 419–436.

Roche, K. M., Mekos, D., Alexander, C. S., Astone, N. M., Bandeen-Roche, K., & Ensminger, M. E. (2005). Parenting influences on early sex initiation among adolescents: How neighborhood matters. *Journal of Family Issues, 26*, 32–54.

Romich, J. L., Lundberg, S., & Tsang, K. P. (2009). Independence giving or autonomy taking? Childhood predictors of decision-sharing patterns between young adolescents and parents. *Journal of Research on Adolescence, 19*, 587–600.

Ryan, R. M., & Deci, E. L. (2000). Self-determination theory and the facilitation of intrinsic motivation, social development, and well being. *American Psychologist, 55*, 68–78.

Samuolis, J., Hogue, A., Dauber, S., & Liddle, H. A. (2005). Autonomy and relatedness in inner-city families of substance abusing adolescents. *Journal of Child & Adolescent Substance Abuse, 15*, 53–86.

Steinberg, L., Elmen, J. D., & Mounts, N. S. (1989). Authoritative parenting, psychosocial maturity, and academic success among adolescents. *Child Development, 60*, 1424–1436.

Van Ryzin, M. J., Gravely, A. A., & Roseth, C. J. (2009). Autonomy, belongingness, and engagement in school as contributors to adolescent psychological well-being. *Journal of Youth and Adolescence, 38*, 1–12.

Wang, Q., Pomerantz, E. M., & Chen, H. (2007). The role of parents' control in early adolescents' psychological functioning: A longitudinal investigation in the United States and China. *Child Development, 78*, 1592–1610.

Way, N., Reddy, R., & Rhodes, J. (2007). Students' perceptions of school climate during the middle school years: Associations with trajectories of psychological and behavioral adjustment. *American Journal of Community Psychology, 40*, 194–213.

Wong, E. H., Wiest, D. J., & Cusick, L. B. (2002). Perceptions of autonomy support, parent attachment, competence and self-worth as predictors of motivational, orientation and academic achievement: An examination of sixth- and ninth-grade regular education students. *Adolescence, 37*, 255–266.

Wong, M. M. (2008). Perceptions of parental involvement and autonomy support: Their relations with self-regulation, academic performance, substance use and resilience among adolescents. *North American Journal of Psychology, 10*, 497–518.

Wray-Lake, L., Crouter, A. C., & McHale, S. M. (2010). Developmental patterns in decision-making autonomy across middle childhood and adolescence: European American Parents' perspectives. *Child Development, 81*, 636–651.

Yu, J. J. (2011). Reciprocal associations between connectedness and autonomy among Korean adolescents: Compatible or antithetical? *Journal of Marriage and Family, 73*, 692–703.

Zimmer-Gembeck, M. J., & Collins, W. A. (2003). Autonomy development during adolescence. In G. R. Adams, & M. D. Berzonsky (Eds.), *Blackwell handbook of adolescence* (pp. 174–204). Malden, MA: Blackwell.

17

YOUTH, FAMILIES, CULTURE, AND CONTEXT

Promoting Urban Adolescent Sexual Health

Rosalie Corona, Michell Pope, Jasmine A. Abrams, and Faye Z. Belgrave

Many adolescents living in urban environments engage in high-risk sexual behaviors that increase their risk of decreased academic attainment, unintended pregnancy and sexually transmitted infections (STIs), including HIV (Frisco, 2008; Miller, Benson, & Galbraith, 2001; Pantin, Schwartz, Sullivan, Prado, & Szapocznik, 2004). However, not all youth living in urban communities have poor outcomes. Appropriate supports, such as close family relationships and family supervision, can help youth develop healthy behaviors. Thus, strengthening these types of supports in urban communities can help promote adolescent sexual health.

This chapter focuses on urban adolescents' sexual health and strategies for promoting sexual health. Using an ecological framework, we review research related to individual, family, cultural, and community risk and protective factors related to urban adolescent sexual health. Throughout, we highlight prevention programs targeting protective factors that promote sexual health.

Adolescent Sexual Behavior: Ecological Theory

Developing evidence-based prevention programs to promote urban adolescents' sexual health requires an understanding of the factors that contribute to their sexual risk behavior. We draw on a theoretical model that combines major social-psychological theories of health behavior change and attends to ecological influences (Fishbein et al., 1991; Guilamo-Ramos, Jaccard, Dittus, Gonzalez, & Bouris, 2008; Jaccard, Dodge, & Dittus, 2002). This model (see Fishbein et al., 1991, for more information on the model) posits that the adolescent is at the center of these influences that can serve as leverage points for behavior change. Social-cognitive factors, individual skills and abilities, environmental variables (such as family, media, and culture that can be barriers or facilitators to adjustment), and intentions influence the adolescent's sexual behavior, substance use, and contraceptive use.

Ecological factors (family, neighborhood) are crucial to effective teen pregnancy and HIV-prevention efforts along with identity and gender development. This chapter next reviews the literature on several components found in this theoretical framework including individual level, family level, and contextual factors (e.g., media, neighborhood) that affect the sexual socialization of urban adolescents.

Adolescents' Conceptions of Self and Future Behavior

A central task during adolescence is the development of self-concept—or perception of the self. Low self-worth and poor self-image are linked to sexual risk behaviors (Laflin, Wang, & Barry, 2008; Salazar et al., 2004). A part of the self-concept is an adolescent's perception of what he/she might become, would like to become, and is afraid of becoming (Markus & Nurius, 1986). These hoped-for and feared possible selves serve to motivate behavior (Markus & Nurius, 1986) and are associated with adolescent risk behavior and academic achievement (Aloise-Young, Hennigan, & Leong, 2001; Oyserman, Terry, & Bybee, 2002). Thus, teaching youth to envision their future possible selves provides prevention programmers with a newer way of promoting adolescent health.

In self-concept interventions, youth are taught to make salient their hoped-for possible selves; linkages are created between possible selves and strategies for attaining them; and a space is created where possible selves are congruent with social identities (Oyserman, Bybee, & Terry, 2006). Adolescents who participate in self-concept interventions are more concerned about performing well academically, are more connected to school, and have better school attendance than youth who are not trained (Oyserman et al., 2002). Intervention effects also are resistant to treatment "wash out" (Oyserman et al., 2006).

Extending this line of work to sexual behavior and health promotion is relevant given that early parenthood and sexual initiation can have a negative influence on youth's academic trajectory and vice versa. Adult Identity Mentoring (AIM; Clark et al., 2005) is a 10-session program based on the theory of possible selves. AIM uses interactive activities (e.g., discussions among participants) to help youth envision their hopes for their future and understand how their behavior promotes or impedes the development of their future selves. Evaluation findings showed that intervention group youth had more positive sexual health outcomes than youth who received a standard health curriculum (Clark et al., 2005). In the Making a Difference curriculum (Jemmott, Jemmott, & Fong, 1998) youth discuss how pregnancy, parenting, and STIs negatively impact one's life goal. Finally, the Carrera Program (Philliber, Williams Kaye, Herrling, & West, 2002) improves life skills in the employment, academic, and communication domains by focusing on seven core components: education, employment, family life and sexuality education, mental health services, medical and dental care, self-expression, and sports.

In sum, possible selves are an avenue to promote adolescent sexual health and academic achievement. Self-concept interventions are well-suited for delivery within a school context, and may provide professionals a different strategy for addressing sexual health within an academic curriculum. Helping youth develop a balance between their hoped-for and feared possible selves is important since this balance is beneficial to youth outcomes. Finally, possible self interventions provide a context for helping youth identify and understand the connection between academic and sexual health outcomes.

Adolescent Sexual Behavior and the Parent–Child Relationship

Families critically shape adolescent sexual behavior through family relationships, parenting practices and by communicating their values and expectations regarding sexual activity (Dittus, Miller, Kotchick, & Forehand, 2004; Miller et al., 2001).When parents and adolescents communicate openly about sex, adolescents are less likely to be sexually active, more likely to use condoms and less likely to get pregnant (Miller et al., 2001; Romer et al., 1999). Thus, parents may be in a unique position to promote adolescent sexual health because they can talk to their children about sexual behaviors and decision making early, often, and can tailor conversations based on their child's current cognitive, social, emotional, and physical development (Kotchick, Shaffer, & Forehand, 2001).

Family-level prevention programs can intervene with the parents alone or with parents and adolescents together, and can be implemented in school, community, and worksite settings (Kirby & Laris, 2009). McKay et al. (2004) developed and evaluated CHAMP (Chicago HIV prevention and Adolescent Mental Health Project) for 4th- and 5th-grade urban youth and their families. CHAMP consists of 12 sessions and focuses on parental supervision, parent–child communication about sexual behavior, and developmental changes. Results suggest that family-level factors (e.g., parental monitoring, comfort communicating) changed as a result of the intervention. DiIorio et al. (2006) evaluated Keepin' it R.E.A.L. interventions that included mothers and children together. Among sexually active youth at the 24-month follow-up, more intervention than control group adolescents reported condom use. Intervention mothers expressed a greater intention to discuss sexual topics with their adolescents and greater comfort than control mothers. *Familias Unidas*, a drug prevention program, was modified to focus on HIV prevention among Latino youth and resulted in an increase in condom use and positive parenting practices (Prado et al., 2012). *Familias Unidas* focuses on four intervention targets shown to be associated with positive youth and family outcomes: parental involvement; adolescent self-regulation and control; adolescent social competence; and academic achievement and school engagement (Coatsworth, Pantin, & Szapocznik, 2002). Although Latino parents are less likely than other parents to talk to their adolescents about sexual behavior, findings from the *Familias Unidas* intervention suggests that Latino parents can learn skills to help them to talk with their adolescent about sexual health.

Finally, involving parents in prevention programs provides them with opportunities to communicate their academic and sexual health values to their children. Romo, Kouyoumdjian, Nadeem, and Sigman (2006) found that mothers spontaneously mentioned academic themes in sexuality discussions with their daughters. For example, messages about "avoiding sex" were often linked to messages to "avoid pregnancy" and "complete educational goals." These findings highlight the relevance of including educational themes in sexual health prevention programs.

Fathers can also play an important role in adolescent sexual health promotion (Rink, Tricker, & Harvey, 2007). A longitudinal study found that girls in father-absent households engaged in more sexual activity than girls in father-present households. Father absence had a stronger impact on adolescent sexual behavior than academic achievement and mental health (Ellis et al., 2003). Dittus, Jaccard, and Gordon (1997) found that African American adolescent girls were less likely to engage in sex if they believed that their father disapproved of premarital sexual intercourse. Including fathers in adolescent sexual health promotion programs should be a priority.

Thus, parents play an important role in promoting adolescent sexual health. Programs designed to increase parents' knowledge and efficacy during conversations have been effective in increasing parent–child communication about sexual topics. More attention needs to be paid to the role of fathers in adolescent sexual health promotion. Developing father–adolescent programs, inviting fathers to program sessions with mothers, or encouraging fathers to participate in discussions that mothers have with their adolescents are some ideas (Corona, 2010).

Media Influences on the Sexual Health of Adolescents

Adolescents are exposed to significant amounts of sexual content through media (Durham, 1998; Flowers-Coulson, Kushner, & Bankowski, 2000). Exposure to sexual content through media outlets is linked to several sexual risk indicators (Escobar-Chavez et al., 2005). For example, increased sexual content in media is associated with more liberal and stereotypical sexual attitudes and greater acceptance of sexual harassment, and sexual behaviors (Collins et al., 2004; Rivadeneyra & Ward, 2005). L'Engle, Brown, and Kenneavy (2006) found that increased exposure to sexual content among youth was associated with more current sexual activity and with greater intentions to engage in sex.

One method of combating the potential negative impact of the media on adolescent sexual behavior is to teach youth to be critical viewers of media messages. Youth are taught to question the intent of the message, who the intended audience is, and whose perspective is being told. An emerging body of research shows that media literacy programs are effective at helping youth develop critical thinking and literacy skills related to violence (Robinson, Wilde, Navracruz, Haydel, & Varady, 2001), disordered eating (Wade, Davidson, & O'Dea, 2003), and alcohol use (Austin & Johnson, 1997). Despite these promising findings, media literacy programs related to sexual behavior have not yet been developed and evaluated (Keller & Brown, 2002) highlighting a significant gap in prevention planning. Further, most media literacy programs are implemented in school and community contexts (as opposed to family), and few media literacy programs have been rigorously evaluated (Brown, 2006).

Media can also be used as a method of teaching assertiveness, self-efficacy, and parenting and communication skills. Media-based interventions deliver intervention content through the use of videos/DVDs, CDs, or internet (e.g., YouTube) and offer flexible interventions so that individuals can tailor the content and sequence of program ingredients. Media-based programs may seem more anonymous and thus less threatening to youth and families. O'Donnell et al. (2005) evaluated Saving Sex for Later, presented on three audio CDs. This parent-education program increased parent–child communication about youth risk behaviors and parental self-efficacy to initiate conversations about sexuality. What Could You Do? (Downs et al., 2004) is a video intervention targeted at increasing adolescents' ability to make healthy sexual decisions. Program participants were more likely to be abstinent in the previous three months, and less likely to report an STI at six months. Finally, Keeping it Safe is a CD-ROM intervention designed to prevent HIV among adolescent females (DiNoia, Schinke, Pena, & Schwinn, 2004). Evaluation findings support the use of computer-mediated programs in increasing HIV/AIDS knowledge and risk reduction self-efficacy.

In summary, media literacy programs can promote adolescent sexual health by helping develop youths' critical thinking skills. Incorporating media into current prevention programs aimed at parents is also warranted. Specifically, programs should encourage parents to monitor their adolescents' media usage, and to discuss resulting media messages. Finally, media-based programs also provide prevention programmers and schools with a newer way of engaging adolescents and parents in adolescent sexual health promotion efforts.

Culture and Adolescent Sexual Health

Prevention specialists must understand how cultural variables relate to health behaviors in order to provide culturally appropriate programs (Kreuter, Lukwago, Bucholtz, Clark, & Sanders-Thompson, 2003). Aspects of culture that affect adolescent sexual health include gender, ethnic or racial group membership, acculturation, and community context. For example, communal and relational values found within the African American culture can promote and deter risky sexual behaviors (Belgrave & Allison, 2010). Personalismo and familismo are related Latino cultural values (Cauce & Domenech-Rodriguez, 2000) that can affect parent–child relationships and families' engagement in prevention programs. The relationship between acculturation and adolescent risk behavior is extremely mixed (Driscoll, Biggs, Brindis, & Yankah, 2001). However, when one considers the interaction of different acculturation variables together, some interesting findings emerge. Guilamo-Ramos, Jaccard, Pena, & Goldberg (2005) found that for recent immigrants, youth from English-speaking homes were less likely to be sexually active than youth from Spanish-speaking homes. An opposite trend was found for US-born youth or those who had lived most of their life in the US. Another example of how cultural values affect sexual health is through the expression of gender role beliefs.

Gender Roles

Gender roles are the traits, expectations, and behaviors associated with men and women and what it means to be "masculine" or "feminine" (Bem, 1993). The distinct gender role expectations supported by traditional Latino culture have important implications for adolescent sexual health (Staples & Mirande, 1980). For example, the traditional emphasis on female virginity may make Latino parents reluctant to give their daughters information regarding sexuality (Baumeister, Flores, & Marin, 1995; Marin & Gomez, 1997) and affect Latino parents' rules about adolescent dating (Villarruel, 1998). This emphasis on female virginity was positively associated with Latino adolescents' inconsistent use of condoms (Deardorff, Tschann, Flores, & Ozer, 2010). Studies with Latina adults have also found that gender-based power imbalances can limit a Latina's ability to negotiate safe sexual practices (Pulerwitz, Amaro, De Jong, Gortmaker, & Rudd, 2002).

In the African American community, girls are socialized to be emotionally strong and self-sufficient (Beauboeuf-Lafontant, 2007; Wallace, 2007). They may believe that emotional strength, caretaking, and independence are important (Kerrigan et al, 2007). This suggests that African American girls are well equipped to assert themselves and negotiate their desires in most situations, including those involving sex. However, the disproportionate rates of HIV and teen pregnancy among African American girls suggests that despite this gender socialization there are more complex factors influencing their sexual behaviors. In fact, societal norms and traditional religion influence African American women to be more submissive in the home environment (Cowdery et al., 2009) where African American girls are likely to adopt their gender role beliefs. The expectation to be strong and independent coupled with the pressure of being submissive may contribute to young African American women's identity confusion and subsequent risk-taking (Dade & Sloan, 2000).

Similarly prevention programming for boys must be responsive to beliefs and values that endorse hyper-masculinity (African American and Latino males) and machismo (Latino males). Hyper-masculinity, the overemphasis of traditional masculine qualities, has been linked to high-risk behaviors such as sexual promiscuity/exploitation and condom refusal (Wolfe, 2003). Therefore, expressions of masculinity contribute to HIV risk by acting as a barrier to safe sex practices (Wolfe, 2003). Adoption of traditional male role beliefs may help youth cope with perceptions of powerlessness associated with living in high poverty, under-resourced communities (Daniels, Crum, & Ramaswamy, 2011; Payne, 2006). Providing educational opportunities and improving the coping skills of youth may help increase feelings of self-worth and re-shape attitudes toward social roles. Additionally, involving male role models and challenging negative media portrayals of African American males may help in promoting sexual health (Brown, Payne, Dressner, & Green, 2010; Kendrick, Anderson, & Moore, 2007).

The terms *macho* and *machismo* are often used when talking about Latino men. For men, the cultural pressure to have children is enormous, even among young Latino adolescents. The extent to which Latino adolescent males endorse a machismo ethic and the effect of this on their sexual behavior has been understudied. In the US the term machismo has a negative connotation. However, a more accurate definition of the term machismo includes men being in control of their own lives, and providing for and protecting their families. Torres, Solberg, and Carlstrom (2002) found that machismo is best characterized as a multi-dimensional construct that includes both positive and negative aspects. Focusing on the positive characteristics of machismo may help promote father or male involvement in promoting adolescent health and reducing risk.

Thus, gender-based programs may be warranted when focusing on adolescent sexual health. Prevention programs for girls should consider how female gender role beliefs of nurturance, compassion, and the importance of virginity may be associated with sexual risk and make protecting oneself more difficult. SIHLE (Sistering, Informing, Healing, Living, and Empowering) is an example of an HIV-prevention program that attends to the culture of African American girls in promoting ethnic and gender pride (DiClemente et al., 2004). An adaptation of this program is currently under way for Latina teens. Also, prevention programs for males should attend to how cultural values and norms affect their beliefs about masculinity. Finally, Cuidate! is an evidence-based HIV prevention program targeted at Spanish- and English-speaking Latino youth that draws on the Latino cultural value of familismo by motivating youth to take care of themselves, their partners, their family, and their community (Villarruel, Jemmott, & Jemmott, 2006).

In summary, attention to cultural factors, including gender role beliefs, will aid us in understanding the best way in which to intervene with racial/ethnic minority youth. Gender role beliefs, such as machismo and hyper-masculinity among males and nurturance and femininity among females can serve to both protect and increase risk for sexual behaviors.

Community Factors

Youth who live in low resourced and disordered communities have earlier sexual initiation, and are more likely to engage in other sexual risk behaviors than youth who live in better resourced communities (Belgrave, 2009; Browning, Burrington, Leventhal, & Brooks-Gunn, 2008). Cooper and Guthrie (2007) found that perceptions of neighborhood disorder were related to African American adolescents' increased sexual risk behaviors, substance use, and other problem behaviors. Finally it is important to note that adolescent functioning even in the most disadvantaged neighborhoods is not always negative (Belgrave, 2009). Community assets and resources, along with personal and family assets and resources, can buffer youth who live in disadvantaged neighborhoods.

Recognizing that adolescents can contribute to positive changes within their communities, some sex education programs include a community component. The Teen Health Project (Sikkema et al., 2005) is an HIV-prevention intervention developed for adolescents living in low-income housing communities. The intervention involves the use of teen opinion leaders who develop and implement monthly HIV-prevention activities and quarterly events in their housing developments.

Conclusions

Using an ecological framework, the literature reviewed highlights several important facets to sexual health promotion for urban adolescents. These include: (1)

strengthening family relationships; (2) incorporating media literacy to buffer negative effects of media messages; (3) helping youth envision their future outcomes and barriers for obtaining future goals; and (4) using adolescents to implement programs within their community. These programs should be culturally tailored for Latino and African American youth in order to have maximum impact (Tinsley, Lees, & Sumartojo, 2004). Although several programs described are culturally appropriate and promote sexual health, these programs do not comprehensively address underlying risk and protective factors for the multiple challenges facing urban adolescents. Programs that promote academic excellence, drug refusal skills, pro-social behavior, and community service while promoting sexual health are desired. Future research is needed to develop, implement, and evaluate multi-level programs.

References

Aloise-Young, P. A., Hennigan, K. M., & Leong, C. W. (2001). Possible selves and negative health behaviors during early adolescence. *Journal of Early Adolescence, 21*, 158–181.

Austin, E. W., & Johnson, K. K. (1997). Effects of general and alcohol-specific media literacy training on children's decision making about alcohol. *Journal of Health Communication, 2*, 17–42.

Baumeister, L. M., Flores, E., & Marin, B. V. (1995). Sex information given to Latino adolescents by parents. *Health Education Research, 10*, 233–239.

Beauboeuf-Lafontant, T. (2007). You have to show strength: An exploration of gender, race, and depression. *Gender and Society, 21*, 28–51.

Belgrave, F. Z. (2009). *African American girls: Reframing perceptions and changing experiences.* London/New York: Springer.

Belgrave, F. Z., & Allison, K. W. (2010). *African American psychology: From Africa to America.* Los Angeles, CA: Sage.

Bem, S. L. (1993). *The lenses of gender: Transforming the debate on sexual inequality.* New Haven, CT: Yale.

Brown, A. L., Payne, Y., Dressner, L., & Green, A. G. (2010). I place my hand in yours: A social justice based intervention for fostering resilience in street life oriented black men. *Journal of Systemic Therapies, 29*, 44–64.

Brown, J. D. (2006). Media literacy has potential to improve adolescents' health. *Journal of Adolescent Health, 39*, 459–460.

Browning, C. R., Burrngton, L. A., Leventhal, T., & Books-Gunn, J. (2008). Neighborhood structural inequality, collective efficacy, and sexual risk behavior among urban youth. *Journal of Health and Social Behavior, 49*, 269–285.

Cauce, A. M., & Domenech-Rodríguez, M. (2002). Latino families: Myths and realities. In J. M. Contreras, K. A. Kerns, & A. M. Neal-Barnett (Eds.), *Latino children and families in the United States: Current research and future directions* (pp. 3–25). Westport, CT: Praeger.

Clark, L. F., Miller, K. S., Nagy, S. S., Avery, J., Roth, D. L., Liddon, N., & Mukerjee, S. (2005). Adult identity mentoring: Reducing sexual risk for African-American seventh-grade students. *Journal of Adolescent Health, 37*, 337.e1–337.e10.

Coatsworth, J. D., Pantin, H., & Szapocznik, J. (2002). Familias Unidas: A family-centered ecodevelopmental intervention to reduce risk for problem behavior among Hispanic adolescents. *Clinical Child and Family Psychology Review, 5*, 113–132.

Collins, R. L., Elliott, M. N., Berry, S. H., Kanouse, D. E., Kunkel, D., Hunter, S. B., & Miu, A. (2004). Watching sex on television predicts adolescent sexual behavior. *Pediatrics, 114*, 280–290.

Cooper, S. M., & Guthrie, B. G. (2007). Ecological influences on health-promoting and health-compromising behaviors: A socially-embedded approach to urban African American adolescent girls' health. *Family and Community Health, 30*, 29–41.

Corona, R. (2010). Moving beyond the mother-child dyad in prevention planning for Latino families: Dads and siblings matter, too! In N. S. Landale, S. McHale, & A. Booth (Eds.), *Growing up Hispanic: Health and development of children of immigrants* (pp. 150–168). Washington, DC: The Urban Institute Press.

Cowdery, R. S., Scarborough, N., Knudson-Martin, C., Seshadri, G., Lewis, M. E., & Mahoney, A. R. (2009). Gendered power in cultural contexts: Part II. Middle class African American heterosexual couples with young children. *Family Process, 48*, 25–39.

Dade, L. R., & Sloan, L. R. (2000). An investigation of sex-role stereotypes in African Americans. *Journal of Black Studies, 30*, 676–690.

Daniels, J., Crum, M., & Ramaswamy, M. (2011). Creating real men: Description of an intervention to reduce drug use, HIV risk, and re-arrest among young men returning to urban communities from jail. *Health Promotion Practice, 12*, 44–54.

Deardorff, J., Tschann, J. M., Flores, E., & Ozer, E. J. (2010). Sexual values and risky sexual behavior among Latino youths. *Perspectives on Sexual and Reproductive Health, 42*, 23–32.

DiClemente, R. J., Wingood, G. M., Harrington, K. F., Lang, D. L., Davies, S. L., Hook, E. W., . . . & Robillard, A. (2004). Efficacy of an HIV prevention intervention for African American adolescent girls: A randomized controlled trial. *Journal of American Medical Association, 292*, 171–179.

DiIorio, C., Resnicow, K., McCarty, F., De, A. K., Dudley, W. N., Wang, D. T., & Denzmore, P. (2006). Keepin' it R.E.A.L.!: Results of a mother-adolescent HIV prevention program. *Nursing Research, 55*, 43–51.

DiNoia, J., Schinke, S. P., Pena, J. B., & Scwhinn, T. M. (2004). Evaluation of a brief computer-mediated intervention to reduce HIV risk among early adolescent females. *Journal of Adolescent Health, 35*, 62–64.

Dittus, P., Jaccard, J., & Gordon, V. (1997). The impact of African American fathers on adolescent sexual behavior. *Journal of Youth and Adolescence, 26*, 445–465.

Dittus, P., Miller, K. S., Kotchick, B. A., & Forehand, R. (2004). Why parents matter!: The conceptual basis for a community-based HIV prevention program for the parents of African American youth. *Journal of Child and Family Studies, 13*, 5–20.

Downs, J. S., Murray, P. J., de Bruin, W. B., Penrose, J., Palmgren, C., & Fischhoff, B. (2004). Interactive video behavioral intervention to reduce adolescent females' STD risk: A randomized controlled trial. *Social Science & Medicine, 59*, 1561–1572.

Driscoll, A. K., Biggs, M. A., Brindis, C. D., & Yankah, E. (2001). Adolescent Latino reproductive health: A review of the literature. *Hispanic Journal of Behavioral Sciences, 23*, 255–326.

Durham, M. G. (1998). Dilemmas of desire: Representations of adolescent sexuality in two teen magazines. *Youth & Society, 29*, 369–389.

Ellis, B. J., Bates, J. E., Dodge, K. A., Fergusson, D. M., Horwood, L. J., Pettit, G. S., & Woodward, L. (2003). Does father absence place daughters at special risk for early sexual activity and teenage pregnancy? *Child Development, 74*, 801–821.

Escobar-Chavez, S. L., Tortolero, S. R., Markham, C. M., Low, B. J., Eitel, P., & Thickstun, P. (2005). Impact of the media on adolescent sexual attitudes and behavior. *Pediatrics, 116*, 303–326.

Fishbein, M., Bandura, A., Triandis, H. C., Kanfer, F. H., Becker, M. H., & Middlestadt, S. E. (1991). Factors influencing behavior and behavior change. *Final report to the Theorist's Workshop*, Washington, DC.

Flowers-Coulson, P. A., Kushner, M. A., & Bankowski, S. (2000). The information is out there, but is anyone getting it? Adolescent misconceptions about sexuality education and reproductive health and the use of the internet to get answers. *Journal of Sex Education and Therapy, 25*, 178–188.

Frisco, M. L. (2008). Adolescents' sexual behavior and academic attainment. *Sociology of Education, 81*, 284–311.

Guilamo-Ramos, V., Jaccard, J., Dittus, P., Gonzalez, B., & Bouris, A. (2008). A conceptual framework for the analysis of risk and problem behaviors: The case of adolescent sexual behavior. *Social Work Research, 32*, 29–45.

Guiliamo-Ramos, V., Jaccard, J., Pena, J., & Goldberg, V. (2005). Acculturation-related variables, sexual initiation, and subsequent sexual behavior among Puerto Rican, Mexican, and Cuban youth. *Health Psychology, 24*, 88–95.

Jaccard, J., Dodge, T. & Dittus, P. (2002). Parent-adolescent communication about sex and birth control: a conceptual framework. *New Directions for Child and Adolescent Development, 97*, 9–41.

Jemmott III, J. B., Jemmott, L. S., & Fong, G. (1998). Abstinence and safer sex HIV risk-reduction interventions for African-American adolescents: A randomized control trial. *Journal of American Medical Association, 279*, 1529–1536.

Keller, S. N. & Brown, J. D. (2002). Media interventions to promote responsible sexual behavior. *Journal of Sex Research, 39*, 67–72.

Kendrick, L., Anderson, N. L., & Moore, B. (2007). Perceptions of depression among young African American men. *Family and Community Health, 30*, 63–73.

Kerrigan, D., Andrinopoulos, K., Johnson, R., Parham, P., Thomas, T., & Ellen, J. M. (2007). Staying strong: Gender ideologies among African-American adolescents and the implications for HIV/STI prevention. *Journal of Sex Research, 44*, 172–180.

Kirby, D., & Laris, B. A. (2009). Effective curriculum-based sex and STD/HIV education programs for adolescents. *Child Development Perspectives, 3*, 21–29.

Kotchick, B. A., Shaffer, A., & Forehand, R. (2001). Adolescent sexual risk behavior: A multi-system perspective. *Clinical Psychology Review, 21*, 493–519.

Kreuter, M. W., Lukwago, S. N., Bucholtz, D. C., Clark, E. M., & Sanders-Thompson, V. (2003). Achieving cultural appropriateness in health promotion programs: Targeted and tailored approaches. *Health Education & Behavior, 30*, 133–146.

Laflin, M. T., Wang, J., & Barry, M. (2008). A longitudinal study of adolescent transition from virgin to nonvirgin status. *Journal of Adolescent Health, 42*, 228–236.

L'Engle, K. L., Brown, J. D., & Kenneavy, K. (2006). The mass media are an important context for adolescents' sexual behavior. *Journal of Adolescent Health, 38*, 186–192.

Marin, B., & Gomez, C. A. (1997). Latino culture and sex: Implications for HIV prevention. In J. G. Garcia, & M. C. Zea (Eds.), *Psychological interventions and research with Latino populations* (pp. 73–93). Needham Heights, MA: Allyn & Bacon.

Markus, H., & Nurius, P. (1986). Possible selves. *American Psychologist, 41*, 954–969.

McKay, M. M., Chasse, K. T., Paikoff, R., McKinney, D., Coleman, D., Madison, S., & Bell, C. C. (2004). Family level impact of the CHAMP family program: A community collaborative effort to support urban families and reduce youth HIV risk exposure. *Family Process, 43*, 79–93.

Miller, B. C., Benson, B., & Galbraith, K. A. (2001). Family relationships and adolescent pregnancy risk: A research synthesis. *Developmental Review, 21*, 1–38.

O'Donnell, L., Stueve, A., Agronick, G., Wilson-Simmons, R., Duran, R., & Jeanbaptiste, V. (2005). Saving sex for later: An evaluation of a parent education intervention. *Perspective on Sexual and Reproductive Health, 37*, 166–173.

Oyserman, D., Bybee, D., & Terry, K. (2006). Possible selves and academic outcomes: How and when possible selves impel action. *Journal of Personality and Social Psychology, 91*, 188–204.

Oyserman, D., Terry, K., & Bybee, D. (2002). A possible selves intervention to enhance school involvement. *Journal of Adolescence, 25*, 313–326.

Pantin, H., Schwartz, S. J., Sullivan, S., Prado, G., & Szapocznik, J. (2004). Ecodevelopmental HIV prevention programs for Hispanic adolescents. *American Journal of Orthopsychiatry, 74*, 545–558.

Payne, Y. A. (2006). A gangster and a gentleman: How street life-oriented, U.S.-born African men negotiate issues of survival in relation to their masculinity. *Men and Masculinities, 8*, 288–297.

Philliber, S., Williams Kaye, J., Herrling, S., & West, E. (2002). Preventing pregnancy and improving health care access among teenagers: An evaluation of the Children's Aid Society–Carrera Program. *Perspectives on Sexual and Reproductive Health, 34*, 244–251.

Prado, G., Pantin, H., Huang, S., Cordova, D., Tapia, M. I., Velazquez, M.-R., . . . & Estrada, Y. (2012). Effects of a family intervention in reducing HIV risk behaviours among high-risk Hispanic adolescents: A randomized controlled trial. *Archives of Paediatric and Adolescent Medicine, 166*, 127–133.

Pulerwitz, J., Amaro, H., De Jong, W., Gortmaker, S. L., & Rudd, R. (2002). Relationship power, condom use and HIV risk among women in the USA. *AIDS Care, 14*, 789–800.

Rink, E., Tricker, R., & Harvey, S. M. (2007). Onset of sexual intercourse among female adolescents: The influence of perceptions, depression, and ecological factors. *Journal of Adolescent Health, 41*, 398–406.

Rivadeneyra, R., & Ward, L. M. (2005). From Ally McBeal to Sabado Gigante: Contributions of television viewing to the gender role attitudes of Latino adolescents. *Journal of Adolescent Research, 20*, 453–475.

Robinson, T. N., Wilde, M. L., Navracruz, L. C., Haydel, K. F., & Varady, A. (2001). Effects of reducing children's television and video game use on aggressive behavior: A randomized controlled trial. *Archives of Pediatric & Adolescent Medicine, 155*, 17–23.

Romer, D., Stanton, B., Galbraith, J., Feigelman, S., Black, M. M., & Li, X. (1999). Parental influence on adolescent sexual behavior in high-poverty settings. *Archives of Pediatric Medicine, 153*, 1055–1062.

Romo, L. F., Kouyoumdjian, C., Nadeem, E., & Sigman, M. (2006). Promoting values of education in Latino mother-adolescent discussions about conflict and sexuality issues. In J. Denner, & B. Guzman (Eds.), *Latina girls: Voices of adolescent strength in the US* (pp. 59–76). New York: University Press.

Salazar, L. F., DiClemente, R. J., Wingood, G. M., Crosby, R. A., Harrington, K., Davies, S., . . . & Oh, M. K. (2004). Self-concept and adolescents' refusal of unprotected sex: A test of mediating mechanisms among African American girls. *Prevention Science, 5*, 137–149.

Sikkema, K. J., Anderson, E. S., Kelly, J. A., Winett, R. A., Gore-Felton, C., Roffman, R. A., . . . & Brondino, M. J. (2005). Outcomes of a randomized, controlled community-level HIV prevention intervention for adolescents in low-income housing developments. *AIDS, 19*, 1509–1516.

Staples, R., & Mirande, A. (1980). Racial and cultural variations among American families: A decennial review of the literature of minority families. *Journal of Marriage and the Family, 42*, 887–903.

Tinsley, B. J., Lees, N. B., & Sumartojo, E. (2004). Child and adolescent HIV risk: Familial and cultural perspectives. *Journal of Family Psychology, 18*, 208–224.

Torres, J. B., Solberg, V. S. H., & Carlstrom, A. H. (2002). The myth of sameness among Latino men and their machismo. *American Journal of Orthopsychiatry, 72*, 163–181.

Villarruel, A. M. (1998). Cultural influences on the sexual attitudes, beliefs, and norms of young Latina adolescents. *Journal of the Society of Pediatric Nurses, 3*, 69–79.

Villarruel, A. M., Jemmott III, J. B., and Jemmott, L. S. (2006). A randomized controlled trial testing an HIV prevention intervention for Latino youth. *Archives of Pediatric & Adolescent Medicine, 160*, 772–777.

Wade, T. D., Davidson, S., & O'Dea, J. A. (2003). A preliminary controlled evaluation of a school-based media literacy program and self-esteem program for reducing eating disorder risk factors. *International Journal of Eating Disorders, 33*, 371–383.

Wallace, D. M. (2007). It's a M-A-N Thang: Black male gender role socialization and the performance of masculinity in love relationships. *Journal of Pan African Studies, 1*, 11–22.

Wolfe, W. (2003). Overlooked role of African-American males' hypermasculinity in the epidemic of unintended pregnancies and HIV/AIDS cases with young African-American women. *Journal of the National Medical Association, 95*, 846–852.

18

PERSONAL, ETHNIC, AND CULTURAL IDENTITY IN URBAN YOUTH

Links with Risk and Resilience

Seth J. Schwartz, Liliana Rodriguez, Robert S. Weisskirch, Byron L. Zamboanga, and Hilda M. Pantin

Urban adolescents face many challenges. They may reside in unsafe neighborhoods, routinely witness crime and violence, and/or are confronted with many barriers that make it difficult to succeed in school and society. Some of the schools that these adolescents attend are under-resourced, and parents may be uninvolved in their schooling. Although not all urban youth are faced with these types of challenges, the present chapter focuses on youth who do face major adversity. It is important to identify ways to help urban youth to succeed. Graduating high school and completing college are required for most professional occupations. The unemployment rate for college graduates (4.7%) is one-third the unemployment rate for individuals who have not completed high school (14.1%; Bureau of Labor Statistics, 2011). However, school engagement is a purposeful choice—and making such a choice requires that school be part of who one is (Destin & Oyserman, 2010). Accordingly, in the present chapter, we draw upon identity theory as a vehicle for predicting school performance, and as a potential target for intervention for urban youth.

Identity is a multifaceted construct (Schwartz, Luyckx, & Vignoles, 2011). Broadly, "identity" may be understood as a sense of oneself in the context of life stages and societal expectations (Erikson, 1959). Identity is an individual's response to questions such as "Where did I come from?," "Who am I?," and "Where am I going?" Identity has been used to refer to long-term life goals (Kroger & Marcia, 2011) and attachment to one's ethnic group (Phinney & Ong, 2007), among many other domains.

This chapter focuses on personal, ethnic, and cultural identity. *Personal identity* refers to one's adopted/considered goals, values, and beliefs (Schwartz, 2001). Personal identity also refers to the possibilities for what one might become (or does not want to become) in the future (Oyserman & Destin, 2010). *Ethnic identity* refers to the extent to which one has a firm idea of what one's ethnicity means to oneself, and to which one regards one's ethnic group favorably (Phinney & Ong, 2007). *Cultural identity* refers to the general set of behaviors, values, and identifications that one adopts regarding mainstream American culture and regarding one's culture of origin

(Schwartz, Unger, Zamboanga, & Szapocznik, 2010). Cultural identity emerges from the ways in which an individual situates her/himself between her/his cultural origins and those of the United States. Given that most urban youth identify as people of color, personal, ethnic, and cultural identities are likely the most salient identities for young people residing in urban environments.

Personal Identity in Urban Youth

Adolescence is a time when identity development is generally initiated: young people are expected to decide on their general adult path (Erikson, 1968). In communities with strong families and support, adolescents may find opportunities to explore potential identity alternatives before enacting major commitments. However, for young people residing in dangerous neighborhoods, attending under-resourced schools, and often facing considerable family turmoil, developing a goal-directed sense of self can be challenging. Difficulties with identity development may also be due to a relative dearth of role models for success.

The most prominent theory of identity is Marcia's (1966) identity status model. Marcia asserted that adolescents must explore potential alternatives and expectations in a number of life domains (e.g., careers) and establish commitments to the alternatives considered (Kroger & Marcia, 2011). The relevance of identity status theory to urban youth is questionable, however, as it assumes that the individual has the psychological "space" to reflect on, and commit to, an array of identity options. Moreover, most identity status research has been conducted on fairly affluent/ educated youth, who have access to opportunities that facilitate exposure to identity options (Schwartz, 2005). Urban youth—for whom daily life is filled with challenges—may not have as much "luxury" in considering identity alternatives (Phillips & Pittman, 2003). If an urban adolescent decides on becoming a doctor or attorney, and then encounters considerable barriers because of lack of resources, the result may be a sense of failure (Oyserman & Destin, 2010).

Oyserman and colleagues (e.g., Oyserman & James, 2011) have focused on *possible identities*: what roles does one want to actualize, does one believe they will actualize, and is one afraid they will actualize? All three types of possible identities—hoped-for, expected, and feared—are based on options that the young person has considered and/or adopted (similar to the identity status model). However, an additional step is *identity-based motivation* (Oyserman & Destin, 2010)—that implies that youth must create a strategy to manifest an ideal identity and to avoid a feared identity. For example, excelling in academic pursuits and in sports are two potential ways of making one's way into college. However, the youth must devise a clear plan to bring the desired identity (e.g., "becoming an A-student") into being. Further, adolescents may choose to assess their strengths and weaknesses, recognize areas where they need help, and secure resources (e.g., finding a tutor) to actualize the desired identities. Without such a plan, the person is unlikely to actualize the hoped-for identity and may wind up actualizing a feared identity (e.g., school dropout). Congruence between actual and feared identities is associated with negative behaviors (e.g., substance use; Oyserman & Markus, 1990). In effect, when a person becomes what she or he is afraid of becoming, the likelihood increases that s/he may "give up" and choose a negative path.

Unfortunately, others often coach urban youth in terms of "what not to do"—don't join a gang, or don't get arrested. However, examples of what one *should* be doing—potential hoped-for identities—are less readily available (Destin & Oyserman, 2010). Moreover, even the introduction of positive future identities may not lead to the pursuit and actualization of these identities—largely because many urban youth do not view professional advancement as consistent with their current views of themselves (Oyserman & Destin, 2010). The task, then, is to expand the young person's identity so that long-term successful goals become consistent with the person's sense of self—and to provide role models to achieve such success.

Fortunately, interventions have been developed to help youth to devise strategies for reaching positive goals (Kurtines et al., 2008). Such interventions involve group meetings with a trained facilitator to identify a range of possible alternatives, to critically evaluate the "pros" and "cons" of each alternative, and to develop a plan for addressing these goals. Indeed, such interventions may be efficacious in helping urban youth to follow positive developmental trajectories—both in school and in other aspects of their lives (Eichas et al., 2010; Oyserman, Bybee, & Terry, 2006).

Ethnicity, Culture, and Identity in Urban Youth

Identity also operates at the collective level, where individuals are influenced by the groups to which they belong (Sedikides & Brewer, 2001)—including ethnic, national, and religious groups—and the concomitant identities that come from them. Group identities are most likely to predict behavior when contextual forces make the group membership salient (Spears, 2011). A powerful way to activate a group identity is to threaten it; discriminating against one's ethnic group is likely to bring that group membership to the forefront of one's sense of self (Rumbaut, 2008). This means not only that being African American, for example, becomes the acute focus of one's identity—but that the identity elements *attached* to the ethnic group become salient within the person's overall sense of self. For ethnic minority, urban youth, this identity threat appraisal may shape one's individual identity. In the US, African Americans and Hispanics are often stereotyped as uninterested in educational/career achievements (Peffley & Hurwitz, 2002). Individuals from these groups might actualize these stereotypes—a self-fulfilling prophecy that has been labeled as stereotype threat (Steele, 1997) and that leads individuals to believe that the established social structure is fair and just (Jost, Banaji, & Nosek, 2004). So, not only might many urban youth feel "trapped by poverty," but they may also often believe (largely unconsciously) that this is "just the way things are."

Many urban youth face considerable obstacles to social mobility. Whereas some African Americans have been successful, they have been historically marginalized in the US. Systemic discrimination—along with stereotype threat and self-fulfilling prophecies—has served to maintain many African Americans in a marginalized social position (Wilson, 2002). As Pratto, Sidanius, and Levin (2006) state, groups in such positions are subjected to "substandard housing, disease, underemployment, dangerous and distasteful work, disproportionate punishment, stigmatization, and vilific-ation" (p. 272). The juvenile justice system is a good example of this. African Americans represent 15% of American youth, but they represent 25% of juvenile arrests and 40% of imprisoned youth (Crutchfield, Fernandes, & Martinez, 2010). African Americans who escape social marginalization are those who are willing to challenge these negative social-structural processes. Such individuals may be motivated, rather than disempowered, by discrimination.

Hispanics, on the other hand, have become socially marginalized through down-ward assimilation (Portes & Rumbaut, 2006). Mexican Americans and Puerto Ricans are often victims of such downward assimilation—owing largely to the circumstances surrounding their original migration to the US. To illustrate, most Mexican migrants to the US have arrived seeking agricultural or unskilled-manual labor (Henderson, 2011). They are most often employed by wealthy White Americans—which only exacerbates their marginalization. Many other Hispanic groups—such as Puerto Ricans and Dominicans—also arrived looking for low-wage jobs (Kasinitz, Mollenkopf, Waters, & Holdaway, 2008) and wound up in a similar disadvantaged social position. Cuban Americans, however, have managed to defy this pattern. Americans more easily accepted Cubans because of their educational status, financial resources, and primarily Caucasian physical features (Stepick & Stepick, 2002). Later waves of Cuban immigrants, many of whom are of mixed racial heritage, are largely protected from marginalization in Florida (where most Cuban Americans live) because of the high social position occupied by the original, affluent cohort of Cubans (Stepick, Grenier, Castro, & Dunn, 2003). Cubans may therefore be one of the few Hispanic groups who are somewhat protected from the effects of urban poverty.

The social marginalization of many urban African Americans and Hispanics, therefore, not only involves personal barriers such as poor schools and dangerous neighborhoods, but also subjects them to discrimination that impairs upward mobility. Because the intergroup processes that occur between Whites and other ethnic groups are often unconscious and self-perpetuating (cf. Pratto et al., 2006), these processes are difficult to change—and many ethnic-minority individuals remain in a subordinate social position. Strategies for helping minority youth to circumvent these barriers must "work around" institutional obstacles while simultaneously empowering youth to believe that success is possible (Destin & Oyserman, 2009, 2010).

One way to maximize their chances of success is for urban youth to be conscious of their ethnic identity—and also distance themselves from their ethnic group's negative stereotypic beliefs about achievement (Altschul, Oyserman, & Bybee, 2008). Identifying with one's ethnicity is not the same as endorsing that ethnic group's stereotypic belief system; indeed, urban youth are challenged with striking a delicate balance between the two (Carter, 2006). Identifying with one's ethnicity allows one to take pride in one's ethnic group (Phinney & Ong, 2007), which may lead to higher self-esteem (Syed & Azmitia, 2008). One study (Oyserman, Harrison, & Bybee, 2001) concluded that urban youth perform better in school if they connect their ethnic identity with academics. African Americans who liked school because it reflected well on the Black community did better academically, even if they were aware of the racism in society. For those urban youth who are successful in completing school and becoming productive citizens, retention of their cultural heritage and maintaining a bicultural identity is important. Relinquishing one's cultural heritage may harm one's relationships with family members who remain identified with the heritage-cultural stream (Rudmin, 2003). Thus, urban youth must be conscious of—and comfortable with—who they are. Rejecting any part of oneself, including one's heritage culture, can lead to compromised personal (e.g., depression) and educational/career (e.g., high school dropout) outcomes.

Resilience and Identity Development in Urban Youth

A commonly invoked construct in the positive development of urban and disadvantaged youth is *resilience*, where individuals with multiple risk factors manage to succeed (Masten, 2001). Masten found that many resilient youth have at least one caring and involved adult mentor. These adults can be parents, teachers, coaches, or other community members (Plunkett, Henry, Houltberg, Sands, & Abarca-Mortensen, 2008). Such mentors are responsible for providing direction while still encouraging youth to make independent decisions (Larson, 2011). Indeed, self-determination theory holds that a balance between autonomy (self-direction) and relatedness (connectedness to others) is necessary for healthy development (Ryan & Deci, 2000).

For Hispanic youth, connectedness to family members helps alleviate identity confusion in adolescence (Schwartz, Mason, Pantin, & Szapocznik, 2009). In turn, decreases in personal identity confusion are associated with lowered risk taking behavior (Schwartz, Mason, Pantin, & Szapocznik, 2008). Further, a strong personal identity is also critical in making career choices (Skorikov & Vondracek, 2011), and to the extent that such choices are linked to one's current sense of self, the individual is likely to take proactive steps to actualize the choices made (Destin & Oyserman, 2010). Thus, a goal that is seen as unattainable will be regarded as such, whereas goals that seem achievable will engender a greater degree of persistence. Indeed, simply *suggesting* to urban youth that college is attainable leads them to work harder in school (Destin & Oyserman, 2009).

Extracurricular involvement also predicts resilience and perseverance in urban youth (Peck, Roeser, Zarrett, & Eccles, 2008). Athletics, school clubs, and volunteering are closely related to higher likelihood of college attendance. All of these activities involve structured participation, commitment, and adult mentoring. In turn, extracurricular activities, and the associated mentorship, often foster a sense of competence and connection to others (Zarrett et al., 2009).

It is important to consider mentoring and extracurricular activity involvement within the context of social-structural barriers and burdens placed on urban youth. Although many urban youth experience uncontrollable, systematic burdens, they are not "required to fail" because of these adverse social-structural processes. Most young people—urban or otherwise—are challenged with making their own way into adulthood with minimal external help (Côté, 2000). Many young people fail to progress in making life choices because they are unable to make or pursue the self-directed choices that are required to enact stable adult commitments. Indeed, the transition from industrial to technological society has phased out the entry-level jobs that young people once took upon entering the workforce (Kalleberg, 2009) and that helped them to sort out occupational, personal, ethnic, and cultural identity choices. Given the additional barriers that many urban youth face due to social dominance processes (Pratto et al., 2006)—poverty, inadequate health care, and disproportionate rates of single-parent homes—support for self-directed decision making is likely to be low among poor urban youth. Conversely, engagement into positive pursuits—particularly structured extracurricular activities—may prevent school underachievement and may keep urban youth away from negative influences by providing supportive social contexts (Randolph, Fraser, & Orthner, 2004). Even in situations where family members are unavailable, non-familial mentors such as teachers, coaches, and neighbors can help adolescents to make positive identity choices.

Perseverance, Agency, and Self-Direction

Perseverance is also extremely important for urban youth (Côté & Levine, 2002; Gestsdóttir & Lerner, 2007). Perseverance is facilitated by a sense of agency and self-direction (Bandura, 1989). Two models of self-direction and agency are relevant to urban youth. The first is Côté's (2000) four-component model of agency—consisting of self-esteem, a sense of life purpose, patience and dedication, and an internal locus of control. Young people who succeed are likely those who believe in themselves, have established a sense of direction for their lives, assume responsibility for their decisions, and delay gratification (Côté, 2002). Moreover, these four components of agency facilitate a coherent sense of self (Schwartz, Côté, & Arnett, 2005).

The second model is Lerner's (Gestsdóttir & Lerner, 2007) three-skill model of agency, which outlines skills that help young people to make self-directed, well-reasoned, and flexible choices. The first skill is *selection*—which represents the ability to choose stimuli that are most appropriate to respond to, and to which a response is most likely to result in success. The second skill is *optimization*, which involves searching for ways to more efficiently and effectively pursue the goal that one has chosen. The third skill is *compensation*, which signifies the ability to "change course" when one's initial course of action is blocked. Gestsdóttir and Lerner (2007) found that these three skills predict competence, character, and connection to others.

The Côté and Lerner models of agency subsume aspects of resilience. Believing in oneself, knowing one's talents, taking responsibility for one's life path, delaying gratification, and identifying the "best" opportunities to pursue, often produce adolescent success. Agency is facilitated by connections to family members and mentors, and by structured activities outside of school. Given Oyserman and Destin's (2010) observation that goals are often pursued when they are self-relevant, a positive and goal-oriented sense of self—facilitated by positive activity involvement and by connections to important others—may help young people to see their future goals as self-relevant. When individuals view their goals as attainable, such obstacles are often framed as challenges to be overcome (namely, Lerner's compensation dimension) (Destin & Oyserman, 2010). Agency is the *route* through which goals are attained, even in the presence of considerable adversity.

The concepts that we review here are likely amenable to application in the school domain. Some urban youth graduate from their high schools and go on to college, despite having attended under-serviced schools. The construct of "educational resilience" (Peck et al., 2008) refers to youth who attend to their schoolwork, establish positive relationships with teachers, and remain engaged in school. Educational resilience embodies many of the same characteristics as the Côté and Lerner models of agency. Young people who display educational resilience have their "eye on the prize"; they complete their schoolwork because it represents a route to educational attainment (Destin & Oyserman, 2010). Without such long-term vision—facilitated by a sense of agency—schoolwork may seem pointless.

Although some interventions have been designed to help urban youth *get into* college (e.g., Oyserman et al., 2006), the challenge does not end there. The U.S. Department of Education (2006) found that, among colleges and universities, the likelihood of graduating within six years of enrollment was 69% for institutions where low-income students comprised 20% or less of the student population, but only 44% for institutions where low-income students comprised 40% or more of the student population. The message here is that, for whatever reason, low-income students are less likely than other students to graduate from college. The U.S. government has also begun to expand programs so that they cover "birth to career" (see http://www.ed.gov/news/press-releases/obama-administration-announces-2011-promise-neighborhoods-grant-winners). However, the picture is not as simple as separating people into those who are and are not invested in school. There is a third category, which Carter (2006) labels as "cultural straddlers"; they are engaged in school but also maintain ties to their peer culture. These individuals engage in what Briley, Morris, and Simonson (2005) have labeled "cultural chameleonism"—where the person tailors behavior to the cultural demands of the situation. Thus, an African American student may be achievement-oriented but may behave in a counter-cultural manner with her/his peers. The cultural straddler approach may, however, carry some cost. A bicultural person may experience pressure from family members to behave consistently with the culture of origin, but in many contexts, members of the larger society may expect the person to behave in an "American" way. Similarly, youth whose personalities change considerably between the school environment and the peer group may be pressured to identify completely with one context.

However, biculturalism is the most adaptive approach to identity for ethnic-minority youth (Sam & Berry, 2010). Such youth might fulfill family obligations within the immediate context, while also participating within the individualistic contexts of school and career planning. Furthermore, biculturalism is associated with the most adaptive outcomes when the youth views her or his heritage and American cultural streams as compatible, and when she or he is able to integrate these streams into a personalized "culture" (Nguyen & Benet-Martínez, 2007). In cases where the two cultural streams are viewed as incompatible and are not reconciled, the psychological costs may outweigh the benefits (Chen, Benet-Martínez, & Bond, 2008). Such individuals may see themselves as "caught between two worlds," rather than as "straddling two worlds"—where the primary difference between the two outlooks is the degree of mastery that the person perceives vis-à-vis her or his cultural environment.

Thus, external forces provide opportunities and guidance (or lack thereof) for young people (Côté & Levine, 2002). Young people need adult mentors to outline the tasks and steps necessary to prepare for college—including preparing for standardized tests and choosing classes that will lay the foundation for college coursework (Torrez, 2004). Youth with moderate amounts of agency can work closely with such mentors to prepare for college, but without adult support, a considerable amount of agency is needed for youth to prepare themselves for college.

Conclusions: So What Can Be Done to Help Urban Youth Thrive?

Because identity is central in the lives of youth (Schwartz, 2001, 2005), and because strong achievement expectancies may increase the likelihood of success (Oyserman et al., 2006), urban youth must develop a positive—rather than negative or oppositional—sense of self. Promoting identity in urban youth is difficult because of some of the structural barriers reviewed above—and as a result, the construct of resilience may be useful to invoke. It is important to capitalize on Oyserman and Destin's (2010) observation that difficulties are viewed differently depending on whether or not the goal in question is self-relevant and achievable. In cases where the goal seems disconnected from the self and feels unrealistic, barriers in the pursuit of that goal are likely to lead the person to abandon the goal. Conversely, in cases where the goal is self-relevant and obtainable, difficulties will likely be taken as challenges to be overcome. Therefore, youth development programs may focus on formulating clear, realistic goals that are consistent with one's identity and conceiving pathways towards achieving those goals. Indeed, Larson (2011) highlights the role of youth development programs (e.g., Boys and Girls Clubs) in helping young people to think strategically and to develop a coherent set of goals. Identity development is central to these programs.

Our focus on resilience is consistent with Lerner's (Lerner, Almerigi, Theokas, & Lerner, 2005) assertion that all youth are capable of living up to their highest potentials. Indeed, there is an abundance of stories of urban youth who have contributed extensively to society (e.g., Jesse Jackson; Frady, 1996). Such individuals tend to be connected to caring adults, self-directed in pursuing long-term goals, and able to identify the choices (e.g., focusing on school success) that lead to the realization of these goals. Thus, it is essential to help youth to see the connections between their current decisions and their long-term goals. Important tasks for adults who play significant roles in the lives of urban youth include: (a) encouraging youth to frame their long-term goals in ways that are consistent with how they view themselves presently, (b) educating them about ways of overcoming potential ethnic/social class marginalization, and (c) helping them to strike a balance between feeling attached to their heritage-cultural groups and succeeding in American society. It is essential to ensure that possible identities *remain* possible, that agency and resilience outweigh despair, and that "beating the odds" becomes a central theme in the lives of urban youth.

References

Altschul, I., Oyserman, D., & Bybee, D. (2008). Racial-ethnic self-schemas and segmented assimilation: Identity and the academic achievement of Hispanic youth. *Social Psychology Quarterly, 71*, 302–320.

Bandura, A. (1989). Human agency in social cognitive theory. *American Psychologist, 44*, 1175–1184.

Briley, D. A., Morris, M. W., & Simonson, I. (2005). Cultural chameleons: Biculturals, conformity motives, and decision making. *Journal of Consumer Psychology, 15*, 351–362.

Bureau of Labor Statistics. (2011). *The employment situation: July 2011.* Retrieved August 10, 2011 from http://www.bls.gov/news.release/pdf/empsit.pdf.

Carter, P. L. (2006). Straddling boundaries: Identity, culture, and school. *Sociology of Education, 79*, 304–328.

Chen, S. X., Benet-Martínez, V., & Bond, M. H. (2008). Bicultural identity, bilingualism, and psychological adjustment in multicultural societies: Immigration-based and globalization-based acculturation. *Journal of Personality, 76*, 803–838.

Côté, J. E. (2000). *Arrested adulthood: The changing nature of maturity and identity.* New York: New York University Press.

Côté, J. E. (2002). The role of identity capital in the transition to adulthood: The individualization thesis examined. *Journal of Youth Studies, 5*(2), 117–134.

Côté, J. E., & Levine, C. G. (2002). *Identity formation, agency, and culture: A social psychological synthesis.* Mahwah, NJ: Lawrence Erlbaum Associates.

Crutchfield, R. D., Fernandes, A., & Martinez, J. (2010). Racial and ethnic disparity and criminal justice: How much is too much? *Journal of Criminal Law and Criminology, 100*, 903–932.

Destin, M., & Oyserman, D. (2009). From assets to school outcomes: How finances shape children's perceived possibilities and intentions. *Psychological Science, 20*, 414–418.

Destin, M., & Oyserman, D. (2010). Incentivizing education: Seeing schoolwork as an investment, not a chore. *Journal of Experimental Social Psychology, 46*, 846–849.

Eichas, K., Albrecht, R. E., Garcia, A. J., Ritchie, R. A., Varela, A., Garcia, A., & Kurtines, W. M. (2010). Mediators of positive youth development intervention change: Promoting change in positive and problem outcomes? *Child and Youth Care Forum, 39*, 211–237.

Erikson, E. (1959). Identity and the life cycle. *Psychological Issues, 1*, 1–171.

Erikson, E. (1968). *Identity: Youth and crisis.* New York: Norton.

Frady, M. (1996). *Jesse: The life and pilgrimage of Jesse Jackson.* New York: Random House.

Gestsdóttir, S., & Lerner, R. M. (2007). Intentional self-regulation and positive youth development in early adolescence: Findings from the 4-h study of positive youth development. *Developmental Psychology, 43*, 508–521.

Henderson, T. J. (2011). *Beyond borders: A history of Mexican migration to the United States.* Malden, MA: Wiley-Blackwell.

Jost, J. T., Banaji, M. R., & Nosek, B. A. (2004). A decade of system justification theory: Accumulated evidence of conscious and unconscious bolstering of the status quo. *Political Psychology, 25*, 881–920.

Kalleberg, A. L. (2009). Precarious work, insecure workers: Employment relations in transition. *American Sociological Review, 74*(1), 1–22.

Kasinitz, P., Mollenkopf, J. H., Waters, M. C., & Holdaway, J. (2008). *Inheriting the city: The children of immigrants come of age.* New York: Russell Sage.

Kroger, J. & Marcia, J. E. (2011). The identity statuses: Origins, meanings and interpretations. In S. J. Schwartz, K. Luyckx, & V. L. Vignoles (Eds.), *Handbook of identity theory and research* (pp. 31–53). New York: Springer.

Kurtines, W. M., Montgomery, M. J., Eichas, K., Ritchie, R. A., Garcia, A., Albrecht, R., . . . Lorente, C. C. (2008). Promoting positive identity development in troubled youth: a developmental intervention science outreach research approach. *Identity: An International Journal of Theory and Research, 8*, 125–138.

Larson, R. W. (2011). Positive development in a disorderly world. *Journal of Research on Adolescence, 21*, 317–334.

Lerner, R. M., Almerigi, J. B., Theokas, C., & Lerner, J. V. (2005). Positive youth development: A view of the issues. *Journal of Early Adolescence, 25*, 10–16.

Marcia, J. E. (1966). Development and validation of ego identity status. *Journal of Personality and Social Psychology, 5*, 551–558.

Masten, A. S. (2001). Ordinary magic: Resilience processes in development. *American Psychologist, 56*, 227–238.

Nguyen, A. D., & Benet-Martínez, V. (2007). Biculturalism unpacked: Components, measurement, individual differences, and outcomes. *Social and Personality Psychology Compass, 1*, 101–114.

Oyserman, D., Bybee, D., & Terry, K. (2006). Possible selves and academic outcomes: How and when possible selves impel action. *Journal of Personality and Social Psychology, 91*, 188–204.

Oyserman, D., & Destin, M. (2010). Identity-based motivation: Implications for intervention. *Counseling Psychologist, 38*, 1001–1043.

Oyserman, D., Harrison, K., & Bybee, D. (2001). Can racial identity be promotive of academic efficacy? *International Journal of Behavioral Development, 25*, 379–385.

Oyserman, D., & James, L. (2011). Possible identities: Possible selves, subjective experience, and self-regulation. In S. J. Schwartz, K. Luyckx, & V. L. Vignoles (Eds.), *Handbook of identity theory and research* (pp. 117–129). New York: Springer.

Oyserman, D., & Markus, H. R. (1990). Possible selves and delinquency. *Journal of Personality and Social Psychology, 59*, 112–125.

Peck, S. C., Roeser, R. W., Zarrett, N., & Eccles, J. S. (2008). Exploring the roles of extracurricular activity quantity and quality in the educational resilience of vulnerable adolescents: Variable- and pattern-centered approaches. *Journal of Social Issues, 64*, 135–155.

Peffley, M., & Hurwitz, J. (2002). The racial components of "race-neutral" crime policy attitudes. *Political Psychology, 23*, 59–75.

Phillips, T. M., & Pittman, J. F. (2003). Identity processes in poor adolescents: Exploring the linkages between economic disadvantage and the primary task of adolescence. *Identity: An International Journal of Theory and Research, 3*(2), 115–129.

Phinney, J. S., & Ong, A. D. (2007). Conceptualization and measurement of ethnic identity: Current status and future directions. *Journal of Counseling Psychology, 54*, 271–281.

Plunkett, S. W., Henry, C. S., Houltberg, B. J., Sands, T., & Abarca-Mortensen, S. (2008). Academic support by significant others and educational resilience in Mexican-origin ninth grade students from intact families. *Journal of Early Adolescence, 28*, 333–355.

Portes, A., & Rumbaut, R. G. (2006) *Immigrant American: A portrait* (3rd ed.). Berkeley: University of California Press.

Pratto, F., Sidanius, J., & Levin, S. (2006). Social dominance theory and the dynamics of intergroup relations: Taking stock and looking forward. *European Review of Social Psychology, 17*, 271–320.

Randolph, K. A., Fraser, M. W., & Orthner, D. K. (2004). Educational resilience among youth at risk. *Substance Use & Misuse, 39*(5), 747–767.

Rudmin, F. W. (2003). Critical history of the acculturation psychology of assimilation, separation, integration, and marginalization. *Review of General Psychology, 7*, 3–37.

Rumbaut, R. G. (2008). Reaping what you sow: Immigration, youth, and reactive ethnicity. *Applied Developmental Science, 12*(2), 108–111.

Ryan, R. M., & Deci, E. L. (2000). Self-determination theory and the facilitation of intrinsic motivation, social development, and well-being. *American Psychologist, 55*, 68–78.

Sam, D. L., & Berry, J. W. (2010). Acculturation: When individuals and groups of different cultural backgrounds meet. *Perspectives on Psychological Science, 5*, 472–481.

Schwartz, S. J. (2001). The evolution of Eriksonian and neo-Eriksonian identity theory and research: A review and integration. *Identity: An International Journal of Theory and Research, 1*, 7–58.

Schwartz, S. J. (2005). A new identity for identity research: Recommendations for expanding and refocusing the identity literature. *Journal of Adolescent Research, 20*, 293–308.

Schwartz, S. J., Côté, J. E., & Arnett, J. J. (2005). Identity and agency in emerging adulthood: Two developmental routes in the individualization process. *Youth and Society, 37*, 201–229.

Schwartz, S. J., Luyckx, K., & Vignoles, V. L. (Eds.) (2011). *Handbook of identity theory and research.* New York: Springer.

Schwartz, S. J., Mason, C. A., Pantin, H., & Szapocznik, J. (2008). Effects of family functioning and identity confusion on substance use and sexual behavior in Hispanic immigrant early adolescents. *Identity: An International Journal of Theory and Research, 8*, 107–124.

Schwartz, S. J., Mason, C. A., Pantin, H., & Szapocznik, J. (2009). Longitudinal relationships between family functioning and identity development in Hispanic adolescents: Continuity and change. *Journal of Early Adolescence, 29*, 177–211.

Schwartz, S. J., Unger, J. B., Zamboanga, B. L., & Szapocznik, J. (2010). Rethinking the concept of acculturation: Implications for theory and research. *American Psychologist, 65*, 237–251.

Sedikides, C., & Brewer, M. (Ed.). (2001). *Individual self, relational self, collective self.* New York: Psychology Press.

Skorikov, V. B., & Vondracek, F. W. (2011). Occupational identity. In S. J. Schwartz, K. Luyckx, & V. L. Vignoles (Eds.), *Handbook of identity theory and research* (pp. 692–714). New York: Springer.

Spears, R. (2011). Group identities: The social identity perspective. In S. J. Schwartz, K. Luyckx, & V. L. Vignoles (Eds.), *Handbook of identity theory and research* (pp. 201–224). New York: Springer.

Steele, C. (1997). A threat in the air: How stereotypes shape the intellectual identities and performance of women and African Americans. *American Psychologist, 52*, 613–629.

Stepick, A., Grenier, G., Castro, M., & Dunn, M. (2003). *This land is our land: Immigrants and power in Miami.* Berkeley: University of California Press.

Stepick, A., & Stepick, C. D. (2002). Power and identity: Miami Cubans. In M. M. Suárez-Orozco, & M. Páez (Eds.), *Latinos: Remaking America* (pp. 75–92). Cambridge, MA: Harvard University Press.

Syed, M., & Azmitia, M. (2008). A narrative approach to ethnic identity in emerging adulthood: Bringing life to the identity status model. *Developmental Psychology, 44*, 1012–1027.

Torrez, N. (2004). Developing parent information frameworks that support college preparation for Latino students. *High School Journal, 87*(3), 54–62.

U.S. Department of Education. (2006). *Placing college graduation rates in context: How 4-year college graduation rates vary with selectivity and the size of low-income enrollment* (Report NCES 2007–161). Jessup, MD: Author.

Wilson, J. Q. (2002). *The marriage problem.* New York: Harper-Collins.

Zarrett, N., Fay, K., Li, Y., Carrano, J., Phelps, E., & Lerner, R. M. (2009). More than child's play: Variable- and pattern-centered approaches for examining effects of sports participation on youth development. *Developmental Psychology, 45*, 368–382.

19

THE ROLE OF PARENTS AND PEERS IN THE PSYCHOLOGICAL AND ACADEMIC ADAPTATION OF YOUTH IN URBAN COMMUNITIES

Darya Bonds McClain, Lorey A. Wheeler, Jessie J. Wong, Anne Marie Mauricio, and Nancy A. Gonzales

Adolescent psychological and academic adaptation is significantly associated with multiple factors within and across interrelated contexts. The ecological systems model, discussed throughout this volume, offers a framework for understanding adolescent adaptation as occurring through the interactions between individual, relationship, and neighborhood factors (Bronfenbrenner, 1979). Family and peer relationships are identified as two proximal contexts (discussed also in Chapters 8 and 9) for adolescent development within this framework (Grotevant, 1998). This chapter focuses on: (a) the impact of disadvantaged (e.g., high rates of public assistance, unemployment, residential instability, and low collective efficacy; Leventhal, Dupéré, & Brooks-Gunn, 2009) urban communities on adolescents' family and peer relationships, (b) the links between the family context and adolescent psychological and academic adaption, (c) the associations of the peer context on adolescent adaptation, and (d) key features of effective family and peer focused interventions designed to promote positive psychological and academic outcomes.

Family Context

The ecological systems framework posits that adolescent adaptation is linked to a dynamic relationship between community and family contexts. Adolescents living in disadvantaged urban communities are often exposed to community crime and poverty with limited access to supportive community resources (Cooley-Strickland et al., 2009). These negative characteristics of such urban communities are considered risk factors and are linked to internalizing problems (e.g., depression, anxiety), externalizing problems (e.g., aggression, delinquency), and poor academic performance across gender and ethnicity (for a review see Cooley-Strickland et al., 2009). Although the majority of research on adolescent development in urban communities is focused on risk factors, positive family relationships and effective parenting practices have been identified as factors that protect against the impact of negative characteristics of urban communities on adolescent adaptation (Gorman-Smith & Tolan, 1998). Below we describe some specific aspects of family and parent–adolescent relationships that are associated with adolescent adaptation.

Family Relationships

Family relationships can either enhance or disrupt adolescent adaptation. Close or cohesive family relationships act as a protective factor against stressors of disadvantaged urban environments. For example, family cohesion is associated with lower levels of externalizing (Henderson, Dakof, Schwartz, & Liddle, 2006) and internalizing problems (Deng et al., 2006), and positively associated with academic engagement (Annunziata, Hogue, Faw, & Liddle, 2006). Research also suggests that families who live in urban communities that show more collective efficacy (e.g., willingness to work together for the common good, such as speaking to unaccompanied misbehaving children or reporting crimes, shared values, social connections) are more cohesive and have children with lower levels of problems (Deng et al., 2006). Mechanisms to promote collective efficacy (e.g., involvement of parents and youth in community enhancement projects) are thought to also improve communication between parents in the community, and thus, relationships and functioning within families (Deng et al., 2006).

Family values also are linked to adolescent psychological and academic adaptation. Urban populations are often comprised of minority families that hold traditional cultural values, such as familism. Familism values, which are relevant to many cultural groups but most often associated with Latino culture, refer to the attachment, identification, and obligation of individuals to their families (Cauce & Domenech-Rodríguez, 2002). A growing body of literature supports familism as a protective factor for urban Latino youth that decreases susceptibility to negative influences and promotes healthy families (Germán, Gonzales, & Dumka, 2009).

Parent–adolescent relationships

Researchers have begun to examine how adolescents' supportive relationships with parents promote positive adjustment among youth in urban neighborhoods (Woolley & Bowen, 2007). Ecological models suggest that positive relationships with parents serve as a resource for these youth. For example, positive parent involvement is associated with greater school competence (Murray, 2009) and negatively associated with adolescents' internalizing and externalizing problems (Kuperminc, Blatt, Shahar, Henrich, & Leadbeater, 2004). Also, parent–adolescent open communication (e.g., adolescents' ability to openly discuss beliefs with parents) is positively associated with adolescent self-esteem (Rhee, Chang, & Rhee, 2003).

Parenting practices are another critical component of parent–adolescent inter-actions and have significant associations with urban adolescents' adaptation. For example, increased parental involvement and monitoring is linked with lower levels of depressive symptoms and externalizing problems, and higher levels of self-esteem, perceived self-efficacy (Swenson & Prelow, 2005), and academic engagement

(Annunziata et al., 2006). Parental monitoring (i.e., parents' awareness of adolescents' whereabouts, activities, and companions) also mediates the relation between exposure to community violence and externalizing problems during adolescence (Fowler, Toro, Tompsett, & Baltes, 2009). Parental warmth (i.e., acceptance, affection, and responsiveness), another widely studied parenting practice that contributes to positive parent–adolescent relationships, is associated with decreased internalizing (McCabe, Clark, & Barnett, 1999) and externalizing problems (Mason, Cauce, Gonzales, Hiraga, & Grove, 1994).

Peer Context

Adolescence is marked by increased sensation-seeking (Steinberg et al., 2008) and conformity to peer attitudes and behaviors (Steinberg & Monahan, 2007) that may be linked to increased risk-taking in disadvantaged urban communities. As purported by the ecological systems framework, characteristics of urban communities are significantly associated with peer relationships that are linked to adolescent adaptation. Social disorganization theory posits that characteristics and social processes (e.g., absence of social cohesion among neighbors) of disadvantaged neighborhoods inhibit prosocial behaviors (Leventhal et al., 2009). For example, less social control of youth groups in urban neighborhoods (e.g., structured, supervised activities and programming) is linked to heightened influence of delinquent peer groups, increasing adolescent risk for delinquency (Sampson, Raudenbush, & Earls, 1997).

Peer Relationships

The links between neighborhood risks in urban communities and adolescent psychological adaptation can be counteracted by positive peer influences. A study of urban African American youth found that support from friends buffers the negative associations of exposure to community violence on aggressive behavior (Benhorin & McMahon, 2008). Involvement in prosocial activities with peers (e.g., school extracurricular activities) moderates the negative effect of neighborhood risks on cigarette smoking among Black and White urban youth (Xue, Zimmerman, & Caldwell, 2007). Unfortunately, urban youth are less likely to participate in school- and non-school-related prosocial activities (Stanley, Comello, Edwards, & Marquart, 2008), and a positive link between peer support and academic achievement has not been found among urban youth living in high-risk neighborhoods (Gonzales, Cauce, Friedman, & Mason, 1996). Yet, contrary to stereotypes that depict urban youth discouraging academic achievement among peers, research suggests that urban students strongly admire high achievement among their peers and that peers who are viewed as academically disengaged are regarded with lower social preference (Becker & Luthar, 2007).

Extensive research suggests that adolescents in urban communities are more likely to associate with deviant peers, increasing their risk for delinquency (e.g., Chung & Steinberg, 2006). For example, the link between neighborhood hazard and anxiety sensitivity is exacerbated by exposure to delinquent peers (Nebbitt & Lambert, 2009).

Furthermore, peer drug use significantly predicted alcohol and marijuana use among African American adolescents (Clark, Belgrave, & Nasim, 2008). Deviant behavior begins to play an increasingly important role in popularity among peers in adolescence (Cillessen & Mayeux, 2004), and research shows an association between peer admiration and substance use (Becker & Luthar, 2007). Urban youth are also more likely to become involved in gangs when they experience peer rejection, academic failure, and antisocial behavior (Dishion, Nelson, & Yasui, 2005). This is linked to elevations in problematic behavior (Esbensen, Huizinga, & Weiher, 1993) that decreases when adolescents leave gangs (Gordon et al., 2004).

Romantic Relationships

Scholars have also proposed that involvement with a romantic partner may lead to positive adaptation given that the experience is positive or the partner is a positive role model (Furman & Shaffer, 2003). For example, Latinos who were dating had lower levels of social anxiety compared to those who were not dating; thus, positive experiences from dating may be linked with feelings of increased social competence, and, thus, to decreased anxiety in social contexts (La Greca & Harrison, 2005). Another study showing a positive association between partner's grade point average (GPA) and respondent's GPA provides further evidence of romantic partners as positive role models (Giordano, Phelps, Manning, & Longmore, 2008). Conversely, studies have also found evidence that suggests that adolescents who date exhibit more internalizing and externalizing behaviors (Swahn, West, & Bossarte, 2009) and lower achievement for girls (Reis & Díaz, 1999). There is also some evidence that it may not be just involvement in dating but over-involvement in dating (i.e., high number of partners) that is linked to increases in externalizing and internalizing behaviors and decreases in academic performance and motivation, with stronger associations for girls than boys (Zimmer-Gembeck, Siebenbruner, & Collins, 2001). Moreover, others link dating with negative outcomes (i.e., lower GPA) through stressors (e.g., breakup) for Mexican American urban adolescents (Gillock & Reyes, 1999). As these studies are correlational in nature, more work needs to be done to disentangle the direction of effects of dating on adolescent adaptation.

Interventions

Historically, interventions have primarily targeted youth exhibiting problematic behavior; however, in recent decades there has been a significant paradigm shift to an increasing emphasis on services that support positive youth development (i.e., a strength-based conception of adolescence focused on promoting healthy develop- ment; Lerner, Almerigi, Theokas, & Lerner, 2005). The paradigm shift was precipi- tated by conceptualizations of diversity in youth development as a manifestation of social and cultural contexts (Bronfenbrenner, 1979), and corresponding theoretical and empirical research identifying risk and protective factors across contexts (Catalano, Hawkins, Berglund, Pollard, & Arthur, 2002). The research on urban youth reviewed in the previous sections has informed the design of programs for this population because it identifies the critical interacting systems (e.g., family, peers) and specific risk and protective processes that could be targeted to alter developmental trajectories. Below we describe evidence based features of effective family and peer focused interventions.

Family Focused Interventions

Evidence from randomized controlled trials offers robust support for interventions that target family interactions and parenting behaviors at different developmental stages to promote positive youth development and prevent problem outcomes (O'Connell, Boat, & Warner, 2009). In particular, this research suggests that close, stable, and open relationships with parents and supportive relationships with other adults and peers can insulate youth during critical transitions when adolescents are at increased risk for risky behaviors and mental health disorders, such as depression (Moore & Chase-Lansdale, 2001). In contrast to programs that target younger children (Webster-Stratton & Taylor, 2001), programs for urban adolescents should target parental monitoring (e.g., awareness of adolescents' whereabouts, activities, and companions) because parents need specific skills to limit adolescents' opportunities to engage in maladaptive or dangerous behavior. Parent–child communication and problem solving are also important intervention targets. These skills facilitate adolescent emotion regulation and decision-making that become even more critical as adolescents undergo biological and social changes that heighten the value and salience of peers, particularly the reward salience of risky peer activities (Brown, Bakken, Ameringer, & Mahon, 2008).

Family focused interventions for adolescents are often part of comprehensive programs that also target the adolescents themselves, their peers, communities, and/or schools. These programs typically teach a core set of communication and effective parenting skills to increase parent–adolescent bonding, use of effective discipline, and monitoring, and to reduce family conflict (Gonzales et al., 2012). Some programs include adolescents and parents together to strengthen family skills to overcome the challenges of urban life (Gonzales et al., 2012). Programs also address specific topics relevant to targeted outcomes, such as open parent–child communication about sex to reduce risky sexual activity in adolescence (Dilorio, McCarty, Resnicow, Lehr, & Denzmore, 2007) or offer parenting strategies to promote school engagement and achievement (Gonzales et al., 2012). Programs that bring parents together with an emphasis on developing supportive networks both within and between families also provide an important source of parent support (McKay et al., 2004). The inclusion of a parent focused component affords additional protection from involvement in adolescent risk behaviors compared to interventions that only target adolescents (Dilorio et al., 2007).

Integrated programs also combine family interventions with components directed at other social contexts, such as neighborhoods, schools, churches, or at the community level through strategies such as media campaigns or community organizing (Sanders, 2008). Findings suggest that multi-component models may be necessary to alter the developmental trajectories of youths who live in high-risk environments because they address risk and protective factors in multiple contexts (e.g., home, school, peer, neighborhood) and involve multiple socialization agents (e.g., parents, teachers) that create contextual changes needed to support individual coping skills (Greenberg, Domitrovich, & Bumbarger, 1999). These programs are often developed in collaboration with youth, families, and communities to ensure the program is relevant and ultimately sustainable within the intended communities (Dumka, Mauricio, & Gonzales, 2007).

Interventions that incorporate the culture, values, and norms of the community are most likely to be successful because newly learned behavior is easier to implement in culturally familiar and supportive environments. For example, extended families are often important in the lives of many African American children and are often an integral part of intervention programs for African American children and families (Black & Krishnakumar, 1998). Culturally sensitive programs for African American youth also have incorporated strategies to enhance racial socialization within families (e.g., involved-vigilant parenting strategies for adaptive racial socialization including teaching children about the realities of racial oppression and the achievement of success under these conditions; Brody et al., 2006). Programs for Latino youth also have addressed unique cultural risk and protective factors, such as implementing strategies to reduce acculturation discrepancies and related conflicts between youth and parents (Szapocznik et al., 1984), build stronger connections between immigrant parents and U.S. schools (Gonzales, Dumka, Mauricio, & Germán, 2007), and incorporate traditional family values and strengths in the design of interventions (Gonzales et al., 2007).

Peer Focused Interventions

The social support derived from peer interaction can have positive, growth promoting associations with adolescent development. Accordingly, peer focused interventions provide an opportunistic milieu to promote the psychological and academic adaptation of youth (Karcher, Brown, & Elliot, 2004). A potential hazard to the success of peer focused interventions, however, is delinquency training that can offset the desired positive effects of group interventions (Dishion, Poulin, & Burraston, 2001). Peer contagion refers to the spread of delinquent behavior among participants in an intervention group constituted for therapeutic reasons (Capaldi, Dishion, Stoolmiller, & Yoerger, 2001). Alternatively, the peer contagion process also applies to the spread of positive behaviors among peers, such that peer focused interventions provide opportunities for adolescents to model positive behaviors and share prosocial norms and attitudes (Karcher et al., 2004).

Peer interventions should be voluntary and structured in ways that promote prosocial engagement with peers to reinforce prosocial behaviors (Fashola & Slavin, 1998). Because context determines exposure to specific risk and protective factors (Bronfenbrenner, 1979), interventions that target urban youth must consider risk and protective factors idiosyncratic to urban settings. Empirically supported peer focused interventions use social influence strategies to change peer group attitudes, norms, and behaviors and are generally administered in a group. Intervention strategies may include skills training (e.g., assertion skills, refusal skills), information on socialization and social learning (i.e., modeling), peer tutoring, peer counseling and mediation, peer support groups, and mentoring (Karcher et al., 2004). While some peer interventions are stand-alone programs (e.g., peer mentoring), others are a component of a more comprehensive intervention (Catalano et al., 2002). Most peer focused interventions are delivered in a school setting, target school-based peer networks, and are effective in strengthening school connectedness (Karcher et al., 2004). However, youth are also likely to have influential peer networks in other settings. For example, ethnic minority youth who live in urban settings report that their closest friends are in their neighborhood and report less connection to school networks (Dolcini, Harper, Watson, Catania, & Ellen, 2005). Accordingly, implementation of peer focused interventions in community settings, such as youth centers, is also critical.

Recommendations

Characteristics of disadvantaged urban communities (e.g., poverty, crime, and lack of resources) can have pervasive, negative influences on adolescent psychological and academic adaptation, thus, research and intervention efforts should focus on the promotion of protective factors that buffer these effects. Below are several recommendations to assist in this process:

1. *Research and interventions should consider context when identifying risk and protective factors.* Family and peer relationships are key sources of strength for adolescent adaptation. However, the links between specific aspects of these relationships and adolescent adaptation are dependent on the community context. For instance, positive peer relationships tend to be positively associated with adolescent adaptation, however peers in urban communities are more likely to be deviant and associations with deviant peers is linked to negative outcomes. Peer focused interventions in urban communities should keep this in mind when deciding on the best approach for delivering interventions, given that group based interventions with deviant peers can lead to increased deviance and poor psychological and academic adaptation.

2. *Research and interventions should consider the reciprocal relations between family and peer contexts in urban settings.* Incorporating research on the relations between family and peer relationships is a worthwhile approach to designing interventions for adolescents in urban communities. Developmental cascade models represent the progressive associations among various domains of adaptation across multiple contexts (Masten et al., 2005). In these models, change in one domain of adaptation is viewed as a trigger that can have extensive developmental effects on other contexts or areas of adaptation. Although early interventions focused on prevention of a single problem behavior by targeting risk and protective factors in one context, these factors could be associated with multiple problem behaviors as the probability for problem behavior decreased consequential to the number of protective factors adolescents experience (Greenberg et al., 1999). Accordingly, interventions that target multiple risk and protective factors in multiple contexts (e.g., family and peer) have the potential to influence a wide

range of adolescent psychological and academic adaptation outcomes, and may lead to interventions that are more effective.

3. *Intervention designs should be flexible to account for diverse life experiences of adolescents in urban communities.* Family structures are varied in urban communities and the availability of prosocial peers may be lacking. Developing interventions that target not only family and peer relationships, but also mentor relationships are necessary to have a broader impact with a larger number of adolescents living in urban communities. Evaluations of mentoring programs that include structured activities to promote emotional support and academic and social skill development show that the youth participating in these programs had a greater sense of family and school connectedness (King, Vidourek, Davis, & McClellan, 2002) that was associated with improvements in academic performance (Karcher et al., 2004). Peer and adult support of motivational change (i.e., developing an interest in and motivation by program activities) is another important component that promotes youth engagement in positive development that encourages success beyond their community (e.g., Pearce & Larson, 2006). Future family and peer focused interventions should also promote positive relationships with extended family members, teachers, and other prosocial adults in an effort to be inclusive of adolescents who do not have a foundation of family or peer relationships to strengthen and improve.

4. *Intervention development should be guided by a strengths-based philosophy and focus on promoting positive youth development.* Prevention scientists, community practitioners, and developmental scholars now agree that positive psychological adaptation during adolescence requires more than avoiding drugs, violence, school failure, or precocious sexual activity; thus, interventions are increasingly aiming to promote positive youth development as well as prevent negative outcomes (Catalano et al., 2002). Adolescents who live in high-stress, impoverished urban neighborhoods are confronted daily with contextual risk factors that could negatively alter their life trajectories. Interventions should contrast adolescents' daily experiences in their neighborhoods, and focus and build on adolescents' strengths and resources. Given that adolescent development is a malleable process influenced by context, directing adolescents to personal, familial, and community strengths, and encouraging adolescents to recognize and proactively use these strengths to shape their development should be integral components of positive youth development interventions that promote competencies, confidence, coping skills, resiliency, connection, and attachment to significant others (Lerner et al., 2005). Increasing awareness of strengths and potential for positive outcomes increases efficacy that desired positive outcomes are possible.

Future research and intervention efforts that follow these recommendations and continue to identify the strengths and risks associated with adolescent development in urban contexts have the potential to improve psychological and academic adaptation among these youth.

References

Annunziata, D., Hogue, A., Faw, L., & Liddle, H. A. (2006). Family functioning and school success in at-risk, inner-city adolescents. *Journal of Youth and Adolescence, 35*(1), 105–113.

Becker, B. E., & Luthar, S. S. (2007). Peer-perceived admiration and social preference: Contextual correlates of positive peer regard among suburban and urban adolescents. *Journal of Research on Adolescence, 17*, 117–144.

Benhorin, S., & McMahon, S. D. (2008). Exposure to violence and aggression: Protective roles of social support among urban African American youth. *Journal of Community Psychology, 36*, 723–743.

Black, M. M., & Krishnakumar, A. (1998). Children in low-income, urban settings: Interventions to promote mental health and well-being. *American Psychologist, 53*, 635–646.

Brody, G. H., Murry, V. M., Kogan, S. M., Gerrard, M., Gibbons, F. X., Molgaard, . . . & Wills, T. B. (2006). The strong African American families program: A cluster-randomized prevention trial of long-term effects and a mediational model. *Journal of Consulting and Clinical Psychology, 74*, 356–366.

Bronfenbrenner, U. (1979). Contexts of child rearing: Problems and prospects. *American Psychologist, 34*, 844–850.

Brown, B. B., Bakken, J. P., Ameringer, S. W., & Mahon, S. D. (2008). A comprehensive conceptualization of the peer influence process in adolescence. In M. J. Prinstein, & K. A. Dodge (Eds.), *Understanding peer influence in children and adolescents. Duke series in child development and public policy*. New York: Guilford Press.

Capaldi, D. M., Dishion, T. J., Stoolmiller, M., & Yoerger, K. (2001). Aggression toward female partners by at-risk young men: The contribution of male adolescent friendships. *Developmental Psychology, 37*, 61–73.

Catalano, R. F., Hawkins, J. D., Berglund, L., Pollard, J. A., & Arthur, M. W. (2002). Prevention science and positive youth development: Competitive or cooperative frameworks? *Journal of Adolescent Health, 31*, 230–239.

Cauce, A. M., & Domenech-Rodríguez, M. (2002). Latino families: Myths and realities. In J. M. Contreras, K. A. Kerns, & A. M. Neal-Barnett (Eds.), *Latino children and families in the United States: Current research and future directions* (pp. 3–25). Westport, CT: Praeger Publishers.

Chung, H. L., & Steinberg, L. (2006). Relations between neighborhood factors, parenting behaviors, peer deviance, and delinquency among serious juvenile offenders. *Developmental Psychology, 42*, 319–331.

Cillessen, A. H. N., & Mayeux, L. (2004). From censure to reinforcement: Developmental changes in the association between aggression and social status. *Child Development, 75*, 147–163.

Clark, T. T., Belgrave, F. Z., & Nasim, A. (2008). Risk and protective factors for substance use among urban African American adolescents considered high-risk. *Journal of Ethnicity in Substance Abuse, 7*, 292–303.

Cooley-Strickland, M., Quille, T. J., Griffin, R. S., Stuart, E. A., Bradshaw, C. P., & Furr-Holden, D. (2009). Community violence and youth: Affect, behavior, substance use, and academics. *Clinical Child and Family Psychology Review, 12*, 127–156.

Deng, S., Lopez, V., Roosa, M. W., Ryu, E., Burrell, G. L., Tein, J., & Crowder, S. (2006). Family processes mediating the relationship of neighborhood disadvantage to early adolescent internalizing problems. *The Journal of Early Adolescence, 26*, 206–231.

Dilorio, C., McCarty, F., Resnicow, K., Lehr, S., & Denzmore, P. (2007). REAL men: A group-randomized trial of an HIV prevention intervention for adolescent boys. *American Journal of Public Health, 97*, 1084–1089.

Dishion, T. J., Nelson, S. E., & Yasui, M. (2005). Predicting early adolescent gang involvement from middle school adaptation. *Journal of Clinical Child and Adolescent Psychology, 34*, 62–73.

Dishion, T., Poulin, F., & Burraston, B. (2001). Peer group dynamics associated with iatrogenic effect in group interventions with high-risk young adolescents. *New Directions for Child & Adolescent Development, 91,* 79–92.

Dolcini, M. M., Harper, G. W., Watson, S. E., Catania, J. A., & Ellen, J. M. (2005). Friends in the 'hood: Should peer-based health promotion programs target nonschool friendship networks? *Journal of Adolescent Health, 36,* 267–277.

Dumka, L. E., Mauricio, A. M., & Gonzales, N. A. (2007). Research partnerships with schools to implement preventive interventions for Mexican origin families. *Journal of Primary Prevention, 28,* 408–420.

Esbensen, F. A., Huizinga, D., & Weiher, A. W. (1993). Gang and non-gang youth: Differences in explanatory factors. *Journal of Contemporary Criminal Justice, 9,* 94–116.

Fashola, O. S., & Slavin, R. E. (1998). Effective dropout prevention and college attendance programs for students placed at risk. *Journal of Education for Students Placed at Risk, 3,* 159–183.

Fowler, P. J., Toro, P. A., Tompsett, C. J., & Baltes, B. B. (2009). Community and family violence: Indirect effects of parental monitoring on externalizing problems. *Journal of Prevention & Intervention in the Community, 37,* 302–315.

Furman, W., & Shaffer, L. (2003). *The role of romantic relationships in adolescent development.* Mahwah, NJ: Erlbaum.

Germán, M., Gonzales, N. A., & Dumka, L. (2009). Familism values as a protective factor for Mexican-origin adolescents exposed to deviant peers. *The Journal of Early Adolescence, 29,* 16–42.

Gillock, K. L., & Reyes, O. (1999). Stress, support, and academic performance of urban, low-income, Mexican-American adolescents. *Journal of Youth and Adolescence, 28,* 259–282.

Giordano, P. C., Phelps, K. D., Manning, W. D., & Longmore, M. A. (2008). Adolescent academic achievement and romantic relationships. *Social Science Research, 37,* 37–54.

Gonzales, N. A., Cauce, A. M., Friedman, R. J., & Mason, C. A. (1996). Family, peer, and neighborhood influences on academic achievement among African-American adolescents: One-year prospective effects. *American Journal of Community Psychology, 24,* 365–387.

Gonzales, N. A., Dumka, L. E., Mauricio, A. M., & Germán, M. (2007). Building bridges: Strategies to promote academic and psychological resilience for adolescents of Mexican origin. In J. E. Lansford, K. Deater-Deckard, & M. H. Bornstein (Eds.), *Immigrant Families in Contemporary Society* (pp. 268–286). New York: Guilford Press.

Gonzales, N. A., Dumka, L. E., Millsap, R. E., Gottschall, A., McClain, D. B., Wong, J. J., . . . & Kim, S. Y. (2012). Randomized trial of a broad preventive intervention for Mexican American adolescents. *Journal of Consulting and Clinical Psychology, 80,* 1–16.

Gordon, R. A., Lahey, B. B., Kawai, E., Loeber, R., Stouthamer-Loeber, M., & Farrington, D. P. (2004). Antisocial behavior and youth gang membership: Selection and socialization. *Criminology, 42,* 55–88.

Gorman-Smith, D., & Tolan, P. (1998). The role of exposure to community violence and developmental problems among inner-city youth. *Development and Psychopathology, 10,* 101–116.

Greenberg, M. T., Domitrovich, C., & Bumbarger, B. (1999). *Preventing mental disorders in school-age children: A review of the effectiveness of prevention programs.* U.S. Department of Health and Human Services: Center for Mental Health Services.

Grotevant, H. D. (1998). Adolescent development in family contexts. In W. Damon (Ed.), *Handbook of child psychology. Social, emotional, and personality development* (pp. 1097–1149). Hoboken, NJ: Wiley.

Henderson, C. E., Dakof, G. A., Schwartz, S. J., & Liddle, H. A. (2006). Family functioning, self-concept, and severity of adolescent externalizing problems. *Journal of Child and Family Studies, 15,* 721–731.

Karcher, M. J., Brown, B. B., & Elliott, D. W. (2004). *Enlisting peers in developmental interventions: Principles and practices.* Thousand Oaks, CA: Sage.

King, K. A., Vidourek, R. A., Davis, B., & McClellan, W. (2002). Increasing self-esteem and school connectedness through a multidimensional mentoring program. *Journal of School Health, 72,* 294–299.

Kuperminc, G. P., Blatt, S. J., Shahar, G., Henrich, C., & Leadbeater, B. J. (2004). Cultural equivalence and cultural variance in longitudinal associations of young adolescent self-definition and interpersonal relatedness to psychological and school adjustment. *Journal of Youth and Adolescence, 33,* 13–30.

La Greca, A. M., & Harrison, H. M. (2005). Adolescent peer relations, friendships, and romantic relationships: Do they predict social anxiety and depression? *Journal of Clinical Child and Adolescent Psychology, 34,* 49–61.

Lerner, R. M., Almerigi, J. B., Theokas, C., & Lerner, J. V. (2005). Positive youth development: A view of the issues. *The Journal of Early Adolescence, 25,* 10–16.

Leventhal, T., Dupéré, V. & Brooks-Gunn, J. (2009). Neighborhood influences on adolescent development. In R. M. Lerner, & L. Steinberg (Eds.), *Handbook of adolescent psychology: Contextual influences on adolescent development,* Vol. 2 (pp. 524–558). Hoboken, NJ: John Wiley & Sons Inc.

Mason, C. A., Cauce, A. M., Gonzales, N., Hiraga, Y., & Grove, K. (1994). An ecological model of externalizing behaviors in African-American adolescents: No family is an island. *Journal of Research on Adolescence, 4,* 639–655.

Masten, A. S., Roisman, G. I., Long, J. D., Burt, K. B., Obradovíc, J., Riley, J. R., . . . & Tellegen, A. (2005). Developmental cascades: Linking academic achievement and externalizing and internalizing symptoms over 20 years. *Developmental Psychology, 41,* 733–746.

McCabe, K. M., Clark, R., & Barnett, D. (1999). Family protective factors among urban African American youth. *Journal of Clinical Child Psychology, 28,* 137–150.

McKay, M. M., Chasse, K. T., Paikoff, R., McKiney, L. D., Baptiste, D., Coleman, D., . . . & Bell, C. C. (2004). Family-level impact of the CHAMP Family Program: A community collaborative effort to support urban families and reduce youth HIV risk exposure. *Family Process, 43,* 79–93.

Moore, M. R., & Chase-Lansdale, P. L. (2001). Sexual intercourse and pregnancy among African American girls in high-poverty neighborhoods: The role of family and perceived community environment. *Journal of Marriage and Family, 63,* 1146–1157.

Murray, C. (2009). Parent and teacher relationships as predictors of school engagement and functioning among low-income urban youth. *The Journal of Early Adolescence, 29,* 376–404.

Nebbitt, V. E., & Lambert, S. F. (2009). Correlates of anxiety sensitivity among African American adolescents living in urban public housing. *Journal of Community Psychology, 37,* 268–280.

O'Connell, M. E., Boat, T., & Warner, K. E. (Eds.). (2009). *Preventing mental, emotional, and behavioral disorders among young people: Progress and possibilities.* Institute of Medicine, National Research Council.

Pearce, N. J., & Larson, R. W. (2006). How teens become engaged in youth development programs: The process of motivational change in a civic activism organization. *Applied Developmental Science, 10,* 121–131.

Reis, S. M., & Díaz, E. (1999). Economically disadvantaged urban female students who achieve in schools. *The Urban Review, 31,* 31–54.

Rhee, S., Chang, J., & Rhee, J. (2003). Acculturation, communication patterns, and self-esteem among Asian and Caucasian American adolescents. *Adolescence, 38,* 749–768.

Sampson, R. J., Raudenbush, S. W., & Earls, F. (1997). Neighborhoods and violent crime: A multilevel study of collective efficacy. *Science, 277,* 918–924.

Sanders, M. R. (2008). Triple P-Positive Parenting Program as a public health approach to strengthening parenting. *Journal of Family Psychology, 22,* 506–517.

Stanley, L. R., Comello, M. L. G., Edwards, R. W., & Marquart, B. S. (2008). School adjustment in rural and urban communities: Do students from "Timbuktu" differ from their "city slicker" peers? *Journal of Youth and Adolescence, 37,* 225–238.

Steinberg, L., Albert, D., Cauffman, E., Banich, M., Graham, S., & Woolard, J. (2008). Age differences in sensation seeking and impulsivity as indexed by behavior and self-report: Evidence for a dual systems model. *Developmental Psychology, 44*, 1764–1778.

Steinberg, L., & Monahan, K. C. (2007). Age differences in resistance to peer influence. *Developmental Psychology, 43*, 1531–1543.

Swahn, M. H., West, B., & Bossarte, R. M. (2009). Urban girls and boys who date: A closer look at the link between dating and risk for alcohol and drug use, self-harm and suicide attempts. *Vulnerable Children and Youth Studies, 4*, 249–254.

Swenson, R. R., & Prelow, H. M. (2005). Ethnic identity, self-esteem, and perceived efficacy as mediators of the relation of supportive parenting to psychosocial outcomes among urban adolescents. *Journal of Adolescence, 28*, 465–477.

Szapocznik, J., Santisteban, D., Rio, A., Perez-Vidal, A., Kurtines, W. M., & Hervis, O. E. (1984). Bicultural Effectiveness Training: A treatment intervention for enhancing intercultural adjustment. *Hispanic Journal of Behavioral Sciences, 6*, 317–344.

Webster-Stratton, C., & Taylor, T. (2001). Nipping early risk factors in the bud: Preventing substance abuse, delinquency, and violence in adolescence through interventions targeted at young children (0 to 8 years). *Prevention Science, 2*, 165–192.

Woolley, M. E., & Bowen, G. L. (2007). In the context of risk: Supportive adults and the school engagement of middle school students. *Family Relations: An Interdisciplinary Journal of Applied Family Studies, 56*, 92–104.

Xue, Y., Zimmerman, M. A., & Caldwell, C. H. (2007). Neighborhood residence and cigarette smoking among urban youths: The protective role of prosocial activities. *American Journal of Public Health, 97*, 1865–1872.

Zimmer-Gembeck, M. J., Siebenbruner, J., & Collins, W. A. (2001). Diverse aspects of dating: Associations with psychosocial functioning from early to middle adolescence. *Journal of Adolescence, 24*, 313–336.

20

ADOLESCENCE AND EMERGING ADULTHOOD

Positive Transitions in Urban Communities

Pamela Aronson and Ashleigh Hodge

The transition to adulthood in underserviced urban areas is a time of both potential and risk. In this developmental period, long-term work and family roles are shaped and there is an opportunity to begin a mature adult trajectory characterized by a positive developmental life path. However, poor youth are also at risk for a variety of negative outcomes, such as school drop-out, teenage child bearing, and unemployment. The life phase of the transition to adulthood has become more variable, extended and unequal (Furstenberg, Kennedy, McLoyd, Rumbaut, & Settersten, 2004). Furstenberg and his collaborators (2004) say that, compared to the past, "growing up is harder to do," especially for young people who lack economic resources. The challenges that young people face are linked to the rapidly changing economy that has resulted in an unstable employment market (Fullerton & Wallace, 2007).

Poor youth are disproportionately likely to drop out of high school, finish their education at the high school level, or enter community college (Horn & Nevill, 2006). About a quarter of first-generation college students attain a Bachelor's degree, compared with over two-thirds of the students whose parents had at least a Bachelor's degree (Chen & Carroll, 2005). Unfortunately for such youth though, a college education is a vital first step toward employment and adequate pay. While 8.4% of college-educated young adults under age 25 are unemployed, 14.7% of young adults with a high school diploma and 26.6% of high school drop-outs are unemployed (Carter, Cox, & Quealy, 2009). Young African American men without a high school diploma face the highest unemployment rate of any group: 48.5% (Carter et al., 2009). A Bachelor's degree increases wages even for jobs that do not require a college education; such as childcare workers (Leonhardt, 2011). Program interventions must be put into place to ameliorate the effects of growing up in underserviced urban areas. It is also crucial that individual-level resources be identified and developed during this stage of life. These steps are important to ensure that the most disadvantaged individuals become contributing members of their communities.

High School Completion

Obstacles

Disadvantage can begin early in life. According to Bowles and Gintis (1976), children are socialized to assume a particular place in the class structure through practices such as academic tracking, gate-keeping by teachers and guidance counselors, and expectations of conformity. Linguistic subcultures learned in the family place middle-class children at an advantage, as they develop a greater sense of entitlement and confidence than their less advantaged peers (Lareau, 2003).

Youth in poor urban areas often experience many obstacles to attaining a high school diploma. Ninety percent of highly segregated minority schools are characterized by high poverty rates and both segregation and poverty predict drop-out rates (Orfield, Losen, Wald, & Swanson, 2004). Many such schools have teachers unfamiliar with urban culture, and a large number of students with health and emotional problems (Orfield et al., 2004). While 75% of White students graduate "on time" with a regular diploma, only about half of African American, Hispanic and Native American students do so (Orfield et al., 2004). Youth drop out as a result of skill deficiency, difficult transitions to high school, and "lack of engagement," as early as sixth grade (Alliance for Excellent Education, 2009). High school drop-out is associated with a significantly lower lifetime income, worse health, higher incarceration rates, and higher reliance on welfare (Chapman, Laird, & KewalRamani, 2010).

Poor women are more likely than middle-class women to have children outside marriage at a young age (Edin & Kefalas, 2005). Teenage mothers who have child care responsibilities experience an "educational penalty"; teenage fathers lack material resources relative to their peers and have lower socioeconomic and educational starting points (Mollborn, 2007). While early parenting is negatively associated with educational attainment (Sandefur, Eggerling-Boeck, & Park, 2005), having a child early in one's college career may primarily serve to delay college completion (Attewell & Lavin, 2007).

Individual-Level Resources

Connection with a caring adult has been found to offer many psychological and achievement benefits, including improved mental health, better school performance, decreased delinquency (DuBois, Neville, Parra, & Pugh-Lilly, 2002), and increased resources and cultural capital (Philip & Hendry, 2000). Mentoring relationships, whether formal or informal, can increase the resilience of at-risk adolescents (Rhodes & DuBois, 2006).

It is important to recognize that what is seen as a negative outcome in the middle class is often viewed positively in poor urban communities. In contexts where there is little opportunity for educational and career attainment, parenthood may be thought of as a positive step in development (Edin & Kefalas, 2005). These cultural beliefs may have the unintended consequence of limiting adult success.

Program Interventions

Some of the best practices in effective mentoring programs are those that are youth-centered, consistent (providing regular contact), long lasting (over one year), and provide links between a mentor and the youth's networks (Rhodes & DuBois, 2006). Programs that do not have these features have the potential to "do harm" (Rhodes & DuBois, 2006). School-based mentoring programs are especially promising (Rhodes & DuBois, 2006).

For all urban students, rigorous high school curricula can facilitate college access and persistence (Choy, 2001). To address the problem of skill deficiency, Ascher and Maguire (2007, p. 5) proposed strengthening "networks of timely support" to increase student competencies—teachers and tutors can assist at-risk students by offering extra lessons, such as before or after school, on Saturdays, and during lunchtime. Community centers or after-school programs can offer after-school help with homework or preparation for admissions tests. After-school homework assistance programs can provide a "protective function" for at-risk youth (Cosden, Morrison, Albanese, & Macias, 2001).

Since a disproportionately smaller number of minority students take Advanced Placement (AP) courses, teachers should provide extra encouragement and schools should provide information sessions for parents and students about the benefit of such courses (Taliaferro & DeCuir-Gunby, 2007). Schools could also enlist academic supports (such as tutors) for homework help and community sponsors to offset the cost of AP exams (Taliaferro & DeCuir-Gunby, 2007). Texas has created an innovative "pay-for-performance" program that offers students and teachers financial incentives when students pass AP courses (Haskins & Kemple, 2009).

Low-income schools often have a student-to-counselor ratio of about 1,000-to-1, while advantaged schools have ratios half that size (Haskins & Kemple, 2009). Establishing a cap on the student-to-counselor ratio would help create deeper relationships and better-equipped students. Since urban adolescents may have parents who lack English-language skills and experience navigating school completion and college access, teachers and counselors have a responsibility to advocate for, and mentor, students (Choy, Horn, Nunez, & Chen, 2000).

Some programs focus on multiple aspects of the transition to adulthood. For example, some target support for pregnant adolescents to continue their education have been effective at reducing repeat pregnancies and increasing school completion (Romo & Segura, 2010). For example, Pittsburgh's Family Growth Center and the Program Archive on Sexuality, Health, and Adolescence involves the extended family and offers frequent social worker visits to strengthen support networks during the transition to parenthood (Romo & Segura, 2010). YouthBuild, which exists in 45 states, supports both the educational and career development of young people as they pursue GEDs[1] or high school diplomas while "learning job skills by building affordable housing for homeless and low-income people" (YouthBuild, 2012).

1   GED: General Equivalency Degree (or diploma); certifies that passing score means the test taker has American or Canadian high school level academic skills.

One promising development has been the establishment of "career academy" high schools that are small (typically 30–60 students) learning communities (often a school within a school) that seek to provide "a college preparatory curriculum with a career-related theme," such as health care, finance, and communications media (Stern, Dayton, & Raby, 2010, p. 5). With linked academic and technical courses and partnerships with employers and postsecondary institutions, these programs may be especially helpful in underserviced areas (Stern, Dayton, & Raby, 2010). Career academies often have positive effects on students, particularly in producing "sustained earnings gains," especially for African American young men (Kemple & Willner, 2008, p. iii).

Policy Recommendations

In its efforts to help disadvantaged students, the No Child Left Behind law provides targeted federal funding to areas with a high poverty concentration (Orfield et al., 2004). The law requires states to enact reading and math achievement tests that are used to evaluate the schools, with the eventual goal of 100% proficiency by 2014. However, to raise test scores, many schools have "'push[ed] out' low achieving students" (Orfield et al., 2004, p. 11). Under the Obama administration, states with low performing schools can request a waiver for the 2014 proficiency deadline in lieu of adopting new academic standards and accountability systems (Dillon, 2011). As states design programs, districts should be rewarded for retention and school completion instead of being penalized for inadequate test scores.

Because public schools are funded primarily by local property taxes, there are significant funding inequalities between school districts in the same metropolitan areas. For example, per pupil spending is over $17,000 in Highland Park and Deerfield, IL but just over $8,000 in Chicago; in Bloomfield Hills, MI it is nearly $13,000, but about $9,500 in Detroit; in Manasset, NY, it is over $22,000 per year, but slightly less than $12,000 in New York City (Kozol, 2005). These funding gaps have significant implications for teacher quality, class size, programming, and building infrastructure. Efforts to expand schools of choice and charter schools have actually increased stratification (Kozol, 2005). Equality in school funding could be achieved if the basis of school funding was changed so that states or metropolitan areas shared a tax pool.

An end to "apartheid" segregated schools is also vital (Kozol, 2005). Currently, the housing agencies that distribute federal Section 8 housing grants encourage minority families to live in segregated neighborhoods (Kozol, 2005). Federal, state and local governments could do more to assist with the construction and acceptance of Section 8 grants in suburban housing (Kozol, 2005). Some court-ordered desegregation programs, where suburban students attend urban schools and vice versa, have been successful after initial resistance on the part of some parents (Kozol, 2005).

College Enrollment

Obstacles

The postsecondary educational process can be conceptualized as a funnel, where cumulative disadvantage results as first-generation and low-income students are disproportionately filtered out of college at each stage (Aronson, 2008). Students whose parents did not attend college are less likely than their counterparts to expect to obtain a Bachelor's degree and to complete even the first steps toward college enrollment (Choy, 2001). Poor students have lower grades in high school, lower achievement test scores, and fewer advanced math courses, which all predict college success and persistence (Chen & Carroll, 2005). Low-income students are more likely to delay college enrollment, attend part time or only part of the year, which makes completion of a Bachelor's degree less likely (Bozick & DeLuca, 2005; Goldrick-Rab, 2006).

Although many high school students expect to receive a college degree, many lack information about the application process for both college and financial aid. Cultural and social capital influence knowledge of the purpose and requirements of postsecondary programs and different social classes "filter out" college choices outside of their "comfort" levels and frame of reference (McDonough, 1998, p. 186). Thus, it is paramount that youth from underserviced urban areas receive expanded support and interventions throughout the entire college process.

Individual-Level Resources

Two individual-level resources that can be encouraged are academic achievement and parental support. Chronic poverty has the greatest impact on college enrollment for academically weak high school students who have not taken college-preparatory courses; it is not as influential for talented students (Baker & Velez, 1996). In addition, the high perceived efficacy of some low-income families can buffer the negative consequences of disadvantage (Crosnoe, Mistry, & Elder, 2002). It is also important that parents have the knowledge and skills to advocate for their children (Choy et al., 2000). When parents serve as role models, this positive relationship promotes health and well-being among their children (Bryant & Zimmerman, 2003). To empower parents, high schools could sponsor workshops addressing the benefits of post-secondary education, routes to obtain financial assistance, and involve parents on college campus tours (Ascher & Maguire, 2007).

Program Interventions

The first step toward encouraging college enrollment is providing basic information to youth and their parents. To do so, high school counselors should have allocated physical space for college advising. Computer stations, with teacher or counselor assistance, could be available at the beginning and end of the day so that students can create resumes, research colleges, and complete applications (Ascher & Maguire,

2007). High school and middle school advising could also be paired with a college resource center to provide information (Ascher & Maguire, 2007).

Schools can also set up mentoring programs to encourage college enrollment. Since urban adolescents have difficulty forming close relationships with non-family members outside of formal programs, many youth turn to friends or peers for mentoring (Philip & Hendry, 1996). When peers encourage college attendance, students are more likely to enroll (Sokatch, 2006). Thus, establishing peer-counseling programs, such as one in which current college students act as mentors in the high schools they previously attended, could be a useful tool (Ascher & Maguire, 2007).

Bridges between high schools and colleges could also be strengthened (Haskins & Kemple, 2009). For example, college representatives and professors could speak in high school classrooms about a wide number of issues, including course load and reading expectations, study habits, and time management (Taliaferro & DeCuir-Gunby, 2007). Forging relationships between high school teachers and college faculty would increase the flow of information between the institutions and help high school teachers prepare their students to address college demands.

Policy Recommendations

Many students place little importance on attaining good grades if they do not see college in their future. Some communities have developed innovative incentives to do well, such as Kalamazoo, Michigan. This city, where nearly two-thirds of public school students qualify for reduced lunch (Miron & Cullen, 2008), provides a tuition scholarship (with the support of anonymous donors) to any public postsecondary institution in Michigan for children who completed grades k–12 within the city and meet minimum grade and attendance requirements. An evaluation study of the "Kalamazoo Promise" reveals that there has been an increase in students' educational aspirations and a 71% increase in students enrolled in AP courses (e.g., Miron, Jones, & Kelaher-Young, 2010). Close to 85% of eligible students have utilized the scholarship benefits, with two-thirds attending four-year colleges or universities and one-third attending community colleges (Miron et al., 2010). The scholarship also appears to be an effective incentive to complete high school (Miron & Cullen, 2008).

State and federal support of higher education could include more direct appropriations and an expansion of need-based grants, whose reductions in favor of merit-based aid and loans (e.g., Choy & Carroll, 2003) has been particularly detrimental to low-income students. While the original goal of federal financial aid was to extend higher education access to low-income families, tuition increases and policy changes have recently expanded the goal to make college affordable for middle-class families (Choy & Carroll, 2003). The assumption of current policies is that parents will assist students in paying for postsecondary education, which places a major burden on poor families (Choy & Carroll, 2003). However, one way to offset this problem rests with college based, work-study programs. Work-study has been shown to positively increase students' connection with the institution, and along with grants, increases retention (Baker & Velez, 1996). If every student in a poor, urban school had access to a highly subsidized postsecondary education, educational achievement would increase.

College Persistence and Completion

Obstacles

College students who come from poor urban areas experience a wide range of obstacles, including difficulty choosing their majors and needing remedial coursework (Chen & Carroll, 2005). They are more likely to major in business, health, and vocational/technical fields (Horn & Nevill, 2006) and avoid courses in mathematics, science, computer science, social sciences, and foreign languages (Chen & Carroll, 2005). They do not perform as well academically as their more advantaged peers and are more likely to withdraw from, or repeat, courses (Chen & Carroll, 2005). Further, students from low socioeconomic backgrounds study less, are less involved in college life, and report lower grades than their counterparts (Walpole, 2003), as daily survival often takes priority over education that can be seen as "optional" or a "luxury" (Lynch & O'Riordan, 1998, p. 454).

Due to lower tuition at community colleges, many low-income college students view these institutions as stepping stones to vocational occupations or four-year universities. Indeed, such colleges provide vocational certifications that lead young adults into productive careers. At the same time, completion rates are quite low: while half of U.S. undergraduates have attended a community college, only one-third will graduate with an Associate's degree within six years (Scrivener & Coghlan, 2011).

Individual-Level Resources

Even when students appear to be mismatched with the university environment, they can exhibit resilience. Goodwin's (2006) study of college graduates from low-income families found that such youth achieved "educational resiliency" as a result of three factors: connections with others (e.g., via student organizations), positive educational competence (e.g., strong study habits), and creating their own opportunities for participation and contribution. Although postsecondary education overwhelmingly reproduces existing class inequalities, at-risk college students who demonstrate educational persistence can break through established class barriers.

Program Interventions

Some of the differences in persistence between first- and second-generation college students may result from a student's "voluntary decision" to scale back their commitment as a result of a lack of integration or "fit" into "the intellectual life of his or her college" (Baker & Velez, 1996, p. 92). Thus, targeting at-risk college students early is essential. African American or Hispanic college students may benefit from mentors or student organizations that are tailored to their unique cultural background (Harris, 1999).

Further, an evaluation of community college programs found that financial incentives and required programs had the most significant impact on student behavior (Scrivener & Coghlan, 2011). Students who received $1,000 for each of two semesters to maintain at least a 2.0 average were more likely to persist in college and earned more credits than the control group (Scrivener & Coghlan, 2011). Students in short-term assistance programs also experienced positive changes, especially when required (Scrivener & Coghlan, 2011). For example, freshman learning communities (with linked courses and shared students) provided an "initial boost" to students (they moved through remedial courses more quickly, passed more classes, and felt more engaged in school than the control group; Scrivener & Coghlan, 2011). Enhanced academic counseling (with mandatory meetings with counselors), had a modest impact on retention and the number of credits completed. Finally, enhanced targeted services for students on academic probation (enrollment in a "success" course and required visits to the "success" center) resulted in gains in academic progress and retention over time (Scrivener & Coghlan, 2011).

To facilitate the transfer process, four-year colleges and universities have developed articulation agreements with community colleges. To allow students to take general education courses at lower rates, some universities allow students with Associate's degrees to waive their general education requirements or permit dual enrollment. Florida and Pennsylvania both offer guaranteed admission to a four-year university upon completion of an Associate's degree at one of the state's community colleges.

Colleges could also expand educational programs (e.g., night classes, more flexible programs and requirements) and support systems (e.g., advising and child care) to help non-traditional students. Developing courses that encourage extra-curricular involvement or relationships with students of similar backgrounds may also enhance connection to the institution.

Policy Recommendations

It is important to recognize that low-income families may be relying on TANF (Temporary Assistance to Needy Families) benefits as they pursue their degrees. In some states, single-parents must be employed 20 to 30 hours a week to be eligible for benefits and college enrollment only satisfies part of this requirement (Romo & Segura, 2010). Thus, allowing TANF recipients to count education as their work requirement would help them move out of low wage jobs.

Preparation for Work

Obstacles

Establishing a stable work trajectory is especially difficult for those who lack resources and opportunities. The decrease in manufacturing jobs in the modern economy has meant that many of the jobs for young people without a college degree are menial, temporary, part-time, and low paying (Fullerton & Wallace, 2007). When young adults cannot find stable work, they have less successful transitions to marriage and parenthood and are more likely to engage in criminal behavior (Mortimer, 2003). Many poor youth work in jobs that are "off the books," which means that employers may not fully follow child labor, minimum wage, and anti-discrimination laws. Some youth who work during high school and college receive little training or guidance that will directly prepare them for particular career paths (Mortimer, 2003).

Individual-Level Resources

Work during high school, especially when it is "steady," of high quality, and less than 20 hours per week, has several advantages: it can help prepare youth for subsequent work, is associated with higher postsecondary educational attainment, and tied to positive mental health (Mortimer, 2003). In contrast, low quality work, especially when sporadic or high intensity (in work hours) is less beneficial (Mortimer, 2003) and may detract from studying or extra-curricular activities. In addition, mentors (in and outside of work) can help teach adolescents important workplace skills.

Program Interventions

Formal linkages between postsecondary education and the world of work need expansion, including the development of internships, co-ops, and apprenticeships, job shadowing, and other "school-to-work" programs (e.g., Kerckhoff, 2002). Since the quality of the work experience matters for vocational development, emphasis should be placed on developing high school and college-supervised programs that help young people develop work skills and explore career goals (Mortimer, 2003). The most effective programs provide close supervision with clear feedback about performance (Mortimer, 2003) and well-defined learning objectives that directly connect school and work (Settersten, 2005).

Policy Recommendations

Our "college for all" culture does not adequately value community college and vocational credentials and often makes high school seem irrelevant (Rosenbaum, 2001). Credential-specific educational programming could provide occupational skills relevant to our economy, especially in growing fields such as health care (Kerckhoff, 2002). Community colleges are "uniquely" positioned to train young adults to occupy a wide range of career paths and greater public funding is necessary (Settersten, 2005, p. 538). For example, many part-time students and those taking remedial courses are unable to utilize grants to pay for community college courses, as student grants are designed for full-time attendance (Settersten, 2005). In an important first step, the Obama administration has pledged $2 billion to support community colleges and career training through the development of partnerships with businesses and online courses. Supporting funding for community colleges and its students is vital in helping disadvantaged young adults.

Conclusions

The transition to adulthood is a vital period of the life course when it comes to educational achievement. Youth growing up in underserviced urban areas experience a wide range of obstacles that impact high school completion, college enrollment and persistence, and the transition to work. This chapter has outlined some of these barriers, along with the individual-level resources, program innovations and policy recommendations that facilitate the transition to adulthood. Individual resilience is important, yet it cannot, by itself, alter the pervasive structural inequalities that exist in school funding.

Many existing programs target certain populations (e.g., children, rather than adolescents) or services (e.g., preschool interventions). This "silo" approach is limited since it does not sustain support over the life course. One exception is the new Promise federal government initiative that supports children and youth from "cradle to career" (U.S. Department of Education, 2011). Although limited at present in its scope, several communities have received funding to develop community-wide, full service programs with the ultimate goal of supporting young people through college and into a career. Also, incentives could be created to encourage educated young adults from poor communities to return to their communities to serve as role models and agents of social change.

To create equality of opportunity for at-risk youth, policy makers usually think about expanding access, equalizing participation, and achieving greater parity in attainment. However, as Lynch and O'Riordan (1998) point out, this approach assumes a meritocratic model of education, where success is measured in terms of effort and ability rather than a "playing field" that is unequal from the start. Efforts at educational reform will not, however well intentioned, remove existing disparities. To close these gaps, policy will need to challenge the inequalities that underlie our educational system.

References

Alliance for Excellent Education. (2009). *High school dropouts in America*. Washington, DC: Author. Retrieved from http://www.all4ed.org/publications/GraduationRates_FactSheet.pdf.

Aronson, P. (2008). Breaking barriers or locked out? Class-based perceptions and experiences of postsecondary education. *New Directions for Child and Adolescent Development, 119* (Spring), 41–54.

Ascher, C., & Maguire, C. (2007). *Beating the odds: How thirteen NYC schools bring low-performing ninth-graders to timely graduation and college enrollment*. Retrieved July 1, 2011, from http://www.annenberginstitute.org/pdf/BTO_report.pdf.

Attewell, P., & Lavin, D. E. (2007). *Passing the torch: Does higher education for the disadvantaged pay off across the generations?* New York: Russell Sage Foundation.

Baker, T., & Velez, W. (1996). Access to and opportunity in postsecondary education in the United States: A review. *Sociology of Education, 69*, 82–101.

Bowles, S., & Gintis, H. (1976). *Schooling in capitalist America: Educational reform and the contradictions of economic life*. New York: Basic Books.

Bozick, R., & DeLuca, S. (2005). Better late than never? Delayed enrollment in the high school to college transition. *Social Forces, 84*(1), 531–554.

Bryant, A. L., & Zimmerman, M. A. (2003). Role models and psychosocial outcomes among African American adolescents. *Journal of Adolescent Research, 18*(1), 36–67.

Carter, S., Cox, A., & Quealy, K. (2009, November 6). The jobless rate for people like you. *New York Times*. Retrieved July 15, 2011 from http://www.nytimes.com/interactive/2009/11/06/business/economy/unemployment-lines.html?emc=eta1.

Chapman, C., Laird, J., & KewalRamani, A. (2010). *Trends in high school dropout and completion rates in the United States: 1972–2008* (NCES 2011–012). (Compendium report). U.S. Department of Education. Washington, DC: National Center for Education Statistics, Institute of Education Sciences.

Chen, X., & Carroll, C. D. (2005). *First-generation students in postsecondary education: A look at their college transcripts* (NCES 2005–171). U.S. Department of Education, National Center for Education Statistics. Washington, DC: U.S. Government Printing Office.

Choy, S. P. (2001). *Students whose parents did not go to college: Postsecondary access, persistence, and attainment* (NCES 2001–126). U.S. Department of Education, Washington, DC: National Center for Education Statistics.

Choy, S. P., & Carroll, C. D. (2003). *How families of low- and middle-income undergraduates pay for college: Full-time dependent students in 1999–2000* (NCES 2003–162). U.S. Department of Education. Washington, DC: National Center for Education Statistics.

Choy, S. P., Horn, L. J., Nunez, A., & Chen, X. (2000). Transition to college: What helps at-risk students and students whose parents did not attend college. In A. F. Cabrera, & S. M. La Nasa (Eds.), *Understanding the college choice of disadvantaged students* (No. 107, pp. 45–63). San Francisco, CA: Jossey-Bass.

Cosden, M., Morrison, G., Albanese, A. L. & Macias, S. (2001). When homework is not home work: After-school programs for homework assistance. *Educational Psychologist*, *36*(3), 211–221.

Crosnoe, R., Mistry, R. S., & Elder, G. H. Jr. (2002). Economic disadvantage, family dynamics, and adolescent enrollment in higher education. *Journal of Marriage and Family*, *64*(3), 690–702.

Dillon, S. (2011, September 22). Obama to waive parts of No Child Left Behind. *New York Times*. Retrieved from http://www.nytimes.com/2011/09/23/education/23educ.html.

DuBois, D. L., Neville, H. A., Parra, G. R., & Pugh-Lilly, A. O. (2002). Testing a new model of mentoring. In J. E. Rhodes (Ed.), *A critical view of youth mentoring: New directions for youth development* (pp. 21–57). New York: Jossey-Bass.

Edin, K., & Kefalas, M. (2005). *Promises I can keep: Why poor women put motherhood before marriage*. Berkeley, CA: University of California Press.

Fullerton, A. S. & Wallace, M. (2007). Traversing the flexible turn: US workers' perceptions of job security, 1977–2002. *Social Science Research, 36*(1), 201–221.

Furstenberg, F. F. Jr., Kennedy, S., McLoyd, V. C., Rumbaut, R. G., & Settersten, R. A. Jr. (2004). Growing up is harder to do. *Contexts, 3*(3), 33–41.

Goldrick-Rab, S. (2006). Following their every move: An investigation of social-class differences in college pathways. *Sociology of Education, 17*(1), 61–79.

Goodwin, L. L. (2006). *Graduating class: Disadvantaged students crossing the bridge of higher education*. Albany: State University of New York Press.

Harris, F. (1999). Centricity and the mentoring experience in academia: An Africentric mentoring program. *The Western Journal of Black Studies, 23*(4), 229–235.

Haskins, R., & Kemple, J. (2009). *A new goal for America's high schools: College preparation for all* (Policy brief). The Future of Children: Princeton-Brookings. Retrieved July 1, 2011, from http://www.futureofchildren.org/futureofchildren/publications/docs/19_01_PolicyBrief.pdf.

Horn, L., & Nevill, S. (2006). *Profile of undergraduates in U.S. postsecondary education institutions: 2003–04: With a special analysis of community college students: Statistical analysis report* (NCES 2006–184). U.S. Department of Education. Washington, DC: National Center for Education Statistics.

Kemple, J. J., & Willner, C. J. (2008). *Career academies: Long-term impacts on labor market outcomes, educational attainment, and transitions to adulthood*. MDRC. Retrieved from http://www.mdrc.org/publications/482/full.pdf.

Kerckhoff, A. C. (2002). The transition from school to work. In J. T. Mortimer, & R. W. Larson (Eds.), *The changing adolescent experience: Societal trends and the transition to adulthood* (pp. 52–87). Cambridge: Cambridge University Press.

Kozol, J. (2005). *The shame of the nation: The restoration of apartheid schooling in America*. New York: Three Rivers Press.

Lareau, A. (2003). *Unequal childhoods: Class, race, and family life*. Berkeley: University of California Press.

Leonhardt, D. (2011, June 25). Even for cashiers, college pays off. *New York Times*. Retrieved July 15, 2011, from http://www.nytimes.com/2011/06/26/sunday-review/26leonhardt.html?_r=3&emc=eta1.

Lynch, K., & O'Riordan, C. (1998). Inequality in higher education: A study of class barriers. *British Journal of Sociology of Education, 19*(4), 445–478.

McDonough, P. M. (1998). Structuring college opportunities: A cross-case analysis of organizational cultures, climates, and habiti. In C. A. Torres, & T. R. Mitchell (Eds.), *Sociology of education: Emerging perspectives* (pp. 181–210). Albany: State University of New York Press.

Miron, G., & Cullen, A. (2008). Trends and patterns in student enrollment for the Kalamazoo public schools (Working paper #4). Retrieved July 14, 2011, from http://www.wmich.edu/kpromise/.

Miron, G., Jones, J. N., & Kelaher-Young, A. J. (2010). Kalamazoo promise: Can a universal college scholarship reform urban education? *Kappan Magazine*, December 2010/January 2011, 50–56. Retrieved July 14, 2011, from http://www.kappanmagazine.org/content/92/4.toc.

Mollborn, S. (2007). Making the best of a bad situation: Material resources and teenage parenthood. *Journal of Marriage and Family, 69*, 92–104.

Mortimer, J. T. (2003). *Working and growing up in America*. Cambridge: Harvard University Press.

Orfield, G., Losen, D., Wald, J., & Swanson, C. B. (2004). Losing our future: How minority youth are being left behind by the graduation rate crisis. Retrieved July 16, 2011, from http://civilrightsproject.ucla.edu/research/k-12-education/school-dropouts/losing-our-future-how-minority-youth-are-being-left-behind-by-the-graduation-rate-crisis.

Philip, K., & Hendry, L. B. (1996). Young people and mentoring—Towards a typology? *Journal of Adolescence, 19*, 189–201.

Philip, K., & Hendry, L. B. (2000). Making sense of mentoring or mentoring making sense? Reflections on the mentoring process by adult mentors with young people. *Journal of Community and Applied Social Psychology, 10*, 211–223.

Rhodes, J. E., & DuBois, D. L. (2006). Understanding and facilitating the youth mentoring movement. *Social Policy Report, XX*(III), 3–19.

Romo, L. F., & Segura, D. A. (2010). Enhancing the resilience of young single mothers of color: A review of programs and services. *Journal of Education for Students Placed at Risk, 15*, 173–185.

Rosenbaum, J. E. (2001). *Beyond college for all: Career paths for the forgotten half*. New York: Russell Sage Foundation.

Sandefur, G. D., Eggerling-Boeck, J., & Park, H. (2005). Off to a good start? Postsecondary education and early adult life. In R. A. Settersten, Jr., F. F. Furstenberg, Jr., & R. G. Rumbaut (Eds.), *On the frontier of adulthood: Theory, research, and public policy* (pp. 292–319). Chicago, IL: University of Chicago Press.

Scrivener, S., & Coghlan, E. (2011). *Opening doors to student success: A synthesis of findings from an evaluation at six community colleges* (Policy brief). New York: MDRC. Retrieved from http://www.mdrc.org/publications/585/policybrief.pdf.

Settersten, R. A. Jr. (2005). Social policy and the transition to adulthood: Toward stronger institutions and individual capacities. In R. A. Settersten, Jr., F. F. Furstenberg, Jr., & R. G. Rumbaut (Eds.), *On the frontier of adulthood: Theory, research and public policy* (pp. 534–560). Chicago, IL: University of Chicago Press.

Sokatch, A. (2006). Peer influences on the college-going decisions of low socioeconomic status urban youth. *Education and Urban Society, 39*(1), 128–146.

Stern, D., Dayton, C., & Raby, M. (2010). *Career academies: A proven strategy to prepare high school students for college and careers.* Career Academy Support Network, University of California-Berkley. Retrieved from http://casn.berkeley.edu/resource_files/Proven_Strategy_2-25-1010-03-12-04-27-01.pdf.

Taliaferro, J. D., & DeCuir-Gunby, J. T. (2007). African American educators' perspectives on the advanced placement opportunity gap. *The Urban Review, 40*(2), 164–185.

U.S. Department of Education. (2011). *Promise neighborhoods.* Retrieved February 7, 2011, from http://www2.ed.gov/programs/promiseneighborhoods/index.html.

Walpole, M. (2003). Socioeconomic status and college: How SES affects college experiences and outcomes. *The Review of Higher Education, 27*(1), 45–73.

YouthBuild. (2012). Retrieved February 7, 2012, from https://youthbuild.org/youthbuild-programs.

CONCLUSION

The urban landscape is a complex space. There are often wide pockets of affluence—yet seemingly a world away, but sometimes separated by a few blocks, are areas marked by poverty and lack of access to adequate employment, education, health care, green space, proper food nourishment, and social services. Many urban residents who live outside of these neighborhoods often avoid these spaces, and often warn visitors to keep their distance as well.

However, these under-serviced neighborhoods are diverse places. A few years ago, the editors passed by two small parks in two relatively poor, urban communities. Some area college students in partnership with neighborhood high school students had constructed both parks. Recently, when touring the area again, it was noted one of the parks was thriving, but the other was choked with weeds and much of the playground equipment was in disrepair. In the latter community, once the college students finished their summer project, and the high school students graduated, no one was in place to sustain the effort. *Nobody seemed to care.* Perhaps this exemplar communicates how adolescents may feel in such communities—something that is started is not finished, adults say "yes" then say "no," a college student mentor is around for one semester, then graduates.

Note we indicate that this is how "adolescents *may* feel," as youth in the first community with the thriving park may host a different perception. Perhaps one major characteristic that separates poor, disordered, under-serviced communities from adjacent neighborhoods that share the same demographics, yet are relatively safe and moving forward is that there are people in the latter community *who do care*. A theme that has been repeated throughout this book is that support from families, teachers, peers, adult mentors, community members as well as university partners—working in tandem—has a facilitative role in promoting adolescent development. Although we are intrigued by the image of the "resilient adolescent"—a young person that can withstand the challenges of poverty and other urban hardships on their own—the major promise for youth living in the communities highlighted in this book pertains to a collective efficacy and empowerment that is shared by multiple stakeholders.

One person cannot address the difficulties adolescents face in under-serviced urban areas. The lesson learned from the more successful communities is that it takes collective action by a group of people, who reside inside and outside of the neighborhood, who all consider the community their "home." Further, involving adolescents in this collective action—via youth development programs, community-based school projects, and mentorship opportunities—also encourages these youth to become active stakeholders in their community. Involvement in these programs has been shown to facilitate identity, pride, and civic commitment in these youth. While we need more research, it is our best estimate that these are the very youth who will eventually serve and live in their community as educators, health care providers, coaches, and community leaders. Such an outcome truly represents "resiliency in the neighborhood."

Gary L. Creasey
Patricia A. Jarvis

ABOUT THE EDITORS
AND CONTRIBUTORS

Jasmine A. Abrams, Doctoral Student in Psychology, Virginia Commonwealth University

Sofiya Alhassan, Assistant Professor of Kinesiology, University of Massachusetts at Amherst

Kevin W. Allison, Professor of Psychology and the L. Douglas Wilder School of Government and Public Affairs, Virginia Commonwealth University

Pamela Aronson, Associate Professor of Sociology, University of Michigan–Dearborn

Daheia J. Barr-Anderson, Assistant Professor of Epidemiology, University of South Carolina

Lisa Barto, Master's Graduate in Clinical Mental Health Counseling, Cleveland State University

Faye Z. Belgrave, Professor of Psychology, Virginia Commonwealth University

Amy Bellmore, Assistant Professor, Educational Psychology, University of Wisconsin

Amanda S. Birnbaum, Associate Professor in Health and Nutrition Sciences, Montclair State University

Keri Blackwell, Senior Program Officer for LISC/Chicago's New Communities Program

Darya Bonds McClain, Research Associate Professor in Nursing and Health Innovation, Arizona State University

Sara Bosch, Madero Middle School Assistant Principal, Chicago Public Schools

Heather A. Bouchey, Director of the Patrick and Marcelle Leahy Center for Rural Students, Lyndon State College

Robert S. Broce, Assistant Professor of Social Work, Southern Connecticut State University

Brad Christerson, Professor of Sociology, Biola University

Rosalie Corona, Associate Professor of Psychology and Founding Director of the VCU Latino Mental Health Clinic, Virginia Commonwealth University

Michael J. Crawford, Doctoral Student in Educational Psychology and Research, University of Kansas

Gary L. Creasey, Professor of Psychology and Assistant Director of the TEACHER+ PLUS Project and CONNECT, Illinois State University (Co-Editor)

Michael Cunningham, Associate Professor in Psychology and African and African Diaspora Studies, Tulane University

Michelle A. DiMeo-Ediger, Doctoral Student, Georgia State University

Richard Durán, Professor of Education, University of California at Santa Barbara

Korie L. Edwards, Associate Professor of Sociology, The Ohio State University

Nancy A. Gonzales, Foundation Professor of Psychology, Arizona State University

Kimberly Goodman, Executive Branch Policy Fellow, Society for Research in Child Development

Bonnie L. Halpern-Felsher, Professor of Pediatrics, University of California, San Francisco

David M. Hansen, Assistant Professor of Educational Psychology, University of Kansas

Barton J. Hirsch, Professor of Human Development and Social Policy, Northwestern University

Ashleigh Hodge, Graduate Student in Social Work, The Ohio State University

Alecia J. Houston, Graduate Student in Urban and Regional Planning, L. Douglas Wilder School of Government and Public Affairs, Virginia Commonwealth University

Cynthia Hudley, Professor of Child and Adolescent Development, University of California at Santa Barbara

Patricia A. Jarvis, Professor of Psychology, Illinois State University (Co-Editor)

Nadia Jessop, Doctoral Student in Psychology and Research in Education, University of Kansas

Jennifer K. Karre, Research Associate at the Social Science Research Institute, Pennsylvania State University

Andrew Kim, Graduate of Tulane University in Psychology, Society for Research in Child Development, France D. Horowitz Millennium Scholar

Wendy Kliewer, Professor and Chair, Psychology, Virginia Commonwealth University

Gabriel P. Kuperminc, Professor of Psychology, Georgia State University

Joann Lee, Postdoctoral Fellow, Centers for Disease Control and Prevention

Robert E. Lee, Founding Director of Illinois State University's Chicago Teacher Education Pipeline™

Miriam R. Linver, Associate Professor of Family and Child Studies, Montclair State University

Anne Marie Mauricio, Faculty Research Associate in Prevention Research, Arizona State University

Holly E. R. Morrell, Assistant Professor of Psychology, Loma Linda University

Nina S. Mounts, Associate Professor of Developmental Psychology, Northern Illinois University

Cristina Pacione-Zayas, Culture of Calm Coordinator, Chicago Public Schools

Hilda M. Pantin, Professor of Clinical and Executive Vice Chair of Epidemiology, University of Miami

Natalie Papale, Psychology Graduate from Tulane University

Dakota M. Pawlicki, Program Coordinator for the Chicago Teacher Education Pipeline™, Illinois State University

Justin Perry, Associate Professor in Counseling, Administration, Supervision, and Adult Learning and Director of the Center for Urban Education, Cleveland State University

Laura Pittman, Associate Professor of Clinical Psychology and Director of Clinical Training, Northern Illinois University

Michell Pope, Doctoral Student in Psychology, Virginia Commonwealth University

Kathryn Reid-Quiñones, Postdoctoral Fellow, Medical University of South Carolina

Liliana Rodriguez, Director of the Multicultural Center, Williams College

Seth J. Schwartz, Associate Professor in Epidemiology and Public Health, University of Miami

JulieAnn Stawicki, Assistant Professor of Youth Development, University of Wisconsin-Extension

Eric W. Wallace, Doctoral Student in Counseling Psychology, Cleveland State University

Tracy Walters, Doctoral Student in Developmental Psychology, Northern Illinois University

Robert S. Weisskirch, Professor of Human Development, California State University–Monterey Bay

Lorey A. Wheeler, Predoctoral Student in Social and Family Dynamics, Arizona State University

Jessie J. Wong, Pre-doctoral Fellow in Prevention Research, Arizona State University

Byron L. Zamboanga, Associate Professor in Psychology, Smith College

INDEX